OLYMPIC COLLISION

OLYMPIC
COLLISION

The Story of Mary Decker and Zola Budd

KYLE KEIDERLING

University of Nebraska Press · Lincoln & London

Library of Congress Cataloging-in-Publication Data
Names: Keiderling, Kyle, author.
Title: Olympic collision: the story of Mary Decker and
Zola Budd / Kyle Keiderling.
Description: Lincoln: University of Nebraska Press, 2016. |
Includes bibliographical references and index.
Identifiers: LCCN 2016012186 (print)
LCCN 2016033151 (ebook)
ISBN 9780803290846 (hardback: alk. paper)
ISBN 9780803296503 (epub)
ISBN 9780803296510 (mobi)
ISBN 9780803296527 (pdf)
Subjects: LCSH: Decker, Mary, 1958- |
Runners (Sports)—United States—Biography. |
Budd, Zola, 1966- |
Runners (Sports)—South Africa—Biography. |
Runners (Sports)—Great Britain—Biography. |
Olympic Games (23rd: 1984: Los Angeles, Calif.) |
BISAC: SPORTS & RECREATION / Olympics. |
SPORTS & RECREATION / Running & Jogging. |
BIOGRAPHY & AUTOBIOGRAPHY / Sports.
Classification: LCC GV1061.15.D42 K45 2016 (print) |
LCC GV1061.15.D42 (ebook) | DDC 796.420922 [B]—dc23
LC record available at https://lccn.loc.gov/2016012186

Set in Lyon Text by Rachel Gould.

This isn't a tale of heroic feats. . . . It's about two lives running parallel for a while, with common aspirations and convergent dreams.

—Ernesto "Che" Guevara de la Serna, *The Motorcycle Diaries* (2005)

CONTENTS

ACKNOWLEDGMENTS

Many people assisted me in the research involved in this book. I am indebted to them for their cooperation and kind assistance in sharing their thoughts and memories with me.

First and foremost I must thank Zola Budd Pieterse, for her help in understanding the events described herein and her willingness to share her insights into what was, for her, a difficult experience many years ago. She also shared her scrapbooks and photos and made available to me the names and addresses of others that I could interview. She graciously permitted me to visit with her at her home in South Carolina on four occasions and replied promptly to all telephone and email correspondence with unfailing good humor. A former world champion, she remains a national heroine in South Africa and will forever be a champion in my mind for her willingness to relive for me some of the most difficult times any athlete ever faced anywhere.

The need to speak with as many participants as possible led me to many places around the globe. In Romania, I was assisted by Simion Alb, Director of Tourism for Romania, who conducted the interview for me with Maricica Puică at her home.

In Germany, David Hein conducted interviews with Brigitte Kraus.

The other runners in the 3,000-meter event at the 1984 Olympic Games were all, with one exception, willing to speak with me at length about their views on the incident as well as their own performance in the race. This group of accomplished athletes, who were largely overlooked by the media at the games, were all cooperative and willing to share their understanding of the event as they saw it as well as the state of the sport in the 1980s. The sole exception was Mary Decker Slaney, who refused to acknowledge numerous requests by mail and email for an interview.

I did have the cooperation of most of those who coached Mary through the years, and I am very grateful to them for their willingness to speak about her and her accomplishments as well as her character. They were an invaluable source of information. Don DeNoon and Dick Brown were especially helpful, as was Rich Castro.

Pieter Labuschagne was willing to participate through an exchange of emails with regard to Zola Budd's career while he was coaching her during the time leading up to and shortly after the Olympics. In Great Britain, John Bryant, a world-class runner, spoke with me at length about Zola's career in that country while he was involved with coaching her and about the many obstacles Zola faced while in Great Britain. Rebecca Biddiss provided research assistance, searching newspaper archives in London for relevant articles on Budd's career. Richard Mayer was of great assistance to me in South Africa, suggesting sources, confirming information, and reviewing the manuscript for accuracy.

Alexander Keating, my attorney and friend, assisted with research on Decker in New Jersey.

Many of the best writers in the United States and Great Britain spoke with me about their coverage of both Mary and Zola and were unfailingly willing to help me.

Richard Pound of the International Olympic Committee (IOC) was a great source of insight into that always secretive organization as well as furnishing insights about the former IOC president, Juan Antonio Samaranch.

In addition to the writers I spoke with, I am thankful that Marty Liquori—a former runner of international repute and the on-air television commentator for the race in 1984—was willing to describe the events as he saw them at the time and honest enough to admit he had erred in his instant analysis under the pressure of a live event.

As my tutor in middle-distance running I was fortunate to have Jodie Bilotta D'Ariano—a former Stanford star and the holder of twenty-five high school state championships in track and cross-country in New Jersey—as my teacher. In addition, Stacy Bilotta Gaynor, a former high school All-American and North Carolina State University star, proved invaluable as a fact checker.

The many reference librarians that indulged my pathetic attempts at retrieving microfilm articles without ejecting me from their presence include those at the Los Angeles Public Library and the staff at the Lamoreaux Justice Complex in Orange, California.

Many thanks to John Frangelli and Ed McManimon, my first

readers, for their comments and suggestions. For their hospitality while researching and writing the book, I am indebted to Linda and Robert Aloia and Helen and John Frangelli.

In the vast majority of cases, I have identified the source of any comment or observation by name. In a few cases, my sources asked not to be identified by name and I have honored that request and appreciate the fact that they were willing to speak with me at all.

My editor, Polly Kummel, once again performed her magic as she has on all my previous books. She is amazing. Thanks to Rob Taylor, Joeth Zucco, and the entire team at the University of Nebraska Press. Thanks also to Karen Brown for copyediting the final version.

My agent, Lawrence Jordan, was supportive of the project throughout the long process of research and writing.

The endnotes to the book identify by name all those who participated on the record, whether in person, by email, or by telephone.

The journey that I embarked upon in researching and writing *Olympic Collision* was long and winding. But it was always interesting, informative, and eye opening in the revelations that were uncovered. I hope you find the journey through these pages as compelling and enlightening as I did.

ABBREVIATIONS

AAU	Amateur Athletic Union
AIAW	Association for Intercollegiate Athletics for Women
BAAB	British Amateur Athletics Board
IAAF	International Association of Athletics Federations
IOC	International Olympic Committee
LAOOC	Los Angeles Olympic Organizing Committee
SAAF	South African Athletics Federation
TAC	the Athletics Congress
USATF	USA Track and Field
USOC	U.S. Olympic Committee
WAAA	Women's Amateur Athletic Association
WADA	World Anti-Doping Agency

OLYMPIC COLLISION

ONE. Starting Line

She was the most motivated and talented runner I have ever seen.

—Don DeNoon on the eleven-year-old Mary Decker

Mary Decker entered the world on August 4, 1958, in a delivery room at the Hunterdon Medical Center in Flemington, New Jersey, about ten miles from the home of her parents, John and Jacqueline Decker, in the tiny crossroads village of Bunnvale. The birth certificate recorded her full name as Mary Teresa Decker. The birth was unremarkable, and Jacqueline and her newborn daughter soon returned to Bunnvale.

Mary would spend her first ten years in a peaceful, bucolic area of the nation's most densely populated state. People in Bunnvale knew their neighbors, and they rarely locked their doors. The four-season climate could produce hot humid summers and bitterly cold winters, but the residents took it all in stoic stride. No parkway or turnpike was then in sight, and many roads in the county were still dirt. The low rolling hills, heavily forested, surrounded acres of farmland under cultivation. Poultry and dairy farms were prevalent, and fields of golden hay, Jersey tomatoes, and tall sweet corn were arrayed in checkerboard patterns throughout. Hunterdon County was bisected by the waters of the South Branch of the Raritan River and bordered on the west by the Delaware River as it made its way eastward toward the Atlantic Ocean, about fifty miles away.

About equidistant from Philadelphia and New York, Hunterdon was one of the least populated of the state's twenty-one counties. With fewer than one hundred thousand people, it had as yet no major shopping malls. Flemington, the county seat, had a population of about four thousand. The medical center where Mary was born had been constructed only a few years earlier through a massive countywide fund-raising effort.[1]

...

Mary attended public school in Lebanon Township. In the late 1950s five county high schools accepted students on a geographic basis.

Lebanon sent its students to North Hunterdon Regional High School in Annandale. Although in later years the school would produce outstanding track and cross-country teams—boasting several outstanding women runners—at the time, no high schools in the county offered track as a sport, and there were no women's track teams.

In 1968, when Mary was ten, her parents decided to leave Hunterdon County and join the many others from around the United States who were making the move to Southern California. The Deckers—John, Jacqueline, their son, Johnny, and their three daughters—became part of a massive influx of people that saw Orange County become one of the nation's fastest-growing areas in the 1960s and 1970s. The climate was pleasant, jobs were plentiful, and housing affordable. To keep up with the demand for housing, builders in the county, which is south of Los Angeles, were bulldozing as fast as they could the orange groves from which the county derived its name. Before they settled in Garden Grove, the Deckers lived for eight months in Santa Ana and for two years in Huntington Beach.

The move, prompted by her mother's desire to join other family members in the area, would prove to be fortuitous. Had Mary Decker remained in Bunnvale and environs, she would not have had an opportunity to develop as a runner: she was born in the wrong place at the wrong time for aspiring young female runners. Had the Deckers stayed in Hunterdon County, New Jersey, it is unlikely we would ever have heard of Mary. Southern California, on the other hand, was arguably the best place a young female runner could be in the United States.

. . .

Soon after John and Jacqueline made the move west, their marriage headed south.

John was not the dominant influence in his daughter's life. "My father is a very quiet person. My mother is a very unquiet one. The atmosphere [at home] was dominated by my mother," Mary would say in later years. However, John had an adventurous streak. A tool-and-die maker by training, he once used his mechanical skills to construct a homemade gyro helicopter, which he flew—and crashed. He also loved to race around on motorcycles, hardly a safer pastime. Mary, riding behind her father when she was twelve, fell off and fractured her skull. The injury resulted in a year of physical therapy and another scare when she resumed running too soon and began to hemorrhage. That was the end of her motorcycle runs with John.

Jackie disapproved of John's hobbies and daredevil antics. And as her marriage crumbled, she grew increasingly unhappy about her circumstances. Her oldest daughter told Kenny Moore of *Sports Illustrated* in 1978: "They stayed together for the sake of the kids. It was the biggest mistake they ever made—besides getting married in the first place. They were never close, as long as I can remember."[2]

While working as a bartender in a watering hole close to the Orange County courthouse, Mary's mother began to seek counsel from the barristers who bellied up to her bar. As she poured them martinis, she poured out her tale of woe. And while they imbibed, she sopped up the spilled gin and free advice.[3]

. . .

When Mary was eleven, she and a girlfriend of the same age spotted a flyer announcing a cross-country event in a nearby park: "We didn't know what 'cross-country' was, but we decided to go," she said. They discovered upon arrival it was a running event, and they both entered. "My friend dropped out, but I won," she recalled years later.[4]

In winning her very first race, with no training or preparation whatsoever, Mary Decker displayed a raw talent that would become the foundation for the greatest career of any female middle-distance runner America has ever produced.

TWO. First Steps

Running is the perfect metaphor for life.
You get out of it just what you put into it.

—Oprah Winfrey

Eight years after Mary Decker arrived on the planet, and eight thousand miles away in a hospital in Bloemfontein, in South Africa's Free State Province, a woman lay dangerously close to dying. She had been in labor for almost thirty-six hours and had received thirteen pints of blood. Finally, blessedly, she was delivered of a daughter by emergency Caesarean section on May 26, 1966.

Fearing the infant had suffered brain damage from oxygen deprivation, nurses and doctors quickly carried the child—undersize, despite being full term—to an incubator to monitor her condition. Her mother also remained under close observation in intensive care, drifting in and out of consciousness for several days after the delivery. Not until her child was six days old was she was able to hold her in her arms. She recalls that the infant was "a tiny little thing." However, the newborn, despite her difficult arrival and diminutive size, was healthy and showed no ill effects from her traumatic delivery. The staff at Bloemfontein's National Hospital watched as the infant thrived and soon were calling her "the miracle baby."

Her father chose her name. Had she been a boy, it was to have been Zero. Since the baby was a girl, he decided instead on Zola, after the nineteenth-century French writer Émile Zola, whose work Père Budd admired.

Zola Budd's difficult arrival in the world foretold her later life.

. . .

When the baby finally left the hospital, she came home to a single-story, white stucco house with a red corrugated roof; it was on a red dirt road just off Route 30, about seven miles outside Bloemfontein—a bustling old city of nearly four hundred thousand located on a high plateau about four thousand feet above sea level, in an area known as the veldt. In addition to the substantial house, the small farmstead included a menagerie of ducks and chickens, which Zola's father, Frank, raised with pride, along with a few ostriches and several dogs and cats. In a small vegetable garden in the back, her mother, called Tossie, grew fresh produce for her home-based catering business.

The Budd family was comprised of the oldest sister, Jenny, who was eleven; nine-year-old Estelle; and twins Quintus and Cara, five. The Budds had had another child, Frankie, who was born in March 1960 with a liver ailment. The prognosis for survival, despite frequent medical care in Johannesburg, where the infant underwent several operations, was poor. When Tossie brought him home for the final time, she knew Frankie's struggles would soon end. He died on New Year's Day 1961, five years before Zola arrived. Pictures of the little boy were on display in nearly every room, making the palpable sadness of the loss ever present in the house. The parents never spoke of him to the other children, and discussions about him and his death were off-limits.

After the difficult delivery of Zola, Tossie, born Hendrina Wilhelmina de Swardt, to a Boer farming family, remained in the hospital until she was well enough to be discharged. But the experience had left her weakened and ill, so Zola's oldest sister, Jenny, assumed responsibility for the little girl's care. When the toddler spoke her first word, Jenny heard it: *Mommy.*[1]

. . .

Frank Budd, tall and balding, with muttonchop whiskers, had inherited a printing business in Bloemfontein from his father, who had immigrated to South Africa from England in the early 1900s. It was never a particularly profitable enterprise, however, and sales continued to decline as Zola grew older. Tossie supplemented their income through her catering business. Zola recalls being "up to my elbows in mayonnaise in the kitchen" as her mother and the few assistants the family could afford prepared an order.[2]

Bloemfontein (the Dutch word means "fountain of flowers"; the city's nickname is City of Roses) was settled by the Boers, who first arrived among the indigenous people of the future South Africa in the late 1600s. With a dry temperate climate conducive to agriculture, by the mid-nineteenth century the town had matured as the focal point of the thriving farmlands that surrounded it. The land around Zola's home was rural and spotted with small farms. The farmers raised potatoes and corn, and cattle farms were prevalent. The veldt, or grassland, was a gently undulating plain that stretched for miles in every direction, though mountains could be glimpsed on the far horizon. The days were sun splashed and warm, and the bright blue of the sky seemed to span the land like an endless azure canopy. The rains that rolled in on angry black clouds each summer were a welcome sight in the afternoons of baking hot days. "You could actually smell the rain before it arrived," Zola remembered.[3]

. . .

The young Zola Budd first experienced the joy of running with the eighteen-year-old Jenny, who introduced her to it when Zola was about seven. The two would ramble off for miles together, romping barefoot through the low grass and along dirt paths in the countryside. Those early runs with her sister Jenny, including frequent trips down Route 30 into Bloemfontein and through its many parks, would remain in Zola's memory as the happiest of her life.

Frank Budd shuttled his family from farmstead to city and back for the first ten years or so of his youngest daughter's life. The constant moving created problems for Zola once she began school: she was always the new kid, and her innate shyness, small size, and quiet demeanor meant she made few fast friends in her early years. Thus, despite her parents' growing marital difficulties, home was where Zola was happiest. Among her pet dogs and cats and the other farm animals she was accepted, safe, and secure.

One of her earliest friends on the farm was the child of one of the women who came to the house to help Tossie. The boy's name was Thipe, and together the two explored the land in and around the farm, playing all the games young children enjoy. But the relationship ended when the Budds moved back to the city. Thipe was black, and the camaraderie they enjoyed out in the countryside was not permitted in Bloemfontein—or indeed anywhere else in South Africa. Apartheid was still the law of the land, and such associations were not acceptable. But Zola learned a different lesson from this friendship, and as she later put it, "My relationship with Thipe taught me, early on, that the color of a person's skin is not what's important."[4]

But the government of her country had determined that it was precisely the color of a person's skin that set him or her apart from others. The failure of others to distinguish Zola Budd's thoughts and actions from those of her government would play a large role in determining how she was perceived in the eyes of the world.

. . .

In essence, during her early formative years, Zola led a sheltered life. Perhaps because of the loss of Frankie, the family was extremely protective of their youngest child, who was generally coddled and treated with utmost care by her siblings and parents, though both

Frank and Tossie were kept busy with their own lives and business ventures.

And Zola always had Jenny. She ran with Jenny, shared her fears and concerns with Jenny. Jenny was always there for her and always would be. While their parents' marriage grew increasingly fragile, and their squabbles more and more frequent, Jenny was the one safe harbor in the home for Zola—her surrogate mother, her anchor, and her best friend. No matter what was going on in Zola's young world, she could count on Jenny to make everything right. But of course Jenny, who was tall and attractive, with dark hair and eyes and a ready smile, was growing up as well. By the time Zola was ten, Jenny was twenty-one and a newly married nurse with her own home outside Bloemfontein, although she was not far away.

Zola was in the early years of primary school in Bloemfontein—attending her third school, in fact, since her education began—when she first competed against others. At the annual race meeting, she was urged to try a longer-distance race against her schoolmates. "It was a three-lap event of 1,200 meters and Daddy, who was there, encouraged me to try it. 'Come on Zola, give it a go.' I was not really that interested. I had only been running in sprints and had just finished running a sprint and a relay race and was not at all sure I could last the three laps. I won by miles," she recalled.[5] For her, running was little more than an extended recess activity she was good at and enjoyed. Though her father continued to encourage her, she was just as interested in books as she was in running: "I would go into town with my mother on her weekly shopping trips, and I saved all my allowance money so I could purchase books in town."[6]

Surrounded by her books and stuffed animals inside, and her pets outside, Zola was happy and content on the farm. At school, however, she was not. Her father had determined that Zola, unlike her older sisters, would attend Oranje Meisieskool, a private school for girls from the upper class—a social stratum Frank had convinced himself befitted his family and his ambitions. But the attempt to turn the tomboyish Zola into a prim and proper young lady soon fizzled. Among girls from wealthy families, the decidedly middle-class Zola, sometimes arriving for classes in her mother's battered old pickup truck, was embarrassed and increasingly uncomfortable: "I really didn't fit in with the other girls."[7]

Placed among the top-level students, the new kid—now in her fourth school—looked and felt out of place. She complained to her mother about the school and the bad dreams she was having because of it. Her marks, for the first time, were poor. She hated it. Making her even more miserable was some surgery to remove a small bone from her arches. The surgery was performed over the Christmas holidays, and Zola, both feet encased in plaster casts, was definitely not feeling the holiday spirit.

Jenny roused Zola from her blue funk. Jenny understood Zola best. They had shared a bedroom, and Jenny had taught Zola to swim and to run. Zola always turned to Jenny, not her parents, for strength, guidance, and love. Jenny had never failed her, and with her sister's stern but gentle urging, Zola soon was back on her surgically repaired feet—and back on the track.

. . .

When her mother arrived to pick Zola up one afternoon a short time later, Tossie had with her a uniform of the coed Dan Pienaar school, where Zola's sister Cara was enrolled. The uniform was for Zola, to her surprise. Tossie had persuaded Frank that their daughter was out of place at the snobbish Oranje Meisieskool, and the finishing school experiment was finally, well, finished. Zola joined Cara at Dan Pienaar.

The following year, at thirteen, Zola advanced to Sentraal Secondary School (the equivalent of high school in the United States), where she soon encountered a young history teacher, Pieter Labuschagne, who also served as Sentraal's athletics coach.

Dark haired and mustachioed, the handsome, well-built Labuschagne was himself a former runner who had a large group of runners under his tutelage: "I represented the province [Free State] while in University at the National Championships in both cross-country and the marathon," he said. "Coaching was just a natural extension of my own experiences, and when I started teaching it was an easy transformation for me into coaching young students."[8]

Among them was Zola Budd: "Several of the girls on my track team told me about her. They had run against her in meets last season and she had beaten them," he recalled.[9] Once aware of her potential, Labuschagne asked her to join his squad of runners, and Zola agreed. However, as she described it, "He started me off in cross-country, and I wasn't that thrilled about it. In fact, I hated it."[10] Her reaction would soon change.

THREE. Off with the Gun

The taste of victory that had come with her first competitive race was sweet to small, pigtailed Mary Decker. That she had to savor it through teeth encased in heavy metal braces mattered little to her: she had found in running something that was at once not boring and deeply rewarding. She was good at it—and she liked being good at something. Mary would soon find that her excellence at track acted as a magnet, drawing attention from coaches in Southern California who were constantly on the lookout for young girl runners with raw potential.

Bob Hickey, then a police officer who doubled as a track official, described the context: "At that time, in the area, there were a number of women's track clubs. They weren't age-group clubs, just women's clubs, and we were under the governance of the AAU [Amateur Athletic Union]. Meets were held all over the area, and it was an active organization." Hickey adds, "We were all trying to develop women who could lift the level of talent in the United States to where we could compete on an international basis with the Europeans and Eastern bloc communist countries that all had state-sponsored and [state]-supported organizations."[1] With names like Cheetahs, Jets, Comets, and Angels, the AAU clubs presented a unique opportunity for young female runners to expand their skills.

Don DeNoon was a volunteer coach with the Long Beach Comets, and he recalled that "Mary came to my attention when she was just ten years old." He was a former race walker with impressive credentials and took over the head coaching job when Ron Allice, a former track star at North Carolina State University, left to take another job.

DeNoon found Mary Decker to be "the most motivated and talented youngster" he had ever seen and encouraged her to join the team. But Mary's home was nowhere near the Comets' training center, so DeNoon had to make arrangements for her transportation so she could train with the team. "When I began coaching her, I hardly ever saw either of [her parents]. They would sign the forms she brought home for permission to travel and train, but that was about the extent of their involvement," he said.[2]

In a home more than a bit unsettled by Jackie's eruptions, which rivaled those of Vesuvius, and John's no-less-damaging periods of icy silence, Mary's parents were too involved in their deteriorating relationship to show much interest in fostering their daughter's new-found pursuit. So for Mary the connection with Don DeNoon was significant. She would find comfort in the company of a man who saw in her the promise of something special. Track could get her out of the hostile atmosphere at home and into a place where her efforts would draw notice and approval—a place where she could channel her confused feelings into something exceptional and attain a sense of self-worth.

. . .

Track did not enjoy the fan support or the financial backing in the United States that the sport—known everywhere else as athletics—had overseas. It was a constant struggle for the AAU coaches, who were largely volunteers, to raise the money to support their clubs. "We literally went with our hands out to stores and malls, asking shoppers for contributions. If someone dropped some money in a girl's bucket, we gave them a team logo decal," Hickey recalled. DeNoon added that, although she was still only ten, "Mary Decker would do her part in soliciting."[3]

Mary was soon doing more than her part in training as well, according to DeNoon: "She started as a sprinter and did well at the short distances. Then we moved her to longer distances, and she showed in training that she could challenge the sixteen- and seventeen-year-olds we had." As DeNoon put it, "Mary had from the outset the most innate talent I'd ever seen. All I could do was try to improve her. She was a gem in the rough. She had natural ability and was able and willing to push herself. It was that attitude that most struck me about her. Mary didn't want to be beaten, in practice or in meets. She always had to be first."[4]

Their partnership would work very, very well for the next four seasons, as Decker ran first for the Comets and then the Blue Angels Track Club in Huntington Beach, to which she followed DeNoon when he took over the top coaching job there. After starting Mary in sprints, he moved her to the mile and then settled on the half mile. His training methods included some long runs on the nearby beach, and for warm-ups he used the perimeter of the mile-square park where they trained. But most of the work was interval training on the track, at the time the accepted method for training middle- and long-distance runners in the United States. It used fast running on the track, followed by periods of rest intervals, stress, then relaxation. Volume (the total workload of an athlete) was generated by the repetitions. Workouts meant running sets of 220 yards, 330 yards, 440 yards, and 600 yards, with occasional longer individual runs.

DeNoon's teams trained four days a week, and they typically covered thirty-five miles a week, followed by racing on weekends.[5] Mary flourished within the system: "She loved the excitement, the spotlight, and the rewards," DeNoon said.[6] She would be in the spotlight often.

Throughout the four seasons that DeNoon coached the girl whom writers would call—appropriately, for her diminutive stature and age—"little Mary Decker," he was astonished by her truly extraordinary ability to "go through any pain threshold to reach her goal."[7]

We have no way of knowing if the physical pain she fought so valiantly to conquer—pain that is the constant companion of all middle- and long-distance runners—was her way of coping with the emotional pain she had to endure at home, but what is certain is that her ability was off the known scale for young female runners. Mary Decker was a gifted, motivated, even obsessed, talent who met every challenge thrown at her and stared it down while accumulating accolades and records along the way. The writer Kenny Moore observed that Decker was "moved by a competitive yearning that rises from so deep within her character that it connects with her will to be loved. Since she was a child, she has tried to transform her hunger for comforting approval into dominating athletic performance."[8] As her successes on the track, indoors and out, mounted, writers and fans joined DeNoon in marveling at her exploits.

. . .

Mary was virtually unbeatable at any distance. Her immature body seemed indestructible no matter how many training miles and races she forced it to endure. But, despite DeNoon's claim that "all I could do was try to improve her," he would be the first in a long line of ever-changing advisers to learn that coaching Mary Decker was anything but easy. In the face of all her achievement, she constantly sought reassurance and required encouragement and flattery. Despite his avowal that "she did it mostly by herself," DeNoon soon found Decker requiring almost his full and undivided attention.[9] He also discovered that reining in her enthusiasm and obsessive need to succeed was nearly impossible. When asked what motivated or possessed his then fifteen-year-old star, DeNoon said, "She has goals other people have never dreamed of having. I learned long ago never to underestimate her."[10]

He would be criticized from afar by coaches and runners alike who thought he was subjecting his superbly talented young runner to abusive and ultimately dangerous training methods. No less than Steve "Pre" Prefontaine, then America's top middle-distance runner, observed from Oregon, after viewing Mary's training schedule, that DeNoon's methods were likely to imperil her career. She "would burn out" early, he cautioned, if it continued.[11]

What Pre and others could not know was that DeNoon had in his charge an adolescent girl with blazing speed, fierce determination, incredible stamina and strength, and an indomitable will that impelled her, as hard as he attempted to control her, to take the bit and *run*. Mary Decker was going to run harder, farther, and faster than anyone around her. Francie Larrieu, a world record holder at 1,500 meters, two miles, and 3,000 meters, had also been a teenage star. Perhaps her own experience colored her point of view, but in 1974, when she was twenty-one, she voiced her doubt that Mary "would fizzle out. Somehow, I have the feeling that Mary is different. You can't be on top all the time. You've got to see how Mary reacts to the downs."[12]

In fact, if Decker had a chink in her armor, it was psychological, as Bob Hickey and Don DeNoon learned early in her development. Hickey, a full-time police officer and part-time track official, had begun running in his thirties with another cop; they often trained with DeNoon's team to keep themselves fit: "One day my friend and I were on a training run with Mary. We were both much older and bigger and were jostling and bumping her and passing in front of her. We were just kidding around. All of a sudden Mary stopped, sat down on the track, and threw a fit, screaming and bawling like a baby," he recalled.[13]

Observing the tantrum, DeNoon rushed to his young star's side to comfort and console her. Then he took the two police officers aside. "He told us in no uncertain terms that we were never, ever, to run in front of Mary under any circumstances: 'You don't run in front of Mary. She always has to be in front,' he said."[14]

Hickey would remember that lecture, and that attitude, years later, when someone else passed Mary in a race that was much more meaningful than an afternoon training run in the park.

. . .

Don DeNoon coached Mary Decker for four—by any measure spectacular—seasons. Now retired in Florida, DeNoon is not a man who is full of himself. He is the first to acknowledge that he benefited from their association, which he later turned into a string of coaching positions at several major colleges and universities. Similarly, he is not unaware of the criticism of those who, in hindsight, point the finger of blame at him, bringing his early training of Mary Decker under attack as the cause of the series of injuries that would hound her for years after they parted ways. "Let me tell you this," he said more than three decades later: "I coached Mary Decker to her first three world records before she was fourteen years old. And while I coached her, she was never injured." DeNoon added, "Mary loved every day she trained."[15]

Expanding on the adolescent's self-determined will to do more than anyone else, Bob Seaman, a world-class sub-four-minute miler and track official in Southern California, offered the following example: "During one seven-day period when she was still twelve, Mary ran a marathon in 3:09 and a 440, an 880, a mile, and a two-mile race."[16] The next day, not surprisingly, she was in the hospital.

DeNoon recalled that "Mary had an attack of appendicitis. She was rushed to the hospital, where she underwent an emergency appendectomy. Two days after her release she was back training, with the blood from her [still intact] stitches staining her jersey. I remember the doctor asking her before the operation if she had been 'under any undue stress lately.' She just grimaced and shook her head."

"Mary Decker," DeNoon added, "had a burning desire to excel. She enjoyed what she did. Most important, she enjoyed the success."[17] Those, as they say, are the facts.

. . .

DeNoon had always described himself as "more like a big brother to Mary," and thus it was appropriate that, when he married Sandy Dean—Mary's best friend on the team he coached—in 1971, Mary was the flower girl at their wedding.[18]

With the arrival of 1972, an Olympic year, it became obvious even to the most casual observer that little Mary Decker belonged on the U.S. team—obvious to all, that is, but U.S. track officials, who declared that their bylaws prevented anyone from participating in the Olympic trials who was not yet fourteen years old. Mary's birthday was in August. The trials were in June. Although she had set the world age-group record for 800 meters at twelve, and had clocked a 4:55 mile at thirteen, Mary was not allowed to try out. "We appealed the decision but got nowhere with them," Bob Hickey recalled.[19]

. . .

That summer Mary developed Sever's disease, an inflammation of the bone-growth tissue in the heel that often afflicts adolescents. Though both her feet were encased in plaster casts, her ceaseless activity soon turned them into rags: the casts had to be replaced, Mary bounced back quickly, and 1973 would be the season that saw the emergence on the national and international stages of the young phenomenon.[20] She finished first in the 1,000 meters at the *LA Times* indoor meet in February at the Forum, and in June at UC Irvine she went on to win a spot on the U.S. national team in the 880-yard race. Both events were televised.[21] When the Americans competed against the Soviet Union at an indoor meet in Richmond, Virginia, she finished third in the mile—and less than two seconds behind the winner, the reigning Olympic 1,500 meters champion, Lyudmila Bragina.

As impressive as that showing was, Decker continued to astound observers when she ran second to Wendy Knudson in the race at

880 yards at the outdoor U.S. championships.[22] Decker followed that with a winning performance in Toronto at the Pan Pacific Games. Knowledgeable track aficionados were slack-jawed at her speed. She clinched the win with a 53.9-seconds 400-meter segment. She was still only fourteen years old.

After that, Decker began a globetrotting tour with the U.S. team that saw her meet West Germany's Hildegard Falck, the 1972 Olympic 800-meter champion, with Decker losing by just a second. Then the American star hopped over to Turin, Italy, where she beat that country's best runners.

Then, in the eleventh in a series of two-nation competitions that were a fixture during the Cold War years, Decker faced the Russians again. In July in Minsk she ran against the Olympic silver medalist, Nijolė Sabaitė, a Lithuanian. At just five feet and only eighty-six pounds, Decker appeared overmatched by the bulky, muscular Sabaitė. Last at the bell for the final lap, Decker moved quickly up to third and then surged into the lead in the stretch, passing a shocked Sabaitė and leaving the Soviet star in her wake while winning in 2:02.9. The meets were popular television fare, and millions of Americans watched and cheered Decker on from the comfort of their living rooms.

It didn't hurt that Mary Decker was white, young, pigtailed, and tiny. She was a child facing and beating Amazon-like Russians, and she reflected a wholesome, all-American image in doing so.[23] A star had been born, and the media loved her. Though America had produced other young runners—Marie Mulder, Doris Brown Heritage, Jan Merrill, and Francie Larrieu among them—they were covered principally by the print media. Mary's appearances at televised events catapulted her further and faster into the limelight than her predecessors. She was a ready-made media sensation with irresistible appeal. *Newsweek*, *Sports Illustrated*, and other periodicals scrambled to put out gushing tributes to the newest track star.

Mary loved the spotlight and basked in its warm, bright glow. But spotlights, as she would soon learn, can also be harsh, and when they expose defects and flaws, they tend to turn away as fast as they arrived.

. . .

Behind the hoopla surrounding his young protégée, Don DeNoon was dealing with stark reality: by the end of 1973, his relationship with Mary Decker was over. The youngster he had developed into a star was leaving. DeNoon succinctly summed up why they parted ways: "It was Jackie."[24]

When Mary's home life had become too much to endure, she had found refuge with the DeNoons. "She stayed with us for a time when the Deckers were battling between themselves," Don said. Now, as Mary's star was rising in Southern California and beyond, Jackie Decker began to take an interest in her daughter's extracurricular activities—and in the perks she was receiving.

"Jackie," according to Don, "didn't have much of a life. She was a bartender and struggling financially. I had a confrontation with her over the travel money and trips we were taking."

Jackie told *Sports Illustrated* in April 1974, "I told Don that I wanted to have a say from now on when anything involves Mary. I want to give the okay for anything pertaining to Mary—interviews, television appearances, anything."[25]

DeNoon's response was, "The better athletes get, the more independent they get. Both Mary and her mother are getting to be more demanding."[26]

Having noted that her daughter was getting all-expenses-paid trips to foreign cities, Jackie demanded that she be allowed to serve as her daughter's chaperone.[27] European capitals and Japan beat the hell out of a dark smoky bar full of sloshed men in Orange County. Bob Seaman, an AAU official by then, also recalled interactions with Jackie in those early years: "She was a tough Italian. Dark-complected and fiery."[28]

Cognizant of the AAU's tight purse strings, DeNoon was reluctant to accede to Jackie's demands. Finally Jackie asked her teenage daughter, "Who would you rather have with you on your trips? Me or your coach?" Forced into a corner by her volatile mother, the youngster not surprisingly sought the easiest route available to her. "You," she replied.

"That was pretty much the end of our relationship," Don DeNoon said.[29]

Jackie asked Bob Hickey to take over as her daughter's coach, but Hickey turned her down. "I knew from my association with her and

Don that she would require full-time attention, and I didn't have that to give her," Hickey explained. "I idolized Mary and was in awe of her ability. She pushed herself as hard as she could push herself. She was an extraordinary competitor. And she hated to lose."

Bob Hickey believed that he "got along okay with Mary and Jackie," even though he had refused to coach her. A few years later, however, when Mary had become really popular, he found out he hadn't been as well liked as he thought.

"I placed a call to Jackie, who was then working as a car salesperson. I called her at work, told her who I was, and asked her for Mary's address," he said. "There was a long icy pause on the line. Then she asked me, 'How did you get this number?'

"I told her a friend had provided it and that I wanted to send Mary some photos I had of her." Another frosty pause.

"'Don't call here again,' she said, and the phone went dead."[30]

. . .

When Mary left Don DeNoon, and after Hickey declined to coach her, she ended up at Pacifica Track Club, where her then boyfriend, a twenty-one-year-old runner named Bill Graves, was training with Ted Devian. "The problem with that was that all the training runs they did were on the road," Hickey said. Though Mary's legs took a terrible pounding, and she was soon hobbled with injuries, "she ran in a meet in Japan with her shins in bandages and in a lot of pain. She did well in spite of it," Hickey remembered.[31]

Mary's 1974 indoor season under her new coach began well enough as she set the world record in the 1,000-yard run, besting the previous mark by nearly three seconds and beating Francie Larrieu and Julie Brown.[32]

In a column in the *Los Angeles Times* on February 5, the sportswriter John Hall noted that the most-used line about Mary for the last year was "She's captured the hearts of four continents." She continued to win hearts and fans as she set a meet record in winning the 880 in 2:07.1 at Madison Square Garden in late February, with "pigtails flying."[33] Three days later a feature article on her in the *LA Times* on February 26 summarized her early success: "The 15-year-old Orange High School sophomore has broken three women's indoor world records this winter—800 meters (2:01.8), 880 yards (2:02.4) and 1,000 yards (2:26.7)."[34] Hall also noted that the meet promoter for the *Times*'s indoor games was risking the wrath of the other 245 competitors when he listed Mary Decker as one of "the top 5 attractions at the meet," along with Steve Prefontaine, Dwight Stones, and two other world record holders.[35] John Walker, a New Zealand miler, commented: "She's been fantastic, but every time she goes out there she's expected to run fast and hard and that must take a toll." The article quoted Jackie as well: "I hope she's not moving too fast. It scares me. I don't want her to be a has-been at 17," she said.[36]

. . .

In March Mary went with the U.S. team to Moscow to face the Soviets indoors. She ran from the front in the 800 and won easily in 2:04.5. It was also at this meet that the first blemish on her charming public persona was caught in the spotlight: coming off the final turn in the women's medley relay race, Mary had been bumped and jostled by the larger Sarmite Shtula of the Soviet Union. As Decker ran anchor, Shtula shoved her out of the inside lane of the track and out of contention. At first Mary seemed bewildered, then angry. In a fit of rage, she tossed her baton at the runner—not once but twice—resulting in the U.S. medley team's disqualification.[37]

Teammates rushed to console her as Mary shouted over the crowd's disapproving whistles: "She hit me in the stomach with her baton!" She later told reporters, "I know I shouldn't have done it but I was so mad. I know I could have caught her easily if that hadn't happened."[38]

This moment, revealing a glimpse of a different Mary Decker, was quickly glossed over by the media as nothing more than evidence of her immaturity; a mean-spirited, spoiled, petulant Mary Decker wouldn't sell on television or in the press. But the spotlight had caught the moment nonetheless. While not given much weight at the time, it would later be remembered as an example of the "real Mary Decker," not the carefully controlled and managed media star her advisers were intent on presenting to the public.

Perhaps it was the image makers at work, perhaps it was just time for a makeover, but when Mary Decker arrived at a Southern California track writers' conference in April, she surprised them. She had been there the year before as a pigtailed fourteen-year-old who often blushed at their questions. Now the girl who showed up was prettier and looked "like someone who knows where she is going." She was quoted as saying that she was happy with Devian because her workouts with DeNoon had been "getting boring." Now, she added, she was training with the boys, and "I have to run to keep up." Asked if she was satisfied with her world records, she replied, "I'm never satisfied."[39]

Mary's 1974 indoor season had been a satisfactory one. She handled U.S. competition outdoors easily, and she beat the Russians in a Durham, North Carolina, rematch before thirty-five thousand spectators and a national television audience in early July. Passed in the home stretch, Mary rallied to beat Sabaitė with a new meet record of 2:02.3. But after that, Decker's season was essentially over. She did not tour Europe with the U.S. team for what she would later describe as personal reasons.[40]

Though she would later tell a writer, "My injuries began when I was fifteen," what she didn't say was that they coincided with two other factors: by 1974 she had left DeNoon and the forgiving grass and cinder tracks where his team trained and had begun to run on the pavement with her boyfriend and his coach, Ted Devian. And little Mary Decker was growing up, emotionally and physically. And she was doing so faster than her body could adjust. She grew six inches between the ages of fifteen and sixteen. "I didn't know what to do with this new body," she said later.[41] The growing and still-fragile bones and muscles were being battered by the abuse she inflicted on them on the road. Her new body wasn't responding like her old body had. It was protesting. Anyone else would have quit, rested her aching shins, and recovered. But not Mary Decker. Mary Decker ran. Indoors and outdoors, in unremitting pain, she ran and ran and ran, until finally she could run no more.

• • •

Dick Bank, a veteran track announcer and journalist, who covered track for *Women's Track & Field* magazine and a half-dozen foreign publications, often accompanied the U.S. team to international meets. "We had seen and developed a lot of good young women runners in California," he remembered. "But when Mary first burst upon the scene, we all agreed we'd never seen anything quite like her. She was just unbelievable. She wasn't just a star, she was Superwoman. She was this tiny little kid, in pigtails and braces, and she was just demolishing the competition. She was running distances we didn't think possible for a girl that age and doing so in times that placed her in world-class company. No one had ever seen anything quite like her."[42]

But like Superman, this Superwoman had a Kryptonian vulnerability, and her growing young body rebelled, soon reducing her to a painful, hobbling shell of the fleet-footed gazelle who had thrown the Southern California track community into spasms of excitement. The pain in her changing body was accompanied by another type of pain whose longer-lasting effect would perhaps prove more debilitating.

. . .

In addition to the physical pain that abruptly ended her 1974 season, she also was dealing with emotional upheaval. After a long period of hostility, her parents were finally ending their unhappy union. Jackie Decker had filed for divorce on December 28, 1973. In her filing, she stated that John "has been subjecting myself and my children to severe emotional pressures."[43]

In an action heard in Orange County Superior Court, Family Law Division, the case, D-78622, was turning out—like many divorces—to be an acrimonious affair. The decree, which was granted in November 1974, stipulated that Jackie would receive one hundred dollars a month in support for each child. But in a motion to have the divorce judgment amended after the decree was granted, John Decker asked in September 1975 to be relieved of the child support he had been ordered to pay for the minor child Mary T. Decker.

His sworn affidavit asserted that she had not been living at home since December 1974, but "had been residing with a male to whom she is not married." John swore under oath that he "was not responsible for child-care payments for Mary as stipulated in the divorce decree."[44]

. . .

Those who knew Mary Decker at that time remember her father's denial of his responsibility for her care and support as devastating news. In the opinions of two men who coached Decker for a number of years, her father's declaration that he was not responsible for her care and support—when she was only fifteen—was tantamount in Mary's mind to his abandoning her as his child. She interpreted it—and later described it to others—as a denial of his paternity.[45]

Though the damage was severe, in her pain, confusion, and anger, Mary Decker did what she had always done: she ran. But this time the physical pain, added to the emotional trauma, would prove to be too much to run through.

Her mother's fears that she would turn out to be a "has-been at 17" were a bit shortsighted. Mary was only fifteen.

. . .

The runner herself would later say, "People think DeNoon pushed me; they think my mother pushed me, but I can't honestly say I was ever pushed. I trained and raced hard because that was me. It was something within myself."[46] That is probably as close to the truth as Mary would ever come. What she didn't say was that inside her was a powerful hurt and the painful recognition that the man she had known as her father had denied her.

. . .

Mary continued to run.

In January 1975—when she still held the world indoor records at 800 meters, 800 yards, and 1,000 yards—Decker was entered in the Sunkist Invitational in Los Angeles, and there she faced Francie Larrieu. One of the first women middle-distance runners to have benefited from television exposure, Larrieu was pretty and personable. She was also very good—the world record holder for the indoor mile, two miles, and 3,000 meters. The matchup between the two stars was a promoter's dream.

Attired in her new Patriot Track Club uniform, Mary, as usual, streaked to the front. Larrieu worked her way through traffic and on the third lap passed Mary and assumed the lead. Decker continued to fall back and was soon passed by Cyndy Poor, who also pulled away from her (Poor would run in the 1,500 meters at the 1976 Olympics). Mary finished a full ten seconds behind Larrieu, who established a new indoor mark, beating the record formerly held by the Russian Tamara Kazachova.

The deep burning pain in Decker's shins wouldn't go away. Rest didn't help, therapy failed; nothing relieved the searing pain. Her season was over.

In the summer of 1975 she tried to come back. Her best time in the 800 meters was only 2:08.2. Now she was chasing competitors she had once breezed by.

The pain persisted, and by 1976 she couldn't run at all. Still, she harbored hopes, however faint: "I want to make the Olympics, even if I have to wait until 1980. The Olympics are what count." This was January 1976. "I still think I have enough time," she said. "[If] I don't have any more trouble. I hope the injuries are in the past."[47]

In reality, hobbled by her shins, Mary was hopelessly out of the picture. The world rankings for those three years—1975, 1976, and 1977—don't even list her name, and they would later be called the lost years of her career. Mary Decker, teenage phenom and media darling, had fallen completely off the charts. "At sixteen," she later would say, "I was a has-been." At the Montreal Olympics and the U.S. Olympic Trials preceding them, she could only watch. "It was hard," she said, knowing she "had the potential to be out there" and seeing Russian and Eastern bloc runners dominate the events she would have competed in.[48]

So it was that the 1976 Olympic Games, like those of 1972, passed Mary Decker by, and the spotlight sought new faces.

FOUR. Healing the Body

Anyone who has ever seen a thoroughbred racehorse injured knows that the magnificent animal, whose legs seem too thin ever to support its weight at high speed, will instinctively attempt to run away from the spot where it experienced the pain, as if by fleeing it can somehow escape the hurt.

A two-legged thoroughbred, Mary Decker fled the place where she felt the pain, both emotional and physical. She removed herself from the sand and surf of Southern California—from a sun-splashed life where swaying palms and warm ocean breezes had brought her such pain. Eventually she found her way to Colorado, surrounded by snow-capped mountains and frosty winters—and a new beginning.

. . .

In the summer of 1976, Mary settled in Boulder, Colorado, with her boyfriend, Bill Graves, and his parents. She found a job waiting tables at a Marie Callender's restaurant. Boulder was home to the University of Colorado, as well as a large group of serious runners who, like the marathoner Frank Shorter, used the high-altitude city as their training base.[1]

Though shunted to the periphery of that world by her injuries, Mary Decker was known and respected there for what she had achieved. While she may have been forgotten by the media that had once fawned over her as America's next best hope, she was remembered by the sophisticated running community in Boulder.[2]

. . .

Rich Castro was starting the women's track program at the University of Colorado in 1976.

"A friend whom I had coached as a runner, John Gregorio, came to see me, and he told me there was a young woman whom I might have heard of living here, named Mary Decker. Being a track nut I knew immediately who she was."

Castro also knew about Mary's reputation for being difficult: "I knew she could be a handful, her reputation was as somewhat of a prima donna, so I told Frank [Shorter], who was working for Nike at the time, to bring her on by and I would talk to her."[3]

Castro invited Mary to an ice-cream social at his home with the members of the women's track team. To his pleasant surprise, Mary was "very personable. I told her after we talked that if she was serious about coming to school, she should come up and see what I was doing with the team. If she was comfortable with that, I told her we'd see about getting her into school," Castro recalled. Mary did come to see the training Castro was supervising and apparently approved of what she saw. Shortly thereafter she enrolled and was given a partial scholarship, and in January 1977 she became part of the Buffaloes track team under Castro's watchful eye. "I wasn't really a distance coach. Most of my experience was with developing sprinters, but I told her I would try to help her as much as I could," he said.[4]

Mary ran for the Colorado Buffaloes that winter and spring. But Castro kept her schedule light. She managed to win a quarter-mile event in 56.7, a record for the meet and for the Big Eight Conference indoors. She finished third to Cindy Worchester of Kansas State in an 880-yard race in 2:15.9, about five seconds behind the winner.[5] While the performances were impressive, considering the lack of training and the pain she was fighting through, the times were a far cry from those clocked by a healthy, younger Mary Decker.

Later that spring the pain in her shins forced her to drop out of the outdoor meets. She had tried about everything she could think of or that anyone had heard of, short of surgery, with no improvement.

Track & Field News, the bible of the sport, which had once carried thousands of words about the wunderkind from Southern California, now took a different tack: "Mary Decker probably won't run this spring following the recommendation of a podiatrist. What seemed to be persistent shin splints are in reality a series of stress fractures."[6] Though the article would turn out to be wrong in its report of the diagnosis, Mary's condition was preventing her from running competitively.

She had always regarded surgery as "a final option"—her obvious concern was that if it didn't work, she might not be able to run at all.

. . .

In May Mary met a friend of Frank Shorter's who was training with Frank's running team—a meeting that would prove providential for her and would have a huge impact on her career. Dick Quax, a New Zealander born in the Netherlands as Theodorus Jacobus Leonardus Quax, had been a silver medalist at the 1976 Olympics, finishing second to the great Finnish runner Lasse Virén in the 5,000 meters. When he encountered Mary at a training session in Colorado and listened to her describe her symptoms, he stopped her in midsentence. "Look at this," he said, pointing to two long scars running down the front of his shins. "I had the same problem," he told her, explaining that the sheath around her calf muscles was too tight. The condition, known as compartment syndrome, could be corrected by surgery.

Having heard from Quax about the procedure that had relieved his pain—with no ill effects—Mary decided to have the surgery. She found a surgeon and, since her parents' insurance covered the operation, made the trip back to Southern California in July 1977. ("I actually paid for her flight back there," Castro recalled, acknowledging that the Association for Intercollegiate Athletics for Women [AIAW], the governing body of women's sports, might have frowned on that had they known about it.) The surgeon would later remark that when his scalpel made the incision into the constraining sheath, Mary's muscle burst free like an overstuffed sausage from its casing.

Within a matter of mere weeks, Mary Decker was running free of pain for the first time in years. It was almost miraculous. The Buffaloes would be the first to get a glimpse of the new Mary Decker, who had moved from Marie Callender's to Frank Shorter's running store in Boulder.

. . .

Rich Castro, a college administrator as well as coach, had moved back into his academic office, and his assistant, Tracy Sumlin, took over the team, but Rich continued to monitor Mary's progress. Under his watchful eye, Mary started the postoperative journey back. "No one knew just how good she would be. She started back slowly, training primarily with the men's team so she could push herself," he said. Gradually Mary's conditioning returned. Not long after, her speed reemerged from the pain-shrouded fog where it had been hidden until the surgery.[7]

The Lady Buffaloes began to become a factor, with Mary leading the way. They finished second in the Big Eight meet and qualified for the AIAW Nationals in Austin on November 19, 1977.

Castro, who tried to get her to adopt a more conservative approach to training, remained impressed by Mary's tenacity and could see the change in her. "Give her a year, and she will challenge anyone," he predicted.

Not even Mary's poor showing in the final fall cross-country race in November—she finished a distant ninth—hurt her growing self-confidence. As Castro correctly put it, "Mary didn't like to lose."[8]

In fact she had already set her own goals for the coming spring:

to run 800 meters in 1:58 and 1,500 meters in 4:05. When Castro saw the numbers she had jotted down as her targets, he immediately realized they would place her in the very top echelon of American middle-distance runners. Mary Decker knew she was coming back—and coming back with a vengeance.

"She was the most competitive athlete I have ever coached," said Castro, who coached for forty years. Mary "had a tenacity you seldom see," and "for sheer talent there has never been anyone better."[9]

But Rich Castro also knew Mary well enough to be aware of her vulnerability. The two had run together a number of times, and he had noted that she always "pushed the envelope." She'd always urge him, "Let's go hard," whenever he tried to get her to throttle back in a training run. "She never eased into anything," he said.[10]

Years after he last coached her, Castro would say of Mary Decker, "I always thought her downfall would be that she pushed her body harder than it could handle. There was no barrier—pain, exhaustion—no problem. She would just push herself through it.

"And," he added, "she always needed to be in control of the race."[11]

. . .

Mary moved on—all the way to New Zealand and then Australia—in late 1977 and early 1978. Dick Quax had arranged several meets for her Down Under, and he was to coach her on the trip. The good-looking New Zealander was tall, lean, blond, mustachioed, and had that singular Kiwi accent. The nineteen-year-old Mary and the man who, in her eyes, had proved to be her savior with his solution to her shin problem, would see a lot of each other.

Bill Graves, her boyfriend, remained behind in Colorado.

. . .

Decker's trip was a smashing success on the track. She followed a training schedule designed for her by Quax and won all seven races she entered. And, more significant, her times were coming down: she ran the 800 meters in progressively faster times, culminating in a 2:01.8 mark in her final start at that distance. She also won the longer races easily, and in January 1978 she posted a winning time of 4:08.9 in a 1,500-meter race.

Mary Decker was back.

· · ·

Nobuya "Nobby" Hashizume, a runner himself, who now heads the foundation devoted to Arthur Lydiard's marathon-training methods in Plymouth, Minnesota, was a friend of Quax's. "I really believe that Dick Quax laid the foundation for Mary's success. He went the Lydiard way—building an aerobic foundation first and eschewing the former Decker plan of speed, speed, speed," Hashizume said.[12]

The Lydiard program emphasized long moderate miles of training runs supplemented by shorter interval-training programs. The results were runners with a solid foundation for endurance and strength. They would be able to sustain their performance over longer distances without risking serious injuries.[13]

The results of Quax's coaching were obvious on the track, but off the track, they led to an ugly scene: "Mary developed a huge crush on Dick," Hashizume recalled. While this was hardly remarkable, given that the two were together virtually the entire time, it did present a problem. The thirty-year-old Quax was married, and his wife was not pleased. "Mary created a big scene and embarrassed Dick."[14]

But even as her personal life took yet another blow, Mary returned to the United States physically fit and with a solid foundation for running under her. After the successful surgery and Quax's training regimen, she had been rebuilt as a runner.

Her transformation extended beyond the track.

The little pigtailed girl in braces who had earned the admiration of writers and track officials in the early seventies was now a slender, five-foot-six, 110-pound woman who would be twenty in August. The braces were gone, and her front teeth were now neatly aligned and surrounded by bright red lip gloss. Her pigtails were replaced by professionally coiffed auburn curls with blond highlights that framed her brown-eyed face. Her eyebrows were plucked and penciled into graceful arches, while eyeliner and mascara added the final touches.

A comparison of photographs of the two Mary Deckers makes it impossible to miss the transformation. The carefully coiffed and made-up Mary was now an attractive young woman. Not only was she ready to resume her former position as the darling of American track athletes, now she had the looks for the role.

Her reemergence into the limelight came, appropriately, in Los Angeles—where people understood star power—at the LA Times meet in February 1978. Admittedly nervous about her homecoming in Southern California, Decker didn't know if her fans would remember her or what their response might be if they did.[15] The question was answered early on, when the 16,333 in attendance at the indoor meet cheered her appearance as she stepped on the track.

But her comeback race would offer a much sterner test than the fields she had conquered in the Southern Hemisphere. The runners in the 1,000-yard contest included Francie Larrieu, Wendy Knudson, Julie Brown, and a West German star, Ellen Wessinhage. Old habits die hard, however, and at the sound of the starting gun, Mary sped to the front.

Leaving little doubt that the "new Mary" was indeed the old healthy one, she stretched her lead to twenty-five yards and passed the 880-yard mark in a blazing 2:05.2 as the crowd cheered her on—as they had when, as a teenager, she first won their hearts. Buoyed by the reaction, she cruised home in 2:23.8, a new world record.[16]

Mary Decker had clearly come all the way back, and the crowd rose in unison, according the victor a standing ovation. "This is elation," she said after the race.[17]

Explaining that she hadn't run with the record in mind, she told reporters, "I hadn't run indoors for so long, I just wanted to avoid the pushing and shoving," she said.[18] Had Bob Hickey overheard her remarks, he would have nodded knowingly.

Decker was still on an emotional high when she told the assembled reporters, "No more injuries and no more losses. I'm looking only upwards." She smiled as the photographers snapped away at the photogenic winner.[19]

. . .

Returning to Colorado after her stunning performance in LA, Mary resumed training with Dick Quax. She followed her LA win with an appearance in Canada before another sold-out stadium for the Toronto Star Maple Leaf Games indoor meet. The field included Larrieu and Jan Merrill, along with Mary, then the three top women in the 1,500 meters.

Wearing the black-and-silver colors of New Zealand, made recognizable to all by the two-time Olympic and world record holder Peter Snell, among others, Mary moved into the lead after a quarter mile. She easily outlasted a challenge by Larrieu in the final lap—as a reporter noted: "[Decker] sort of shrugged her shoulders and sprinted away to win by five yards." After the race Larrieu remarked, "Mary is just too strong right now."[20]

. . .

Back in Colorado Mary donned the Buffaloes' colors and added a Big Eight Conference title to her comeback, setting a new conference record for 880 yards, chopping a full five seconds off the previous mark and finishing in a time that was ten seconds better than she had posted when she finished third in the previous season's injury-plagued effort. At the same meet she also smashed the conference mile record by posting a 4:41.2 mark, a full eight seconds better than the old mark for that distance.

An article in New York's *Newsday* that was reprinted in Boulder's *Daily Camera* contrasted her remarkable comeback with her long absence. "People shook Mary Decker and rattled her, and bounced her a few times, curious about the inner works. That the damage was done as innocently as a child would do it (to an object) did not undo it. Decker was broke and forgotten."[21]

The broken Mary Decker was a thing of the past. With her image refined and her dramatic comeback from injury seen as nothing short of miraculous, Mary was quickly becoming a media icon. The story was irresistible: A teenage phenom who had been disastrously damaged recovers to take back her spot as America's best hope to defeat the Eastern bloc runners dominating middle-distance track. Oh, and by the way, she looked good doing it.

Great story.

And the 1980 Olympic Games were coming up fast.

. . .

Mary, never a motivated student, had withdrawn from the University of Colorado during the indoor meet season to devote more time to her running. Still training with Quax, she upped her workouts to two a day and her distance to ninety miles a week over the road and mountain trails. In June 1978 she told Elizabeth Wheeler of the *Los Angeles Times:* "My goals in racing are basically the same that I've always had. Every time I run, I hope I can run fast enough to win. It's a good thing to run for personal records. But I want to go one step further. I want to make a personal record but I want to run faster than anyone else."[22]

Though the new Big Mary sounded a lot like the old Little Mary, she would soon resemble her old self in another way: her shins were aching again. Despite finishing third in 2:03.1 for 800 meters in the U.S. national championships, her overall results were not satisfactory, and she was in pain. In August 1978 she had another operation on her legs.[23]

That fall she returned to classes at Colorado and ran cross-country. At the AIAW nationals at the end of the 1978 season, she ran in unusually warm weather in Boulder and beat Julie Brown and Kathy Mills of Penn State. The field Decker defeated was populated with other strong runners, including North Carolina State's Joan Benoit and Julie Shea, Lynn Jennings of Princeton, Margaret Groos of the University of Virginia, and other standout performers, but Mary Decker triumphed despite the strength and experience of the field.[24] Her success was quickly followed by more pain, in what would become, through the years ahead, a never-ending saga. Back in New Zealand shortly after the AIAW meet, she developed sciatica, a pinched nerve in her back, which was compounded when she slipped and fell on a wet road. After those injuries healed, she tore a muscle in her back. She managed to finish her semester at Colorado and then sought Rich Castro's advice again.

"She had received an offer from Athletics West [Nike's sponsored track team], which she wanted to speak to me about," Castro said. "She was only getting a partial scholarship from us, and the offer from Athletics West was for $15,000. I told her there really wasn't any reason for her to stay here. She wasn't particularly interested in academics, and I thought she should move on."[25]

. . .

Mary left Colorado and joined Athletics West in May 1979—the first woman to do so—moving to Eugene, Oregon, and starting a new training regimen. She was seeing a chiropractor weekly as well as getting massage therapy and making regular visits to the orthopedist as well as to Dick Brown, the Athletics West physiologist who monitored her well-being through regular blood samples. She and Quax shared scars on their shins and an apartment in Eugene near the Athletics West training complex—although Quax was still married, his off-track relationship with Decker was so well known it was mentioned in the sports pages. But after a rather messy row, the demise of their on-track relationship soon followed that of their romantic one.

Despite her physical problems, Mary had run a 4:23.5 mile, establishing a new American record, and had captured the 1,500-meter title at the Pan American Games in 1979. But Mary wasn't the best American middle-distance runner that year: Francie Larrieu held that honor—and she was ranked only fourteenth best in the world. That meant that Mary's best 1,500 time of 4:05 left her far behind a host of Eastern European runners, as well as Norway's Grete Waitz, Great Britain's Chris Benning, and West Germany's Brigitte Kraus. In terms of the international rankings, Decker was an also-ran.

Fortunately for Decker, she was in a place where coaching track athletes was a religion. And the high priest—also in Eugene, Oregon—was willing to take her on. His name was Bill Bowerman.

Raised by his mother in the small Oregon town of Fossil, Bowerman was the coach at the University of Oregon. He had developed unique training methods—"train, don't strain"—that included rest days between interval-training sessions and a program aimed at peaking runners for major events.

Bowerman's teams at Oregon won four national titles, and his athletes had set thirteen world and twenty-two American records. The most successful track coach in America, he was also an inveterate tinkerer who, dissatisfied with the running shoes that the European and Japanese countries produced, designed a "waffle-soled" running shoe in his garage with a waffle iron. His prototype would form the basis for the success of a small Oregon company he cofounded with an accountant friend, Phil Knight. The company's original name was Blue Ribbon; then, on the advice of a coworker, it adopted the name of the Greek goddess of speed. Nike would soon outdistance all competitors and grow to be the dominant company in the field, its Swoosh trademark becoming a ubiquitous presence at all track events.[26]

Fittingly, for a man whose company was named for a goddess, the woman once seen as filling that role arrived in Eugene to ask Bowerman and Dick Brown, sports physiologist and director of Athletics West, to assume control of her career. Decker had gone to Eugene because Pre had always urged her to do so. Also, the Olympic trials were to be held there, and she had great Nike friends there.

According to Brown, Dick Quax had shed himself of Mary after a final falling out in the summer of 1980—he had decided that the current Mrs. Quax was preferable to the aspiring next Mrs. Quax. Now Mary Decker would have as her advisers the taciturn, quirky, and enormously successful Bowerman as well as Brown, whose discipline as an exercise physiologist was something the often-injured Decker needed more than most.

Though Bowerman would say later that he "felt honored to be entrusted with her talent and a little burdened with her temperament," after about six months as Mary's coach he had changed his mind. Brown recalled that Bowerman said, "'I don't need this in my life anymore, Dick. Find her another coach.' That's when I became her coach."[27]

Bowerman had become the sixth man to learn that coaching Mary Decker was not an easy proposition. Her talent was never in question, but her need—which amounted to an obsession—to have her coach devote his full and undivided attention to her was more than Bowerman could handle, although he is acknowledged to have been the best in the business. Bowerman would continue to help Brown plan training and strategy, but he removed himself from the onerous all-consuming demand for attention that Mary insisted upon.

Brown would become Decker's seventh coach and, as it turned out, her best, by doing what no one else had been able to do: he kept her healthy enough to run to her full potential. That potential would prove to be unprecedented in women's track.

. . .

Dick Brown had the training and knowledge to understand exactly the stresses Mary had been putting on her body through her rigorous training methods and her refusal ever to ease up, no matter the pain or the circumstances. She had always pushed through it all until she inevitably broke down. Brown would be the man who gained her trust and convinced her there was a better way.

"I had gotten to know her first as her exercise physiologist, before I coached her. She had confidence in me from that relationship. I also understood that she was one of the most gifted natural runners this world has ever seen," he said. Brown would also describe his new charge—and challenge—as "from the knees up . . . a great thoroughbred. From the knees down her legs were full of scar tissue. What we had to do," he said, "was to keep her healthy, so she could participate in the major meets."[28] Brown adapted the system Bowerman had used to perfection with his runners, with some important modifications by Brown to meet Decker's special needs, and, more important, to persuade Decker to follow it.

The results would make history.

. . .

One of the things Brown is proudest of is that Decker "met every goal I set for her for major meets, with one exception." That exception would not manifest itself for four more years, and in the interim Decker and Brown would set forth on a series of seasons that had no equal.

In Brown's opinion, "Mary Decker either saw people as wearing white hats or black hats. I was one of those few she saw as wearing a white hat for many years."

Running, he believed, was what "defined Mary. Mary needed that [success] because there were a lot of things in her life that had produced insecurity."

When he was running with her, he would insist she run behind him. "I wasn't a very good runner, but she did it, and that kept her at a slow pace. In intervals I told her if she would run [ten sets of four hundred yards] in eighty-five seconds for each, which was very slow for her, I'd give her a prize. That held her back.

"That was the biggest thing I had to do with Mary—hold her back," he said. Dick Brown became the first coach to rein in her overarching obsession with speed and her need to finish first no matter what. He was able to do it, he believes, "because she trusted me." Planning a schedule for her workouts, "we would discuss it and agree to it and she would do it."[29]

The formula proved wildly successful and worked for five years, until a third party entered the scene and Brown became yet another ex-coach. But that lay in the future.

Under Brown's restraining guidance, and with intermittent counsel from Bowerman, Mary Decker would enjoy a remarkable—by any standard—five seasons at the pinnacle of her sport. In 1980, an Olympic year, despite occasional heel pain, she ran well for the entire season. But as had happened in the past, there would be no Olympic Games for Mary Decker.

The year started promisingly; she began the indoor season in fine form as she set a world indoor record of 4:00.8 in New York for the 1,500 meters. She continued her dominance by becoming the first woman to break the two-minute barrier, winning an 800-meter race in 1:59.7, which included a blazing first lap of 56.9. In the Houston Astrodome, on February 16, she ran a mile in 4:17.5, which bettered Francie Larrieu's previous world record by almost eleven seconds and left the closest competitor thirty-three seconds behind. "I had broken all of Doris Brown Heritage's records, and then Mary came along and broke all of mine," Larrieu said.[30]

In April, Mary added a 32:53 victory in a 10K road race in San Diego—a race she ran "just for fun." At that late date she was still clinging to a hope that she would finally get to the Olympics: "If there's any way I can go, I will. I've waited a long time to make the trip."[31] But as things developed, she'd be waiting a little longer.

. . .

Even before the relationship with Quax ended, Mary had been discussing her return to fame with Elliot Almond of the *Los Angeles Times*: "I'm supposed to be nice to everyone I meet. I'm not a mean person. I like people. But, there's a limit. When I was younger," she told Almond, "people wanted to know what classes I was taking, what I ate. They weren't asking me who I was sleeping with."[32] By the time the summer 1980 outdoor season arrived, both Mary and Quax were training in Oregon, but the romance was over.

Mary was nursing an aching Achilles tendon that Dick Brown treated with exercises in a pool and on roller skates for as many as six miles a day. He nursed her along with these and other alternative training methods that enabled her to continue to compete without doing any further harm, a monumental achievement in and of itself. She was a lock for the Olympic team, but there was one problem: no U.S. team would go to Moscow in 1980.

"At first I thought it was a little unfair. President Carter hasn't been president as long as some of us have been training. It's been my whole life for a lot of years, and a lot of other people's. You feel a little cheated, that somebody who really doesn't know what it takes to win a medal in the Olympics has complete control. But you can't be naive and say that sports and politics don't mix. They always have. You just have to take it in stride," she said in late February as news of the potential boycott leaked out.[33]

Soon after, in retaliation for the Soviet Union's invasion of Afghanistan, President Carter decided to boycott the Moscow games, announcing that any American athletes who tried to attend would have their passports revoked.[34] For the third straight Olympics since she began running, Mary Decker would be denied the chance to compete for an Olympic medal.

"I would love to win an Olympic medal, but if it isn't possible, it isn't possible. Maybe I can just prove I am the best in other ways," she would say.[35] "The Olympics have been my goal since I was eleven years old," she told the Southern California track writers' luncheon in March.[36]

It would be one of the rare personal goals that Mary would fail to achieve, and she felt keenly her disappointment at being denied the opportunity coveted by all world-class athletes.

Decker overcame the lost chance by running as only she could. In July she posted a winning time—4:04.9 over 1,500 meters, the second-best time ever recorded by an American woman—in the televised but meaningless U.S. Olympic Trials. On July 12, in Stuttgart, before a crowd of ninety thousand under the lights, she set a new American mark by running at the front of a weakened field to notch 4:01.7, erasing Jan Merrill's old mark by nearly two seconds.[37] Three days later Decker was in Oslo, where another capacity crowd watched as she added the American record at 3,000 meters to her growing portfolio of bests.

Returning to America, she ran in the Liberty Bell Classic, an event designed to soothe American feelings at being denied the chance to view their athletes in the Olympics. On a hot muggy day in front of more than twenty thousand fans and a national television audience, Mary defeated a strong field for the 1,500-meter race that included Francie Larrieu, Julie Brown, and a Kenyan, Rose Thomson, who was representing the University of Wisconsin.

Decker set the pace early, and as the field dropped away she sped to another American record in 4:00.87, with Brown finishing second nearly ten seconds back. Afterward Decker told reporters she had hoped to go under four minutes and brashly announced, "The world record is definitely on my mind."[38] Revealing just how upset she had felt when denied the chance to run in Moscow, she also said she wanted to race the three Olympic medal winners after the games concluded. Even after two Soviets and an East German posted the winning Olympic medal times—which were faster than Decker had ever run—she maintained that, while maybe the gold wasn't yet in her range of possibilities, "I do believe that I would have won a medal."[39]

Mary's audacity was in sharp contrast to the growing number of runners in the West who believed—correctly, as it turned out—that the Soviet and Eastern bloc women were running with an advantage that rendered futile all efforts to compete with them. But she would get her chance at a meet in Rome on August 5, just a scant few days after the Olympics had concluded. The Olympic gold medalist, Tatyana Kazankina, and Gabriella Dorio of Italy, the host nation, were entered in the 1,500. Bothered by a still-sore Achilles tendon, Decker managed only a third-place finish. Next she ran an 800 meters in her personal best time of 1:59.10 and then tried once again to better 4:00 in the 1,500 on August 11 in Budapest. She came close, finishing in 4:00.4 and setting another new American record.

In Zurich, in the prestigious Weltklasse meet later in August, Decker would get her chance to test herself again against Kazankina. However, the Russians used a rabbit—a runner who is in the race solely to set a furious early pace and then generally drops out—to assist Kazankina and drain Decker's energy. The strategy worked. Though she set a new American record and finally ran under 4:00 (3:59.43), it was small consolation. The flying Kazankina had thrashed her by nearly fifty meters. Later Mary would announce, "I don't know if I will ever beat her. She is so strong."[40]

It would fall to Mary Decker, not surprising given her competitiveness, to do what others had failed to do with regard to the Eastern bloc runners. "Mary had gone to look for the women's locker room," Dick Brown recalled. "She was directed to the door, and when she walked in the Soviets were getting dressed. She turned around and walked right out. 'They don't look like women to me,' she said."[41]

Noting their bulky muscles and buttocks, the willowy long-legged Mary said, "Their muscle definition is so pronounced. I don't doubt that they are women biologically speaking, but, shall we say, chemically, I'm not so sure."[42]

With that, Mary Decker had thrown down the gauntlet.

FIVE. Dirty Little Secret
· ·

Nothing can be written about twentieth-century track, or sports in general, without acknowledging the very thing that Mary Decker had brashly dared to express publicly: the playing field was uneven.

Decker knew it and everybody else involved in track knew it, including those entrusted with the purity of friendly competition between representatives of member nations. In Lausanne the International Olympic Committee (IOC) held the franchise for the hugely popular Olympic Games, which were founded in 1892 by a French aristocrat, Pierre de Frédy, Baron de Coubertin, who thought an international meeting of athletes would promote cooperation between nations and world peace. In 1894 he convened a meeting at which seventy-nine delegates from twelve countries agreed to form a committee to reinstitute the games that had been held in ancient Greece. Two years later the IOC would hold the first modern Olympics in Athens, chosen for its symbolic representation of the original games.

From that early beginning, the Olympic Games became a quadrennial event that rotated among host countries, bringing together athletes from various disciplines to test themselves against the best in the world. All competitors were, of course—in keeping with the initial charter of the body—to be amateur athletes competing for nothing more than olive wreaths and, later, medals. Alas, the well-intentioned de Coubertin was a man destined to be disappointed by reality: the games soon were interrupted by World War I.

In 1912, however, when hope was still stirring in his breast, the games were held in Stockholm, where a young American, Avery Brundage, competed in the decathlon and pentathlon, finishing well behind his fellow compatriot Jim Thorpe in those events.[1]

Avery Brundage was an Ivy League–educated patrician of dubious sensitivity and judgment. A hard-liner on amateurism, by 1932 he had risen to the top positions in the Amateur Athletic Union and the U.S. Olympic Committee (USOC). In 1934 he made a fact-finding tour of Nazi Germany to evaluate the situation in advance of the 1936 games, which Berlin was to host. He returned to the United States to assure the USOC that in his view all was fine in the Third Reich and that Americans should indeed compete. Behind his back he became known as "Avery Slavery," for his vow to keep athletes from earning any money in their chosen sport and for his contemptible, privately held anti-Semitism and racism.

In 1936 Brundage stood nearby as Adolf Hitler and his henchmen filed out of the stadium when Jesse Owens was supposed to receive his first of four Olympic gold medals from the Führer. Three years later, when the Nazi Germany that had received Brundage's seal of approval began World War II, the games again were suspended, resuming in 1948. They did so in a much-altered world.[2]

The USSR and the United States, former allies, began a decades-long period of uneasy peacetime competition in which the two superpowers jockeyed for preeminence. In the East the communist governments soon realized that, after eschewing participation in the postwar Olympics because they regarded the games as bourgeois, competing, in fact, offered some political advantage: they could prove, through their excellence in sports, that their communist system was superior to that of the capitalist West.

In the years following the end of World War II, the battle for the military, economic, and political allegiance of other nations was fought not with intercontinental ballistic missiles just a jumpy trigger finger away, but in an apparently harmless worldwide forum in which it was possible, every four years, to display for all to see the dominance of the Soviet system. In this the Soviets had a distinct advantage in that their governments, unlike that of the United States and others in the West, fully supported the funding and training of their athletes.

While most Western runners were forced to beg, borrow, and otherwise scrabble for government support and training facilities, the athletes from communist countries were rewarded handsomely—in what might seem to be an inverted form of capitalism—for their prowess on the fields of athletic strife. At least for as long as they won, they received better housing, handsome monetary allowances, and other displays of regard from their otherwise ruthless rulers. The results began to show almost immediately.

But the true domination by Eastern Europeans would come in the midseventies and beyond, when the communist governments that administered the programs decided better results could be attained through pharmacological enhancement of their athletes.

The use of drugs in the Olympics can be traced to the 1960 games in Rome, when a cyclist died and the results of an autopsy showed he had been using drugs. The IOC was alarmed. According to then-IOC member Dick Pound, "They thought, 'Wait a minute. You are supposed to come to the Olympics to compete. You aren't supposed to come here to die because you're using drugs.'"[3]

The IOC established a medical commission, which had a subcommittee on doping and biochemistry. It assembled a group of experts and told them, "Here is what we think is being used," and asked the commission to look at the drugs. From that information, the IOC developed a list of prohibited drugs: whatever wasn't prohibited was permitted.

Once rules had been established against the use of certain drugs, "it all went underground," Pound said. "The first drugs were obtained from veterinarians, the logic being if steroids could beef up cattle, we can beef you up, too," and the early use of anabolic steroids, including Dianabol and others, was centered on those athletes whose strength was of the utmost importance: weight lifters, hammer and discus throwers, and shot-putters all began to use steroids to perform better. The word quickly spread to other sports, and countries traded information.[4]

The IOC conducted its first tests at Grenoble during the 1968 Winter Games. "The difficulty was that the IOC could only test at the games," Pound said. "Other than that two-week period the tests were under the control of the various countries' national Olympic committees or the various international federations for each sport." Accordingly, for the period of three years, eleven months, and two weeks between games, the testing—if there was any—was done by those bodies. Most didn't even have tests or, if they had them, used them only during competitive meets. This system, such as it was, allowed athletes to make certain that any drugs they were using would be cleared from their bodies before Olympic competition and testing.

"I've always said if you fail an in-competition drug test, you've failed two tests. You failed a drug test and you failed an IQ test," Pound joked.[5]

Athletes using drugs were assisted by their sophisticated knowledge of the detection methods and the various ways to beat the system, including the use of agents that masked the drugs in the early rudimentary tests of urine samples.

As the testing became more sophisticated and effective, so too did the efforts to beat detection.

. . .

In his book *Faust's Gold*, Dr. Steven Ungerleider, a sports psychologist who served on the USOC registry of sports psychologists and has advised numerous Olympians, documents in detail the intricacies and efficacy of the programs to improve athletic performance through the use of drugs and the horrific price paid by those subjected to them.[6] The East German women swimmers would be the first examples of the success of the program in bringing home the gold.

The young women selected for the East German team were monitored intently by the secret police, the Stasi, and were tested rigorously through government-sponsored monitoring of their blood. Anabolic steroids were the drug of choice for the Eastern bloc nations. In East Germany the program was carried out under the then-secret State Planning Theme 14.25. Under this seemingly innocuous-sounding program, more than ten thousand unsuspecting young athletes were given massive doses of anabolic steroids. Their success in competition was immediate and miraculous. They soon dominated swimming, and as the advantages became apparent, usage spread to other sports and the science to other iron-curtain countries.[7]

Incredible as it seems, the IOC's policy of having member nations, their Olympic committees, and their sports federations administer the drug tests between Olympic Games was so loose that, in East Germany, for example, the same doctor who oversaw the drugging of athletes also was in charge of testing those athletes. The lab the East Germans used to process the urine samples was the same lab in which they compounded the drugs and masking agents. That was the system.

In addition, the international sports federations, the governing bodies for sports, were reluctant to make positive test findings public. "They had no appetite whatsoever for acknowledging that there was drug use, or acknowledging that there was a problem, or that there were positive tests," Pound said. "The IOC, I thought, could have used the considerable leverage of participation in the games more effectively. But [they were] very reluctant to have any sort of confrontation with the international sports federations.

"Remember, this was all Cold War conditions. It was very difficult to attack the Soviet bloc. You knew you were dealing with state-imposed and -administered programs in that world. So, all the others, where there wasn't much oversight by sports bodies or governments in the West and in the United States, said, Well we're playing against a stacked deck and we have to do what we have to do to be competitive," Pound added.[8]

Thus the risks to the athletes—and those administering the drugs were aware of them—were secondary to the goal of proving to the world that the communist athletes, and by extension the communist political and economic systems, were superior to any others—most pointedly to America's brand of capitalism.[9]

The results were so obvious it is astounding to think that those administering the Olympic Games were unaware of the massive state-sponsored doping. Astounding, that is, until we recall who was at the head of the IOC from 1980, the very summer that Mary Decker became the first world-class track athlete to openly draw attention to the Eastern bloc women runners whom she was constantly chasing.

The IOC, as Pound explained, was not naive, nor was it oblivious to the blatant doping. The IOC had known about it since the 1960s and had deplored it and established commissions and subcommittees to combat it. But the IOC was waging a battle it was certain to lose, and the man who headed the IOC knew it.

. . .

Juan Antonio Samaranch, a member of the IOC since 1967 and most recently its first vice president, had become president of the organization eight years after Avery Brundage's reign ended in 1972, and after the Irishman Lord Killanin had served.

By 1980 the Olympic Games were well established, if not wildly successful financially. Increasingly seen as the opportune public forum in which to display conflicting political and economic philosophies, the games were light-years removed from the vision of Baron de Coubertin. Samaranch would alter the games even further.

A wealthy, ambitious Spanish grandee and businessman, Samaranch had obtained his position with the strong support of Horst Dassler, a German who headed Adidas, the company that makes athletic shoes, apparel, and equipment. Dassler had used his contacts throughout the developing African, Caribbean, Middle Eastern, and Soviet bloc nations to deliver the presidency to Samaranch. Samaranch and Dassler had become friendly after Samaranch, who had served as sports minister under Franco, was dispatched to Moscow as ambassador after Franco died. When the IOC presidency opened up, Dassler was able to secure it for Samaranch because Dassler's efforts on behalf of Adidas had introduced him to the leaders of the international sports federations in the developing world. Dassler's marketing tactics should have given considerable pause: in an era when amateurism was still the rule, at least nominally, his free athletic shoes often came stuffed with dollars. When he courted countries, gifts to prominent leaders of their sports federations were lavish and frequent. He made lots of friends with his "sports assistance."[10]

Dassler was the first to bring to the IOC's attention the intrinsic monetary value of the Olympic brand. In 1982 Dassler secured the marketing contract for World Cup soccer through his marketing company, ISL (International Sport and Leisure), which he parlayed into the marketing contract for the Olympic Games, thanks to his good friend Samaranch. Dassler, ISL, and the IOC then teamed up, and the results were a financial windfall for both parties. TOP (The

Olympic Program) was the result, and in 1988 it received $100 million from sponsors. Not long after, however, the Spaniard relieved Dassler of the marketing rights. Loyalty, Samaranch had learned in his days as a stiff-armed, fascist-saluting member of Franco's regime, worked only one way.[11]

. . .

Under Samaranch there proved to be another money-spewing faucet to be tapped. The tool he used was something called television—and with television came money. (Although the Olympics had been televised for years, whichever network had the contract paid little for the privilege, and the television rights were barely profitable for the IOC.) Samaranch, the newly elected head of the IOC, knew instinctively that money, more than anything else, was what he needed to continue in his lofty position.

Samaranch ruled an organization headquartered in super secret Switzerland, and little was known about the IOC other than that it held the franchise for the Olympic Games. In fact the IOC was an exclusive club made up of representatives—mostly male, mostly wealthy or politically connected, and mostly white—from about seventy-five countries, both superpowers and obscure third-world islands in the far-off Pacific or Caribbean.

The IOC membership, in turn, elected the president by secret ballot. In so doing, the members gave him virtual carte blanche for its governance and financial affairs. Samaranch rewarded their support by parceling out plum committee assignments that would entail all-expenses-paid first-class travel to international cities and accommodations at five-star hotels while on IOC business. (Samaranch's experience in Franco's fascist regime, and as Spain's ambassador to the Soviet Union after the dictator's death, had well prepared him for this system of rewards.) He ruled his domain pompously and autocratically with little opposition. Certainly most of those enjoying the perquisites of their positions on his various committees—per diem, plus expenses for travel—were not going to do anything but rubber-stamp his decisions and plans. They met as a whole only once a year in Switzerland, and those meetings were lavish parties as much as business meetings.

Samaranch had learned from a master during his tenure under

Franco, and he would run the IOC with a velvet glove—but one that barely covered the steely reality of raw power that was all too obvious to those who knew where to look in Lausanne.[12]

By 1980, when Samaranch assumed his post, the recent history of the Olympic Games had been marked by tragedies and a variety of unpleasantries: In 1972 a group of Palestinian terrorists had murdered members of the Israeli Olympic team in Munich. In 1976, in Montreal, the host city went into the red by a billion dollars after hosting the games. The 1980 Moscow Games, just concluded, had been a monumental bust because the United States had refused to attend, and American TV viewership—in what was the games' largest commercial market—plummeted.

Dick Pound, a prominent attorney and IOC member from Canada (he had rowed for his country in the 1960 Olympics), was instrumental in obtaining for Samaranch and the IOC the first significant television contracts and commercial agreements for the licensing of the Olympic logo.[13]

Pound also was enlisted by Samaranch to head the World Anti-Doping Agency (WADA) in 1999. As czar of the effort, he would be placed in an untenable position. It was not in the interests of Samaranch and the IOC to have their games sullied by a massive number of drug cheats testing positive. The IOC system of leaving the testing and enforcement between the games to the international sports federations and national Olympic committees served as an insurance policy that no such embarrassing disclosures would be forthcoming.

The television contracts that Pound secured for the IOC produced a wellspring of hundreds of millions of dollars that funded Samaranch's feudal fiefdom. Television revenue provided the money he needed to dispense to his supporters on the IOC in the form of "developmental grants" and other lofty-sounding names, often to third-world nations where—coincidentally—the same IOC members often served as the administrators of the funds. Finding concrete evidence of new or enhanced facilities and programs that resulted from such grants would, in many cases, prove difficult.

It was, however, vital to Samaranch that the money Pound produced keep flowing. Nothing must be permitted to dampen the interest of the television networks or corporate partners of the IOC. Everyone from credit-card issuers to candy bar makers, and every conceivable product or service in between, had joined the rush to share in the luster of being associated with the famed Olympic five-rings logo and of proclaiming themselves "the Official [whatever product or service—one company per category, please] of the Olympics." Through skillful negotiations by Pound, the influx of television dollars to the IOC would escalate exponentially, from $10 million in 1968 to more than $325 million by 1984.[14] This veritable deluge of dollars—which made the secretive IOC a cash cow—could not, in Samaranch's view, be jeopardized by anything—including the revelation that Olympians were doping. It would surely result in diminishing the value of the franchise and, correspondingly, the amount of money corporate sponsors and television networks were willing to channel to Switzerland.

It should be noted that the IOC had made statements as far back as 1960 against the use of performance-enhancing drugs. But they were statements without any clout. With the exception of the two weeks of each quadrennial Olympics, the international athletics federations for each sport were responsible for enforcement and detection. When a country hosted an Olympics, its Olympic committee was in charge of testing on behalf of the IOC. Thus it was almost a self-fulfilling prophecy that, while the IOC maintained a public posture of sanctimonious opposition to doping, it had perfect deniability when anyone like Mary Decker pointed an accusing finger.

Pound would prove to be a well-meaning, talented, and loyal IOC member who, more than anyone else, had made the IOC one of the most successful organizations on the planet. But in his later role as the committee's drug czar, he fought a losing battle. He was hamstrung by the very organization he served: the IOC found it more convenient—indeed, desirable—to leave responsibility, and blame whenever it came, to the international federations and national Olympic committees.[15]

. . .

The IOC was not the only organization to be tainted by the proliferation of drug use. Few sports would escape its pervasive damage.

In the United States baseball players posted numbers that made a mockery of time-honored records, only to be accused of doing so (or admitting to having done so, in some cases) while using steroids.

Drug use to enhance performance was a cancer that spread across national boundaries and reached virtually every competitive sport. While those in the West condemned the blatant usage in the East, they were hardly, in the end, blameless. As Pound said, "If you ask a European about drug use, he will tell you if the Olympics gave out medals for drugs, the Americans would win them all."[16]

Lance Armstrong, Barry Bonds, and Mark McGwire, among others, later showed that the Europeans had good reason for their suspicions. The simple fact was that drugs were pervasive in sports: as masking agents grew ever more sophisticated, always a step ahead of the detection process, those who felt they needed to join the dopers to have any hope of winning sought to do so. In baseball, football, boxing, track and field, swimming, bicycling, and virtually everywhere else, the rush to juice was on. It has continued unabated. Drug use by athletes is as common as yesterday's—or tomorrow's—headlines. From the summer of 1980, when Decker spoke out, until the present day, it has been a factor in all Olympics and in most sports worldwide.

• • •

In 1980, however, it was desirable, if not mandatory, for the IOC's purposes (at least as seen by the self-important Samaranch), for the extent of drug use in the Olympics to remain a dirty little secret for as long as possible.[17] That secret would, in a strange way, play a part in the 1984 games—Mary Decker's next opportunity to go for gold.

SIX. Running for Jenny

She was the most dedicated runner I have ever seen.

—Pieter Labuschagne on the thirteen-year-old Zola Budd

"I had produced a couple of national champions in cross-country and on the track when Zola first joined the team [in 1980]," Pieter Labuschagne said. "I noticed immediately that she had above-average talent. But in the beginning she was only the second- or third-best runner in the group."[1] Never having had any real coaching, Zola was starting behind the others.

In her first competitive meet, a local affair in Bloemfontein, she finished fourth to her teammate Stephanie Gerber and was bitterly disappointed. "I finished so far behind that when I crossed the finish line Stephanie had already put on her warm-ups," Zola recalled. "I decided then that if I were going to run, I was going to run to win."[2]

If you ask world-class middle-distance runners what motivates them to run, you will receive similar answers from most. They are as a group decidedly humble despite accomplishments that placed them among the best in their chosen sport. Some cite the pure joy and feeling of freedom that comes with running. Others will tell you that it was a chance to prove themselves and to accomplish something worthwhile and noticeable to others. Almost without exception they are without a trace of hubris. By the very nature of the sport, running competitively at the elite level has produced a humility in them.

Many will tell you that achieving a personal best time in a race held as much or more appeal as winning a race. While winning produced a great sense of self-satisfaction, it was also a fleeting feeling that could, and likely would, be lost in the very next race, when a runner could fail to cross the line first. Eventually, as competitors knew too well, they all would fail. So the defense mechanism they tapped to deal with that failure was to judge their performances by a different standard than where they had finished in front of an audience of fans.

In Zola Budd's case, her motivation is easily traced to a life-changing event that occurred when she was just beginning to run in serious competition. That event, which launched her on a path to the pinnacle of success, had nothing to do with joy.

Jenny Budd, Zola's big sister and role model, had married Barney Fourie in October 1979 and moved to a small farmstead near Zola's home. A qualified nurse at the time, she and Zola still saw each other frequently. "I would go to her home, and we would just chat and sip coffee together. Sometimes I helped her with her small garden. We still spent a lot of time together," Zola said.[3]

Then Jenny discovered a small lump in her arm. Doctors who examined her suspected a malignant form of melanoma, and surgery was scheduled to remove it; she entered the hospital on September 3, 1980. The operation was successful. The tumor they removed was benign.

But something was terribly wrong: Jenny had a rare but severe allergic reaction to the anesthesia.

Zola had not visited Jenny while she was hospitalized. Everyone had told her that it was just a routine, minor surgical procedure and that Jenny would be fine. "I only realized the severity of her condition when I wasn't allowed to visit her in the hospital. I knew she had become ill, but no one had told me how serious her condition was," she said.

At 4:00 a.m. on September 9, she learned: "Ma woke me up and told me that Jenny was gone."[4]

. . .

For Zola Budd, just fourteen, her world would never be the same.

Always quiet, she didn't cry. She didn't scream. Jenny was the only person with whom Zola had ever shared her feelings. And Jenny was no longer there. "I just shrank within myself. I was numb and could neither believe, nor accept, the fact that she was gone. I felt as if my brain had been shattered."[5]

Losing her sister—the woman who had literally raised her from infancy, who had been her rock through the years in a home that was filled with sadness and the tension of her constantly at-odds parents—was a blow beyond belief. In a household where the loss of an infant was never discussed but was omnipresent, the loss of Jenny now added another layer of grief to suffer silently. Tossie, always the quiet parent, grew quieter.

To put the pieces of her shattered life back together, to cope with the unthinkable pain and loss she felt, Zola turned to the gift her oldest sister had given her. Jenny had started Zola running on the paths and fields around their home. With Jenny, Zola had first experienced the feeling of freedom from the strife and sadness at home that came with running. But Jenny, the one person in her family to whom Zola could always turn when she needed someone, was now gone.

It is impossible to overestimate the effect Jenny's death had on Zola Budd. It would be seven years before she could bring herself to visit Jenny's grave, and more than thirty years later, even a gently probing question about their relationship by an interviewer still produced tears.[6]

The loss that Zola felt, the pain that loss produced in her heart and soul, was nearly unbearable. The only way she could cope was to do what Jenny had first taught her to do. "I wanted to prove to her I had found something that I could do well," Zola recalled.[7]

She would run. Away from the pain. Away from the hurt. Away from the loss. From the depths of the darkness that enshrouded her, Zola Budd ran . . . and ran . . . and ran.

She began to rise at 4:45 and ran before school for forty-five minutes. After school she did her homework and ran again from 5:00 to 7:00, when it became too dark to see. This she did in addition to her training with Labuschagne. He noticed his new runner's improvement: "It came gradually at first. We built a strong foundation for her by running longer distances," he said.[8]

Pieter told Kenny Moore and Frank Hawthorne in an interview for *Sports Illustrated* four years later that Zola "didn't smile very much, or joke with the other kids. When she began to run, she took on that great frown of concentration from start to finish. Her determination came across like an army of safari ants on the march. She was the most dedicated runner I have ever seen."[9]

Zola had run competitively in the months leading up to Jenny's death and had won the South African schools cross-country championship in July 1980; in August she had come in second in the Free State under-fourteen age group. Selected to represent her province in the national junior championships in Pretoria, she had finished twelfth.

After Jenny died, Zola was certain Jenny would have approved of her youngest sister's successes on the track. The prizes were nothing more than ribbons and small sports duffel bags, but to Zola each was a prized possession.

. . .

Zola's running with increasing success in South Africa would become a big problem for her. In 1948, almost twenty years before she was born, the white minority that ruled the millions of indigenous people of the vast mineral-rich country had enacted a policy that was to stamp it and its residents as despotic racists. The policy was apartheid.

As the name implies (in Dutch-derived Afrikaans, one of the two official languages of South Africa), it was a government-mandated policy of separation of rights for blacks from those of the white minority. The policy was enforced vigorously, and those protesting it would soon find themselves incarcerated or worse. One, Nelson Mandela, a left-leaning black activist imprisoned for twenty-seven years, would become the symbol of the antiapartheid movement at home and around the world. By 1962, as the South African government continued its strong-arm tactics to keep power in its hands and the black population under its control in almost every facet of their lives, protests against the ruling minority were spreading around the globe.

In the United States students picketed Wall Street and college campuses to attempt to force firms and college endowment funds to divest themselves of South African investments. Europe and communist bloc countries imposed sanctions that set South Africa apart from the rest of the modern world despite its vast, sought-after mineral resources—uranium, gold, and diamonds, among them.

South Africa had become an island—a racist island, many would say—unto itself, with few friends and allies and countless critics and enemies of its policies. It was cast out of international bodies of every sort, including the International Association of Athletics Congress (IAAC), the forerunner of the International Amateur Athletics Federations (IAAF) and the governing body of the sport the young Zola Budd was pursuing.

Just as Mary Decker's move with her family to Southern California would have tremendous impact on her development as a runner, so too would Zola Budd's birthplace influence her subsequent career. In Budd's case, the happenstance of being born in South Africa would dog her steps on the track like a faster runner she couldn't shake off no matter how she tried.

But that lay in the future. For now Zola Budd was content just to be among the best of her gender in her own insular world in and around Bloemfontein.

• • •

The sense of hopelessness that had dominated her thoughts after Jenny died was slowly replaced by a desire to achieve, if not for herself, then in Jenny's memory.

On September 19, just ten days after Jenny died, Zola ran in a 3,000-meter race in Bloemfontein and finished fourth in 10:19.8, far behind Sarina Cronje, who had won in 9:32.9. "Just wait," Zola said to herself after that race. "It won't be too long before I will be running as fast as Sarina."[10]

On October 8 Zola finished first in both the 800 meters and the 1,500 meters in Bloemfontein, before meeting Stephanie Gerber again in a 3,000-meter race. Stephanie prevailed again in 9:59.9, with Zola at third in 10:06.5. In the same meet, in the 800 meters, Stephanie was first, Zola close behind. She hadn't caught Stephanie yet, but Zola's time was improving with each meeting.

On November 11 she again chased Stephanie, this time over 1,500 meters, the metric mile, which Zola ran in 4:24.3, another personal best yet still only good enough for runner-up. Progress, though, was apparent, and Zola felt a growing sense of confidence as the 1981 season approached.[11]

Under Labuschagne she trained increasingly harder. "I used a variation of the [Arthur] Lydiard system, not slavishly, but with an eye toward building up her base to prepare her for the track," he said.[12] His training techniques, which emphasized aerobic conditioning, combined with Zola's burning desire to produce increasingly better times and results, made 1981 a turning point in her athletic development.

On February 3, 1981, she came in third in the Free State senior 1,500 meters against older competitors, and six days later she earned her first provincial title when she won the Free State championship at the Bill Troskie Meet, in a time of 4:20.7 in the 1,500 meters, a new under-sixteen record. Two more wins in the 800 and 1,500 followed, and she was rounding into form as the South African junior championships in Bloemfontein approached.

In front of her home crowd on April 3, she would compete in her first major championship against her old rival Stephanie Gerber. "I was tired of snapping at her heels," Zola recalled. "I wanted to prove to myself that I was capable of beating her."[13]

With her adrenaline surging, she nearly managed to do so. The 1,500 meters had been her main focus at the meet, but she finished second to Stephanie again. Still, the gap separating them was narrowing: Gerber had run the race in 4:22, and Zola finished a mere 0.9 seconds behind.

Labuschagne had entered her in the 800 meters as well, which followed not long after. Zola got through the heats and lined up for the start of the 800 with little expectation of success. "I warmed up well, and in the first lap I kept up with the leaders quite easily. With 300 meters to go, I put on a spurt of speed and surged ahead. I wondered why the others weren't coming up on me. As the finish line approached, it dawned on me that I was going to win. All I could think of was, Finally, I'm going to get the red [duffel] bag that is given to the winners."[14]

Zola, not quite fifteen, got her red bag. She also collected her first national championship, as the fastest under-sixteen girl in the country at 800 meters. People started to notice the five-foot eighty-pound girl who ran barefoot.

While running barefoot was perfectly natural to her—it was the way she had always run from the outset with Jenny—it would later become a trademark so attached to her that it would seem a prefix to her name in sports pages around the world.

Pieter and Zola's parents celebrated the national championship. Her mother, Tossie, had been shuttling her to training and back while juggling her catering chores. Zola's father, Frank, attended most of her events and had watched with growing interest and encouragement his slight, sad, shy, young daughter's improvement.

With her victory and a national title in hand, Zola's relationship with Labuschagne, as well as that with her father, started to change. "With Pieter, after that race, when we both realized I had the talent to do well, we took each other more seriously."[15] A bond began to develop between them that would grow stronger and closer as the years went on. And Frank, who loved to tell his mates—when liberally lubricated with liquid refreshment—that his goals in life were to earn a million pounds and have tea with the queen, became much more focused thereafter on his daughter's development and growing reputation.

Both Pieter Labuschagne and Frank Budd saw something in Zola that afternoon that would have a profound effect on her, something she couldn't begin to imagine in the afterglow of the celebration: dollar signs. People who are not dedicated track fans seldom know it, but coaches, like racehorse trainers, receive a percentage of their runner's winnings. Zola, on the other hand, was content to share

her new status with her favorite cat, Stompie, who purred content-
edly at the news—or more likely at Zola's gentle stroking—while
leaving cat hair all over her tracksuit.

...

Cross-country season began in June, and Zola continued to show
marked improvement, winning at Potchefstroom in June and again
at Bloemfontein in the Free State Championship on August 8, eighteen seconds faster than her time the previous season. She won
again in Cape Town on September 5 and capped the cross-country
season by finishing third behind Diane Massyn, on September 19,
at the Prestige Meet in Pietersburg.

In races over the road that fall, Zola won the Free State Championship for 10 kilometers on August 1 and finished a respectable
second to Massyn in the South African Championships. Back on
the track in October, Zola garnered wins at 800 and 1,500 meters
on October 30 and 31. The season ended with Zola in a familiar
spot. She had finished second to Stephanie Gerber once again in
the 1,500 meters in the final event of the season on November 14.
But even in defeat the vast improvement in Zola was obvious. Gerber needed a new national record to hold Budd off as she finished
just two-tenths of a second behind.

"Second again wasn't good enough," Zola said. "I was determined to do better."[16]

That determination was evidenced by a stepped-up training
program designed by Labuschagne. He increased her training
runs to one hundred kilometers a week, or about nine miles a
day, a significant load for a fifteen-year-old, but Zola handled
it easily. She was beyond determined, strictly focused on winning. Everything else was secondary to her goal to be the best
she could be.

"Running had taken on a new meaning in my life," she would
say. What had begun as a normal thing to do at school and later
became her escape from Jenny's death had become her way of life.
For the two months of the off-season, she trained intensely. The
season-ending defeat by Gerber had given her all the incentive she
needed. She was determined not to lose again.

Under Labuschagne's tutelage Zola returned for the 1982 season fit and ready to resume her racing career. The off-season training, increased miles, and intense focus on success paid immediate dividends.

At the first meet, in her hometown, she won her first two starts and in a 3,000-meter race eclipsed her time for that distance by a full minute. On February 19, 1982, at the Bill Troskie meet, she defeated Stephanie Gerber and set a South African under-sixteen mark as well as an under-nineteen mark, when she clocked 4:09.1 in the 1,500 in just her third event. She had knocked a full ten seconds off her time in her last race of the previous season. The improvement was extraordinary and proved, to Pieter and to Zola, that they were on the right path.

The dominance of Zola Budd, over runners in her age group as well as older girls in open events, continued throughout the season. The national under-sixteen mark for 800 meters fell in March, when she clocked 2:06.5, and the under-nineteen mark for 3,000 meters fell when she won in 9:05.7 at Pretoria on April 2. Her record-breaking year continued the very next day, when she lowered the under-nineteen record for 1,500 meters to 4:15.7. On April 16 and 17 she won the South African championships in both the 1,500 and 3,000 meters at Stellenbosch.

When road racing began in June, she showed her versatility and her ability to run longer distances as she finished first in a 16K race. In July she set a new record in the 10,000 meters that earned her the South African best mark at the Free State Championships. Back on the track in September, she remained undefeated at both 1,500 and 3,000 meters while lowering the mark for the under-nineteen age group to 9:03.5 at Bloemfontein in October.

On the road and on the track she had an unblemished record of success. In cross-country the skein continued as she added the under-sixteen age group championship in Alberton in September. In December she was back on the road with two more wins at ten and then five kilometers to cap off the extraordinary campaign.

Zola Budd's 1982 season was the best any South African girl had ever produced. She was not just beating girls her age but was handling older, open competition and setting records while doing so.

Her star was on the rise. Reporters in her country had followed her exploits with growing coverage, and hers was becoming a well-known name in a country where track was a major specta-tor sport, second only to rugby in popularity. Unlike the United States, where—other than friends and family members—only a few hard-core track fans attended meets, in South Africa the meets attracted large numbers of avid and knowledgeable spectators. Since the country was barred from international competition, its national championships substituted. Thus Zola was adding to the country's already-high fan interest as she assaulted records and mowed down competitors.

She was a major sports figure in a nation that was intimately involved with the sport. Zola's reward came when she was presented with the coveted Springbok Club colors that represented the top athletes in her country. The famous green-and-gold blazer looked a little large on her, as if she were a little girl playing dress-up. But by virtue of the club's acceptance, she was recognized as among the best in her nation.

She was just sixteen.

. . .

As Zola's phenomenal season progressed and her star rose higher and higher in the firmament of track athletes, the two men who orbited around that star, her father and her coach, began to clash. Frank Budd, always a dreamer, had proudly noted the headlines and feature stories that his daughter had earned. As her popular-ity soared, so did his pride in her accomplishments. Labuschagne, a relatively unknown high-school history teacher and part-time coach, now found himself to be the coach of the biggest name in South African track. He too was basking in the reflected glory of his young charge.

Success, it is said, has many fathers. In Zola's case there were two. And their struggle to control her future began during that undefeated season of 1982. "I had been asked to travel with the Springbok team to a meet, after which I was going to return to Bloemfontein by car with Pieter," Zola recalled. "My school, Sentraal High [Dan Pine-aar had merged with it], wanted to have a reception for me, and my father wanted me to fly home with him. In the end my father won the argument, and we flew back to a warm and wonderful recep-tion. But the argument between my father and Pieter took some of the glow off the moment."[17] That discord, seemingly unimportant at the time, was the first sign of what was to come.

As good as her undefeated 1982 season had been, 1983's would be even better. From January 26 through December 1983, Zola Budd raced thirty-eight times on the track and the road, and over cross-country trails. In doing so she would establish herself as the best female runner of any age in her native land.

Soon, as it turned out, she would add "world champion" to her list of accomplishments. (Though South Africa was banned from international competition, it still measured its sports records against those of other nations.) Her 1983 season would see her set a world junior record for 5,000 meters at Durban in January and a world junior record for 3,000 meters in February at Stellenbosch.

Her only loss came in a 1,000-meter race in early February, to Ilze Venter, by half a second on the same day that Zola ran, and won, an 800-meter race. The odd distance, seldom run, was the only blemish on her record that season. It was also the only loss she incurred on South African soil since her second-place finish to Gerber in November 1981.

Zola would not lose there again.

She tore through the 1983 season barefoot and running from the front with astounding ease. Her competitors often found themselves lapped by the flying form of the tiny runner as she blazed by in the longer-distance races. Her only real competition was with herself.

In the middle of her magical 1983 season, with the victories mounting and national and world marks falling before her onslaught, her father, now constantly in attendance wherever she went, attempted to assert himself as the gatekeeper to Zola's career.

"We were to go to Durban as part of the Orange Free State team for the South African National Junior Championships," she recalled. "I spent the first night there with my parents at my father's insistence. I was supposed to be with the rest of the team members at a hostel, but my father insisted I stay with him. The next morning I was warned by our team officials that I would be withdrawn from the championships if I did not stay with the rest of the team."[18]

The ultimatum led to a rush of tears. Zola, who was unstoppable on the track, was being stopped by her intransigent father. After a tear-filled argument with Frank, Zola, now pleading with her father, prevailed. But it came at a cost. Frank Budd reluctantly gave in to his daughter, but he was upset at being treated as just another parent of a track team member. "He packed up all my clothes for the five-day meet in one huge suitcase and drove me to the track, where he dumped me and my oversize suitcase unceremoniously, and drove off in anger."[19]

Years later Zola could look back and laugh at the absurd scene her arrival created, but at the time, it wasn't funny at all. Pieter, certain Zola's stubborn father would not relent, was shocked when she arrived. "He helped me turn the situation into an advantage," she said. Pieter told her, "It's quite simple. You either let what's happened affect you negatively or you turn it into a positive."[20]

Zola chose the latter course, and her results prove just how determined she was not to let her father's intransigence hurt her. In late January she had already established what would have been her first world junior record for 5,000 meters and followed that with what would have been a world junior record in the 3,000 meters in early April had her marks been recognized outside South Africa. Still, her times could not be ignored.

At Durban for the national junior championships, she showed her resilience and determination not to allow her father's churlish attitude to affect her performance. Following her coach's advice, she set new world, South African, and South African under-nineteen marks for the 3,000 meters with a time of 8:39. She followed it with a new South Africa under-nineteen mark in the 1,500 preliminary heats and then proceeded to better it by sixteen seconds in the final, with 4:09.[21]

Her victories, while sweet, were rendered a bit hollow by the absence of her parents. After Frank sped off with Tossie, Zola was left to bunk with a teammate, Elizna van Zyl, on the night before her record-shattering performance. Van Zyl consoled a lost and confused Zola before the race.

Frank's angry departure would not forestall his daughter's best effort, but it certainly did nothing to aid it. Zola and Pieter, on the other hand, were drawn closer by her triumphant performance at the national junior championships.

She continued to improve her time and to lower even further the records she already owned. Her strength and stamina, built up through racing and training, never flagged. By season's end, she had lowered the world junior mark for 5,000 meters from 15:35 in January to 15:10 in October at Port Elizabeth, at sea level. By season's end, her national best time in the 1,500 was 4:06, which was just shy of her own goal of 4:05 for the distance.[22]

When the 1983 track season ended in South Africa, she had won thirty-three races on the track, the road, and cross-country. She was without question the preeminent track star in a nation that valued track athletes highly. A national name, a teen phenom capable of beating older, more experienced runners over almost any distance, at any time, Zola Budd was the object of her nation's affection. But as acclaimed as she was at home, fans and sportswriters could only speculate how their waifish heroine would fare when pitted against international competition. South Africa, a maligned island unto itself, was still barred from those events.

But those who had watched her development most closely couldn't be faulted for speculating. Frank Budd was among those musing as he scanned magazines and newspapers to compare Zola's impressive 1983 marks with those of runners from other countries. He could hardly have missed the accounts of the American runner who had run through competition all season like a warm knife through butter. Her name, he knew, was Mary Decker.

With his printing business struggling to remain profitable while his daughter continued to be a record-breaking sensation throughout the land, who could blame the garrulous dreamer for the thoughts that swirled constantly through his restless mind?

SEVEN. The Kid Comes Back with a Swoosh

. . . .

As it happens, Mary Decker's thinly veiled, public finger pointing at drug use by some of her competitors begged the question of support. Decker herself was competing in 1980 for a Nike-owned-and-sponsored track team, Athletics West. It was lavishly funded and had the latest world-class equipment and facilities. The athletes were compensated for their endorsement of Nike by being paid in retainers, public appearances, performance bonuses, and

Nike stock and stock options. In addition they earned prize money from meets and appearance fees from promoters just for showing up (all permitted since a change in IOC bylaws had finally but quietly acknowledged that USSR and Eastern bloc athletes were state-sponsored professionals, putting American and other Western athletes at a disadvantage).

There was no hotter property in track in 1980–84 than Mary Decker, and she cashed in. In exchange for the Nike largesse, Mary wore Nike uniforms and shoes and performed where Nike told her to. Her coach was a Nike employee. "When Mary came to me in 1980," Dick Brown said, "she was earning $15,000 from Nike. When she left me five seasons later, her income was in the mid-six figures."[1]

. . .

The year 1980 was the beginning of a remarkable run that would see Nike's modest investment in Mary pay handsome dividends. The summer season continued, as did Mary's quest to prove to herself and to others that, had she been permitted to compete in Moscow, she would have had her Olympic medal—dopers be damned. She'd run them all down if given a chance—assuming, of course, that she stayed healthy. And that was Dick Brown's job.

. . .

After the Weltklasse meet in Zurich in August 1980, when Decker had failed to catch the Russian Tatyana Kazankina but had run a 1,500 in less than four minutes, Mary defeated the Soviet runner Nadezhda Olizarenko in a 1,500-meter race in 4:00.3. Decker followed that with a world record attempt over 3,000 meters in Brussels on August 22, but the pain in her Achilles tendon flared up again, forcing her to withdraw. Upon her return to the United States, she underwent another surgery to repair the partially torn tendon. Brown instituted a carefully constructed training regimen to keep her fit while her Achilles healed: "She would swim and lift weights. After a time we started her back with just easy jogging," he said.[2]

However, the 1981 season had hardly begun when the pain in her shins returned. She underwent yet another surgery, but the 1981 season was essentially lost. Dick Brown, by now the person who held Mary's future in his skilled hands, had quite a challenge before him. He was an Annapolis graduate, a former U.S. Air Force officer, and a coach who understood that keeping Mary Decker on the track was going to be a difficult assignment. A skilled exercise physiologist, he also understood the value of scientific tests for measuring fitness.

He would use the same tests the Eastern Europeans had developed within their programs—without the accompanying drug enhancements—and add his own refinements to manage Mary Decker. He knew he had a woman of spectacular talent, naturally gifted and strongly motivated from within to succeed.

"My training regimen was based on the work of a man named Hans Selye, a pioneering Hungarian endocrinologist who developed a theory he called general adaptation syndrome.

"There are three stages: There is the alarm stage, where a person goes through a workout and uses a lot of energy. Then they stop the workout and have a recovery phase that lasts twenty-four to forty-eight hours. If they repeat the phase intelligently over nine to ten months, they are then in the adaptation phase, and they improve their performance.

"You are constantly challenging the body and having it recover. Then, if you continue stage 2, or put too much effort into the adaptation phase, or if there are other stressors in your life—that don't have to be athletic—you will probably go into the third, or exhaustion, phase" instead of adaptation, Brown explained.

Exhaustion, according to Dick Brown, is the phase that must be avoided at all costs: "Once you get into that stage, sometimes it takes a year to get back on track again. I understood how to balance the challenge and recovery, how to work the adaptation stage, and then I had some formulas I developed and patented to prevent the athlete from getting into the exhaustion stage," he said. "In training Mary Decker, in addition to the Selye philosophy, I would keep track of just how many effort points she was getting. Each exercise—running, swimming, weight lifting—had effort points assigned. This way I monitored the physiological stresses she was enduring and how she was handling the challenges to her body." Brown's system kept Decker from the exhaustion phase: "Before I coached her she had about seven surgeries. After I coached her, she had about five more. When I took over her full-time coaching, and employed the system I developed, she had none."

Managing Mary was not difficult for Brown. "I was wearing a white hat in her eyes. I told her the truth, and she understood that," he said. "We got along really good. Mary was a nice person trying to get out. She wanted desperately for her niceness to get out. But she was so protective because she had been hurt so many times. I know when she went over to Europe, meet promoters would hit on her. She was a young girl. Consequently she built up a big defense. And as a result, unfortunately, the part of her personality that people saw was, 'Don't mess with me.'"

Brown speculated that the attitude that Mary showed the world (at least in public) could in large measure be traced to John Decker's denial, years earlier during the divorce trial, that he was responsible for her support: "Her home life, I understood, had been chaotic, and then that denial was put out there at the trial."[3]

The torn Achilles, compartment syndrome, and other physical injuries she'd suffered were nothing compared to the emotional pain she must have felt. Brown was dealing, very gingerly, with an athlete whose injuries extended well beyond the physical. He did so with great empathy and success, at least with regard to the physical aspects of managing Mary Decker. Brown is a quiet, sincere man. His job in coaching Decker would prove his ability not only to monitor and regulate her physical well-being but also to care for, nurture, and support an athlete who needed care, nurturing, and emotional support as much as any he'd ever dealt with. Measuring Mary's physical fitness would be the component of his care that was readily visible, as evidenced by her performance on the track, but the rest of the work he did with her, largely undetectable by others, was of at least as much benefit, if not more.

The foundation of the program Brown constructed for Mary would prove to be sturdy and enduring: it would lead to the most remarkable single-season performance by a woman middle-distance runner that the world has ever seen.

. . .

At the same time, another episode was unfolding in Mary's ongoing soap opera–like life.

Shortly after returning to Eugene in 1980, and after she and Dick Quax had parted company, Mary met someone. Whether she was on the rebound can't be said with certainty, but there are some clues. In a lengthy article in *People* magazine, Mary gave her version of events.

Ron Tabb, a marathon runner of some repute, had recently moved to Eugene to train. After a night of partying, he knocked on Decker's door. "It was 11 p.m. and I thought he was nuts," she said. "But I had nothing going on that night, so we went out dancing and drinking." She forgot to take her keys and spent the night at his place.[4]

"Mary was dating Tom Wysocki at the time we met," Tabb recalled. "There had been a few others between Quax and me." Wysocki was a world-class, long-distance runner who would eventually marry one of Mary's running rivals.

Mary's aggressive athleticism wasn't confined to the track: "We had the wildest sex I've ever had that night," Tabb said, adding that all his friends had told him that "getting involved with her was a bad idea."[5] He didn't heed their advice, and they were married six months later, in the fall of 1981.

The two had something in common, however, apart from their vigorous athletic activities in the bedroom: there was running, and then there was running, and—let's see—oh yes, there was running.

He hated her dog and made her send it to live with his mother out of state. And Mary confessed to *People* and its readership of millions that "he was a little pigheaded." But, what the heck, every couple has a few differences—especially one in which, as Tabb described it, they were together almost around the clock. He further told *People*: "Everyone says a relationship as close as ours won't work. But I love our togetherness. I really miss Mary when she goes shopping."[6]

Mary and Ron trained together while Mary was under Dick Brown's care and preparing her return to the track. They did so at the training facility Nike maintained in Eugene, where Dick Quax was still in residence. Eugene's winters are relatively mild, if damp and drizzly, but when those three encountered one another, there must have been some icy days.

Brown commented that husband and wife were "a little overaggressive" at times but that he'd managed to slow them both down.[7] And Ron's friend, the Houston businessman Craig Christopher, told

People, "They're still very independent. But they both realize they have to give a little."[8] Or not. The marriage lasted twenty-one months.

. . .

Tabb claims that while training with Brown, he and Mary were offered the option of trying steroids—an offer they both declined.[9] Brown denies that he offered pharmacological aid and insists that, at least while under his care, "she ran clean." According to Tabb, while he and Mary were together as a couple he obtained a job for Mary's brother, John, with Craig Christopher's pharmaceutical company: "[John] was kind of a bum and needed a job. John was getting drugs from Christopher's company, and he became a major supplier to athletes who all knew he was Mary's brother." (The athletes John allegedly supplied, according to Tabb, included Richard Slaney, whom Mary would later marry.)[10]

Though Tabb denies ever seeing Mary use drugs during the time they were together, if he is to be believed, the family connection to the availability of drugs does raise questions.

Tabb pointed out that later in her career, when Mary was being trained by the Brazilian Luiz de Oliveira, she refused to take the weekly drug tests he insisted on because he suspected something was amiss: "When she refused repeatedly to be tested, he quit as her coach."[11] Decker turned down an opportunity to respond to her ex-husband's allegations.

"Ron used her," said Bob Hickey, who was by then an official with the Athletics Congress (TAC), which had succeeded the AAU as the governing body for track and field in the United States. "Mary was so much better and well known than he was. He couldn't stand being Mr. Decker. He even tried to use her to blackmail us. He told us, 'If you don't pay me more money for training and expenses, I'll go public and say she wasn't an amateur'" when she was setting records earlier.

"Ron Tabb," said Hickey, the ex-cop-turned-track-official, "was an asshole."[12]

Maybe Mary should have known that when a drunk knocks on your door at 11:00 p.m. and soon after makes you get rid of your dog, there might be a problem, but it took her a while to figure it out.

. . .

All through 1981 the building blocks for Mary's comeback were carefully measured and laid by Dick Brown. By the late fall of that year Mary was following a training schedule that would convert her unlimited potential into performances that were worthy of her promise. The regimen Brown designed and monitored would combine speed and endurance runs tempered by his cautious, patient concern never to have her reach the exhaustion phase, from which she might not recover.

Together they added mileage, working from just thirty-seven miles a week in July but never exceeding more than sixty-eight miles a week by November. Brown added intervals only after a six-week period showed that her base (her conditioning for distance races) had been safely established. Though her mile runs were in the molasses-slow range of six minutes or a little better at first, she was staying healthy. And her times would continue to improve with each passing month.

The results would be seen in 1982. After a year and a half out of the spotlight of competition, Mary Decker was ready to return. Little Mary, fatherless Mary, damaged Mary, jilted Mary, divorced Mary, injured Mary, and invisible Mary were gone. After Dick Brown's caring and calculated ministrations, a new, healthy, and healed Mary Decker emerged. In this latest incarnation, wrought by Brown, she would prove, finally, to be the Mary Decker who had always been there but was hidden from sight by her numerous physical and emotional injuries.

This Mary Decker was a sight to behold.

She served notice at her very first indoor meet in January 1982, winning a 1,500-meter race in 4:08.32. In case no one had noticed, she added a world indoor record, running a mile in 4:24.6 on January 22. To that she would later add a record for the 3,000 meters in 8:47.3 and would lower her mile mark to 4:20.5. The outdoor season produced more of the same: at her home base in Eugene, she bested Paula Fudge of England, the 5,000-meter record holder, and set a new record for that distance of 15:08.26.

Decker Tabb's amazing comeback (amazing to everyone but Brown, that is) continued on a European tour during which she ran two separate mile races, another at 3,000 meters, and a fourth at 800 meters—and won all of them. Mary returned to Eugene on July 16 after exhausting flights that had taken her from Lausanne to London to San Francisco before reaching home. Nevertheless, she persuaded Dick to allow her to enter an all-comers meet at her track that day, where a 10,000-meter race was on the program. Demurring at first, Brown finally agreed, if Mary would wear track shoes without spikes and quit at the first sign of a twinge anywhere.

Running that way, and after that plane ride, she proceeded to blast around the track, clocking evenly paced miles in the five-minute range to finish in 31:35.3. It was, she figured, as good as if she'd done her normal seven-mile training run. It was also good enough for a new world record, her seventh that season.

Mary shrugged off the news, saying, "It just proves that the records aren't that stiff yet."[13] By the conclusion of her latest and most successful comeback season, Mary held the world records for both the 5,000 and 10,000 meters.

Sports Illustrated put Mary, identified now as "Mary Decker Tabb, World Record Holder," on the cover of its July 26, 1982, edition. The photo, accompanied by the caption, "Sets Her 7th World Mark of '82," portrayed her in an Athletics West tracksuit, standing with her hands on her hips and staring cockily at the camera with a look that was easily understood to say to the world, "Bring it on. I'm back. Catch me if you can."

Still, Mary wanted to improve. The rankings for the 1,500 meters revealed her best time—the only time she had run that distance—to be only ninth best, trailing the times of seven Eastern bloc runners. And over 3,000 meters, she was listed as fourth behind three Eastern bloc athletes, including one from Romania named Maricica Puică.

Decker finished the year as the Associated Press (Female) Athlete of the Year and as the Sullivan Award winner, an honor bestowed each year on the top amateur athlete, male or female.[14]

. . .

The International Association of Athletics Federations had announced that for the first time a women's world championship for track and field would be conducted under its auspices in 1983. Brown's careful and caring work with Decker Tabb had paid off, but more remained to be done. With his philosophy of training proven, he needed only to continue the program and point her toward peak conditioning—the whole purpose behind his work—by the time that meet arrived.

He would do so but not without some difficulty (no matter his demurrals about the difficulty): with Mary, the one reliable constant was that there was always going to be some difficulty.

Brown had carefully nursed her back to health, or at least what passed for health in her damaged scar-crossed body. He watched vigilantly for any early signs of illness, and any soreness was cause to taper off. He kept a trained eye on the effort points she was earning with each workout and monitored her daily. Together they plotted a carefully spaced indoor season that would see her peak for the TAC national championships that summer in Indianapolis and for the world championships later in Helsinki. "She had some minor soreness at times, but we made adjustments for that, and she stayed healthy and fit," Brown said.[15]

Decker Tabb was straining at the bit as the TAC meet approached: she wanted to run in races at both 1,500 and 3,000 meters. Brown, however, wasn't that sure about the effort that would take, especially since there was only about an hour between the two races. Decker Tabb was insistent and Brown relented but with conditions: "I wanted her to run the 3,000 with restraint, stay in the pack and not race out front as she always wanted to. I wanted her to get used to what it felt like running in the pack and get a feeling for what it's like."[16]

She won the 1,500-meter race easily in 4:03.5, with Cindy Bremser of Wisconsin finishing a full six seconds behind. Decker Tabb may have heard and even agreed to Brown's instructions for the 3,000 meters when he delivered them but could not, or would not, follow them. Despite Brown's cautioning her to run with the pack, less than an hour later she streaked to the front in the 3,000 meters and stayed there, finishing in 8:38.36—the best time in the world that season. Later Decker Tabb would tell reporters, "I went into the 3,000 meters more relaxed than I usually go into an event."[17] She ran as she had always run, and whatever lessons she might have taken from running in the pack and becoming accustomed to the different conditions there remained unlearned. In fact, in August

1983, when *Track & Field News* acknowledged Decker Tabb's dominance at that point in the season, the magazine touched on that very issue, raising a question about her future when she'd be facing fields of international runners: "She can run the pace, but can she stay with the pack?"[18] Thus far she had not demonstrated that ability. She continued to run in front from start to finish. And that bothered *Track & Field*'s knowledgeable staff.

It also bothered Dick Brown. But apparently it didn't bother Mary.

Decker Tabb was moving easily through the early season, adhering strictly to Brown's program in training, even when she ignored him in races, but it was working. In the summer of 1983 in Los Angeles, in a televised dual meet—the United States and East Germany were the only competitors—she would have an opportunity to send a strong message to the world in advance of the Helsinki world championships.

In the 1,500, racing with Cindy Bremser against East Germany's Christiane Wartenberg and Astrid Pfeiffer, Decker Tabb set the pace in Los Angeles. When Wartenberg made her challenge, Decker Tabb held her off and ran the last lap in 60.3 seconds to leave Wartenberg a distant second.[19]

As her 3:59.43 time was fixed in place on the timer at the finish line, she could say to herself, Hey, world, look at that!

Thus far no one had been able to race with her. She was undefeated and seldom challenged. As Margaret Groos, another elite runner for Athletics West, noted, "I wish, for her sake, we could give her some competition. But we've learned to pretty much let Mary do what she wants to do. If you can't do her workouts, you certainly can't fool yourself and try to race with her."[20]

Brown still had his focus on the Helsinki meet—the sternest test of the season for Mary—and thus far the program was proving to be as good as he could hope. Her workouts were gradually increased; her conditioning and speed picked up, her effort points studiously accounted for, with pauses inserted when appropriate. He was upping her training regimen in small increments, pointed toward her peaking at the meet in Finland while avoiding the exhaustion phase that would compromise any chance she had.

But experts, including those at *Track & Field News*, remained unconvinced that Decker Tabb, even in the best of condition, had what it would take to defeat the Russian and Eastern bloc runners. "She hasn't been in this kind of competition since her teenage days . . . except for a good stretch run against Christiane Wartenberg in the DDR [GDR] dual at 1500," they observed, adding that "a Soviet sweep [of the middle-distance events] is expected."[21]

Francie Larrieu, who had been competing against the Soviet bloc runners as a member of the U.S. team for years, said, "We often joked among ourselves that in international meets we'd try to be the best in the West, because we knew the Eastern bloc runners were doping and we couldn't beat them."[22]

Despite the experts' opinion, however, Mary Decker Tabb was, as always, confident she would prove them wrong.

She flew to Europe on July 20, landing in London and then flying on to Stockholm, the site of another made-for-TV event (the first was the meet with East Germany), between the United States and a team representing the Scandinavian countries. On July 26, in front of a crowd of nearly fifteen thousand, Decker Tabb did what she had always done. Leading from the outset, she finished the 1,500 meters in a sizzling 3:57.12, more than ten seconds ahead of her closest follower.

After her victory, Mary addressed a question about the world championships, which were moving inexorably closer. She announced that she believed "her best chance" would come in the 1,500 but that she fully intended to compete in the 3,000 as well, "just for fun."[23] Dick Brown wasn't asked to comment.

When queried about racing from the front against the experienced Eastern European runners, she calmly said, "If I have to kick, I'll be able to kick. I'm fast enough and strong enough. They will not run away from me."[24]

As if to prove her point, she set a new American record in an 800-meter race on July 31 at Gateshead, England. "She was coming down with a cold and her Achilles was a bit sore," Brown recalled.[25] Doing what he did best, Brown immediately advised her to rest and recover.

The time frame was far from ideal: Helsinki and the IAAF world championships were just a week away. There, more than fifteen hundred athletes would meet in the largest gathering of talent at a track-and-field event since the 1972 Olympic Games. Forty-one nations would be represented. (South Africa wasn't one of them, having been banned by the IOC since 1960, and from international competition by the IAAF since 1976.) Mary Decker Tabb still had plenty of competitors to think about. Most of her serious challengers were from the communist bloc countries, whose runners everyone knew would be racing with a pharmacological edge.

The president of the IAAF, an Italian named Primo Nebiolo—a man whose ego rivaled that of Samaranch, and whose ethics were questionable at best—he was known to have rigged results when Italian competitors needed a boost—issued a statement saying that the IAAF would be conducting random drug tests at its events.[26] This would, he asserted, add an element of surprise. Nebiolo's proclivity for prevarication made the statement laughable: the only surprise would be if anyone *failed* an IAAF-supervised test—and that was how the 1983 IAAF World Championships in Athletics would be remembered: "A drug-ridden championship," according to the 1992 book *Dishonored Games*. Dr. Robert O. Voy, a sports medicine specialist who would become the chief medical officer for the United States Olympic Committee in 1984, told the authors, "The IAAF must have covered up the results in Helsinki. There is no doubt in my mind that, at least in 1983, Nebiolo would not have pressed for honest, accurate testing in Helsinki."[27]

Predictably the IAAF would find no positive drug test results to reveal to the world.

A year later Cliff Wiley, an American 400-meter runner in the championships, would say that "at least thirty-eight people tested positive, seventeen were Americans. But they were so big the organizers didn't dare name them."[28]

Despite the widespread belief that the championships would be yet another demonstration of the IOC's dirty little secret, the meet would provide Mary Decker Tabb with her chance to test herself against the best—if they showed up. For instance, where was Tatyana Kazankina? Some newspapers reported that she had retired, and others wondered why she hadn't appeared at the 1982 European Championships and why there had been no sign of her at all in the early months of 1983.

But, as the field assembled for the heats of the women's 3,000, there she was. Explanations from Soviet officials included the news that she had taken time off to have a second child and to heal an injury. "They often made women have babies," Dick Brown said. "They felt it made them stronger afterward."[29]

Whatever the real reason for Kazankina's disappearance, she was present and apparently fit to run again; she had run a 3,000 in 8:32 in Moscow in July.[30] Mary and Tatyana found themselves in the same preliminary heat. They finished in a dead heat at 8:42.7 and easily qualified for the finals. Svetlana Ulmasova of the USSR, the current world record holder, had won the first qualifying heat in 8:46.65.

The stage was set for the finals. Decker Tabb had a day to rest, recover, and summon herself for the event that she and Dick Brown had been pointing toward all season.

The 3,000 meters held high drama for the crowd and the reporters covering the event. All the elements were present: Mary was having an outstanding season, Tatyana was back, Svetlana looked fit and ready. What else could the crowd ask for?

Brown had done his job. Decker Tabb was poised to do hers. But would it be enough against the strong Soviet runners, who were known to gang up on challengers and use rabbits to burn them out in international meets, which the Soviets had dominated since 1976?

Decker Tabb hadn't faced those tactics yet. She had always been in front, setting the pace and staying out of trouble. After checking her condition and assuring himself of her fitness, Brown talked strategy with Decker Tabb. In the end, she would use the tactics that had sustained her almost from the first race she had ever entered and won back in Orange County nearly fourteen years earlier. At the gun she would take the lead and accelerate progressively to control the race as it wore on and to remove the threat of the Russian runners' finishing spurts of speed.

Decker Tabb led from the start, putting in a fast first lap and then slowing down to a more leisurely but even pace for the next five laps. By that time, the runners behind her had separated, and only Wendy Smith-Sly of Great Britain, Brigitte Kraus of West Germany, and Agnese Possamai of Italy, along with the Russians Kazankina and Ulmasova, were in striking distance. When the bell rang for the final lap, onlookers felt certain that Mary Decker Tabb, having set the pace and borne the brunt of the work, would fade under the Russians' powerful finish. She had done all the work, and logic dictated she would fade out of contention as they surged by.

"Setting the pace in middle-distance races is generally thought to be suicide for the pacesetter. The races are tactical, and those running behind often make their move and start their finishing kick toward the end, leaving the pacesetter, who has done all the work, behind," Francie Larrieu said.[31] At least that's what people thought who didn't know Mary's mind-set.

She hadn't faltered. Not on the backstretch or around the last turn. Though the Soviet runners had patiently waited for logic to assert itself—for Decker Tabb to fade—she didn't.

The announcer was calling the event with an increasing sense of urgency, his volume rising as the finish line approached. Kazankina had finally found a hole past Smith-Sly on the inside, and Ulmasova was roaring up the stretch on the outside. The experts nodded knowingly. The Russians would do as expected to the tiring pacesetter: they would run her down. But Decker Tabb sensed the attack coming. With just fifty meters to go, Kazankina appeared at her shoulder.

The announcer was screaming into the public-address system: "And—here—comes—Kazankina!" drawing out the words for dramatic effect. Kazankina was doing what she had done so often before when an announcer exclaimed, "Here—comes—Kazankina!" as she stormed down the stretch.

And then, with the finish line rushing toward them, something different happened. Logic failed, expectations were dashed, and so were the Russian hopes. As Kazankina drew up to Mary Decker Tabb, the Russian hung there for a second, poised, it seemed, to make the final move to kill Mary off. Kazankina hung there for a little spirit-breaking moment longer—and then fell back.

Decker Tabb "took a deep breath, relaxed and went," is the way *Sports Illustrated*'s Kenny Moore described the moment when the Russians realized they were beaten.[32]

Kazankina, shocked by her failure, was passed by Kraus, whose time knocked more than eight seconds off the West German national record.

Two Western runners had toppled Kazankina and Ulmasova, who finished fourth, from their perches. Decker Tabb had won her stiffest challenge by holding off the best the Eastern bloc could throw at her. Her time was 8:34.26, which was well off Ulmasova's world record of 8:26.7 but enough to put the Russians away.

After the event was over, a solemn-looking Kazankina, her ever-present KGB handler standing close by, said, "I was sure I would win it. But I lost in the final sprint to an American, Mary Decker, who proved to be stronger at the finish."[33] Decker Tabb told reporters, "I wasn't worried when Kazankina came up to me in the stretch because I know I have a strong kick."[34]

Dick Brown smiled.

. . .

The 1,500-meter race lay three days dead ahead. The Russians would throw three fresh runners at Decker Tabb, who would have to hold them off as well as Great Britain's Wendy Smith-Sly, who was also trying to double.

The race was a tactical one from the start. Decker Tabb at first grabbed a slight lead, but her pace was not fast. The field was tightly bunched, and all seemed to be waiting for someone to take command. When no one appeared willing to do so, Mary moved out in front.

The Russian, Zamira Zaitseva, certain that her finishing kick would prove to be Decker Tabb's undoing, ran stride for stride with her, their bodies brushing occasionally as they raced around the three-tiered stadium. Neither runner was giving in. The pace wasn't blistering, with a Russian once again assuming that Decker Tabb would fail in the end.

As they entered the bell lap, the pace, set by Decker Tabb, quickened, Zaitseva matching it on her outside.

Together they swept up the backstretch with the crowd on its feet, carrying the two runners on. Zaitseva, the Russians' strongest finisher, signaled with her shorter, choppier stride that she was about to pounce and finally did so.

With about two hundred meters to go as they came out of the shadow cast over the track by the stadium, off the final turn and headed for home, Zaitseva brushed past Decker Tabb. The Russian's lead lengthened to nearly five yards. Behind Decker Tabb the other two Soviet runners were also gaining ground. There it was, the pundits thought: the American has been beaten.

But they thought too soon.

Most runners who have set the pace spit out the bit and quit when they are finally caught and passed. For her entire career Mary Decker Tabb had run from the front and never failed. She had left them all in the dust.

Now they wondered how she would respond once she had been passed.

The Russians, the crowd, and the vast TV audience would soon find out that a new Mary Decker Tabb was running. One who wasn't hurt. One who knew she was fit and ready. And one who never, ever quit.

With each passing meter Decker Tabb surged closer to the Russian. From almost two meters behind at the top of the stretch, Mary was within a shortening meter with only twenty meters to go. Her stride remained as smooth and controlled as it had been when she was leading. She glanced down once, her face set in intense concentration. Her eyes closing for a second, she surged onward.

From somewhere deep within herself, Mary Decker Tabb summoned the courage, determination, and tenacity that had defined her since she was only eleven years old. Brown's preparation, the counting of the effort points, the persistent, patient urging for her to stay within herself, to peak at the right moment, surfaced in those final strides.

With Zaitseva struggling to reach the onrushing finish line, Decker Tabb surged back at her from the outside. She gained ground on the Russian with every step. Finally, with the line just feet away, the Russian made one last desperate attempt to hold her off. She threw herself forward with her arm stretched out as if to reach for the finish line and went sprawling and sliding across it.

But she was too late: Mary Decker Tabb, in a performance that ranks among the best ever seen, had won the final with a long elegant stride.

She had done it. The Russians were defeated. Mary Decker Tabb had won. Dick Brown, the architect of the reconstructed runner, finally relaxed enough to allow a smile to appear on his face.

Decker Tabb's time was 4:00.9. She was a two-time world champion. Writers searched for superlatives to use to describe her extraordinary accomplishment and failed to find one that was appropriate. So they invented a new one. Forever after, her supremacy over the Russians in both the 1,500 and 3,000 meters would be known as "the Decker Double."[35] It may sound too much like a greasy product ordered at a fast-food outlet, but to track fans around the world it said it all.

The invincibility of the pharmacologically enhanced Eastern bloc runners had been shattered in her double victory over the best they could throw at her. Mary would recount the thrilling final lap, as she saw it, to reporters. Zaitseva, she said, had cut her off as they were coming off the last turn. "I don't think it's personal," she said. "It's just the way they are trained. She was running with me and leaning on me and I had to back off."[36] She complained that Zaitseva had been elbowing and pushing her the entire race when they ran side by side. "She hit me practically every stride the whole way," Decker Tabb told reporters.[37]

In the 1,500 she had demonstrated to the Russians, and to the world watching, that she was not just a runner who could control a race and win from the front. She proved that day that she was also able to come back and win from behind. For the rest of the runners around the world, drug enhanced or not, such a realization had to have been bone shaking.

For Dick Brown the double victory was confirmation of everything he believed in. The complex formulas to measure performance, the calculations for assigning effort points for every exercise, the monitoring of stressors, and, most important, the certain knowledge that if Mary Decker Tabb could be persuaded to trust him and his methods, no one in the world could beat her.

The rest of her 1983 competitions in Europe proceeded like those that had gone before. She finished undefeated in finals twenty times that year. By the end of the season she was number one in the world rankings for the 1,500 and the 3,000 meters. No runner has ever had a season like hers in 1983. She established world and national marks at distances from 800 to 10,000 meters.

Once again, though, that season provided a glimpse of the "other Mary Decker"—of the dark side that surfaced from time to time and that would be remembered by writers and track fans a year later. In the Millrose Games in February in New York, she was sweeping toward victory when she came up behind Angelita Lind, whom she was about to lap. Lind failed to move outside fast enough to suit

Decker Tabb, and Mary pushed the Puerto Rican runner violently across the track and down as she rushed past.[38]

That was the Mary Decker Tabb her handlers sought to keep concealed. But it was always there, bubbling just beneath the sunny façade they helped create, waiting to erupt in ugliness. However, her sensational season left the dark side behind as if it were the other side of the moon. She bathed in the warm light of her celebrity, earned in victory after victory. She was showered with accolades and awards, including the Jesse Owens Award and her third appearance on the cover of *Sports Illustrated*, proclaiming her selection as "Sportsperson of the Year."

Back in Eugene, Mary tapered off, and Dick prescribed easy workouts and training programs for her. She seemed to be a healthy woman—as well as a happy one. While in New York, she had met a British discus thrower named Richard Slaney. The burly six-foot-seven, 235-pounder was a huge step up from the five-foot-six gaunt marathoner she was about to divorce.[39] And, after her previous failures in the romance department, Slaney would be a strong contributor to her sense of well-being.

"I think she needed someone like Richard after all she had been through. She saw in him someone who genuinely cared for her and would protect and shelter her from everything around her," Dick Brown said.[40] In Richard Slaney, Mary Decker found what she had been searching for since she was a teenager. "I think she thought she needed a bodyguard," one writer said.

Though Richard Slaney certainly fitted the role in simplistic terms, according to Brown, it was much more complex than that. What Decker needed was someone who would provide her with security, safety, protection, and a sense of caring only for her. Someone who would love her and hold her safe from harm, real or imagined. In that capacity, Richard Slaney would perform to Olympic standards.

But difficulties arising from their relationship would nonetheless have serious consequences for Mary Decker.

. . .

Back in wet and chilly Eugene, as the 1983 holidays approached, Mary basked in the glow of Richard's affection and that of her unique accomplishments on the track. But one thing was lurking in the back of her otherwise satisfied mind. One thing remained for her to do, and, lest she become too comfortable, she was reminded of it often by the media.

"The only things missing from Mary's stat collection are Olympian in nature: an Olympic title and world record at an Olympic distance. Guess what's coming up?" a writer mused in a *Track & Field News* article that looked back at her amazing year in its December 1983 issue.

Mary, as much as anyone, knew she wanted, needed, to win a gold medal. She had wanted one since at least 1972, when she was prevented from competing. In 1976 she was hobbled and hurt, and the games passed her by. In 1980 Jimmy Carter had stopped her from another chance.

Now, at the end of 1983, she was literally on top of the track world. From her lofty perch as Queen Mary, she surveyed the kingdom she ruled. In the not-too-distant future she could see the 1984 Olympic Games looming in Los Angeles.

This time, she thought, nothing can stop me.

EIGHT. Out of Africa

. . . .

She had the face of an angel, the legs of an
antelope, and the luck of a leper.

—William Oscar Johnson, *Sports Illustrated*, on Zola Budd

Not unlike Mary Decker in the United States, Zola Budd had been the recipient of just about every accolade her country could bestow upon an athlete after her 1983 season. She had been named South African woman athlete of the year, cross-country athlete of the year, and South African junior athlete of the year. The South African magazine *Fair Lady* named her sportswoman of the year.[1]

But unlike their American counterparts, South African sportswriters never even speculated about how their country's best female middle-distance runner might fare at the 1984 Olympics in Los Angeles. They knew it was pointless: because of their government's policy of apartheid, South African athletes were barred from competing in international meets. South African sports fans noted the Olympic Games, if at all, as only the latest lost opportunity for their athletes, who wistfully viewed the games as yet another inequity imposed on them by the rest of the world.

In the past, a few South African athletes had managed to compete in the games and at international meets but only after leaving their native land. Sydney Maree, an outstanding miler, had gone to the United States and entered college at Villanova, where he became a seven-time All-American. He was on the U.S. team for the 1984 and 1988 Olympics and still holds the record time for the Fifth Avenue Mile, which he set in 1981.[2]

Cornelia Bürki, a middle-distance runner, had left for Switzerland. Once there she married a Swiss citizen, thus making it possible for her to compete for that country.

But they were the exceptions.

. . .

As January 1984—summer in South Africa—began, Zola had been running almost without a break for twelve months, pausing only in November before resuming competition in December.

During that time she had run almost every time against the clock, lapping the other runners who simply could not keep up with the runner the press had anointed the Bloemfontein Bullet.

. . .

Coetzenburg, Stellenbosch, South Africa, is nestled in a tranquil verdant valley surrounded by mountain peaks. It is home to a university and is known for its wines; grapes are grown throughout the surrounding area, which resembles California's Napa Valley.

The Danie Craven Stadium at Coetzenburg, which had an all-weather surface, was the site of Zola Budd's first race, 5,000 meters, in the Olympic year of 1984. On January 5, twenty thousand track-savvy fans packed the stands to capacity as they eagerly anticipated the appearance of the runner they had read so much about.

Conditions were far from ideal as gusty winds swept down the Stellenbosch mountains. "I had to use [the wind] when I ran downwind and then fight against it as I ran upwind into it," Zola recalled.

"Because of the poor conditions I decided to treat it as just another race and not worry about the time."[3]

She ran the race in typical Budd style. She went out fast, quickly putting a large gap between herself and the other competitors. The announcer kept the boisterous crowd apprised of her time after she completed each lap, and the crowd began to clap in time with her every barefoot stride.

Excitement crackled through the stands as the times announced after each lap indicated Zola was on a world-record pace. As the gun sounded for the final lap and she passed more lapped runners, Zola Budd raced on alone.

In a moment worthy of Hollywood, the track announcer played a tape recording of the theme music from the popular movie *Chariots of Fire* as Budd flew across the finish line and the crowd reacted with wild cheers.

Her official time: 15:01:83. No woman in the world had ever run 5,000 meters faster. The former record holder was Mary Decker. Zola hadn't just broken Decker's record—Budd had smashed it to smithereens, lowering it by more than six seconds.

She was only seventeen years old.

"I thought after that, maybe I'm not too bad," she said.[4]

. . .

John Bryant was executive features editor of the *Daily Mail*, a London tabloid with a circulation of about two million. Bryant was also an amateur runner and had been reading for some time about the performances of Zola Budd in *Runner's World* and brief mentions in the *Times* of London.

When word of Zola's January 5 performance in South Africa cranked out of the teletype, he immediately contacted the *Mail* correspondent in South Africa, Peter Younghusband, and instructed him to do a feature on her.

"The feature ran on March 2 in the *Mail*, and it revealed that Frank Budd's father was born in Great Britain. This nugget of information was recognized immediately by our editor, David English, as a possible opportunity to have Zola run for Great Britain," Bryant recalled. "He instructed Brian Vine, a senior correspondent, to telephone Frank Budd and dispatched Neil Wilson, our athletics correspondent, to ascertain whether, in fact, Zola could run for Britain."[5]

Vine quickly confirmed that Frank Budd's father, Zola's paternal grandfather, was British, which made Zola eligible for British citizenship.[6] Vine told David English what he had learned, and they hatched a plan to make Zola Budd a British citizen. The effort undoubtedly was part of English's long successful plan to give the *Mail* one of the highest circulations in London by providing must-read stories, but he also ran a paper that disapproved editorially of sports boycotts of South Africa.

Bryant recalled that, in early March, Ian Wooldridge, the *Daily Mail*'s widely read sports columnist, described Zola Budd as "the hottest property in world athletics." Meanwhile English and John Simpson, head of the London office of IMG—the world's leading sports management agency—met in London to discuss the possibility of getting Budd to England and having her race for the United Kingdom.

English then sent the reporters Vine and Wilson, as well as a photographer, to South Africa, less to write and shoot stories than to seal a deal to bring the young runner to England.

. . .

Zola Budd would look back at the night that changed her life and say ruefully, "It was the worst night of my life."[7]

But that assessment would come later.

"She was such a shy person," Cornelia Bürki recalled of her young friend and future competitor. "All she ever wanted to do was to run and run fast."[8]

What Zola wanted wasn't what Zola got.

. . .

While Zola continued to race and run against the clock twelve more times between January 5 and March 21, establishing even more records, events around her but not known to her were moving nearly as fast as she did on the track.[9]

When the emissaries dispatched by the *Daily Mail* arrived in South Africa, they found Frank Budd a genial and welcoming host. Discussions began almost immediately about making the arrangements necessary for Zola to compete in the Olympic Games as a representative of Great Britain.

The *Mail* was not the only suitor for young Zola's services. Mark McCormack, founder of IMG, had contacted Frank Budd earlier about representing Zola. Frank had already signed a deal with the South African appliance manufacturer Defy and its marketing manager, Bill Muirhead, for promoting its wares in South Africa. The Defy sponsorship included a car, which Frank promptly appropriated. Zola didn't even possess a driver's license.

Offers by mail and telephone arrived daily at the Bloemfontein farmstead from U.S. universities that promised a scholarship and ultimately U.S. citizenship, the route Maree had taken a few years earlier. Italy was another hopeful suitor.

"It was the master stroke that Zola could get an instant British passport through David English's political connections that swung it for the *Mail*," John Bryant said.[10]

Thus the *Daily Mail* held the upper hand, and that hand was offering an inducement that caught Frank Budd's eye.

Money. A lot of money.

The negotiations would take seventeen days and involve the *Mail*, Defy's Muirhead, and John Simpson. Simpson urged the others to slow down in the belief that Zola was too inexperienced for the 1984 Olympics and should point toward 1988 instead. Pieter Labuschagne, who was also present much of the time, agreed. Zola was an infrequent attendee, and it was obvious to her that her opinions were not valued by the men who debated and plotted her future.

At first "I thought it was all just silly," she recalled. She wasn't the only one who felt that way. Simpson's was the sole voice of caution among those debating Zola Budd's future. "I was a little skeptical about it," he said. "She was very young, and taking her out of her rural country home and relocating her abruptly to England seemed to me to be a bit much for her to handle.

"I also told Frank that I thought having a newspaper organize the move wasn't the right way to go. It would alienate all the other papers. There was also the time angle in getting a passport for her. I thought at that time that she should wait until 1988 to run in the Olympics," Simpson said.[11] He was overruled.

In a recent interview, Simpson recalled his feelings of misgiving as the entire scheme was hatched. "Parents of athletes should really remain in the background, making sure that everything [is] being done correctly for their child, not leading it. It always ends in tears," Simpson said.[12]

• • •

"When I told them I didn't really want to run in the Olympics," Zola said, "there was just silence."[13] She withdrew to her room alone, save for Stompie, her favorite cat, while talks about her future droned on.

• • •

Frank Budd found himself the father of a daughter who ran like the wind and who consequently was in great demand. He soon also discovered, as the talks went on, that he was much more than a father. He was in possession of a commodity eagerly sought by the men from the *Daily Mail*.

He was where he had always dreamed of being. His young daughter's opinion be damned: Frank Budd was going to cash in.

• • •

As negotiations between Frank and the *Daily Mail* progressed toward the inevitable question of just how valuable Frank's commodity was, the men continued to brush aside Zola's participation and softly voiced opinion.

"He was offered 100,000 British pounds," Zola said. (That would have been about US$140,000 then, or about US$352,000 today.)

In return, Frank would grant the *Mail* exclusive rights to his daughter's story. He couldn't sign the papers fast enough. The deal was done. Frank Budd was rich.

"The contract was to pay him eighty thousand pounds, and I was to receive twenty thousand in a trust fund that he and Pieter would administer," Zola explained. "I remember at the end asking the men from the *Mail* what the reaction of the people in Great Britain might be. They assured me that there wouldn't be a problem. Oh, a few people might protest, they told me, but it's nothing at all to worry about. We were so very isolated from events around the world at that time that I didn't have any basis on which to question them further."[14]

Once the deal with the *Daily Mail* was done and the participants had a celebratory drink, they held further discussions about how to handle getting Zola out of South Africa and into Great Britain.

In a move that would lead some South African media representatives to criticize the young woman whom they had all been praising, the men from the *Mail* decided that they would secretly spirit Zola and her parents out of the country. The *Daily Mail* wanted, above all, to protect its investment and to avoid the South African press. After all, the group reasoned, they had just paid a considerable amount of money for exclusivity. Why would they give the papers and television and radio stations the story for nothing?

• • •

As she reluctantly prepared to leave the home and family surroundings in which she was most comfortable, Zola Budd surveyed her small bedroom one last time. On the bed and scattered around the room were the numerous stuffed animals characteristic of a teenage girl's bedroom. One Raggedy Ann–type doll was nearly as large as she was.[15]

On the wall were posters, pretty standard fare for a teenager's room. But among the photos pasted on the walls—prominent were Sebastian Coe and Steve Ovett, the two British runners whose fierce rivalry and record-setting races had dominated British papers for years—was one that held special significance for Zola Budd.[16]

It occupied the place of honor above her head. Each night when she retired, it was the last thing she saw before extinguishing the lights. And in the morning, as the strong South African sun streamed into her room, it would be the first thing she saw.

It was a large color photo of her idol, the person whom she most admired.

Mary Decker.

• • •

In late March, Zola and her parents were accompanied by the *Daily Mail* representatives to Johannesburg immediately after a race arranged by the *Mail* in Welkom.

A day before the race, when she was made aware of the planned clandestine escape from South Africa, Zola had made one last effort to voice her opinion. "I told Pieter that I didn't think the plan [to leave South Africa for England] was a very good idea," she recalled. Her coach, who played an integral role in developing the plan, replied, "We've gone this far, it's too late to turn back. You might as well go along." Zola would recall years later that she was left feeling "like a puppet on a string."[17]

The group stayed with Zola's aunt and uncle in Johannesburg overnight. They told no one outside the family about the plan to flee for England.

On March 24, 1984, Zola boarded a KLM flight in Johannesburg bound for a new life in Great Britain. "I had never been out of the country before. My mother was not happy about the trip. She hadn't been part of the decision and had no say in the matter at all," Zola said.

The *Daily Mail* began taking photos of Zola at every opportunity throughout the trip. "I hated it," she said.[18] Indeed, Frank was the only Budd who enjoyed the trip. Tossie was seething because the *Mail* team had taken all the family photos that they could lay their hands on to use in the official Zola Budd biography that Brian Vine would be producing as part of the agreement with Frank.

John Bryant, the *Mail*'s features editor, later would tell a BBC reporter on Radio 4, "You have to give credit to Sir David English. He spotted the story from 3,000 miles and saw its potential." Interviewed years later for Zola's autobiography, Bryant pointed out that hers was one of the "longest running and most headline grabbing news stories of all time."[19]

While the *Daily Mail* was gloating at the prospects of soaring circulation and revenue that lay ahead, Zola was glimpsing, if only briefly, what was awaiting her when they reached their destination and her new life.

No one, least of all Zola Budd, could have imagined the living hell that life would become.

. . .

Bedlam.

In its lowercase form it has become part of the English language. In the mid-thirteenth century a wealthy Brit who had experienced a religious epiphany during one of the numerous crusades of the era donated land to a religious order for the establishment of a hospital.

The parcel was located in London's Bishopsgate Ward, and the hospital erected by the Priory of St. Mary of Bethlehem became known as Bethlehem Hospital, later shortened to Bethlem by Londoners and finally Bedlam, which was the phonetic pronunciation at the time.

It would operate on the two-acre site for more than four hundred years until it relocated to Moorfields, also in London. At some point in its early history, the monks began to admit patients with mental problems, and eventually that became its sole function. The hospital struggled to survive and in 1346 was taken over by the city as a hospital specializing in madness. Plagued by scandals, ill treatment, and mismanagement, Bedlam gained the reputation that would lead to its becoming the term we still use today to describe "any place or condition of noise and confusion."[20]

Unfortunately for Zola Budd, that definition fit the circumstances she found herself in upon arriving in Great Britain. However, in retrospect even *bedlam* might not be a strong enough word.

. . .

It is difficult to imagine in hindsight just how chaotic Zola's life became from the moment her father decided it was in her (and decidedly his) best interest to immigrate to England.

The Cold War was still hot, England was facing the difficulty of a coal miners' strike that threatened to paralyze the country, and the government was taking action to break off relations with Libya, but one story transcended all others and occupied a prominent place in the press for months.

The Zola Budd affair.

From March onward, her arrival, and the *Daily Mail*'s involvement and plan to have her become a citizen of Great Britain and represent the United Kingdom in the Olympics, was hotly debated and not just in the press.

The venerable Parliament of the United Kingdom itself took up the topic of Zola Budd. Fierce debate about the seventeen-year-old raged. Margaret Thatcher, the prime minister and leader of the Conservative Party, led the defenders of Zola against attacks from the left-leaning Labour Party, communities governed by Labourites, and representatives of the antiapartheid movement in Great Britain.

The arrival of a seventeen-year-old warranted this attention?

Unfortunately for Zola the answer was a resounding yes. Zola, whom the journalist Ian Wooldridge had described as "looking like a bewildered 12 year old," was going to have to grow up fast.[21]

. . .

The widely read *Daily Mail* was supportive of the Thatcher government, and English, its editor, wasted no time in calling in favors from the administration.

At a time when a typical application for British citizenship entailed waiting months and even years for approval by the Home Office, English managed to move the process through the bureaucracy at lightning speed.[22]

Zola was scarcely over jet lag from the flight from South Africa through Amsterdam to England when she was directed to quietly apply for citizenship at the Croydon Immigration Office, accompanied by *Mail* representatives and photographers, on March 26.[23]

When the *Daily Mail* trumpeted the news on April 7 that Zola had been granted British citizenship, all hell broke loose. The anti-apartheid lobby, small but vocal and highly visible, screamed. The Labour Party saw an opportunity to further castigate the Conservatives and demanded an investigation. The press, effectively shut out of the story by the *Mail*, saw a chance to throw darts at the process and in an oblique way at the *Mail*, whose blocking of their access rankled them all.

But Zola was the target of opportunity.

The *Daily Mail* was hard pressed to restrain itself in announcing that it indeed had exclusive access to "the hottest property in athletics." The March 27 edition had carried a banner headline on the front page: "Mail Brings Wonder Girl Zola to Britain."

The next day another British daily's take was typical of the rest of the pack: its banner headline had screamed, "Zola Go Home."[24]

. . .

It was just the beginning.

News that Zola's application for citizenship had been personally handled and decided by Home Secretary Leon Brittan set off a firestorm of protest throughout the country. The Home Office spokesperson didn't help matters when he announced, "We understand that she is an exceptionally talented athlete who needs to participate in competitive running as soon as possible."[25]

The understanding supplied by the *Daily Mail* was misunderstood by many. When the outrage spread to include near-universal condemnation in the press, the *Mail* responded with a front-page story crowing about Zola's new status as a British citizen. On April 7 the banner headline, accompanied by a bold black reverse-type box reading "EXCLUSIVE," proclaimed, "I'll Run My Heart Out for Britain." A secondary headline for the piece announced, "Day of Joy for the Barefoot Girl the Mail Brought Here."

. . .

That may have been the way the *Daily Mail* saw it. It is also the way the paper hoped the public would come to see it, but in the residence the paper provided for the Budds, there was little joy.

During the next three months, Zola Budd would become the biggest news story in Great Britain. Hardly a day passed without some story somewhere about her. An inordinate amount of coverage was devoted to the story of Zola's arrival in England, but one must remember the climate in which the stories were written.

In 1984 Nelson Mandela was still in prison. South Africa was an international pariah for its brutal apartheid policy of racism. Anglican bishop Desmond Tutu of South Africa was a rallying voice against the white government. Whenever unrest occurred, retaliation was brutal and swift.

In the United States, liberal voices of protest left college campuses and picketed Wall Street to protest investments in South Africa. Students and professors frequently purchased a single share of stock so they could attend shareholders' meetings and question corporate leaders about their South African holdings and demand divestiture. The numerous African nations ruled by black majorities saw the Zola Budd story as an opportunity to further isolate South Africa from the rest of the world. They threatened to boycott the Olympic Games in Los Angeles if Budd was permitted to compete. They were quickly joined by other nations, ranging from Norway to Spain, that were protesting her eligibility.

David English was right: Zola Budd was one big honking story.

. . .

Zola retreated behind the walls of her rented flat, provided and guarded by the *Mail*. Inside were Brian Vine and a photographer; outside were private security guards hired by the *Mail* to keep other reporters away from the young woman the paper regarded as its property.

She emerged from the prisonlike apartment only to run—after all, wasn't that what she had gone there to do?

. . .

Meanwhile the subject of the stories, who soon was moved to a rented house with more privacy in Guildford, also selected for her by the *Daily Mail* and guarded by a security team outside, was finding that her new residence was anything but a serene and tranquil refuge from the angry world outside.

As the cacophony of criticism of her arrival on British soil ascended to a crescendo in the media, the one thing she needed at the time, and for the difficult months ahead, was a place where she was safe, secure, and insulated from the hostile world outside her door. Instead she got "a house filled with tension," she would say.[26]

. . .

Zola had always found in running a means of escape, a way to feel free and secure. She had run in South Africa at first to escape her dysfunctional family. Then she had used running as a healing balm for the pain and sorrow of Jenny's death.

Now, when she went out to do her 5:00 a.m. training run in England, the difference between her new environment and her former home was stark. Instead of running freely through the veldt under an endless sky with the South African sun warming her shoulders, she dodged cars on narrow streets with running rivulets of rainwater and standing puddles. It was dark, gloomy, foggy, cold, and wet.

"It was such a contrast to what I was used to and it was depressing," she said.[27]

And when her morning run was over, she found conditions at home anything but ideal.

Vine, the portly, monocled *Daily Mail* reporter designated to produce the official Zola Budd biography, was a constant presence and irritant as he poked and prodded her to produce details for the manuscript. "I was wretched," she recalled. "I felt my running ability was being exploited by people who did not share my belief in the sport. Running was very important to me, and for me it was private."[28]

Once again she told Labuschagne about her unhappiness with the entire arrangement. "I told him I wanted to go home. I didn't want to stay there any longer. He told me it would be the wrong thing to do, and leaving would just subject me to even more criticism," she said.

"If it had been my decision to make, I would have just called the whole thing off. But it wasn't. My father and Pieter had a great influence on me then, and I couldn't manage to assert myself with either of them."[29]

Ensnared by those who had used her prodigious talent for their own purposes—the *Daily Mail*, her father, and her coach—she was effectively trapped. She could not even find comfort and solace from her mother.

"My parents were constantly fighting. The house was a place of constant tension. My parents fought over everything, and my mother was extremely unhappy and upset." She even made a poster with the number of days remaining before the Olympics and put it up on the wall, where each day she would cross out another day to remind herself that "we were getting closer to home."[30]

In retrospect Budd realized that the entire "Budd project" conceived by the *Mail* and her father lacked any semblance of long-term planning. "They had assumed everything would just fall into place neatly for them. They could never admit that the image they portrayed of me, as a little English girl returning to her roots, was hollow and false.

"I could barely speak English [her first language was Afrikaans] and needed time to get comfortable with the language, but I didn't have it. I reacted strongly when pushed. I just wanted to be myself, but I couldn't be because that didn't fit the image they had contrived," she said.[31]

John Simpson visited the Budd residence in Guildford often and recalled his impression of how Zola was living. "It was a chaotic, nerve-jangling existence," he said. "There were arguments over just about everything. Her father and coach would get into shouting matches over her schedule, and her mother always seemed to be upset and crying over the way her daughter was being treated."[32]

Seeking to join the mix were others who sought to enrich themselves through forging an association with Zola Budd. "Andy Norman and Sven Arne, two of the top race promoters in Europe, were on the scene, often trying to arrange for Zola to appear at their meets, where they knew her very presence would mean a large crowd," Simpson said.[33]

At the center of all the tumult and shouting was a young girl who in a matter of days had seen herself become a household name. And it made her miserable. "Even though I was the focus of all the attention, I felt that I was being treated by everyone as if I didn't count as a person," she said.[34]

Running, the root cause of it all, lost its appeal. She became moody and petulant and would contrive reasons not to train. Labuschagne "tried everything to get me to go on my morning runs, but I was so upset by what was going on, I didn't feel like running anymore," she recalled.

And when he could cajole her to run, she would fall into an easy jog behind him instead of running with him, which irritated her coach even more.[35] Zola's petulance and her adamant refusal to comply with her coach's wishes were obviously directly connected to her effort to gain some sense of control over her increasingly unhappy, chaotic life.

"I had sunk so far into the depths of despair that all I really wanted to do was to go home," she recalled.

Once she realized she wouldn't be going back to South Africa anytime soon, she set a new goal for herself: "I saw the Olympic Games as being not the great opportunity every athlete dreams about but as the end to my torment. I would watch Ma cross off each day and know that I was one day closer to returning home."[36]

NINE. Gathering Storms

In Eugene, Oregon, Mary Decker and her coach at Athletics West, Dick Brown, were preparing for the 1984 Olympic Games in Los Angeles. They were following a regimen that Brown devised that would have Decker fit and ready to peak in the summer.

In the small insular world of track-and-field athletes and coaches, her unparalleled 1983 season was the topic of much whispered discussion. "There were rumors that Mary had opted to 'level the playing field' by resorting to the same methods and means that the Eastern bloc runners had used when they were dominating the sport," said one elite athlete who asked to remain anonymous.

Was it possible?

In their pathbreaking look at Nike, *Swoosh*, published in 1993, the authors J. B. Strasser and Laurie Becklund recount experiments with the use of steroids, and other performance-enhancing drugs, as well as other techniques, on behalf of the athletes under the Nike-sponsored umbrella organization.[1]

Tom Sturak, who headed the Nike running promotions program, found disturbing evidence in the form of bills submitted to Nike from a Southern California chiropractor for "injection, injection, injection." Sturak called Brown, Mary's coach and the head exercise physiologist at Athletics West, and asked about the bills for what he feared were steroid injections. The next bills that arrived from the chiropractor reflected charges for "adjustment, adjustment, adjustment."[2]

Brown has steadfastly denied that Decker had used drugs to achieve her spectacular 1983 results.

According to Strasser and Becklund, Brown acknowledged that around 1980 he had investigated blood doping, a practice in which oxygen-enriched blood is injected into the athlete to improve stamina and performance. He even drove two unnamed athletes to Portland, where he had a doctor give the injections. Brown said the injections did not seem to improve performance, according to the authors.[3]

When I interviewed him, Brown also denied ever giving Decker any performance-enhancing drugs. Yet it is not unreasonable to assume that Decker, living in Eugene among the various other athletes whom Nike housed there, was aware of the benefits that blood doping could provide, despite Brown's opinion that it didn't work.

In blood doping the athlete's own blood is injected before a competition. Urine samples and blood tests at that time would not have detected any anomalies if an athlete had indeed used blood doping.[4] Iron-curtain countries used it at home in the early eighties, but its benefits could not be obscured for long, and the Eastern bloc runners used it, along with other enhancements, to dominate distance-running events—except for 1983 when Decker stunned the world with her performances time and again.

Athletes at various international meets in 1983 overheard Mary and Ron Tabb "make references to drug use," according to several elite runners who were present but declined to be named.

Mary Decker, the oft-injured athlete, had remained relatively free of injury during that spectacular season. She and Brown credit his strictly supervised regimen and monitoring, through periodic blood tests, for the results.

Her history of injury after injury throughout her career made her 1983 season even more fascinating and gave rise to the rumors and questions, never spoken publicly, about her ability to best the Eastern bloc runners and everyone else that year.

Brown maintains to this day that Decker did not use any drugs, but questions about her record-shattering performance that year remain in the minds of competitors and track reporters.[5]

In 1982 a new coach from New England arrived in Eugene to work for Athletics West. "Bob Sevene and his secretary were going over insurance records when they discovered a request for an insurance copayment for testosterone tests on one of AW's female athletes out of state," according to Strasser and Becklund; they do not identify the athlete in question.[6]

. . .

If the rumors and questions reached the ears of Nike executives, they apparently did not shake corporate confidence in Decker. Nike had upped the track star's income package and would use her in its advertising before the Olympic Games. She was believed to be a heavy favorite for gold in Los Angeles, and the Oregon shoe company, battling Adidas for supremacy in the marketplace, relied on her and a few others in its ad campaign leading up to the games.

The ad campaign belied what Nike, like almost everyone else, had learned about Mary Decker: she was difficult to handle. In one memorable incident in the early 1980s, she had a screaming fit when Nike refused to pay for a first-class ticket for her then-husband, Tabb, who was an Adidas athlete. She confronted Sturak about this in the Lausanne hotel where the elite Nike athletes were staying.

She entered the Nike executive's third-floor room, where he had Nike equipment and paperwork spread out across the bed, and screamed at Sturak about his refusal to provide the ticket for her husband.

"Why are you making my life miserable?" she yelled.

When Sturak tried to explain that she had a contract with Nike and that providing plane tickets "to an Adidas athlete wasn't part of the deal," she became even more enraged. She began to pick up the sneakers and apparel and files and throw them out the open window of Sturak's room while a crowd gathered below to watch the theatrics. Finally, Sturak, like so many others who would face Decker's petulant rage, relented.

As insane as her demands sounded to the Nike executive, she was, after all, their athlete, and she was by all accounts expected to make the Nike brand proud at the Olympics. But she was not, and never would be, easy for Nike to handle.[7]

A year later, when Decker was divorcing Tabb, she insisted that Brown serve the divorce papers on Ron. She seemed to feel, Brown said, that Nike was her surrogate family and that they should provide the support she needed—or demanded but never received—from her own dysfunctional family.[8] The divorce was so acrimonious that a judge issued a gag order to stop the two from contesting it in the media.[9]

. . .

Mary Decker would get her chance to fulfill a dream she had held since she was a teenage phenom in 1972. Injuries and circumstances had prevented her from competing in the Olympics, which had always been her dream. Now, in 1984, back in her home area, she would get her long-delayed due—an Olympic gold medal—the defining achievement of every middle-distance runner.

In early 1984 few among the astute observers of the scene doubted her ability to win, not just the 1,500-meter race but the newly installed 3,000 meters as well. For Nike it was to be her long-awaited coronation as the queen of women's track, so long as she managed to stay healthy.

But could she?

Her injury-plagued history would give everyone pause and cause them to always qualify her chances with "if she is healthy."

It was a big if.

Dick Brown had managed through persistent persuasion and adept training methods to harness Decker's previously unbridled insistence on hard training. The results had been self-evident in 1983.

Now, as Brown, who had managed to keep her healthy through her spectacular 1983 season, plotted strategy for the Olympic Games, his job would become even more difficult. Richard Slaney, the British discus thrower and Mary's future husband, was constantly coming between Decker and her coach. A bulky, muscular discus thrower makes a formidable wedge.

At least one prominent writer who covered track regarded the pairing of Slaney and Decker as an example of Mary's desire to have a bodyguard, as much as a boyfriend. If so, Richard fit the bill.

He was born about thirty miles from London to a middle-class British family; his father was an engineer and his mother a book-keeper. He had studied aeronautical engineering in England before earning a scholarship to San Diego State University. Richard Slaney was no stranger to injuries. He had sustained a serious one when he fell at the age of eleven and a fence post pierced the back of his leg nearly to the hip. It took four pins on one side and three on the other to stabilize the injury. He underwent more surgery at twelve and fourteen. So Richard could empathize with the oft-injured Mary.[10]

But for Brown, Slaney's presence would pose new difficulties in the effort to rein in Mary's demands that she do more than Brown's program called for. Keeping Mary healthy was never easy. Now, with Slaney on the scene, Brown would have to contend with his interference and insistence that he, a discus thrower, knew more about what was proper for Mary than the coach who had guided her to the best season any woman middle-distance runner had ever had. Their clashes became commonplace, and invariably Mary would defer to her discus-throwing boyfriend.

The pressure on Brown had been mounting since the end of the 1983 season. Now, with the Olympic Games looming, he was facing the difficult task of preparing his fragile charge for the games while attempting to temper Slaney's influence. It was a task no one would welcome, and, not surprisingly, Slaney turned out to be the more influential of the two men.

Brown wanted Mary to concentrate on a single event, the 3,000-meter race, while Slaney was adamant in his opinion that Decker should attempt a double gold-medal effort in both the 1,500 and the 3,000 meters in Los Angeles.

Brown also faced problems created by Mary's agent at IMG, Drew Merens. "He wanted Mary to do appearances and events that I felt were not in her best interests. I had to work through all that with her," Brown said.[11] Her income from Nike, along with performance bonuses and appearance fees, as well as the endorsement deals IMG secured, had Decker's income in the high six-figure range.[12] She was a hot property and everyone at Nike knew it.

Mary Decker, Joan Benoit, Alberto Salazar, and Carl Lewis were the stars of the large Nike stable of talent. Lewis was difficult to deal with and surrounded by an omnipresent entourage. He was stand-offish with the press as well. Benoit, an immensely talented New Englander, was a shy taciturn marathoner who was never really comfortable in the spotlight. Salazar was confident and charismatic; he had won three consecutive New York City Marathons, 1980–82.

Mary, a narcissistic, spotlight-craving athlete, was the brightest of the Nike stars. She was the living, breathing epitome of Nike—a company named after the winged goddess of speed in Greek mythology. It just didn't get any better than this, and Nike had invested a lot in her.

Despite her reputation with the media for being difficult, or, more commonly, a bitch to deal with, her story was a soap opera that resonated with the public. The tale of a teen phenom who had been injured and had come back time and again appealed to the public even if the press disdained her self-centered attitude.

It didn't get easier for reporters once Richard Slaney was on the scene. "I had been dispatched to Oregon in advance of the games [about a week before they began] by the *LA Times* to do a story on Mary," Rick Reilly recalled. "I made an appointment to see her and flew up to do the interview. I was there three days in a small motel room, and she kept putting me off. My editor asked me every day for the story, and I had nothing to give him. Finally, the day I was to return, she agreed to do it on the plane to LA. I packed in a hurry and met her for the plane ride down to LA.

"As I got on the plane, I saw that Mary was seated next to the window and her boyfriend, big, burly Slaney, was in the middle seat. I took the aisle seat and tried to do an interview with her while Slaney's ample girth made just seeing her almost impossible," Rick said.[13]

Dick Brown observed what was going on. "I told her, 'That is no way to treat the press,' he recalled. "She didn't pay any attention to me."[14]

Mary, who had been portrayed and described in the media as America's sweetheart, was in fact anything but. "If she was America's sweetheart," Reilly offered, "America needed body armor."[15]

But except for reporters who had to deal with her and Richard, Mary Decker remained a compelling and fascinating story. Her wild career swings and dramatic comebacks from injury, coupled with her ascendancy to the top of the world of women's middle-distance running, were hard to ignore.

The public loved her.

And, to make certain everyone was fully aware of her, as part of the advertising build-up for the games, Nike had images of Mary Decker painted on the sides of buildings throughout LA several months before the games began. Hundred-foot photos of her in midstride were installed along the route to the Coliseum. She was also one of the Nike athletes shown in a television commercial that featured Randy Newman's "I Love LA."

To his credit, Brown did a remarkable job preparing Decker for the Olympics, but it was evident to him after Slaney arrived that coaching her was going to be infinitely more difficult.

Everyone at Nike, the Athletics Congress, the U.S. track and field organization, and Olympic organizers had great expectations for Decker to succeed in LA. It fell to Brown to see that those expectations were met. He carefully selected meets and monitored Mary's condition leading up to the Olympic trials in June in Los Angeles.

To him, as well to others, the Olympic Games without the participation of the Eastern bloc countries—they had pulled out in support of the Soviet Union's retaliatory boycott of the games—didn't "feel like a real Olympics," and he was pointing her toward the post-Olympic season in Europe where she would defend her titles against all comers.

Mary agreed with Dick, at least at the outset. "But Richard interfered," Brown said. Slaney prevailed in his argument that Mary should compete in both the 1,500 and 3,000 meters at the Olympic trials.

Entering both events meant that she had to run heats and a final for both events.

The final for the 3,000 came before the 1,500. The meet had fallen behind schedule by about forty-five minutes by the time the athletes assembled for the final of the 3,000. After cooling down for a long period, the athletes were hurried out to the track. They were permitted only the briefest time to do some strides and loosen up before the race.

Although she was healthy coming into the trials, "Mary injured her Achilles tendon in the race," Brown said. She still won the race, but Brown believed her Achilles injury validated his contention that she should not have entered that race as well as the 1,500.

On the ride back to the hotel, the three talked about Mary's options. Brown insisted that she forgo the 1,500 final the next day. "I told her it would just make her injury worse and she shouldn't do it. "Mary looked at Richard," Brown recalled. Slaney turned to Brown and said, "I want her to run in the 1,500."[16]

Kim Gallagher, a talented young American runner at 800 and 1,500 meters, was in the field for the finals as well.

Mary elected to run against her coach's advice. In the final of the 1,500, Mary was defeated decisively by her longtime rival Ruth Wysocki. Gallagher, who would go on to capture a silver medal in the 800 at the Olympics, faded badly and finished ninth.[17]

Decker aggravated the Achilles injury in the race. "No one knew she was injured," Brown said. She had qualified for the Olympics in both events, but her injury made her participation problematic.

Back in Eugene, Brown had to try to remedy the problem that Richard's decision had caused. Brown had a saline solution injected in her Achilles tendon, where she had a buildup of scar tissue from old injuries. As the procedure was performed, Brown remembered, "You could clearly hear the 'pop, pop, pop,' as the scar tissue was dissolved in the area."

The injury left her Achilles very sore and tender. Brown immediately stopped her track workouts and put her in the swimming pool. "She did all her training in the water, weighted down to maintain her aerobic fitness and to avoid aggravating the Achilles."

For the next month Brown supervised her workouts in the pool. On July 28, the day of the opening ceremony for the games in Los Angeles, Mary Decker returned to the track in Eugene, where the Nike coaches had gathered five others to join her in a race at an all-comers meet.

"I think I can beat Zola's 2,000-meter record," Decker told Brown before the race.[18] "She [Decker] then set a world record in the 2,000 meters in the race just three days after getting out of the water," he said. "She was ready to run."[19]

Her training continued under Brown's watchful eye. He had her run three 400-meter workouts on a track outside Los Angeles two days before the heats for the 3,000-meter race. "She was supposed to run a sixty-second lap, then jog and run a fifty-eight-second lap, jog and complete the workout with a fifty-six-second lap. She ran the last lap in fifty-two seconds," Brown remembered.[20]

Same old Mary.

She was as ready for the world stage as she could be. And she would compete only in the 3,000 meters, having decided to drop out of the 1,500 after her most recent injury.

Brown had done his job—against all odds and despite the near-disastrous meddling of Slaney—and Mary Decker was poised and primed to claim what she believed was her long-delayed due.

As the heats for the 3,000 meters approached, Mary Decker was the brightest star in a firmament of stars burnished to a high glow by the media and by her IMG and Nike handlers.

To further whet the appetite of American viewers, most of whom viewed track meets about as often as curling contests, Decker would be paired in print and on television with Zola Budd. The tiny barefooted and controversial runner from South Africa would be scripted by the media as the opponent with whom Mary Decker would duel for gold.

It was a story worthy of nearby Hollywood.

TEN. Rings of Fire

Regarding the Olympics as her ticket back to South Africa was not the ideal mind-set for an athlete preparing for the grandest event in her sport, but that's how cornered Zola Budd felt.

But first she would have to qualify to compete for a spot on the British Olympic team despite her dismal state of mind.

Asked three decades later how, in view of all the negative energy around her at the time, she was able to compete, she said simply, "I have always had the ability to dissociate myself from my surroundings."[1]

That attribute, which would be sorely tested, would prove to be Zola Budd's salvation in the months leading up to the games.

It is difficult to imagine any elite athlete preparing for a series of important races under more adverse circumstances. Budd had been racing and training with virtually no break for a year. She would now have to divorce herself from the chaos and clamor surrounding her at home and in the media and race to prove her ability to represent her new country.

She needed to race within the Olympic qualifying times for her distances first and then to run well enough in the British Olympic Trials to be included on the British team.

. . .

Only two weeks after she arrived from South Africa, the *Mail* arranged for Budd to join one of England's numerous running clubs. Membership in a club was a prerequisite for competitive running, and the clubs were the traditional means through which Britain developed athletic talent. Zola joined the Aldershot, Farnham and District Athletic Club. "We are delighted to have her as a member," the club secretary said.

Not everyone shared his enthusiasm. Wendy Smith-Sly, twenty-three, was a leading contender for the British Olympic team. She was off training in the United States but issued a short statement about Zola Budd. "It's got to be unfair and so discouraging if Zola Budd can come in at such a late juncture, get a British passport at incredibly short notice and take a place on the team," said England's top middle-distance runner, adding, "I intended to run in the British Olympic Trials in June, but now I'm considering pulling out as a matter of principle."[2]

Smith-Sly joined another British middle-distance runner, Jane Furniss, who had said only days after Budd's arrival that other British athletes "should make a stand" if Zola was allowed to gain citizenship and a spot on the Olympic team. Furniss, another aspirant for a spot on the British team, was a 3,000-meter runner and was quoted as saying bluntly that her rival was "not welcome here."[3]

In a letter to the editor of the *Daily Express* one reader asked, speaking of Furniss, "Where is her Olympic spirit which says the best athletes—from everywhere—may take part? Surely all ... should be only too happy to help a fellow athlete, particularly one who is otherwise prevented from entering the games."[4]

Despite the criticism from other runners, Budd planned to run in the 3,000 meters in a meet on April 14 at Dartford in an effort to establish her qualifying time for the Olympic trials at that distance; her South African time of 8:37.5 was not recognized anywhere outside that country. Worse, she would have to qualify on a third-rate track. Judging from a photograph, she said, "It was a dirt track and it looked to be in terrible condition."[5]

Two days before the meet she, and more directly the *Daily Mail*, were attacked by the Labour MP Denis Howell, who termed the rapidity with which Budd had been granted citizenship by the Home Office an example of "a disgraceful newspaper stunt and an obscene marketing operation."[6]

. . .

A horde of reporters and photographers assembled in Guildford on race day. As Zola prepared to leave home for the race, she shot pictures of the picture takers through the parted curtains of the rental.

The *Daily Mail* hired a car to drive her to Central Park, Dartford, and a police escort awaited her there and accompanied her to the track from a secluded area where she had warmed up. The police were essential because the large crowd, estimated to be about six thousand, surged forward to get their first glimpse of the tiny girl who, one writer observed, had a birdlike frailty.[7]

The *Mail* used the music from *Chariots of Fire* to ignite the large crowd's enthusiasm. The race was also televised by the BBC, which Andy Norman, the race promoter, had induced to participate.

When Labuschagne told Zola to run a few strides on the outside of the track before lining up, she refused. "I was too embarrassed with all those people watching me," she said.

As the call to the starting line was approaching, Labuschagne whispered his final advice: "All the calmness is over now, and you have to prepare yourself for the future."[8]

She must have wanted to smack him.

. . .

The BBC beamed the race live on its afternoon *Grandstand* show. With a television audience of millions and the cameras of twelve international networks trained on her, Zola Budd more than exceeded the expectations of the sophisticated British track audience.

Running in spikes over a surface that many runners felt was the worst in Great Britain, Budd easily bested the small field. Though her time of 9:02.6 was slow by her standards, it was easily within the Olympic qualifying time for 3,000 meters. She also set a new British junior record.

After the race she was presented with a large bouquet and reluctantly found herself the star of a press conference called by the *Daily Mail*. It was the *Mail*'s attempt to both quell the media uproar its actions had caused and trumpet the emergence of its "wonder girl" as the next great British runner. No one thought to ask Zola what she thought about participating in such an event. *Daily Mail* editors and executives simply pulled a string on their puppet and told her to appear and speak to a horde of hostile newspaper and television reporters.

The *Mail* made a concerted effort to manage what it called the introduction of Zola to the press, which included surrounding her with *Daily Mail* representatives, her coach, and her parents. Large signs bearing the *Mail* logo were placed on either side of the table where she was seated, ensuring that the paper would get maximum exposure. However, apparently no one had made a concerted effort to prepare her for what was coming. Or perhaps the men from the *Mail* never considered it, focused as they were on pulling off their circulation-boosting coup and lording it over all the media outlets that wanted a piece of the Zola Budd story.

One reporter who attended the press conference thought Zola looked "like a doe caught in the headlights of a speeding car," as she sat stiffly and read, with a heavy Afrikaans accent in her barely audible voice, a statement written for her by the *Daily Mail*.[9]

When she finished reading the statement, the *Mail* attempted to throw a few softball questions at her and call it a day. But the rest of the reporters wouldn't let the *Mail*, and by extension Zola, off the hook that easily. Shouting to be heard over the *Daily Mail* representatives, the cranky reporters hurled a tumult of questions at her about racism and South African politics.

Zola, John Simpson recalled, visibly recoiled before the onslaught and was shaken by the entire experience, which did little to assuage the rival newspapers' displeasure with the *Daily Mail*. She was startled and shocked at the volume, intensity, and relentlessness of the questions hurled at her. Moreover, although she could speak and understand English, she was not comfortable with it. But Zola understood that most of the questions coming at her dealt with apartheid, a word she could understand all too well.

"What are they asking me about that for?" she thought. "I am a runner. I'm here to run, not to explain a government policy in which I have no part."[10]

Even under the best of circumstances, her timid voice was barely a whisper. Had she tried to reply to the insistent demands shouted at her, the answers would have been inaudible and delivered in heavily Afrikaans-accented English that few in the unruly mob could understand. She chose to remain silent, but her silence and the *Daily Mail*'s prepared statement cost her dearly.

The media melee into which her father and the *Daily Mail* had thrown her set the stage for speculation about her views on racial policies in South Africa. Some construed her silence as acceptance of apartheid. Others, fewer in number, would understand her reluctance to address political issues about which she was poorly informed at best.

Although the *Daily Express*, the *Daily Mail*'s bitter rival, described Zola's appearance at the press conference as "a circus act," and despite the verbal battery to which reporters had subjected her, the *Express* was in the minority.[11] The pendulum had already started to swing in Zola's favor.

. . .

Now the top tier of British sports organizations joined in the rush for membership in the Zola Budd fan club.

Only days earlier Sir Arthur Gold, a member of the European Athletics Association, had questioned her ability to get clearance from the International Olympic Committee to run for Britain. "I have misgivings," he gravely told the BBC.[12]

In fact the eligibility of Zola Budd to run in the Olympics represented a thorny problem for Juan Antonio Samaranch. The former fascist could not afford to alienate the large number of African nations whose support he needed to maintain control of the International Olympic Committee. One can only imagine the look on Samaranch's face at the prospect of having to rule on the matter.

But in the wake of Budd's winning performance, no less than the chair of the British Amateur Athletics Board (BAAB), took up her cause. Charles Palmer said he would write to the IOC to seek permission for Zola Budd to represent Great Britain.[13]

When the BAAB declared Zola eligible for competition, now that she was a British citizen, Samaranch passed the buck and said the matter had been decided and the IOC would not be overturning the British governing body's decision.[14] And because the BAAB considered Budd a "British national," the International Association of Athletics Federations (IAAF), her sport's governing body, did too, because in its eyes South Africa didn't exist. This ironic subtlety let the IOC off the hot seat. A few feeble letters of protest arrived from obscure African Olympic committees and were quietly ignored.

Samaranch, fearful the Soviet Union's retaliatory refusal to attend the LA Games would become a more widespread boycott, was relieved.

Now all Zola needed to do was make the British Olympic team.

. . .

Just before the Budds left South Africa for England, Pieter Labuschagne (and Simpson) had warned the *Daily Mail* team that she was not yet ready for international competition.[15] Nonetheless Andy Norman and the *Daily Mail* entered her in a series of races designed to help her gain international experience and improve her conditioning. The contract her father had signed with the newspaper ran for only a year (it would expire in November), and the *Mail* was eager to get what it had paid for. Her next race, at 1,500 meters, over a newly constructed track, was to be at Crawley, near Gatwick Airport. But the Labour Party–controlled town council was, the mayor said, "worried about Zola's connection with South Africa" and wanted to ban her from the race.[16]

Labuschagne withdrew her, and Norman quickly found another one for her, at the Crystal Palace National Sports Centre, the site of many major track meets. The change in venue was announced, giving the antiapartheid lobby time to mobilize.

On race day, April 25, she was confronted before the race by about twenty demonstrators carrying a large banner reading "No to Zola Budd," and she was subjected to chants of "Go home, South African trash," and "You'd be better off dead." She was in tears.[17]

But the rest of the crowd of about a thousand was supportive, cheering her each time she passed in front of the main grandstand as she easily outdistanced her competition and finished in 4:10.82, a new British junior record. She was also now easily within the qualifying time for the 1,500 meters at the national championships, which also served as the Olympic trials and were scheduled for May.

Despite the roars of support, Norman said, "she was in tears before the race and after the race she was visibly upset." He said Zola was upset by demonstrators' comments at the end of the race—among them, "Go home, you white South African trash"—which she could hear over the cheers of the crowd.[18]

Norman and the *Daily Mail* representatives ushered Zola quickly away, avoiding the press conference that they had planned. "If you had a 17-year-old daughter who has just been given a verbal bashing, would you expect her to come to a press conference?" Norman asked.[19]

Zola's ability to run and run well despite the ever-present protesters gradually changed attitudes in the press and among the public in Great Britain. The ugly scene at the Crystal Palace only brought Zola more support and sympathy from the British public.

As the track writer Christopher Hilton remarked two days after the event, "Certainly what happened . . . at the Crystal Palace was a freak event which left a sour note in the mouth, and nothing but pity for a superb young athlete surrounded—trapped—and maybe exploited beyond her knowledge." He added, "That she can really run is beyond all reasonable doubt."[20]

Hilton and the other sportswriters knew greatness when they saw it. With each race and each win and each new record, Zola's enormous and undeniable talent would win them over.

Though they would never be able to let go of their animosity toward the *Daily Mail* and the tactics used to freeze them out of a great story, all the sportswriters would eventually concede that Zola Budd was becoming one of Britain's best hopes for a medal in the Olympics.

The antiapartheid forces, however, never were converted. They continued their harassment and stalked her presence at every meet. Their insults and threats grew in intensity and ugliness.

Despite her success on the track, or perhaps because of it, the protesters found her an easy target. She would wear that bull's-eye throughout her schedule in 1984 and beyond.

• • •

As the voices of antiapartheid lobbyists in Great Britain and abroad assaulted Budd, it is logical to ask why she didn't succumb to the persistent demands that she denounce the racism enshrined in law in her native land.

"It was a no-win situation," she said. "If I denounced apartheid publicly, as I was asked repeatedly to do, I felt that next they would insist I denounce the government, the president, the legislature, and it would never end [and] would naturally offend my friends and everyone back home. And after doing so I would lose their support, which was important to me at the time.

"I really didn't want to antagonize anyone. I didn't even know until I arrived in England who Nelson Mandela was. I was being asked to air my political views publicly, and I thought that the political views of athletes were not something anyone else in athletics was being asked about, so why should I be compelled to do so? I may have been naive to assume that I had a right to my own political views and didn't need to make them public."[21]

Zola's reluctance was a festering irritant to the antiapartheid lobby, which used her silence on apartheid to advance the antiapartheid position. Sam Ramsamy, leader of the antiapartheid lobby, would repeatedly characterize her as "a representative of a racist government." Ramsamy, a South African of Indian heritage, was living in exile in London.[22]

Zola Budd's personal view of apartheid was based on her firm Christian values, which taught her that "it is wrong to discriminate against people because of their color or race."

Her decision not to publicly state her position, denounce her country, and appease the mob impaled her firmly on the horns of a dilemma from which she would not shake free for years. "The irony was that I abhor apartheid as much as those that criticized me do," she said. "But the attacks on me for my silence on the subject, which I felt was my right, only stiffened my resolve not to make a statement."[23]

Budd would point out that other prominent athletes in Great Britain, such as Wendy Smith-Sly and Sebastian Coe, never were asked for their political views but were accepted as just great athletes. "I was not afforded that courtesy," she said.

But that was only one reason for her silence. "It would have been very foolish of me to speak out at that time on a subject I knew so little about as a seventeen-year-old. I was not an expert on political systems. I had no firm grasp on the social issues or on international affairs. I had never studied apartheid in school, and I was certainly not knowledgeable enough to comment on the subject when everyone was demanding it of me."[24]

Zola was also feeling pressure from those in South Africa who thought she should speak out, including Archbishop Desmond Tutu of the Anglican Church. Zola concedes that her stance played right into the hands of her critics by supplying them with still more ammunition to fire at her. "But my conscience was clear, and that was the main thing."[25]

. . .

Margaret Thatcher was among those who were shocked at the treatment Budd had received. "I think the treatment meted out to the 17-year-old girl was utterly appalling and a disgrace," the prime minister declared in the House of Commons.[26]

Although the tide of public opinion was changing, damage had been done. Years later Budd would tell a reporter, "They always hated me there and I never knew why."[27]

It's only natural for her to recall the ugliness and the verbal and written assaults that she endured. Yet video footage of her races in the early months of her residence in England makes clear that she had the support and approval of those who turned out in record numbers to watch her compete. Television cameras and still photographers may have focused on the vocal few that protested, but the vast majority at her races gave her standing ovations at nearly every meet that drowned out the few protesters chanting filthy slurs.

But Zola would hear only the ugliness and wonder why. "All I could hear were jeers, and the shouts and the taunts. It was very personal. And it came close to ruining me," she said.[28]

. . .

After Zola's impressive win at the Crystal Palace, Wendy Smith-Sly, who was training and racing in Florida, joined Zola's growing group of admirers.

"I'm Not a Super-Bitch" was the headline in the *Mail* on April 23. An article filed by Rim Miles from New York quoted Smith-Sly as saying she had no intention of boycotting the Olympics to protest the preferential treatment of Budd.

"I have spent the last three years totally dedicated to one ambition . . . to bring a medal home for my country," Smith-Sly said. "I've never said I would refuse to run in the same team with her. I have absolutely nothing against her. I've never met her but I'm sure she's a very nice person."

. . .

Oslo was the next stop arranged by the race promoter Swen Arne for Zola. On May 6 she ran in a 10K road race against stiff competition there and once again faced demonstrators along the route with signs that said, "Zola Budd Runs with Apartheid," and "Zola's Apartheid's Golden Girl." Norwegian politicians protested Budd's presence. However, most spectators cheered her efforts.[29]

Competing against the Norwegians Grete Waitz and Ingrid Kristiansen, two of the best distance runners in the world, Zola finished a respectable third. She had led at the halfway mark and finished in 31:42, more than a minute and a half in front of Rosa Mota, the 1983 European marathon champion, and won praise from Waitz, who finished behind Kristiansen.

Budd's strong showing against two of the world's best distance runners firmly established her as one of Great Britain's best chances for a medal in the rapidly approaching Olympics.

"I think Zola Budd is going to shake the world," Waitz said. "I could never have done that when I was seventeen." Then she added, "She could put every world record in danger from the 1,500 m[eters] up. I hope people will leave her in peace so that she can develop her talent—she is just startling."[30]

. . .

On May 15 newspaper readers awoke to the news that Zola Budd had renounced her South African citizenship shortly after she became a British citizen. She responded that she had "assumed that when I got my British citizenship I was automatically no longer a citizen of South Africa, so these formal steps are really just tying up any loose ends." She added, "I think, however, it must be made clear to everyone that I am British and intend to remain so."[31]

. . .

The week or so before her eighteenth birthday on May 26 was happier for Zola. She had a visit from her sister Estelle, and Elizna van Zyl, Zola's friend from South Africa, came over to help Zola celebrate her birthday. The event was duly recorded, as usual, by the *Daily Mail*, which provided the cake.

"It was a fruit cake with green icing around the top that was supposed to look like a track and a small figure stuck on it that was supposed to be me. It was in very bad taste, and didn't taste that good either," Zola recalled.

Elizna, Estelle, and Zola repaired to the kitchen and enjoyed the pastries Estelle had brought from South Africa while the adults devoured the cake.[32]

•••

Two days later, on May 28, a Monday, Zola ran in the UK National Championships in Cwmbran, Wales, in bad weather.

More than ten thousand packed the grandstands and hundreds more, ten deep, jostled for a good spot on hillsides around the track. About thirty demonstrators bearing homemade placards paced outside the gates as Budd won the 1,500-meter race in 4:04.39, a British junior record and the fastest by any woman in the world so far that year. The press was quick to point out that "it was also better than the best time this year by American Mary Decker, the world champion," who had run 4:05 in San Jose over the weekend.[33]

Gillian Green, who led during the early part of the race and was pressed the whole time by Budd, dropped out, demoralized, after Zola breezed by her. Green was "torn apart," Ron Pickering, the BBC commentator, remarked.

Jane Furniss, who had criticized Budd when she first arrived in Britain, finished far back in third but gave Zola a kiss on the cheek after the race, which, Zola said, "made me feel welcome."[34]

Zola not only won but survived being tripped and nearly falling in the first lap before completely demolishing the field of talented runners. Budd finished thirty meters, or six seconds, in front of her closest pursuer, Jo White, who ran for the University of Richmond in the United States.

The BBC again telecast the race nationally, and after watching Budd dominate the race, Pickering declared that "she is truly a remarkable, highly talented runner."[35]

The coach of the British national team, Frank Dick, was present and observed happily, "This time was worth well under 4 minutes on a more reasonable day. She is in a different class. What an incredible running machine."[36]

•••

While her running was coming along better than anyone could have hoped, the Guildford household was still chaotic and showed no signs of improving.

The never-ending tension between Frank and Tossie now had infected Labuschagne. Frank, full of himself and growing more so each day with the attention he was getting as Zola Budd's father and the money from the *Daily Mail* for his daughter's story, was at constant odds with Pieter. "Both were constantly arguing over my schedule, and there was no peace at all," Zola said.

Forced to choose sides in the interminable arguments between her coach, in whom she had placed her trust for her career, and her father, who had given her every reason not to trust him, Zola sought to move out.

She approached her father about buying a small one-bedroom home for herself. He flatly refused to discuss it. Although Zola had reached the legal age of emancipation, she was anything but emancipated. Frank controlled all the *Mail* money as well as the money from the Defy sponsorship. He was living large in England, visiting relatives and basking in the reflected glory of his daughter, all the while spending her money and enjoying her new car. He had not yet been invited to tea with the queen, but Frank had pretty much everything else he wanted—at Zola's expense.

When she asked for an accounting of the funds, he refused to supply it.[37]

. . .

The Guildford residence became a bit more comfortable when John Simpson arrived one morning with a kitten for Zola.

"I'd been to her farmhouse in South Africa and had seen how she was always surrounded by animals there. They had dogs, cats, ducks, chickens, ostrich, and even a talking parrot," he recalled. "I knew how lonely and homesick she was for that place and those surroundings and thought the kitten might cheer her up."[38]

Zola promptly named the kitten Johnnie in honor of Simpson. Johnnie later produced kittens.

. . .

But the kitten at least gave her some comfort, which was difficult, if not impossible, for her to find in the chaos of the house.

Ian Wooldridge, the *Daily Mail* athletics writer, visited the house and later wrote a story about what he found. "Her coach and father were yelling at each other over her training schedule. A writer from *The Mail* was hurling questions at her from the kitchen where he was typing a manuscript for her 'official biography,' and, in the background from another room, her mother, Tossie, could be heard weeping," he reported.[39]

After one nasty morning of conflict between her coach and her father, Zola jumped on her bike and headed out. She stayed away all day, returning in the late afternoon after sitting alone in a movie theater for hours.

Her father promptly assured her he had only her best interests at heart.

Frank, of course, blamed Pieter. Pieter in turn blamed Frank. The two men who had put Zola squarely where she now found herself were forcing her to choose between them. It wasn't something she was eager to do, not least because she was in the middle of a series of events that would decide her eligibility to run for Great Britain in the Olympics.

The decision would wait. The running continued. So too did the silent tears she shed in her bedroom, where she snuggled with her kitten in the dark room that reflected her mood.

. . .

In early June, on the eve of her appearance in the Olympic trials at the Crystal Palace, a Labour politician announced that he wanted Zola Budd to denounce South African racism or he would move to cut all funding for the Crystal Palace.

"I don't understand why certain people in this country always try to drum up a big row just before I run. It seems very cruel and unfair," she said.[40]

. . .

The Olympic trials were yet another affirmation of Budd's talent as she easily won her way, running barefoot over a wet surface and onto the team. She finished first in both the 1,500 and 3,000 meters.

Her performance impressed many who cheered her efforts and drowned out the small group of protesters whose handmade banner, held aloft on the first turn, urged, "Zola Leave."

A few days later Chris Brasher wrote in the *Observer*, "I have met her twice. Her voice is so small that you have to bend your ear to her lips; her complexion is as delicate as the proverbial English rose; her spirit is still and quiet. You feel the need to cocoon her from the world, to wrap her in care and love. And then you see her on the track, purposeful, remorseless, and toweringly talented."

Brasher, a former world-class athlete himself, had secured his own place in history by being one of the two runners who had paced Roger Bannister to the first mile ever run in less than four minutes. Now Brasher decried the "political blackmail" Zola had been facing.

"To me, and I hope the vast majority of British athletes and spectators, the issue is simple. Here is a girl of wondrous talent; sport provides an arena in which talent can flourish; so let us help to bring that talent to its rightful place in the world and that place is the Olympic Stadium."[41]

The Los Angeles games were less than two months away.

. . .

At the trials, Zola had been forced to use a back entrance to the stadium to avoid the demonstrators assembled out front.

Aware the event would be televised, the small group of protesters that managed to gain entrance hurled epithets at her as she warmed up. "Racist scum" and "fascist bitch" were but two that were ringing in her ears when she faced the starter.

She still won with ease.

. . .

In a race in Belfast promoted by Norman on June 19, Budd ran in the 3,000 meters and coasted to victory.

Four days later she wore the colors of Great Britain for the first time at the Villa Park stadium in Birmingham, where Great Britain, Wales, Scotland, and Yugoslavia faced off. Zola romped.

The stands were packed on Saturday, June 23, and as usual fans were greeted at the gates by a small group of demonstrators carrying a placard that said, "Zola Can Run, Nelson Mandela Can't," and passing out antiapartheid pamphlets.

In Birmingham, which was the incubator of the Industrial Revolution, she raced through air pollution that must have left her even more mindful of the contrast to her homeland. In the 1,500 meters she ran away from all the competitors, including Wendy Smith-Sly, who pulled out with an injury. Budd took a thirty-yard lead on the field that she extended to about sixty yards at the finish as she flashed across the line in 4:14.22 to a standing ovation.

Asked after the race whether she was homesick, Budd replied, "No, but I do miss my animals from the farm." This prompted a quip from a British team official surveying the large crowd of reporters and photographers threatening to engulf Budd: "She's got a few animals around her now."[42]

. . .

Across the pond in the United States Mary Decker ran the 1,500 meters at the U.S. Olympic trials a few days later and was beaten by Ruth Wysocki. Decker then announced that she would run only in the 3,000 meters at the Olympics.[43]

Fans in Great Britain would have known, upon reading of Decker's decision, that Zola Budd would be competing in the 3,000 meters for Great Britain.

. . .

Zola was almost a no-show for the Peugeot Talbot Games, a prestigious televised event at the Crystal Palace in July that was to serve as a final warm-up before Los Angeles.

Her life at home was anything but good. Even seemingly little things now produced nasty arguments between Pieter and Frank. An innocuous invitation to a fondue party at Pieter and Carin Labuschagne's just weeks before the Olympics finally forced Zola to make her long-delayed decision to sever ties with her father.

Carin and Elizna van Zyl had asked Frank if Zola could attend, and Frank, who had his own plans for her, objected loudly. Carin was not one to be intimidated, and a loud shouting match ensued during which Frank asked what right Peter and Carin had to organize his daughter's life—a job he sought for himself.

The fight ended with Frank slamming the door in Carin's face.

The argument came on the heels of yet another nasty comment from Frank that put Tossie down and left her in tears and an argument with Zola about his callous treatment of her mother.

It was all too much.

Later Zola would say that the door slamming became symbolic because it represented the end of her domination and exploitation by her father.

Zola walked out of the house to stay with the Labuschagnes. Once there she wrote a letter to Frank telling him that she did not want to see him or speak to him again until after the Olympics. Although others tried to mediate, Zola had made a clean break and would not retract her decision. It cost Zola even more when her friend Elizna van Zyl chose to stay with Frank and Tossie after Zola moved out. She continued to visit Tossie, now more miserable than ever, after first calling to ensure that Frank was out. Now, save for Pieter, who had his own agenda, Zola essentially was alone.

With the ugly scene and the banishing of her father still fresh in her mind, she faced a 2,000-meter race at the Crystal Palace in London in the Peugeot Talbot Games on July 13. Labuschagne had committed her to run there.

. . .

"I didn't want to run," she said. "I had told Pieter I didn't want to race on the way to the track. I had used the argument that I wasn't feeling that well that I used before. Again it didn't work with him, and another argument took place in the car. During the argument Pieter told me in a raised voice that this was my big chance.

"I told him I just wanted to go home. He then said, 'If you don't make the most of this, you'll just end up on that small farm back in Bloemfontein with your mother.'

"When he said that to me, it was the moment I realized that he felt that I, as a person, really didn't count. I only had value to him as a runner. I thought it was emotional blackmail, and we ended up screaming at each other.

"After the break with my father, I now had a huge wedge driven between me and my coach, whom I had trusted for years, and [the man whom I had] chosen over my father [turned out to be] just another person who was using me for their own benefit."

Labuschagne had arrived in Great Britain shortly after Zola and her parents. The money the *Daily Mail* had paid Frank also covered Labuschagne's expenses. He had taken leave from his teaching position at the University of the Orange Free State, where he had secured a position after inducing Zola, who did not want to attend that college, to join him there.

Once in England Pieter promptly seized the opportunity to enroll in graduate school at a local university; an advanced degree would mean higher wages. The classes occupied much of his time, and he juggled his schedule to accommodate Zola's training schedule, but there were always conflicts. He was there to help her adjust and to run and to supervise her training, but, like Zola's father, he quickly saw the move as one that would benefit him personally and seized the opportunity.

Zola's father was now effectively shut out of her life. Her coach, she now realized, had little empathy for her as a human being. Her mother, who was to have been her rock and source of comfort in the transition to a new land, was constantly depressed and weeping, hardly able to cope, let alone assist her young daughter. Zola's friends from home had left.

As she waited at the starting line, surrounded by the large field and facing a huge crowd, Zola Budd was alone in the Crystal Palace.

. . .

Fourteen runners, including four Americans, lined up along the all-weather track before a capacity crowd on a cloudy late afternoon in mid-July. The race, over a distance seldom run, 2,000 meters, was televised by the BBC. Cameras from numerous other networks and a horde of still photographers were on hand to document what the BBC announcer termed Zola Budd's "first real test," against a field that would, he claimed, "test her to the limit" at the Crystal Palace.[44]

Wendy Smith-Sly, the current UK record holder, was missing from the field, as was Mary Decker, but the race promised to be a true indication of Zola's ability both against international competition and to navigate a crowded field.

At the start, the American runner Jill Haworth, a 1,500-meter specialist, sprinted to the lead. Budd, back in the pack, moved up slowly through the crowd until she was third by the end of the first lap. By the end of the second lap, she was second behind the pace-setting American, with Christine Benning of Great Britain right behind Budd. By the time they passed the start-finish line in front of the grandstand for the third time, the pace had slowed somewhat, and Budd started to move. As they moved in front of the crowd facing the backstretch she accelerated past Haworth with Benning following on Budd's right shoulder. Passing the start-finish line again, she was greeted with loud applause as the large timer board flashed that they were just outside world record pace.

Benning maintained contact and continued to shadow Budd on the outside, prompting the BBC announcer to note that Zola had always been a front-runner and then ask, "How will she respond to the pressure?"

They were about to find out.

With 600 meters to go, Benning and Christina Boxer were right with Budd, continuing on near-record pace. Budd accelerated and Benning dropped back. Boxer, still to Zola's right, hung doggedly on as they headed for the last turn before the homestretch. Again Budd accelerated and Boxer tried to respond, but Budd pulled farther in front, opening a gap of about five yards down the homestretch and flashing across the finish line in 5:33.17 for a new world record.

The announcer and the crowd appreciated what they had just witnessed: Zola Budd had eclipsed the old mark by almost a half-second.

"She is a true racing talent," the BBC announcer declared, adding, "Zola Budd is no myth."[45] The crowd gave her a standing ovation.

Budd pulled off the track and into the infield, where she was surrounded by photographers and camera crews as she pulled on a light blue t-shirt emblazoned with the Brooks running shoe company's logo.[46] Thus attired, she took a victory lap around the track with applause greeting her every step.

She waved in response, but she wasn't smiling.

. . .

Coming as it did just a few short weeks before the start of the Olympic Games, the news of Zola Budd's record-breaking effort was headline news around the globe.[47]

Mary Decker read about it in the United States, as did the woman whose record Zola had erased, Maricica Puică of Romania. In that police state behind the iron curtain, the only communist bloc country to defy the Soviet Union's boycott and attend the Olympics, Puică learned the next morning that she was now a former record holder.

Her preparation for the games gained a new intensity.

Reporters had peppered Decker repeatedly about Zola Budd in recent months. When Decker deigned to speak to reporters, her answers were always innocuous and deferential. But it had to be apparent to Queen Mary that someone was getting a little too close to her throne.

In fact Dick Brown, her coach, recalled that in her final preparation race in Eugene before the games, Decker singled out Zola Budd's record in the odd distance of 2,000 meters as one she wanted to erase.[48]

. . .

Zola Budd's participation in the Los Angeles Olympics had survived challenges by a score of African nations that had threatened a boycott, criticism from politicians and athletes in Great Britain, her dysfunctional family, betrayal by her coach, and the tumult and shouting of demonstrators who stalked her every public appearance.

Her stay in England had been nothing short of an ordeal by fire, and she had managed to survive. She had done so, as she explained, through her "ability to dissociate from my surroundings."

According to Dr. Bradley Donohue, a professor of psychology at the University of Nevada–Las Vegas, all elite athletes possess the ability to dissociate so they can accomplish the task at hand. In Zola's case that would mean focusing on her race plan and the tactics for each race she entered after arriving in Great Britain.

"All elite athletes are able to do this," Donohue said. "They must process whatever adverses [adversities] they face and be aware of the consequences of hurting their performance if they do not discard or dissociate those adverses in order to perform at the high level called for in competition."

Aware of the numerous adversities Zola Budd had to overcome, Donohue concluded her ability to dissociate was extraordinary.[49]

The girl who had arrived in England at the end of March was

emotionally and physically drained by late summer. She had raced twenty-one times since January and had gone virtually without a break in training and racing for nearly eighteen months. She had done so under conditions that would have destroyed almost anyone else.

"As the Olympics approached, and my mother was making the last few large black X's on the wall poster over the days remaining before we'd be going home, I just wanted it to be over," Zola recalled. "All I wanted was to go home."[50] Accompanied by her mother and representatives of the *Daily Mail*, she flew to LA.

D. B. Prisloo, an accomplished steeplechase runner, had gone to England from South Africa to help Zola train for Los Angeles. She impressed him. "She was doing very well considering the circumstances," the tall rangy runner said. "Zola was very strong in her mind. I am not sure I could have managed to deal with the things she had to deal with. Zola could succeed at anything. She is the most dedicated person I have ever known."[51]

She had to be.

On July 28, the day before she arrived in Los Angeles, an article in the *Times* of London informed readers that her South African citizenship (and Frank's) had been officially revoked two months earlier.[52] Nonetheless, and despite her own renunciation of her South African citizenship, "in my heart I was still a South African," she said.[53]

But thanks to the actions of her father and the *Daily Mail*, she was now, without any doubt, a British citizen with a British passport. She was also a world-famous eighteen-year-old without a real home anywhere. Her ability to continue to dissociate and focus on running would be tested in the extreme in Los Angeles.

ELEVEN. Dream Chasers

· ·

Los Angeles would mark the second straight Olympic Games with no competition between the United States and the Soviet Union. The Soviets boycotted the Los Angeles games in retaliation for the Carter administration's decision to boycott the 1980 Moscow games, after the Soviet Union invaded Afghanistan; and many felt the Los Angeles games were diminished by the Soviets' absence.

Tit for tat was but one of many games played by the superpowers during the Cold War era.

Only one Eastern European nation, Romania, led by Nicolae Ceausescu, a former shoemaker turned iron-fisted dictator, defied the Soviets and sent a team to LA. Juan Antonio Samaranch greeted the Romanians with open arms, kissed their cold-blooded leader on both cheeks, and gave him an Olympic medallion.

The African nations had threatened to withdraw if Zola Budd participated, but their threat had fizzled. South Africa was absent once again, of course.

But the rest of the world was there.

. . .

In the first week of the Olympics, the massive hype engineered by ABC, which had won the rights to televise the games, focused on the gymnast Mary Lou Retton, as did the rest of the U.S. and international media. In the second week of the Olympics, it's fair to say, all eyes were on the women's 3,000-meter race.

Fittingly conducted in an arena named the Coliseum, with all the bloody images the original edifice evokes, television and newspaper coverage cast the race as the classic duel in the sun.

ABC executives led by Roone Arledge had brought us sports "up close and personal" for years with award-winning television. The network had paid an enormous sum for the television rights and can be forgiven for focusing its attention on Mary Decker and Zola Budd to the exclusion of all other middle-distance runners. It was, as so many writers have pointed out, a great story.

ABC milked it for all it was worth.

If the popular radio commentator Paul Harvey voiced an opinion about the 1984 games, it has been lost in the mists of time. But we can easily imagine his dramatic pause, followed by the familiar words in his distinctive mellifluous tones: "And now for the rest of the story."

. . .

The women's 3,000-meter race would see twelve women from around the world line up along the track in the Coliseum in the glow of the late afternoon's slanting sun. All would be chasing a dream.

. . .

Under ordinary circumstances, Maricica Puică would have commanded the attention of the media. She was then thirty-four and a multiple world champion at various distances. Her times in the 3,000 meters in 1984, before the Olympic Games, were the best of any athlete in the crowded field.

She was one of thirteen children and came from Iasi, a city of about three hundred thousand that had been inhabited since 400 BC. Under the oppressive Ceauşescu regime life was harsh. Her parents had clerical jobs in the city, and Maricica worked at home, tending a vegetable garden on their small plot.

She had begun running at sixteen when her coach at school, John Puică, recognized her raw talent and athleticism and took charge of her training. She won her first Romanian senior championship before she turned seventeen. Three years after they met, they were married. "It was the happiest day of my life," she would say later.[1]

Under her husband's tutelage and with the support of the state-sponsored athletics program in communist Romania, Maricica Puică flourished on the track and at cross-country meets. "Life in Romania at that time was not easy. But once I was accepted into the national sports program, things became easier and I had good training conditions," she said.

When she was eighteen she was chosen for the Romanian national team. "I don't think I was given any special benefits," she said. But she acknowledged that once she was in the program, "everything was taken care of."

By August 1984 and the LA games she had accumulated a load of medals and records, and Maricica Puică—"Luka" to her friends— was well known throughout Europe and the Balkans as a genuine threat to capture gold in LA.

Her inability to speak English, and the constant presence at her side of the Romanian secret police, who feared she would defect, kept her out of the public spotlight in the weeks leading up to the games. Puică would tell an interviewer years later that she "lived in horror at times" under the watchful eyes of the Securitae, Romania's ruthless secret police during the Ceaușescu years.

She knew she had the "good luck to be an athlete in Romania at the time," and to enjoy the perks that status afforded, but "there was someone who watched me at every meet," which made her very uncomfortable.

Despite her low public profile, savvy writers and the runners who had competed against her in Europe knew that Puică had a legitimate shot at winning the 3,000-meter race as well as the 1,500, which she also would enter.

A long-legged, powerfully built blonde with an awe-inspiring kick in middle-distance races, she denied ever having been part of a state-sponsored drug program. "I was coached by my husband all the time. I never took anything other than vitamins, which he gave me during training," she said.[2]

Asked directly about drug usage, she replied heatedly, "Why do you always ask only the Eastern bloc runners about drugs? Doping was present in the West too." Puică claimed that her country didn't have "the specialists like East Germany had" to help its athletes avoid detection and added that she was "so afraid to take substances that were forbidden. If I did and was detected, I would then lose the privileges I had gained as a member of the national team, and the Communist Party would have held me responsible for bringing shame to Romania."[3]

She didn't say what the consequences for her family would have been, though it is apparent they also would have suffered. "We [athletes] had a good life compared to others in Romania and didn't want to speak out against the regime about anything," lest their statements cause problems for themselves, family members, and friends, she said.

Puică claimed that "90 percent of the East Germans" she ran against were using drugs, "but after each meet they would test them and find nothing."

Puică recently described her posttraining regimen: "After each session they would take a blood sample to see what was missing. Then I would be given vitamins to make up for any deficiencies they found."[4]

Of course, the East German women athletes were told the same thing while being injected and given so-called vitamins by their secret police, the Stasi. One elite international runner after another told me "the Romanians were the worst" when it came to using drugs to enhance performance.

In any case, Puică was a talented middle-distance runner at the very peak of her career, whether she was actually taking only vitamins or was given something else. Had most sportswriters not been seduced by the Decker-Budd sideshow, they would have noted, as Pat Butcher of the *Times* of London did in a recent interview, that Puică "was the clear favorite going into the games based on her recent race results."[5]

But the other competitors all recognized Maricica Puică as a major contender, and they were right.[6]

• • •

Wendy Smith-Sly, who had been part of the chorus of detractors when Zola Budd arrived in Great Britain, had hurt her ankle while training in April and sought treatment at the University of Colorado. When she returned to Great Britain in May, it was like walking into "a media frenzy," she recalled. The phone never stopped ringing with calls from newspapers and television reporters. "They wanted me to be 'the bad guy' in the whole affair," she said. "It was very distressing. All I wanted to do was run. I didn't need all the distractions."

Smith-Sly was just twenty-five and "had never been exposed to anything like this," she said. "It was all alien to me. It was constant, and I got really sick as a result. I was in bed with flulike symptoms and a 102-degree fever. The stress really got to me and I was running badly. The mental part was the biggest factor for me. I didn't deal with it well."

Smith-Sly realized she had to get away from the circus and flew back to America. "If I had stayed in Britain I wouldn't have made it to the games," she said. "Almost immediately after I got to the U.S. and away from it all, my times began to improve. I decided to just stay there until the Olympics, and that decision was the right one for me."

She was born Wendy Smith in 1959 in suburban West London. "Ours was an ordinary blue-collar family. My father was an engineer and my mom a housewife," she said. "I was about eleven and belonged to a swimming club when one of the teachers told me, 'You should join an athletics club.'"

Her parents couldn't afford both the swimming and athletics clubs; she decided to join the South Feltham athletics club in 1970 and began running cross-country. "The club became my social life," Smith-Sly said. "I loved the outdoors and by the age of thirteen I was becoming quite good at running."[7]

She continued to improve in a sport that was popular in Great Britain. By 1975 she was gaining attention as she finished second in her age group in the national championships. Three years later she made the national team and was coached by Neville Taylor (who would continue in that role until 1986), and she continued to improve. By 1981 Wendy Smith was racing at least once a month in Europe and finished second in the Commonwealth Games that year.

In 1982 she married the miler Chris Sly and would run in the United States to earn enough appearance money to continue training. She gained a sponsor in Brooks athletic shoes and also ran road races in the United States.

"By 1983 I was in the best form ever and ended up breaking British records twice while winning a 10,000 meters road race in San Diego," Smith-Sly said. "I was in Florida, training, when Budd arrived in England. I didn't know anything about it in advance and when told I was shocked to hear she was in the UK.

"My initial thoughts were what effect her presence would have on the other British middle-distance runners, and it seemed unfair to me that they might be denied an opportunity to make the Olympics because of the preferential treatment given to Budd," she said.[8] Smith-Sly was quoted as commenting in a rather negative way about Zola, and those comments would dog her for months.

As the Olympics neared, she moved into a house in Manhattan Beach that Brooks had secured, and she continued her preparations. She felt healthy again and confident about her chances.

"Mary wasn't in the same shape she had been in 1983. She had a slight injury and didn't look the same as 1983. I knew Puică from the 1982 European championships, and I was certain that she and Mary would be the ones to beat," Smith-Sly said. "I wasn't really concerned about Zola. She was in her first big international meet and she was quite young.

"I felt I could win a medal. I was ready to win, and I was in great shape. I'd run an 800-meters time trial a few days before the [Olympic] heats and knew I was peaking at the right time." Besides, she said, "I loved racing in championships. I relished the whole Olympics experience."[9]

Overlooked, and hounded from Britain by the Zola Budd media frenzy, Wendy Smith-Sly was as ready as she could be. Ignoring her would turn out to be a mistake for everyone.

. . .

Lynn Kanuka Williams came from an athletic family—her brother, Michael, was a swimmer, and her sister, Kerri, a world-class gymnast. Lynn was born in Regina, Saskatchewan, a Canadian city of about one hundred thousand. Her dad was a lawyer of Ukrainian heritage and her mom, who grew up in the ubiquitous wheat fields of Saskatchewan, was of sturdy German stock.

"At first I liked swimming best," said Kanuka Williams, who had won a provincial championship in the sport. "But by fifteen I stopped swimming. I had started to mature physically and put on some weight, and one day my dad asked me what I was going to do now that I no longer swam. I decided on track."

When she was in twelfth grade, the cross-country coach asked her to come out for the team. "At first I was reluctant—I liked volleyball better. But I did go out and had immediate success. I found I enjoyed myself even though at first I didn't like it that much. But I did like that I was good at it without putting in too much effort," she said.

Eventually Kanuka became a city and provincial champion and did well at the nationals. From 1973 to 1981 she never finished worse than third in any race at any distance and garnered eleven provincial records.

"Larry Langmore, the high school coach in Regina, told me I should consider doing more running," she recalled. "He was my first real coach, and that summer [1978] was very influential on me. I went to the Canada [Commonwealth] Games, traveled a lot, and enjoyed it all."

Langmore continued as her adviser after she went off to the University of Regina in 1979 and found that the track team was not great and the team wasn't committed to running even in bad weather, which in Saskatchewan meant a lot of time spent not running. He advised her to transfer to the University of Saskatchewan and go out for its track team. "Lynn, you've gotta run," he told her.

Lynn met the Canadian coaching icon Lyle Sanderson at Saskatchewan. "They had a great program—I had a great year," she said of 1980. But with all the classes she was taking, she wouldn't get a chance to train until late in the day and then the outside temperatures in winter were thirty degrees below zero.

Kanuka did well in the conference championships, but she was not crazy about having to continue to train in subzero weather in Canada. Sanderson told her she had great potential and she needed to keep running.

"My coach said he would send my résumé out to American schools for me. 'Maybe you can get a scholarship.'" She heard from several schools and decided on San Diego State, in balmy Southern California, the antithesis of shivering Saskatchewan. When she told her parents her plans, they were shocked—even more so when she said she had won a scholarship.

At San Diego State Kanuka had three years of eligibility remaining, and she trained under Fred La Plante, who had an outstanding roster of athletes. She also continued to run cross-country in Canada, where she won the national cross-country championships in 1980–82.

At San Diego State she was injured a lot. "I always ended up injured at the end of the season, but I ran my heart out for my coach," she said. The result was a series of stress fractures, and she didn't think she would continue running after getting her degree in kinesiology in 1982. Then she met a 10,000-meter runner, Paul Williams, who urged her to keep running. They became a running couple and soon after became a married couple.

Her new husband had relatives in British Columbia, and the couple moved to Vancouver. "When I was healthy again, I began to train hard." Her new coach was Thelma Wright, a former Canadian record holder in the 1,500 meters and longer distances who had experience at 3,000 meters. "She became my coach and I ended up breaking her record," Lynn said.

By 1984 she was running better than ever. When the Olympic trials for Canada were held in Calgary early that summer, she and Evy Scott Bowker qualified to represent Canada.

"I'd been working full time in an athletics shoe store and was on my feet all day. I had to train around my work schedule, which only allowed for about eight miles a day," Kanuka Williams recalled. "I finally got a job as a waitress near Stanley Park, Vancouver, where I could train with a lot of high school and college men runners, which helped my conditioning and speed" for the Olympics.

Eventually her coach set up some time trials for Lynn in Vancouver—informal races against the clock to gauge her conditioning and readiness—before her departure for the Olympics.

She ran a 1,500 in 4:04 and, later, in a 3,000-meter race with two rabbits pacing her, she clocked an 8:42, which was as fast as anyone in the world had run that year. Wright, who was in her eighth month of pregnancy, smiled and said, "Lynn, you're ready."

Lynn Kanuka Williams couldn't wait for the Olympics.[10]

. . .

Cindy Mae Bremser, the fourth of twelve children, was born in the small rural Wisconsin community of Hubertus, near Milwaukee. Her dad worked as a brewmaster in a Milwaukee brewery, but the work was seasonal. When she was in the fifth grade, the family moved eighty miles north to Manitowoc, where her father had been offered a full-time job.

Her dad was always a sports fan and had been a good baseball player in his youth. At her local high school of four hundred students, Bremser found little opportunity for girls' sports in the days before Title IX, the 1972 amendments to federal education law barring discrimination in education.

"The first time I knew I had potential was when we ran a 600-yard race. They all took off and I thought, 'Wow,' but I passed them all, and my teacher said it was a new record. So I knew I had ability, but there was no official competition for girls, just intramurals.

"My first year in college at UW-Green Bay, they had unofficial track and basketball teams. It was pretty low-key. I even did hurdles but didn't really know what I was doing," she said.

A year later, in 1973, she transferred to the Madison campus of the University of Wisconsin. Peter Tegen, who had international experience as a women's track coach, had just been hired to start a women's track and cross-country program. Bremser saw a flyer and went out for the team.[11]

She did well, was injured, and came back for her senior year. After she came in sixth in a big meet, "my coach told me if I stuck with it, I could be real good some day. I ran track and made the nationals and came in third in the mile in the collegiate nationals, the AIAW [the Association for Intercollegiate Athletics for Women] then."

Bremser later ran in the 1,500 and 3,000 meters. She finished second in a race that was being used to select the U.S. national team. When she made the team in 1976, she was working full time as a nurse in Madison.

"I went to the Olympic trials in 1976 and missed making the Olympic team in the 1,500 by eighteen-hundredths of a second. It was devastating," she recalled.

She returned to nursing while training and still competing under Tegen at UW, but no one on the team there could compete with her.

She frequently entered international competitions in the late 1970s. "I know in my early years the Russian women were the studs. They looked a lot different than the rest of us. They were very muscular. We weren't tested a lot, and they knew when to stop taking the stuff, and to cover it up, and there really wasn't that much sophisticated testing then," Bremser said.

"You have to remember it was the Eastern bloc, and they had to do what they were told. It was their only way out of poverty, and they were told it was good for you. The women from the Eastern bloc countries had very spectacular but very brief careers then."[12]

Bremser had always run clean. "I was doing it for health reasons, and I never considered doing anything just to beat them. I did improve and if I couldn't beat the Russians, that was okay. I just continued to improve and that was important to me.

"Mary [Decker] was suspected for a while, but nothing was ever proven, and I was so disappointed when she eventually flunked a drug test," Bremser said. "It does make you question what she did."

Bremser continued to run well until the 1980 Olympic trials but ran terribly there—"I was gung ho about the 1980 Olympics until the boycott was announced." But she kept racing.

At the 1983 Pan-Am Games, she won the silver medal in the 1,500 and a silver at the world championships held by the International Association of Athletics Federations. "In 1984 I decided with my coach that I would just run the 3,000 in the Olympic trials." She qualified second in the trials behind Decker; Joan Hansen was third.

"I was so relieved, because I didn't think I could hang around another four years," Bremser said. "It was a lot of work and everything revolved around your training. It was not easy." She was running seventy-five miles a week in training, and three times a week she ran twice a day and had track sessions (practices) as long as four hours. "It was a lot, and I was so tired at times I didn't think I could run another step."

But the training paid off. Literally.

"I wasn't Mary Decker, but I was happy to get anything. I had a small contract with Nike and ran for Nike North," Bremser said. "I got some money from them for graduate school so I was really grateful."

By the 1984 Olympics, Cindy Bremser was feeling good and running really well.

"I was aware of all the attention being paid to Mary and Zola. The way I looked at it was, 'Good. I don't have any pressure on me at all.' I turned it around to a positive, which you have to do to be competitive," she said.[13]

Cindy Bremser was finally going to the Olympics.

• • •

Zola Budd wasn't the only top female middle-distance runner to come out of South Africa. Cornelia Bürki was born Cornelia de Vos in 1953, the middle child in a family of three children, in Humansdorp, a small town of about two thousand about 160 miles west of Port Elizabeth.

Her parents, of Dutch heritage, were sheep and vegetable farmers, as were many other residents of the area. On the farm Cornelia played with the black kids whose parents worked there. "They were my friends," she said. "Then, when I started school, I found that they were all segregated. We were not allowed to play with black children and were not allowed to say anything against it [apartheid]." It was then that she realized that whites and blacks had vastly different rights in South Africa.

She played all kinds of sports, and was good at netball (an early offshoot of basketball), in school in South Africa. In her last year in school there, she ran an 800-meter race and won. In the summer she outran the boys at local meets. A teacher noticed her and told her she could be good at it.

At eighteen, she married Jurge Bürki, a Swiss citizen, and moved to Switzerland with him. Only then did she realize "how big a problem apartheid was."

When she learned no one played netball in Switzerland, she started running. Three years later she began competing in small races. She was twenty-one. "I ran road races and cross-country in the forests," she said. "I ran my first cross-country race and won, and that qualified me for the Swiss championships."

In the 1970s and 1980s track was quite popular in Switzerland. Cornelia Bürki would become the biggest women's track star the country ever produced, and she did it in a unique way. At first a local sprint coach helped her, but after 1975, "I coached myself. I knew how much my body would take. I had a little child and I knew how much I could do," she said. Sometimes she would run with men because there were no women who could train with her then.

Bürki specialized in the 1,500- and 3,000-meter races and competed in international events whenever she could. She was running the 1,500 in less than four minutes and running well at 3,000 meters. She qualified for the Olympics in 1976, but the Swiss team was small and got so little support that she decided to stay home. "I knew my own capabilities and was able to pace myself within races to get in a good position to have a chance to win—the time was secondary," she said.[14]

In international meets she ran tactically and tried to stick close to the pacesetters while conserving enough to have a closing kick. "Decker," she said, "was always a pacesetter, and if she was in the race you just tried to stay behind and stay as close as possible to her. Zola always preferred to be in front too, neither wanted to be back in the pack, and that was what created the problem [in 1984]."

In the early 1980s Cornelia Bürki was one of the few female runners who got some money for expenses and some appearance fees and prize money. It never was much, "maybe $200," at the beginning. "In 1984, after the Olympics, I ran in Sacramento, California, and finished fifth and got $2,000, and that was the most I ever got," she recalled.

From 1974 until the 1984 Olympics in Los Angeles, Cornelia Bürki accumulated virtually every award and record available for women runners in Switzerland. She had run internationally for years with success, competed in Moscow in 1980, and was a thirty-one-year-old veteran at the time of the Los Angeles games.

"I had thought about retiring after the Moscow games. It was proving to be very tough to compete against women who were shaving, and whose voices from year to year were getting deeper," she said of the Eastern bloc runners who were, in her mind, corrupt.

"The eighties were the worst. It was very difficult to compete against those who were using drugs. They would get caught and then always lie their way out of it," Bürki said.

"In 1980 they caught two Romanian women middle-distance runners who failed their drug tests. But somehow they were allowed to compete in the Moscow Olympics. The Romanians were among the worst," Bürki asserted. "It was so unfair to the rest of us."

She insists that Puică "knew what was going on."

"If you saw her close up and listened to her talk, you would notice, immediately, the difference."[15]

But short of quitting the sport, there was little Bürki could do. "You just had to try to keep your concentration and do the best you could against them," she said, adding, "It was very difficult. It still upsets me today as a coach."

Bürki arrived in Los Angeles a week before the opening ceremony on July 28. "I knew I was in good shape, and I knew I would be able to run my personal best in the games," she said.

As August 8, the day of the qualifying heats for the 3,000 meters, approached, Cornelia Bürki was relaxed and ready. "I was very excited to be there."[16]

. . .

Aurora Cunha is the second most famous woman runner in Portugal after the marathoner Rosa Mota. Cunha has held every Portuguese record from 800 meters to the half-marathon.

Aurora grew up in Ronfe, a village of about three thousand northeast of Porto on Portugal's north coast. She was the eighth child of ten, born in 1959, when Portugal was ruled by the dictator Antonio Salazar.

In a 1990 interview she did through a translator with *Chicago Tribune* writer Phil Hersh, she talked about her childhood in Portugal. When she began her running career, Salazar was still in power and women were still discouraged from athletics in the conservative country. "My family, and society in general, didn't see it as appropriate for women to run."

Eventually her parents realized she was determined, and with the overthrow of Salazar in 1976, just a year after Cunha began competing, being a female athlete became easier.

In 1976 she set national marks in both the 1,500 and 3,000 meters. When Portugal's Carlos Lopes won a silver medal in the 10,000 meters at the 1976 games, the first Olympic medal for his country, attitudes began to change.

"When my parents saw that my name was getting into the paper, they [too] changed their attitude," Cunha said. Her parents worked at menial jobs in a fabric factory, and their help was the only financial assistance she got in the early years. The Portuguese national athletics federation was an unreliable source of support for her. She pushed on alone and eventually would set forty-two national records.[17]

By the 1984 Olympics, the short stocky runner had considerable international experience and was well known among elite athletes. "She had a reputation as a dirty runner," Joan Hansen said, and others recalled unpleasant encounters with Cunha on the international circuit.[18]

In 1982 she won the Indoor European Championship at 3,000 meters. Cunha was better suited for longer distances, but at the 1984 games the 3,000 meters was the longest middle-distance race available. She was eligible and she would compete.

The Los Angeles games would be her first Olympics; if reporters didn't pay much attention to her, it didn't matter. Back in Portugal she was well known, and the whole country would be watching on television.

In a race, Cunha knew from experience, anything can happen.[19]

. . .

Joan Hansen was born three months early in Kansas City on July 18, 1958. The surprise of her arrival was quickly topped by the emergence, just minutes later, of her identical twin, Joy.

Their father was a manager at a bakery company in Wichita and was shocked to learn he had not one, but two, additions to the family. "No one knew my mom was carrying twins," Joan Hansen said, "and at first my dad, who was in Phoenix, refused to believe it. He thought it was a joke."

When the bakery shut down, her father found a new job in Arizona, and the family moved when Joan and Joy were about six.

"We were always very sports minded in our family. My dad encouraged us all, and my brother, George, was an excellent swimmer. He was six years older and my sister Joy and I just followed him into the sport," she said. "Our brother drove us to practice, and we swam with older kids at long practice sessions."

The twins excelled at swimming and soon were coached by Doc Councilman, who would develop Mark Spitz. The twins enjoyed being on a coed team, but when they got to the University of Arizona, they found women had a separate team under Title IX, didn't like it, and quit swimming, Joan Hansen said.[20]

But their aerobic fitness from swimming would serve the twins well. Both began running for fun and fitness, and soon a track coach noticed them. "We were walk-ons. We ran cross-country at first, and Joy kept on after I sprained both ankles. It was very hot in the desert, and I ended up quitting the cross-country team," she said.

In the spring of 1977 both went out for the track team. "It gave us the chance to do something we loved," she said. "But we were clueless about track running."

Dave Murray was coaching both the men and women. After two years, during which Joan suffered through a lot of down time from injuries, Joan and Joy came into their own as juniors.

"I found my body type was prototypical of middle-distance runners. I had problems at 400 meters but at longer distances—800,

1,500, and 3,000 meters—I was able to carry my speed through in all of those races. The 1,500 and 3,000 became my favorites. It didn't hurt at all," Joan Hansen remembered. "While I ran the shorter distances, Joy concentrated on the longer ones, and we both got steadily better. We both became focused on the process of performing in competition and at the same time enjoying it."[21]

Although Joan's legs were not yet strong enough to hold up under all the training and racing that college teams do, she showed early signs of brilliance. At the Aztec Invitational in San Diego, in 1981, she ran a 5,000-meter cross-country race, setting a record that still stands thirty years later.

"College racing was fun," she recalled. "We didn't realize then that we couldn't really do well running so many races. We just performed when and where we were told."

Joan Hansen set an AIAW indoor record at 3,000 meters in 1981. She would also set a new world record indoor mark for two miles in San Francisco in the winter of 1981. She thought that after her record-smashing performance, she was sure to get mentioned in *Sports Illustrated*. "But Mary Decker, injured at the time, was there as an official starter and when the magazine came out and I grabbed a copy, I saw there was a picture—of Mary shooting off the gun, not me!"

Joan Hansen was running, setting records, improving steadily, and just having fun—until she encountered a series of calamities: "At UA I was majoring in PE and planned on going into coaching, but they changed the program I was in and after 129 credits I had to decide what to do. In 1981 the assistant track coach, Willie Williams, committed suicide in the equipment shed at the track. . . . After that I couldn't run on that track anymore." Not long after, two of her friends were killed in a car crash.

Joan Hansen needed to get away and transferred to Kansas State in 1982. She shared an apartment with a few other women runners. She also attracted a stalker, who broke into the house twice. After the second time, she hurriedly moved to Dallas, where she had friends.

She enrolled at Southern Methodist University in 1983 and through Francie Larrieu met Robert Vaughn, a local coach, and he developed a training program for her. When named to the national team in 1983, Joan prepped at SMU for the Olympic Games.

Injuries in late 1983 forced her off the track and into a pool, where she continued to train in the water and lift weights, but she did no running. "I started to ride a bike in February [1984]. On February 10, I was riding with a partner, and as I turned to look behind me, another student riding in front of me stopped short. I hit her and was thrown from the bike.

"I landed on my tail bone, and it broke and [I] dislocated it. A car speeding by just missed my head by inches. As I tried to get up, my body froze up in spasms. I was paralyzed. Cars were speeding by within inches of my head, and I couldn't move."[22]

Taken on a backboard to the hospital, Hansen was given muscle relaxers and her body started to loosen up. A friend picked her up at the hospital and took her home.

Four days later, still moving like she was ninety, Joan and her friend went out to get groceries. The Olympic trials were just four months away.

"I was a passenger, and all of a sudden a car in front of us made an abrupt U-turn. My friend stepped on the gas hard to avoid her, and my tailbone slammed against the doorframe. The impact split my pelvic girdle. My two hips were floating. I went back to the hospital on a backboard, paralyzed again. I wasn't scared, or angry, I was just looking at the moment and the process of training for the Olympics."

Back in the pool a few weeks later, she worked with trainers and started running in mid-March, just two weeks before her first race. She ran that 3,000-meter race in a snail-paced 9:42.

"I was somebody who was a veteran and a record holder, but at that time I was just a newcomer that nobody considered. I had only six more weeks to train. I was so under the radar and nobody had a clue who I was. All the spotlight in the U.S. was on Mary."

The Olympics still just a dream, Joan Hansen kept racing and getting faster.

She went to Oregon in the spring of 1984 to train at a camp Nike was running there. On the way back she developed blood poisoning from a blister she had developed. "The pain was a lot like a red hot poker being pushed into my leg." She was given massive amounts of antibiotics to save her leg. Then she got the flu.

The Olympic trials, held June 16 to 24 in Los Angeles, included the women's 3,000 meters for the first time. All the elite U.S. runners showed up for the trials, which had the runners on the track three times over five days for the 3,000 meters. They began with the three-heat quarterfinals; then came a semifinal with two heats and then the finals.

"We all marveled that, although it was supposed to be random selection, all the slower runners were in Mary Decker's heat," Joan Hansen recalled. "In the other semi you had all the better runners stacked together against each other."

Hansen advanced to the finals. There she ran negative splits—she built her pace through each portion of the distance. "It put me in position to move through the pack. Along with Cindy Bremser, who won our heat, I finished second and made the team. I set a personal best of 8:51, and was in the Olympics."

Joan Hansen had lived through a torturous few months. She had endured and overcome obstacles both physical and emotional that would have stopped most others. She took a victory lap after making the team. "It was the only time I ever did that. After getting through all the situations I had to endure and then to make the team was so exciting."

Joan Hansen would have six more weeks to improve her time before the Olympics. "I was so happy. My dream had been realized."[23]

. . .

Dianne Rodger, who was born on New Zealand's North Island in the town of Napier in 1946, began running in grade school.

"We used to do a lot of swimming in the summer, but the water was always so cold, I started running," she said. "A teacher at our school recognized me and encouraged me to run with the team. I began running on the team at twelve and was beating everyone."

By the time she was in high school, she had left 800-meter races behind to run cross-country. By seventeen she was good enough to try out for the national team—individuals who qualified to compete in various events—in 1974. She didn't make the team, but she did make the national cross-country team and competed in the cross-country team event at the Commonwealth Games in Christchurch. The next year she made the field for the world championships in cross-country. "That sparked my interest," she said, "and I begin training seriously."

The work paid off, and Rodger made the New Zealand national

team for the 1976 Olympics in the 1,500 meters, then the longest distance women could run at the games. It was only the fifth time she had ever run in a race on a track, and she was eliminated in the first round. After that Rodger, then nineteen, decided, "If I'm going to run, I have to do a lot more."[24]

But then her career was slowed by a series of injuries that caused her to miss the 1980 games. Meanwhile, she got married in 1979 and moved to Hamilton, New Zealand, to work with a running coach there.

Once healed, she began to lower her times and was in the World Cross-Country Championships in 1981 and 1982.

Dianne Rodger knew Mary Decker well. "She had come down here [New Zealand] with Dick Quax, who was training her, and I trained and raced with her when she was here during our summer in 1980," she said.

Speaking of Mary's sensational 1983 season, Rodger, who knew Decker's capabilities, said, "I'm not too sure how it [Decker's 1983 season] was assisted, though."

At the World Cup in 1983 Rodger finished fifth behind Grete Waitz and three Romanians. "After the race was over we had to go give a urine sample for the drug test. Grete looked at me and said, 'Dianne, we're going to be here a long while. They,' pointing toward the Romanians, 'will be in and out.' And they were. We knew not one of them was clean."

Of the lone Romanian she would face in the Olympics in the 3,000, Maricica Puică, Dianne Rodger said, "I doubt she was clean."

Rodger had been on the international circuit and had observed the stark differences between the Eastern bloc runners and their Western competitors. "You only had to look at [the Eastern bloc runners]. All the signs were there," she said.

Later, when discussing Mary Decker, Rodger observed with regard to drug usage, "All the warning signs were there. She was very high strung, and her complexion was like those you saw on the Romanians and others. You could kind of tell just by looking at her. Then, of course, she went from being a very good runner to an unbelievably good runner."

In 1984 Dianne Rodger was the only New Zealand runner to have met the minimum qualifying time for the Olympics. She would wear the distinctive all-black singlet that Peter Snell, the great New Zealand miler, had made famous.

"I stayed in the Olympic Village, and we trained at UC Irvine before the games. I was in the best shape I had ever been. I was injury free. We had a few pre-[Olympic] races, and I did well and I was feeling great."[25]

. . .

Agnese Possamai of Italy was born in the village of Lentai on July 17, 1953. She developed slowly as a runner, moving up from 800-meter races—she competed in the 800 at the Moscow Olympics—to races at longer distances. By the 1980s she was one of Italy's best female runners.

In 1981 she won the 1,500-meter race in Grenoble. The next year she ran indoors in the 3,000 meters in Milan and in Budapest.

In 1983 she won both the 1,500- and 3,000-meter races at the Mediterranean Games in Casablanca. That same year she ran a personal best, 8:37.9, in the 3,000 meters at the IAAF world championships in Helsinki, finishing sixth behind Mary Decker, Brigitte Kraus of Germany, the two top Soviet runners, and Wendy Smith-Sly.

Possamai had an atypical body for a middle-distance runner. Her legs were muscular, of the type more frequently seen on sprinters than distance runners.

She would eventually garner twenty-two national titles in her career in Italy and was a seasoned veteran by the time of the 1984 games.

Like most of her competitors, she was mostly ignored by reporters. But she was in the Olympics, and she would wear her country's colors proudly in the 3,000-meter race.[26]

. . .

Brigitte Kraus was born in Bensberg in 1956 in a divided Germany. Her home was in the West, and she would represent the Federal Republic of Germany, as the Western part of the nation was then known.

She began running at thirteen after first trying rhythmic gymnastics. Her running ability attracted the attention of the coach, Lutz Muller, and he convinced her to take running seriously. In 1971, only a year after starting, "I won the German youth cross-country championship," she said. That was the beginning of a remarkable career that she and Muller shared. He was the only coach she ever had in twenty years of running.

"The more success I had, the more I wanted to do better," she recalled. All told, she would garner sixty-three German national titles during her career.

She was a 1,500- and 3,000-meter runner who emerged on the international scene in 1976 when she won the European indoor championships in Munich. She would place third there in 1978 and fourth in 1979. In 1980 Kraus thought about quitting rather than compete against the dopers. "I just stood there at the starting line looking at them and thought, 'Man, what are you doing here?'" she said, laughing at her choice of colloquialism.

Kraus did not compete in Moscow in 1980, but she was a recognized factor in the international community of middle-distance runners. In the early 1980s she trained for a summer in New Zealand and was highly regarded in competitive racing there.

In 1983, in Budapest, she again won the European indoor championship at 1,500 meters.

"I never was interested in using any drugs," she said. "I heard all about the rumors of what was going on in the Eastern bloc, but I was never tempted. But I still have rage in my stomach from when I think back and remember looking at all those women on the starting line with deep voices and hair on their faces. It always made me furious. I still get angry when I read about some of these drug cases."

Puică, against whom she competed many times, was "absolutely a drug user," Kraus declared. "All the Romanians were. I am certain that they did not accomplish what they did with normal training. They all ran regularly under four minutes [for 1,500 meters]. That was too extreme to be normal."[27]

In Helsinki, at the world championships in the 1,500 in 1983, Mary Decker's triumphant undefeated season, Brigitte Kraus caught the attention of the world. She finished a strong second to Decker in that race, posting a personal best and a German record, 8:35.11, and besting the two Russians, Tatyana Kazankina and Svetlana Ulmasova.

By the time the 1984 Olympic Games arrived, Brigitte Kraus of Germany was a legitimate contender for a medal based on her past performance. Of course that would require her to duplicate her best performance, something that is not, as all runners know, easy to do.

"I arrived in LA in good physical condition, at least that's what I thought. It turned out I was sick but didn't know it yet," she said.[28]

. . .

At the Olympics the field for the finals of the 3,000-meter race was determined through a series of three elimination heats. The first three finishers in each race qualified automatically, while the remaining three places in the field for the final were filled by runners with the next best times.

. . .

The first heat on August 8 featured hometown favorite Mary Decker, and she didn't disappoint.

As usual she set a blistering pace and won the heat in 8:44.38, a new Olympic record (the race was being run for the first time at the LA games). Her winning effort pulled along Lynn Kanuka Williams, 8:45.7; Agnese Possamai, 8:45.84; Aurora Cunha, 8:46.38; and Dianne Rodger, 8:47.9. All would advance to the final.

Brigitte Kraus of Germany won the second heat in 8:57.53, followed by Joan Hansen, 8:58.64, and Wendy Smith-Sly, 8:58.66. All three advanced even though their times were far slower than those posted in the first heat.

The third and final heat, which had eleven starters (the first two had only ten runners each), was won by Maricica Puică in a blazing 8:43.42, eclipsing Decker's record before the ink was even dry. Following Puică home in second was Cindy Bremser, 8:43.97, and then Zola Budd in 8:44.62. Cornelia Bürki finished fourth in 8:45.82 and gained the last spot for the final.

Among the thirty-one who ran and did not advance were Jane Furniss of Great Britain and Rosa Mota of Portugal.

The field for the final would have three Americans and two British runners and would be a fair representation of the very best runners at the distance outside the Eastern bloc communist countries, which were boycotting. It promised to be a highly competitive and entertaining race with all eyes focused on Mary Decker and Zola Budd.

The times recorded in the heats were not a surefire guide for handicapping the final. Heats, these veteran runners knew, were just to make certain you made it to the finals. No one expended more energy and effort than necessary to do that.

Zola had, as was her normal strategy, taken the early lead in her heat. When she was assured of qualifying, she eased up in the stretch and was passed by Puică, who rushed home, and Bremser, who passed her as well. "I just wanted to make sure I would qualify, and I glanced back and saw I was clear," Budd said.[29]

Bremser was surprised when she passed Budd. "'Wow,' I thought, 'I just went past Zola Budd,'" she recalled thinking at the time.[30]

Reporters who followed the sport with their eyes and not their hearts noted Puică's time and knew she would figure in the medal count somewhere. The rest of the media, including ABC, which would beam the race worldwide, was still focused on a Decker-Budd duel, and that was where the focus remained right up until the starting gun was fired.

TWELVE. A Split Second That Will Live Forever

The prospect of a Mary Decker–Zola Budd matchup in the 3,000-meter final had reporters across the United States and around the globe in utter thrall. After the two had qualified for their respective national teams, scarcely a day passed when someone, somewhere, failed to speculate about the outcome of the race.

The *Los Angeles Times*, in the host city, gave its prime space in the sports section to coverage of the Olympics. Bill Dwyre, the sports editor, had a stable of talented writers that produced a staggering number of features about the games. Many were devoted to Mary Decker and her looming confrontation with Zola Budd.

Randy Harvey was one of the young writers designated to provide an Olympic preview piece for the paper's ongoing pre-Olympics series. On July 30 he noted in a story that ran before the heats for the 3,000, "This showdown has been the stuff of dreams since last January, when the barefooted Budd shattered Decker's world record in the 5,000 by almost seven seconds."

Harvey, a gifted journalist who later would become the sports editor of the *Baltimore Sun* and then the *LA Times* before taking a similar position at the *Houston Chronicle*, was one of the few to show restraint. His article conceded that Maricica Puică was "somewhat overlooked" and that Brigitte Kraus "has excellent credentials." Still, Harvey acknowledged, the emphasis in the race would be "on Decker, Puică and Budd."

Harvey added presciently that "this should make the race more interesting because Budd and Puică," along with Decker, "also prefer to set an early pace. If they go out together, the winner could be the one who is still standing at the finish."[1]

In South Africa in the week leading up to the games the papers were full of articles about the Olympics from which all South African citizen-athletes were barred.

Writers from South African papers who sought credentials were denied, and the IOC told the South African Broadcasting Company that it could air only six minutes of coverage per day. The IOC's moves didn't dampen the enthusiasm of the South African press.

"The Olympics have just taken over the sports pages here," Ian Cameron, a reporter for the *(Cape Town) Argus*, told the *Los Angeles Times*. "It's phenomenal. It's very, very big. I've never known it this big."[2]

The British press was of course awash in articles that centered on the Budd-Decker matchup. While a number of stories focused on British middle-distance stars Steve Ovett and Sebastian Coe, whose intense rivalry was eclipsed only by Budd's arrival, the British papers were preoccupied with Budd's chances against Decker.

The *Daily Mail* ran a feature story headlined "Zola Versus Mary" on July 22. The lengthy article contained a side-by-side analysis of the two in which Zola was labeled a "speed machine" and Mary a "fiery champ" on the track, and Zola the "shy tomboy" and Mary "the sexy image" off the track.

The last sentence in the piece asked, "Can America be denied a coronation?"

For weeks before the games, papers around the globe filled page after page with stories about the 3,000-meter race. "It was a fascinating story and was the biggest story in track," recalled Amby Burfoot of *Runner's World*. "It was David versus Goliath—only of the wrong sexes. The two would be dueling on the track in the Coliseum."

As for the lack of coverage afforded the rest of the field, Burfoot, who covered track for more than thirty-five years, said, "Puică was not very into talking with journalists, there were too many barriers around her. Sly was glamorous and fast but largely overlooked because of the Budd story."

But mostly the focus remained squarely on Budd versus Decker because, as Burfoot said, "There is no room in a duel for a third person."[3]

· · ·

After the heats were completed on August 8, and the field for the final established, the runners had only one day off.

At a press conference on the day of the final Mary Decker was asked again about Zola, "Zola Budd, Zola Budd, why do you keep asking me about Zola Budd?" she snapped at the reporter who had asked.[4]

"I'm tired of always seeing my name in the same paragraph as hers," she told a reporter.[5] Clearly Queen Mary was not happy sharing the spotlight, especially with Zola.

Mike Waldner of the *Daily (Torrance CA) Breeze* recalled the buildup: "The race had become bigger than life."[6]

In a feature for the *LA Times* on August 8, the writer Betty Cuniberti observed accurately what everyone except Mary seemed to acknowledge: "The world most certainly will be watching. The anticipation is electric."[7]

· · ·

Decker was staying with her boyfriend, Richard Slaney, in a house near the Coliseum that Nike had rented for the games.

Dick Brown spoke with Mary about the race strategy he thought she should follow. "I had had her run with a group of five men in a pack to get her acclimated to that in advance of the games. We spent weeks on it," he said. In analyzing the race, Brown told Decker "the only way Zola Budd could win was to take Mary and Puică's kick away from them."

He added, "I knew Mary would want to lead, and that it would eventually happen, but I didn't want her to lead all the time. I felt Zola was toast. She'd been overraced and would tire. Puică was the key, as I saw it. She depended on her sprint at the end." So, Brown told his runner, "Concentrate on her [Puică]. You are faster."

His final instructions to Decker were "If Zola wants the lead, let her take it."[8]

. . .

Zola Budd arrived in sunny Southern California a few days after her coach did. The two had been having some difficulties back in England.

"Pieter had become quite possessive after my father was out of the picture, and [Pieter] resented me having anything to do with other people. When I struck up a friendship with a former Olympian, Lynn Davies, he became upset. I thought at first he was just being overprotective but decided to do as he suggested, even though it cost me a friendship I valued. I depended on him and respected him, but the closeness was getting stifling," she said.[9]

After she arrived in California, Zola and Pieter went to the British training facility in Point Loma outside San Diego, although he had no official status with the British Olympic Team. The sun was warm—no more dreary English mornings to contend with—and her mood brightened to match the warm California sun.

She visited the San Diego Zoo and even met Princess Anne, who had arrived with the British Olympic Committee. Zola recalled that she was "too nervous to say much" to the royal, so teammate Fatima Whitbread, a javelin thrower, did most of the talking.[10]

Frank Budd had yet to be invited to take tea with the queen, but his daughter had rubbed shoulders with royalty.

. . .

Zola trained in parks and on grass wherever she and the British team coach, Harry Wilson, could find it.

When she joined the other athletes on the track, Pieter unofficially supervised her workouts. "Things were going good," she said. "My mood had lightened up and I was training well and felt fit.

"One afternoon after my track work in preparation for the race was over and I was just doing strides to keep my muscles loose, Pieter told me to do another track session. It wasn't on the sched-

1. Tossie and her "miracle baby." Zola's difficult entry into the world foreshadowed troubles to come. Zola Budd Pieterse collection. Used with permission.

2. Little Mary, in pigtails and braces. No one could catch her. Photo by Walter Iooss Jr., *Sports Illustrated*. Getty Images.

3. Mary with her mother, Jackie,
surrounded by her trophies.
Photo by George Long. *Sports
Illustrated Classic*. Getty Images.

4. Zola was always most comfortable with her pets. Zola Budd Pieterse collection. Used with permission.

SUID-AFRIKAANSE AMATEUR ATLETIEKUNIE

SPRINGBOKLANDLOOPSPAN
1983
SPRINGBOK CROSS COUNTRY TEAM
MIDDELBURG — 17 SEPTEMBER 1983

Agter/Back (vlr):
Matthews Temane (Wes-Transvaal), Jan Olyn (Oranje-Vrystaat), Mark Plaatjes (Transvaal)

Voor/Front:
Zola Budd (Oranje-Vrystaat), mnr Chris van Wyk (Bestuurder), Angela Thirion (Noord-Transvaal)

5. Zola made the South African national team at fifteen. Zola Budd Pieterse collection. Used with permission.

6. Running for Jenny. No one in sight. World record, 15.01, 1984. Zola Budd Pieterse collection. Used with permission.

7. Mary defeating the Russians. She was the best in the world. Photo by Bob Thomas. Bob Thomas Sports Photography. Getty Images.

8. Breaking the tape at South African Championships, 1983. Zola Budd Pieterse collection. Used with permission.

9. Zola takes the lead in LA. Photo by David Madison. Getty Images Sport Classic. Getty Images.

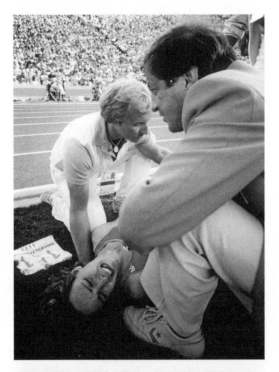

10. After the fall. The bib to Mary's left is the one she tore off Zola's back. Photo by Pat Downs. *Los Angeles Times*. Getty Images.

11. The rematch the world wanted to see, 1985. *Sports Illustrated* cover. *Sports Illustrated Classic*. Getty Images.

12. Nice, France, 1992. After her injury, Zola donned Brooks running shoes and never slowed down. Zola Budd Pieterse collection. Used with permission.

13. Zola with Tossie, 1990s, at home in happier times. Zola Budd Pieterse collection. Used with permission.

14. Mary outside at her home in
Eugene, Oregon. Photo by Rich
Frishman. *Sports Illustrated
Classic*. Getty Images.

ule we'd been following, but I did it anyway. During the session I felt a sharp twinge in my hamstring.

"Later I was doing some stretching exercises and I couldn't do them right. I told Pieter I was injured. Pieter got upset with me. I got the impression that he didn't believe what I was telling him," she said.[11]

She visited a physiotherapist, who gave her some ultrasound treatment, and he told her she had a strained hamstring. Limited by the injury, Budd tapered off to just some light workouts with easy jogs and strides. "Pieter was not at all convinced I was hurt," she recalled. The well-being she had felt since arriving in the United States turned to doubt—doubt in her ability to run her best with an injury. But she carried on with her training.

A day or so before the heats, she and Labuschagne went over the list of the entrants in the 3,000. "It was the first time I had seen most of the names," she said. In retrospect she acknowledged she wasn't very well prepared to face the likes of Puică, one of the few names she did recognize.

"I knew of her and that she was fast, but I knew nothing about the way she raced," Budd said. Her coach was similarly uninformed about the capabilities of many of the thirty or so runners entered in the qualifying heats.

But Budd was aware of the buildup that had her matched one-on-one with Mary Decker. "I wondered why I was seen as one of the favorites," she said. "I hoped to do well enough just to win a medal of some sort."[12]

Her easy race in her heat on August 8 had enabled her to ease up at the end and not further strain her hamstring while still safely qualifying for the final. "One thing I remember was that Puică looked so big to me. Not just in size but in her physical presence. After she sped past in the stretch I knew I would have my hands full with her in the finals," she said. She told Pieter she felt less energetic than usual, "and he assured me it was okay," she recalled. "'It's perfectly normal,' he told me. '"It means you will be fine in the final."'[13]

Zola now was living with the British team in the Olympic Village on the UCLA campus in Westwood. "There was mass confusion there. Helicopters were always flying over because of security measures, and it was impossible to get any peace and quiet. I moved to an apartment nearby with some friends." Her coach wasn't a part of the British team so he and Zola lost contact as race day approached.

The inevitable press conference was scheduled, and Budd was required to participate. "It seemed to me like a pilot episode for the *Zola and Mary Show*," she said.[14] All that the reporters seemed to want to know about was her upcoming confrontation with Mary Decker. Nigel Cooper, a member of the British Olympic Committee, helped her get through it, but it wasn't easy for her.

The *Daily Mail* dogged her every step while she was in LA. The *Mail*'s photographer became a veritable shadow, which she found unnerving and a nuisance, as he snapped pictures at every opportunity. Her "personal diary" of Olympic events had been running in the *Daily Mail* all along, and the Olympic Committee issued a ruling that she couldn't continue to publish her diary any longer and remain eligible.

"It was all a farce," she declared. "The *Mail* writers just made it up to suit themselves and said I was doing it. It was a relief when it finally stopped."[15]

. . .

The headline on the story in the *Los Angeles Times* on August 9 said, "Win or Lose, Citizen Budd Already Has Her Medal."

Jim Murray, one of the paper's veterans, called the Budd-Decker showdown in the 3,000 meters "one of the great sport matchups of these or any Games." He compared Budd's treatment by the British protesters to that accorded the witches of Salem, who were burned at the stake, and he then declared, "Blaming Zola Budd for apartheid is like blaming Shirley Temple for the Johnstown Flood."

Citing her sacrifices to make it to the Olympic Games, Murray said, "Zola Budd's sacrifice gave new meaning to the word."

Then he turned to Mary Decker.

"You wish, somehow, she looked more like she was enjoying herself. Mary approaches a race as if she is awaiting a call from the Warden. Her eyes seem desperate, staring at something she doesn't really want to see. It's as if she fears the worst."[16]

. . .

Zola rode a bus to get to the warm-up area outside the Coliseum.

"It was a warm day, and there was a delay. They had a room where we could relax before loosening up. It had cots set up in it so we could lie down. I was too nervous to get any rest, but Wendy [Smith-Sly] was so cool she was able to get a nap," Budd recalled. "It may have been nerves, but I felt so tired when I went to warm up. My legs felt like lead. I wasn't used to that feeling and wondered how I could possibly race feeling like that.

"Mary looked great warming up. She was in an all-red warm-up outfit, and she looked great doing her exercises. I thought, 'How am I going to beat her feeling like this?'"

Budd's hamstring pull limited her ability to do the exercises she always did before racing. "Pieter finally showed up in the exercise area, and I was relieved to see him there," she said. "I know it sounds incredible but he didn't discuss strategy with me at all before the race. We both knew Mary was a front-runner, and I guess we just assumed she would go all out from the start and try to hang on as she normally did.

"I could feel the pressure from Pieter on me. I knew I was good enough to win a place on the medal stand, but I knew that I was not, at that stage of my career, good enough to win against that strong field. It was the wrong attitude to have. I went into the final thinking, 'Just get it over with,' instead of thinking of running to win. After the Olympics, I thought, the *Mail* would be out of my life, and things would be back to normal again. Apart from Mary I didn't really think about the other runners at all."[17]

In the holding room deep in the bowels of the Coliseum, Budd and the others waited silently to be called to the starting line. There was some delay and the wait seemed interminable, which only added to the already tense surroundings.

One moment of levity broke the tension when an IOC inspector asked to see the running spikes each competitor wore. Zola lifted her bare feet, with two toes on each wrapped in bandages, and said, "Here they are."

In the late afternoon they finally were summoned to the track. "As we walked out of the tunnel, I remember all the noise. The crowd started chanting, 'Mary, Mary, Mary' over and over again,"

Budd recalled. "I felt bad for all the other runners because it made it seem like they didn't even count.

"Then we were rushed through the final warm-up strides on the track and hurried to the starting line with little time to get loose."[18]

. . .

"I was in the stands and watched Mary and Zola as they warmed up. They didn't speak," Amby Burfoot noted.[19]

Steve Bisheff, who had covered Mary Decker since she started running in Southern California, was seated on press row in the Coliseum and, like most of the other reporters, "couldn't wait to see it."[20]

When the track announcer introduced Mary Decker, the roar from the crowd was deafening, leaving little doubt who the favorite was. The hometown girl had returned to her Southern California roots and was expected to shortly reap the reward long denied her.

Above the noise of the crowd, the track announcer pleaded for quiet for the start. "You could hear a pin drop," Wendy Smith-Sly said.[21]

An eerie hush falls over the ninety thousand in attendance as all eyes focus on the twelve women bunched along eight lanes of starting line. The stadium crowd is joined by nearly two billion more viewers around the globe.

This was what everyone has been waiting for.

The starter's pistol fires, and twelve runners speed off, chasing their dream.

. . .

No one is surprised when Mary Decker gains the lead almost immediately from her starting position near the middle of the track. Propelled by a troubled past and twelve years of pent-up frustration, injuries, and perceived injustices, she bolts like an arrow shot from a taut bowstring straight into the lead, Dick Brown's cautious instructions discarded in an adrenaline-fueled instant. As Don DeNoon had said fifteen years earlier of his tenacious and temperamental eleven-year-old prodigy, "Mary always needs to be in front."

:06 Mary sets a blistering pace, hoping to break the will of those behind her.

"It was the only way she knew how to race," said Rich Castro, her coach at Colorado, who was in the stadium that day.[22]

Mary speeds on with long, graceful, seemingly effortless strides as the field, moving now to the inside lanes, strings out behind her.

Zola moves up on the outside of the pack, out of the danger of flying elbows and spikes. Her bare feet strike a rhythmic tattoo on the track surface as she moves through the field, safely passing Cunha, to gain a position in lane 2, just to Decker's right.

:34 Puică is on the inside behind Decker.

"I thought [Decker] went out like a shot," Zola said. "I remember thinking, 'This is way too fast. I hope it doesn't continue like this.'"[23]

Conventional coaching wisdom for middle-distance racing at the time taught that pacesetting was akin to suicide. But as Mary Decker had demonstrated with her dominance in 1983, and whenever else she had been healthy, it could also be a winning strategy.

Most conceded that middle-distance racing was more about strategy than speed. But others had used Decker's tactics with success. Harry Wilson, who coached the great British miler Steve Ovett, noted, "A point very few people make in track and field is that front running is actually a tactic in itself. It isn't a negation; it is utilizing a strength."[24]

Both Decker and Budd had used the tactic successfully on different continents and at different times throughout their careers. Of course, any given race can have only one front-runner at a time.

Two women embracing one and the same strategy, in the same race, was, as you would surmise, not going to work. Someone, at some point, would have to give in.

. . .

Moving toward the front on the outside from sixth place is Wendy Smith-Sly as she follows Budd.

"I knew Mary wanted to be in front and that it would be fast. I didn't want Zola and Mary to dominate the race," Smith-Sly said. "I wanted to make sure I stayed on pace with them."[25]

1:06 Decker, Budd, and Puică are out in front and the rest of the field is settling in behind them, trying to maintain contact with the three favorites.

Lynn Kanuka Williams of Canada is stuck in the middle of the pack.

"It was very tight in there. There was a lot of bumping going on. I was where I wanted to be, and I knew it would open up for me soon at this pace."[26]

1:20 As they come off the last turn of the first lap, Decker takes a quick look over her right shoulder to see who is stalking her. She quickly turns her eyes back to the front. She knows now it is Budd.

Cindy Bremser, in tenth place, is following Kraus down the straightaway just ahead of Dianne Rodger of New Zealand and Joan Hansen, the other American runner.

"I was tucked in and focused," Bremser said. "I felt comfortable with my position. I knew I couldn't let there be a break between me and the front-runners. If there were, I'd never be able to make it up in time."[27]

As they pass the stands again, the order is still Decker, Budd, and Puică. Budd is on Decker's right shoulder, both runners within the first lane. Puică is directly behind Decker; both are on the far inside, with Puică about a stride behind.

1:41 Wendy Smith-Sly has continued to run on the outside of both Agnese Possamai of Italy and Kanuka Williams.

The Brit begins to accelerate, moving past Possamai and coming almost abreast of Puică.

3:18 Zola Budd on the outside and Mary Decker on the inside are nearly side-by-side as they continue in front. Scarcely a foot separates them as they race on.

A stride and a half behind, Puică on the inside and Smith-Sly now on her shoulder, shadow the leaders.

Next are Kanuka Williams and Possamai, also racing side-by-side.

4:01 As she speeds past the start-finish line, Smith-Sly continues to move up outside Budd's right shoulder.

4:07 Hansen is just past the start-finish line and heading to the first turn when she goes down.

"I had begun moving up, and just then Cunha decelerated in front of me," Hansen said. "She drifted back, and my foot landed on her, and I went down. My solar plexus landed on top of my knee."[28]

Hansen falls to her hands and knees directly in front of Dianne Rodger, who has moved up with Joan and is carefully eyeing Cunha and her sharp elbows.

When Hansen fell, "I had to jump over her body and swerve far to the right, way off stride," Rodger said. "When I got back on stride everyone else was gone. I struggled to get back in contact with the field, who had moved far ahead. I thought, 'This race has turned into a nightmare.'"[29]

Hansen recovers almost instantly from the fall. Bracing herself on her right arm, she quickly pops upright and runs on.

"When I had come down on top of my knee, it had knocked all the wind out of me," she said. "I tried to get air but I couldn't. I tried to stay as calm as possible, but I could not breathe. I was trying to catch up to Cindy Bremser up ahead, but I had no air."

Amazingly, Hansen runs on, covering another 200 yards before she is able to breathe normally again. But ahead she can see her dreams disappearing. Her adrenaline surge as she forced herself to a faster pace while in oxygen debt has used up her remaining energy. But Hansen races on as best she can.[30]

4:20 *By now the field is stretching out behind Decker, Budd, Smith-Sly, and Puică, with Kanuka Williams still in contact about two strides behind the lead pack.*

The three front-runners are beginning to bunch up.

4:33 *Decker, Budd, and Smith-Sly are in a virtual dead heat, three abreast on the track and all crowded toward the inside lane. Puică is a step behind Decker, who is on the curb between the inside lane and the infield.*

Decker's pace has slowed since her first lap; Budd senses the change, as does Smith-Sly.

Budd makes her move.

"We were on world record pace after two laps, and then Mary slowed down," Puică said. "Zola didn't have a great finishing kick, and she wanted to increase the pace to give herself a chance to win."[31]

4:37 *Budd sweeps ahead of Decker.*

"With the pace slowed and Wendy coming up on my right and bumping elbows with me, I was afraid I was going to get boxed in," Budd said. "So I accelerated to get away from trouble and to take the lead."[32]

4:51 *Budd is leading; right on her barefoot heel is Decker. Smith-Sly stays on the outside and moves up on Zola's right elbow. Puică is immediately behind Decker. All four runners are tightly bunched along the same inside lane as they come off the last turn and head down the* *stretch. They have separated themselves from the rest of the runners by several yards and are alone in front.*

From her position in fifth place on the inside, Lynn Kanuka Williams has a clear view of what is ahead of her. "They were all vying for the front. I didn't want to be in there," she said. "It was way too tight. I thought, 'Something's going to happen.'"[33]

4:54 Coming off the last turn and heading into the stretch, Decker's foot strikes Budd's leg from behind. Budd momentarily loses her balance but quickly regains it and is back on stride. Decker's arm shoots out to stabilize her balance, and she too is back on stride. Smith-Sly, running on the outside next to Puică, sees what is happening and moves a bit farther right to avoid Budd's slight stutter step.

Mary Decker is no longer in control of the race. Budd has taken that role, and as Decker's long history has shown, she is not where she wanted to be.

4:58 Just a few strides beyond their initial contact, Decker's spiked right shoe comes down just above Budd's Achilles tendon as Decker comes up on Budd from behind.

This time Decker cannot recover.

"Mary had hit her once and then again. The second time [Decker] fell," recalled Puică, who was closest to the two runners. "Mary Decker wanted to increase the tempo and she caused the incident."[34]

Decker falls toward the infield at an odd angle. Her last-ditch move to save herself is to grab Zola Budd's singlet. In the process Decker rips the number from Budd's jersey and takes it with her as she tumbles over the curb into the infield. She lands hard, breaking her fall with her right hand, which is still grasping Zola's number, and lands on both knees. Then she sprawls forward a full body length on her belly, still clutching Budd's number, and turns her head to the infield. As the field speeds by her, she rolls over and watches them pass. She takes one fleeting look at them, grimaces, and rolls over on her right side. She grabs her left thigh just below the hip and rolls away from the track and the race she had expected to win.

Her race is over.

Her dream denied yet again.

Little Mary, proud Mary, Queen Mary was down.

. . .

Amby Burfoot is watching from press row as the race develops. "There was a lot of jockeying going on." When Decker, Budd, Puică, and Smith-Sly broke free from the pack and began to move, he remembers thinking, "'Now it's gonna start.'

"And then it happened. There was an audible gasp from the crowd. Everyone jumped up from their seats and looked at where Mary had fallen. We all expected her to get up and go on."[35]

She doesn't.

. . .

Budd has been knocked to the right by Decker and has nearly fallen herself. She struggles to regain her balance and within a few strides is back on pace but has dropped behind both Smith-Sly and Puică.

"When Mary fell, I was right behind her. I had to jump over her leg. My first thoughts were to stop and help her," Puică said.

She dismisses the thought as fast as it occurs. "I thought if I did I'd be disqualified, and the communists would not be happy with me," Puică said.[36]

Smith-Sly, who has been racing outside Puică, also is impeded by Decker's fall because Puică swerves right into Wendy, bumping her briefly off balance. "I thought, 'Oh my God. We're here in America and Mary's fallen. I didn't know she hadn't gotten up,'" Smith-Sly said.[37]

Smith-Sly and Puică run on, with Puică taking the lead briefly as Budd recovers from the bumping from behind. She recovers quickly despite having two spikes driven into her right foot just above the Achilles. With blood streaming from the punctures that resemble a snake-bite, she accelerates once more and retakes the lead.

"*It shows a remarkable attitude,*" the BBC *commentator says, as Budd leads Puică and Smith-Sly past the start-finish line.*[38]

5:09 *The booing begins.*

. . .

The crowd has recovered from its initial shock.

Decker is sprawled on her back, crying loudly, her chest heaving with each tortured sob. Her demonstrative act is impossible to misinterpret, even from the seats farthest from the track.

The majority of the crowd is now focused on Decker and not the race.

And as spectators grasp that Decker's race is over, they react. The boos start to rain down.

Like a giant wave cresting and crashing down, they pummel Zola Budd as she races around the track. The boos grow in intensity, following Budd and battering the eighty-four-pounder with violent force every step of the way.

. . .

"'Oh my gosh,'" Lynn Kanuka Williams was thinking, "'America's favorite is down.' I got a surge of energy. When I saw Mary fall, I thought she would get up and rejoin the pack. Then I heard the booing begin. It was deafening."[39]

Still, Budd holds the lead as the three front-runners pass the spot where Decker is lying, now attended by a small crowd of officials.

With two laps remaining, the field races past the start-finish line in a tight bunch with Budd holding the lead.

In the back of the pack the German runner, Brigitte Kraus, has stepped off the track into the infield and slumps into a sitting position on the grass.

"I had difficulty breathing," she said. "I started to get dizzy and couldn't get any air. I thought it might be the smog. I couldn't go any further. Later they found I had pulmonary hypertension."[40]

Kraus sits there gasping, one leg folded under her. She does not cry out, makes no theatrical gestures. Only defeat registers on her face.

7:07 *Boos continue to wash over the leaders.*

7:16 *The leaders pass the still-prone, still hysterically weeping form of Mary Decker again.*

Wendy Smith-Sly grabs the lead and Puică follows her, both passing Budd on the outside of lane 1.

Zola Budd feels that the combined enmity of the ninety thousand fans in the stands is aimed directly at her.

"It was just awful," she said. "I just wanted to get it over with and get away from there."[41]

She slows down.

Her ability to dissociate from her surroundings has been exhausted in the face of controversy and hostility in England. Now ninety thousand angry fans are focusing their combined hatred on her. Her reservoir is drained dry.

She slows even more.

"I thought if I continued to race, and won a medal, I would have to get up on the medal stand and face those boos again. I couldn't do it. I slowed down. I just couldn't face that."[42]

Smith-Sly and Puică run on.

. . .

In the infield Decker, whose mother had once harbored the hope that her daughter would be an actor, continues to draw attention from the crowd and officials with her performance. Photographers rush to capture her contorted face as she cries out in huge heaving screams.

While Smith-Sly and Puică race on in the battle for gold, Decker steals the spotlight with her hysterical performance.

In the stands Jackie Decker looks on, her hands over her mouth.

As the bell sounds for the final lap, Budd is in third place, about ten yards behind the leaders; if she remains there, she will claim the bronze medal.

With a lap remaining, she is ahead of the next pursuer by about fifteen yards.

She slows even more.

"We ran the last two laps with all the booing going on," Lynn Kanuka Williams said. "I thought it was awful."[43]

7:56 Puică finally breaks free of Smith-Sly and speeds away from her and the fading Budd with an astonishing sprint toward the finish line, increasing her lead with every powerful stride.

As Zola slows to what she described later as a jog, Kanuka Williams is sprinting.

"I just wanted to get past her. I was sprinting as hard as I could go, and I made up a lot of ground over the last two hundred meters," Kanuka Williams said. "I saw her [Budd] coming back to me, and I passed her. I knew I was now in third and the others were far behind me."[44]

Safe from the medal stand, Zola Budd continues to slow, and others begin to catch up and pass her.

Cindy Bremser is sprinting toward the line. "After the incident everything was disrupted. I lost my concentration," she said. "I thought I blew it. I passed Zola with about 700 meters left. I still felt pretty good." [45]

She finishes fourth.

• • •

The race was over.

But the controversy it stirred became a boiling pot of outrage, sympathy, and finger-pointing.

Under the pressure of live television, ABC's Marty Liquori, a former world-class miler providing expert commentary, had been forced to remark on what had taken place as it occurred.

"I had spoken with Dick Brown before the race, and I asked him if he'd spoken to Mary and if he was worried about her being able to race tactically. He said, 'No, we didn't even discuss it.'"

As Decker tumbled into the infield, Liquori told the vast television audience, as ABC's cameras focused on Mary rolling about on the ground: "It was Zola Budd's inexperience. Zola cutting in on Mary too soon. Mary had stepped on her once and stepped on her again."

Over the clearly audible boos Al Michaels, another ABC commentator, said, "The crowd booing as Mary Decker is in agony in the infield."

He also told viewers, "Obviously after the race is over we'll replay the race for you of what is undoubtedly going to become a very famous scene."[46]

He had no idea just how famous.

The comments from Liquori, and the ABC camera's focus on Decker as the race was continuing, had much to do with the controversy that ensued.

To his credit, after the race, Liquori asked for a tape so he could watch it again in his hotel room. "Around midnight I called Chuck Howard, our producer, and told him, 'I think there's more to this. My call might have been wrong,'" he said.

Liquori then asked Howard to arrange for Decker to come in the next day at 2:00 p.m. for an interview in which he would review the incident with her. Howard said he'd try.

Millions had heard Liquori place blame on Budd's inexperience. Only Howard had heard Liquori say that he might have been wrong.[47]

• • •

"Mary was someone the media had always portrayed on the positive side," said Richard Perleman, who headed media relations at the LA games. "She had always been seen as bright, shiny, terrific, and accessible.

"When the incident occurred, it was just unbelievable. I knew we were going to have a big problem."[48]

. . .

When Puică crossed the finish line, she lifted a hand and waved at the crowd. Smith-Sly lifted both arms in triumph as she captured the silver for Great Britain, and Lynn Kanuka Williams took bronze for Canada.

As the rest of the field was crossing the line about 80 meters up the track, Mary Decker, now surrounded by a dozen or more people, walked across the track, her left hand holding her hip area. On both sides of her were men with their arms on her but not really helping her walk.

To the right of Decker, who was still weeping as she walked across the track, was Slaney in a striped polo shirt. He'd come to Decker's side in the infield.

As the entourage around Decker moved across the track to the tunnel beneath the Coliseum, ABC replayed the race in slow motion with Marty Liquori saying again that Zola "is not giving Mary enough room."

As Puică, the happy Romanian, took her victory lap, the cameras again cut to Decker, still crying and lightly supported by Slaney and an official in a blue blazer. Neither was lifting her. Her limp was slight, barely noticeable. Her sobs were readily visible.

"Mary is of a very delicate constitution," Marty Liquori told the television audience. "This has got to be very hard on her."[49]

. . .

Zola Budd had finished seventh, passed by Cornelia Bürki at the end. "She was barely moving," Bürki said.[50]

When Budd finished, she bent over and grabbed her thighs, her head hung low. Then she straightened up, her hands on her slim hips, her eyes closed and squeezing back tears as she struggled for composure.

A black woman in African dress approached and gave her a warm hug.[51] A few of the runners patted her on the back, offering support as they passed.

"She was emotionally drained," said Nick Whitebread, a British team official.[52]

. . .

As Decker crossed the track under her own power, Slaney picked her up, cradling her in his arms. Still in view of the crowd, he carried her until they disappeared into the tunnel.

The latest installment of the soap opera life and career of Mary Decker had ended in a tear-jerking moment before an audience of nearly two billion.

Procter and Gamble would have been proud.

. . .

Slaney placed Decker on one of the benches lining the walls of the tunnel, then hovered protectively by her side.

As the rest of the runners filed in through the tunnel, they had to pass Decker. Some offered their condolences.

Cornelia Bürki, the veteran Swiss runner, walked through just behind Zola Budd.

"I was right there next to her," Bürki said. "Mary was still crying. Zola approached her and said, 'I'm sorry.' Mary screamed at her, 'Don't bother. Go away! Go away!'

"Zola then moved on and I saw she was very sad and hurt," Bürki said.[53]

Bürki remained behind and told Decker, "It wasn't Zola's mistake. It was your own!"

Decker shot back, "Yes, it was [Budd's fault]. You know it was."

"All people remembered was what they saw and heard on television," Bürki said. "Everyone saw her [Decker's] husband carrying her off the track, and heard her blaming Zola [later] for the accident. No one cared about the little girl who just wanted to be a runner."[54]

Zola Budd, head down, shoulders slumped, moved away with tears raining down her cheeks and staining her white British singlet.

. . .

After Decker fell, an IOC official on the track nearby raised a red flag to indicate a foul and disqualification.

After the race, the track announcer revealed to the crowd that Budd had been disqualified, setting off yet another loud round of boos.

The British team protested immediately. "There was a meeting of about six officials," Rich Perleman recalled. "They viewed the race and decided to overturn the disqualification."[55] No official finding of blame was made. Officially, Zola Budd was absolved of any responsibility.

Unofficially, well, that was another story, one that would rage for days.

· · ·

Stung by Decker's angry dismissal, Zola Budd went into a small booth beyond the drug-testing area and sat with her head down, looking like a puppy who'd been kicked.[56]

She had her spike wounds cleaned and disinfected by a doctor on the medical staff. He told Budd her puncture wounds would heal quickly. He did not have any healing balm for the deeper wounds she had sustained. The psychological wounds hurt far worse than the spike marks Decker had left on her leg and would be slower to heal.

British team officials collected Budd and escorted her and her *Daily Mail* handlers away from the stadium after a short press conference at which her handlers issued a conciliatory statement for her that said, "I am upset that Mary fell and that the crowd seemed to think it was my fault. She just seemed to run into me."[57]

"She didn't speak at all," the sportswriter Steve Bisheff recalled. "She sat there looking like a frightened child. I felt very sorry for her."[58]

As British team officials left to take Zola back to the hotel where her mother and Pieter were staying, she looked up through reddened eyes and asked, "How's Mary?"[59]

· · ·

On the bus ride from the Coliseum to the hotel, a young girl was quietly crying.

"Why are you crying?" Zola asked her.

"Because of what they did to you," she answered.

"It was one of the nicest things that ever happened to me," Zola said.[60]

. . .

Decker was taken to a nearby hospital, where X-rays were taken and she was examined.

Greg Harney of the Los Angeles Olympic Organizing Committee (LAOOC) rode with her. "She was in a little pain but seemed okay to me," he said.[61]

The diagnosis was a slight sprain of the hip muscle. She was told to use ice on the area and was assured that she would be running again in a few days.[62] Accompanied by Slaney, Decker left the hospital with a pair of crutches.

They went back to the press area at the Coliseum to attend a post-trace press conference.

. . .

Dick Brown was with Decker and Slaney before they entered the packed press area to make the first public comments about the incident. About 130 reporters were on hand when she arrived around 10:00 p.m.[63]

"I cautioned her about the press conference before they entered the tent," Brown said. "I told Mary she could take this incident and turn it around and make it into something positive."

"Just be gracious" were Brown's final instructions.

"I'll try to be," Decker replied angrily and dismissively.

Instead of walking into the press conference or using the crutches she'd been given, Decker arrived in Slaney's arms. "He carried her in as he had carried her off the track," Brown recalled. At their side was a physician from the LAOOC, Dr. Tony Daly.

Steve Bisheff of the *Orange County Register* was present. "It all seemed so stage-managed," he said.[64]

At first the reporters were, as you would expect, sympathetic toward Decker. But that began to change almost as soon as she opened her mouth to declare, tears welling up, "I hold Zola responsible. I don't think there's any question she was in the wrong."

Decker went on, unrelenting and ignoring Brown's advice, with venom and spite dripping from every answer.

"She tried to cut in when, basically, she wasn't ahead of me," Decker claimed, whining, "I do hold her responsible. I didn't do anything wrong."[65]

Decker described her injury as "a muscle strain, tear or pull," and went on to say, "The first thing that went through my mind was 'I have to get up.' When I did that, it felt like I was tied to the ground."[66]

The writers present included many veteran track reporters who were well aware of the unofficial yet time-tested rules of the road: a runner wishing to pass a slower runner reaches out and taps the slower runner to flag their intention.

"If I had done that the headlines the next day would have said, 'Mary Decker Pushes Zola Budd,'" she snapped at a writer who dared question her account.

When Chris Brasher, a former runner who was covering the games for the *(London) Observer*, thanked Decker for "having the courage to come here," she again broke into tears and heaving sobs.[67]

Slaney gathered her up in his bulky arms and carried her out of the tent. After less than ten minutes, the press conference was over.[68]

But the damage she inflicted on herself with her comments was far greater than any muscle pull she might have suffered. The deconstruction of Mary Decker began the very next day.

. . .

Dick Brown had watched Decker's performance before the world's press and knew it had gone badly. "I thought she could have handled it a lot better than she did," he said.

He was certain the next day when he saw, as he remembers it, "headlines reading, 'Cry Baby Mary,' and similar treatments of her performance" at the abridged press conference.

He did damage control as best he could. He tried to ameliorate the runner's remarks by telling writers it was an accident and while he thought Zola Budd was at fault, he didn't blame her. Brown's remarks were duly reported, but while he was trying to repair his runner's battered image, she was inflicting more damage.

Decker had granted Kathleen Sullivan of ABC an interview the morning after the race. "Good, I thought, now she can give a clarification of what she said and repair the considerable damage," Brown said.[69]

He was wrong.

Sullivan treated Mary in an empathetic manner and tossed her some softball questions that Decker batted back at her with an animosity that shook Sullivan. When Sullivan asked Decker if she felt the race was "a confrontation," the runner snapped, "It's people like you and others in the media who are the ones who set up a confrontation between Zola and me."[70]

No graciousness, but bitterness and acrimony were present in abundance, accompanied by the requisite tears.

"It was a disaster," said Brown, who was prevented from joining Decker on the set, where only her chiropractor accompanied her.

The damage Decker did to her reputation "was her own fault," Brown said years later. "She had no compassion for Zola, and that hurt her a lot."[71]

Decker's wasn't the only reputation damaged by the interview. Kathleen Sullivan's star had risen after her performance at the 1984 Winter Olympics in Sarajevo. The reviews of her Decker interview were not favorable, and Sullivan, admitting she was puzzled by the reaction, told the *LA Times* a year later, "They [media critics] felt I should have been tough on her. [But] this wasn't some criminal I was interviewing. It was a woman who had fallen and seen her dreams disappear. She was in terrible shape. She'd been shaking and crying and arguing with her coach before we went on. She was someone who obviously needed help."[72]

. . .

Decker's fall from grace was immediate and dramatic. She was now viewed as a whiny, nasty, spiteful bitch.

In a column wrapping up the *LA Times* coverage of the games, Mike Littwin said that even Decker's most conciliatory comments had an accusatory edge. "We found the woman, I think, in Mary Decker. She whined, she cried, she blamed everybody but herself for her Olympic disaster. . . . I don't feel sympathy for Decker anymore," he wrote. "I feel sympathy for Budd, who so many people will blame for the mishap."[73]

He was echoed in New York by Mike Lupica, then a young reporter for the *Daily News*, who asked in his popular column, "Was Zola guilty? Not a chance."

"Mary," he wrote, "deserved to settle her fate on the track, not on her back. But she must take the rap. She did it to herself."

Lupica's analysis reflects the consensus of those who covered the event. Rodney Hartman of the *Rand (South Africa) Daily Mail* wrote, "Why did she have to force her way on the inside with two laps to go? The replay shows it. She steps on Budd once, then again. Then came the platform dive."[74]

Writing in the *Guardian* of London, Frank Keating said, "Miss Decker's head-girl vanity . . . got her into the mess and the agonized come-uppance. No barefoot pipsqueak was going to lead the grand dame of front running."[75]

Decker and Brown continued to deny that Mary had tried to force her way past on the inside. But anyone who saw the tape knew otherwise.

John Holt, an IAAF official who had seen hundreds of races, noted in a prepared statement that the international jury of appeals had reinstated Budd after viewing the tape. His statement referred to Decker's "aggressive tactics" and then added, "Decker was her own victim."[76]

Following the twin fiascos of the press conference and the Sullivan interview, any remaining support for Decker in the media evaporated faster than water in the desert.

She still had some supporters, especially in her former home area, as Steve Bisheff of the *Orange County Register* found after penning a column in which he ascribed blame to Decker for "trying to squeeze through a hole that wasn't there." The same day his paper received multiple death threats aimed at Steve.[77]

. . .

Sometimes those who write the first draft of history are also those who rewrite or revise that history. Those whose prose helped shape a public image can also, if they feel they've been deceived, reshape that image in a less flattering way.

Decker had enjoyed the support of reporters for years despite being, as one writer described her, "a sour, bitter person." She had always been prickly and difficult to deal with. "She was always pissed off at somebody," one said. The writers had put up with her because she was good copy.

Almost immediately their stories began to reflect the Mary Decker they had always known.

. . .

As soon as Decker aired her bitter accusations, Zola Budd's stock began to rise.

Several notables weighed in on her side. Thomas Wessinhage of West Germany, the World Cup 1,500-meter champion, saw it happen right in front of him. "First of all, who is in the lead in lane 1 is not to be blamed for anything that happens behind them. When you are running in the pack, you must not get too close to the runner in front of you . . . because the runner in front does not have eyes in the rear," he said.[78]

Mal Watman, of *Athletics Weekly*, Europe's most respected track publication, said, "Without being nationalistic about it, if anyone was at fault it was Mary. She was trying to move up on the inside when there was no room to get through. My sympathy goes out to her. She's a runner whom I've admired for years, [but] I thought she was less than gracious in her press conference."[79]

David Miller in the *Times* of London said flatly, "The responsibility is Decker's. Mary overreacted to having Zola in front of her."[80]

America's great miler Jim Ryun had suffered a fate similar to Decker's in the heats for the 1972 Olympic Games in Munich. He'd been elbowed aside and tripped over another runner, fell, and had gotten back up after regaining consciousness. He and his wife, Ann, were watching the race at home when Decker went down.

"We were both yelling, 'Get up, Mary, get up!'" Ryun said.[81]

In the same race, Joan Hansen had somehow managed to summon the will to get up and continue in the race after having the wind knocked out of her when she fell.

Decker had stayed down, "pinned to the ground," as she would describe it, after making an attempt (not visible on any tape replay) to get up.

No one but Mary Decker can know if she was physically able to continue. Had she done so and tried to finish the race, she would have been lionized for her effort, and her star would have shined even brighter.

Instead the tarnish set in almost immediately.[82]

An article in the *San Diego Evening Tribune* the day after the race carried the headline, "Somebody Ought to Be Asking: Is Zola All Right?" The writer summarized Mary's tearful performance at the press conference, then noted, "Tears were flowing from another pair of eyes. There was another human being, too, whose emotions were so many split ends. Is Zola all right? Nobody seemed to care."

Noting that Decker had already mentioned plans to go to Europe and collect her next big payday, the article observed, "If you want to talk tragedies talk no more of Mary Decker. The greater sadness of last night was the continuing trauma that threatens to squeeze the spirit from the soul of Zola Budd, the little farm girl who merely wants to run, the two legged international incident who recently sighed, 'Some days I wake up and wish the whole world wasn't watching me.'"[83]

. . .

Budd rejected a proposal by ABC that she appear on a live program with Mary Decker.

"It was the first time I had stood up to Pieter," Zola said. "He had told me I should go on and do it so I could present my side of the story. But I was not going to do it. I was not fluent in English and not at all comfortable with the press and television. Mary was very good at public appearances, and I knew I couldn't do an adequate job defending myself if I appeared with her.

"Pieter was quite upset with me when I turned down the offer he proposed from ABC. It was the first time I had ever disagreed with him about anything."[84]

. . .

The closing ceremony of the LA games was another David Wolper production befitting Hollywood. Wolper's lavish opening ceremony with four thousand pianos and a huge flock of doves was nearly outdone by the finale for the games. The lights were extinguished as sparklers flared and fireworks set the night sky ablaze with color. The crowd delighted in seeing an actor dressed as an alien suspended from a mock spaceship carried by a helicopter. Lionel Richie performed with a large orchestra. He closed the Olympics with his megahit, "All Night Long."[85]

. . .

The Los Angeles Olympic Games were a financial success. The work of the LAOOC, led by Peter Ueberroth, founder of one of the largest travel businesses in North America, had returned a profit of $100 million. The IOC received $33 million of that. After the debacles of 1972, 1976, and 1980, the IOC couldn't have been more pleased.

But one thing that happened would come back to haunt the IOC pooh-bahs. The drug test results on athletes at the games were somehow lost when the Coliseum offices of the drug-testing commission were cleaned out.

Samaranch was not interested in drug-testing results and thought the IOC Medical Commission was dangerous. "These people," he would say, "all they live for is to find a positive sample," Dick Pound wrote in his book, *Inside the Olympics*, in 2004.

"He [Samaranch] agreed with Primo Nebiolo, president of the IAAF—the athletics international federation—to hold off the announcement of any late positive test at the 1984 Los Angeles Olympics, so that the Games would not end with a bad image," Pound writes.

Pound adds that the "records of several tests were removed from the IOC's storage place (the LAOOC did not provide a safe) immediately after the Games, before they could be acted upon."[86]

The results would have included those of Maricica Puică and other Romanians who had defied the boycott and taken part in the games, much to the delight of Samaranch.

The results never did turn up.[87]

In a recent interview, Dr. Don Catlin, the head of the drug-testing facility at the Los Angeles Olympics, said, "The test results [of the athletes in the later events] were sent by Fed-Ex to Switzerland by me. There were positive test results included. They were shredded by the IOC."

Catlin had also supervised a drug-testing program for the U.S. Olympic Committee of a large sample of prospective Olympians in the early months of 1984. "The program went on for six weeks, and the results were transmitted to the USOC. When I found out they were using it to warn the athletes of the possibility that they would fail the tests at the Olympics, I stopped it," he said.

At a press conference in Switzerland a year after the LA games, a writer asked the then head of the IOC Medical Commission, Prince Alexandre de Merorde, if the results from LA had been shredded.

"I can't deny this," he replied.[88]

Of course, had the supposedly lost results revealed positive drug tests for the Romanians, the IOC would have had a huge black eye.

. . .

Because of death threats made against her, Zola Budd had a police escort to Los Angeles International Airport.[89]

When she got to London Heathrow Airport, police accompanied her as she moved through the large cadre of reporters that had been waiting for her. Death threats against her had been received in London as well.[90]

She arrived at her mother's apartment and began packing and preparing to go home to South Africa.

As she boarded the plane for South Africa, the *Daily Mail* contingent was there, waving good-bye.

She wouldn't miss them.

Zola remembers feeling "so relieved to have it all over and be going home."[91]

THIRTEEN. Coming and Going

Before Zola left England for South Africa, she made one last attempt to reconcile her differences with her father.

It didn't go well.

"I had purchased a lighter and another souvenir for him in Los Angeles, and I went to his home to give it to him," she said. "I thought he would be excited, but he was very sarcastic and nasty to me."[1]

Zola was stunned by her father's attitude, and she left almost immediately. The gulf between them widened.

· · ·

The Zola Budd who returned to South Africa was far different from the one who had been secreted away in the night a little more than four months earlier.

She had left an innocent—a trusting, shy, animal-loving teenager who just wanted to run and was going to get a chance to chase her dream. Now the innocence was gone, the trust broken, the dream shattered, her psyche torn to shreds, and her desire to run was virtually gone.

Zola had grown up fast. Four turbulent months in Great Britain and one incident in LA had changed her life forever.

· · ·

As she walked through the airport in South Africa, a large contingent of writers and photographers was waiting for her.

The exclusive contract with the *Daily Mail* was still in effect. Zola walked straight through the throng, staring straight ahead from behind her oversized glasses, prohibited by the terms of the contract from saying a word.

The twins, Quintus and Cara, greeted Zola and Tossie. Quintus told reporters he expected his younger sister to remain in South Africa until after his wedding on September 22.[2]

Zola was home.

· · ·

Mary Decker was back in Eugene, where she would prepare for the European fall season. She had reservations to fly to Zurich for a 3,000-meter race on August 30.[3]

On August 17 the *Los Angeles Times* and other California papers published an open letter from two former Olympians to Zola Budd that criticized Decker for her behavior and actions.

The letter, which papers worldwide picked up from news services, was from Kate Schmidt, a javelin thrower, and Debbie Brill, a high jumper, who said they felt "like apologizing for [Decker's] actions" after the collision with Budd.

The authors expressed their concern that "so much has happened to you at such a young age, it can be difficult to sort out."

"We feel like apologizing for Mary Decker's lack of graciousness, for the otherwise polite Coliseum crowd booing," the letter said. Schmidt and Brill urged Zola to continue to pursue her passion and wished her luck.[4]

Decker was quick to respond. "I don't feel like my behavior was that wrong," she retorted.[5]

It would be, with little amelioration, her story and she was sticking to it.

. . .

A few moments in sports retain their importance long after the cheering stops.

After the incident in LA, race promoters realized immediately that they had a golden opportunity to profit from the controversy raging around Decker and Budd. The *Washington Post* columnist Tony Kornheiser observed, "There's gold in them thar spills," for promoters who could arrange a rematch of the two principals in the drama.

Noting that Zola had been invited to participate in the 3,000-meter race that Decker was scheduled to run in Zurich, Kornheiser added that "the world's top promoters see the chance of the greatest showdown in athletics history."

To questions about the coming rematch, Decker's forceful reply was, "I don't give a damn if I ever set foot on a track with her again."[6]

In December Decker sent Budd a private letter saying she "wanted to apologize to you for hurting your feelings in the Olympics. . . . It was a very hard moment for me emotionally, and I reacted in an emotional manner. The next time we meet I would like to shake your hand and let everything that has happened be put behind us. Who knows? Sometimes even the fiercest competitors become friends." Budd did not respond to the private letter but Decker would refer to it from time to time to try to place herself in a better light.[7] With Mary's public comments greatly at odds with her private ones, and Zola's lack of desire to run against anyone anytime soon, it would seem the race was improbable at best.

But the world was salivating at the possibility.

. . .

When Zola and Tossie got to Bloemfontein, they were greeted by a large crowd carrying a banner that said, "Welcome Home Budd Camp," and friendly applause and cheering.

Although she was now officially a British citizen, in Bloemfontein she was still "our Zola." There was talk of erecting a statue in her honor and a meeting with the mayor and an announcement that she was to be named the unofficial ambassador of Bloemfontein. A South African film producer announced he had acquired rights to her autobiography, which had been written with Brian Vine of the *Daily Mail* and rushed into print.[8]

"In South Africa Zola was a huge heroine," said Leon Botha, a South African writer and track official.[9]

It was good to be home.

. . .

But her presence in South Africa prompted questions about her intentions. Was she staying just until the fall season and then returning to Britain, or was she home for good? Reports of the rift between her and her father surfaced, and Zola and Pieter made only a vague assertion that she planned to return to Europe for the fall season.

Speculation was rampant in Great Britain that she was gone for good. But it was all based on rumors, and neither Pieter, who had returned to his teaching job, nor Zola was confirming them.

. . .

Despite the crowd of photographers that haunted the front of her house, Zola was happy to be home. She was reunited with her pets and was beginning to feel better.

One of the first things she did when she entered her bedroom was tear "the photo of Mary Decker off my wall." That improved Zola's mood significantly.

. . .

The marriage of Tossie and Frank Budd was all but over. Tossie was seeking a divorce, and her health was deteriorating after all the tension and verbal abuse she'd endured while in Britain. She would take no more.

When Frank returned in October, Zola moved out. "I rented a

small apartment in town to be way from him," she said. So great was the animosity between them that they could no longer live in the same house.

The split caused tension between Zola and Quintus, but she stood her ground. "He didn't really know what I had gone through with my father," she said.

When Tossie told Frank to get out of the house almost immediately after his arrival, he converted the garage into an apartment for himself. Zola returned to be with her mother, staying some nights to comfort her, but the arrangement was anything but ideal.

Not long after, Zola's friend Elizna van Zyl arrived at Zola's flat and insisted Zola move in with her. "It was a great act of kindness," Zola said, "and I was grateful to have someone with me who knew me and understood what I'd gone through"[10]

Soon the desire to run returned and she began training with Pieter's track team. However, she had no desire to run internationally.

A wealthy South African vintner, Jannie Momberg, who knew Zola because she had often raced in Stellenbosch and stayed with the Momberg family on their large nearby estate, hatched a plan for a comeback race for Zola there.

Momberg was also an official of the South African Athletics Federation (SAAF), and plans were moving ahead when Momberg changed his mind after officials in the Orange Free State insisted Zola's comeback be staged there, in Coetzenburg.

John Bryant, the features editor at the *Daily Mail*, had gone down to South Africa to talk with Zola and Momberg and to protect his paper's interest in Budd. Also on hand was Nigel Cooper of the British Amateur Athletics Board.

If Zola ran in South Africa, she would be banned from running internationally anywhere. "[The *Mail* and the BAAB] wanted me back in England, and racing overseas," she said.[11]

Just before the *Mail* agreement expired on November 1, Zola issued a statement saying she had "decided to stay in South Africa, mainly because I enjoy my athletics here much more." She added that her "experience in Great Britain was instructive, but I choose rather to stay in South Africa."[12]

The announcement triggered immediate reaction. A spokesperson for the South African Non-Racial Olympic Committee said,

"We knew she would be dishonest. She refused to condemn apartheid. She used the British passport as a flag of convenience. She committed an international fraud with the help of the British Government."[13] "Bye, Bye, Miss Budd," the *(UK) Daily Mirror* headline read when word of her announcement arrived from South Africa.[14]

Not all the press in England was happy about Zola's decision. "She had won a lot of fans while here," said John Simpson, head of the London office of IMG. "She was seen favorably by most track fans. It was the *Mail* that was seen as the bad guy, not Zola."[15]

. . .

"I wanted to stay in South Africa, of course, and my mother wanted me to stay with her, but we eventually worked out a compromise," Zola said. "I could stay and train there and still race internationally. It was a sort of come-and-go arrangement.

"I agreed as long as I could continue my studies by correspondence for my degree through UNISA," the University of South Africa.[16]

Financing international travel was a problem. "My father still had control of the money, and I couldn't afford to fly back and forth," she said. Zola, Labuschagne, and Momberg arranged for another wealthy South African, Graham Boonzaier, to foot Budd's travel bill as well as the cost of plane tickets for her friends to visit her occasionally in England.

A Zola Budd Trust was formed and it took effect in November 1985, with Momberg, Boonzaier, and Pieter Labuschagne as Budd's sole representatives. It was to last four years. Among the clauses in the trust agreement was language that stated the trustees would act in cooperation with the BAAB, which had full knowledge of the plan.

After Cooper returned to England and discussed the compromise plan with the BAAB, the members sent Zola a letter at the Momberg estate in Stellenbosch, where she was staying. It said, in part, that the BAAB agreed to the compromise plan and was granting "permission to compete in a road race in Zurich on 30th December 1984." The letter closed with a wish "for a most enjoyable and successful visit to Switzerland."[17]

As Zola's departure date for Europe drew near, her apprehension increased. She was still conflicted on the day of the flight. "I went to my mother's house, found some sleeping pills, and took a handful. I thought if I fell asleep and missed the flight I would be able to stay home," she said.[18]

But one of her sisters awakened her and urged her to go.

. . .

Zola Budd's decision to return to Europe and continue racing was the result of "a lot of pressure from my coach and advisers to keep on running. My mom and dad were splitting up. I really had no place to stay and no money of my own. I felt like I really didn't have any other choice. I knew the promoters in Europe were offering a lot of money to come back and race there, and I thought that going back was the easiest, and really the only thing, I could do at the time," she recalled.[19]

Although she said she "just wanted to get [the race] over with," her return to racing was successful. On December 30, 1984, in Zurich, Zola ran eight kilometers in 26:27 and defeated her friend Cornelia Bürki of Switzerland.[20]

Still, she found little joy in her victorious return to racing in Europe.

. . .

After the race Zola and her advisers—Momberg, Boonzaier, and Pieter and Carin Labuschagne—went to an upscale ski resort in Austria for two days.

As they were getting ready to leave, they held a meeting in Momberg's room. "They asked me if I was ready to resume my international racing," she recounted. "'No,' I told them. 'I just want to go back home.' I said."[21]

Her statement shocked everyone. They continued to pressure her to return to racing in Europe, and she once more felt like she had no control over her future. Finally the four wore down her resistance, and she agreed to their plans.

"I had no other hobbies, interests, or skills. Running was all I knew," she recalled. "It was one of the loneliest nights of my life. I cried my eyes out."[22]

In the back of her mind was Pieter's prediction that without running she'd be just another nobody on a farm back in Bloemfontein with her mother.[23]

Zola decided to go back into the fire.

. . .

The group arrived in London the next day, and on January 3, 1985, Momberg issued a statement, ostensibly from Zola, though she never saw it in advance, saying that she would continue to race in Europe for Great Britain while training and spending her off time in South Africa.

The statement outlined her racing schedule for the coming year and indicated she would enter an indoor race in January in Cosford and would like to run for England in the World Cross-Country Championships, held by the International Association of Athletics Federations in February. She also would compete in the United States in a road race in Phoenix in early March, then return to South Africa to train, and return to England in June for the summer season.[24]

. . .

Her advisers had put together the schedule based on negotiations with race promoters, and it assured her of a steady income stream in the months ahead. Zola Budd's name and drawing power had increased exponentially since the Olympics, and promoters were eager to capitalize on it.

The final paragraph of the statement Momberg released to the press included this thought: "My final wish is to be treated and accepted as any other British athlete."[25]

. . .

The British mostly greeted Zola's plans with approval. She had won over many fans with her world-record performance at the Crystal Palace before leaving for LA and had won even more to her side after the games and the shabby treatment she'd received there. Even the media had been treating her more kindly since the *Daily Mail*'s exclusivity expired in November.

However, a few Brits still saw her as a South African and as the embodiment of all the evil that represented.

Her announcement that she would, in effect, be commuting to Britain to race while living and training in South Africa made her once more the target of the small but vocal and highly visible anti-apartheid lobby.[26]

FOURTEEN. The Phoenix Rises

· ·

What we do does not define us. What defines
us is how well we rise after falling.

—Author unknown

Mary Decker's recovery from the fall had begun in her room that very night. Surrounded by Richard Slaney and a horde of Nike executives and friends, she sat on her bed holding a glass of champagne.

"Here's to the European campaign and the '88 Olympics," she toasted. Cheers rang out as she downed her bubbly.[1]

• • •

Dick Brown would once again rehabilitate his high-strung filly.

Always mindful of Decker's physical limitations, he urged a conservative approach. She canceled plans to race in August, only weeks after the debacle at the Olympics, and Brown ministered to Decker's strained muscle with great care. Mary and Richard were not pleased with my approach," he said.[2]

As she had done throughout her career, with every coach she had ever had, Decker bristled and chomped at the bit.

• • •

On New Year's Day 1985, Richard Slaney and Mary Decker were married in a church in Eugene. About two hundred people, including Jackie Decker and Dick Brown, attended. The couple would repeat the ceremony in England for Richard's family.

Mary was now Mrs. Richard Slaney and was quick to point a warning finger at any writer who addressed her, announcing, "Don't call me Decker," or she would have nothing to say.

The writers quickly took to giving her name as Mary Teresa Decker Tabb Slaney. Mary was no longer the untouchable queen of track, and they would get their private laughs at her expense, something that they'd long wished they could do but had never dared before the incident in LA.

She had been on the scene since she was twelve years old. She had set records and endured injuries and always had come back. After her 1983 season, when she had turned in the greatest performance of any middle-distance runner, writers had exhausted all superlatives in describing her and had crowned her Queen Mary. After her performance at the Olympics revealed her to be less than regal, her reign was cut short.

Although the incident in LA had done serious damage to her image, she compounded the damage every time she opened her mouth to take another whining swipe at Zola Budd.

. . .

Mary Slaney would begin her latest in a seemingly unending number of comebacks in Los Angeles at an indoor meet in January.

About a week and a half before the race, the promoter threw a luncheon for track reporters. Among those in attendance was the runner Ruth Wysocki. Asked to comment on the unfavorable press Slaney had received since the LA Olympics, Wysocki began by saying she had always admired Mary's talent and ability to overcome injuries. Then Wysocki dropped a bombshell in the reporters' laps.

"The attitude she portrayed after the fall is an attitude we, as competitors, have seen all along. And, in a way, some of us are relieved that the public knows the Mary we all know. She's no ideal," Wysocki said. Continuing to address the furiously scribbling writers, she added, "[Slaney] should apologize to Budd for her comments."[3]

Steve Scott, America's top miler, joined the criticism the next day, calling Mary Slaney spoiled and "a baby." He added, "Mary is an animal. Don't get in her way or you'll pay."[4]

The promoter couldn't have been happier. The race now would be seen as a grudge match between Wysocki and Slaney.

"I really wasn't in shape to race her," said Wysocki, who was slated to run in the 800, not against Mary. "After the furor caused by the comments the promoter called and asked me to race in the 2,000. I said, 'No, I'm not doing it.' He insisted so I just threw out what I thought was an outrageous number that it would take to get me to race her, and he agreed. I only did it because they had offered me $20,000 to do so. I knew Mary was in top shape and I wasn't, but I took the money and ran," she said.[5]

Mary Slaney had responded to Wysocki caustically and continued to insist, in reference to the Olympics, "That's a dead horse that's been beaten enough." Then she reminded everyone that she planned to participate in the Seoul Olympics in 1988.

A capacity crowd greeted Slaney's return to the track with cheers and some boos. She then demonstrated to everyone that she was indeed back and in vintage form by demolishing the field and leaving Wysocki a half-lap behind at the finish.

"She beat my butt," Wysocki recalled. Slaney also set a new indoor record of 5:34.5 for 2,000 meters, besting the previous mark of 5:43.4, held by the Russian Yekatarina Podkopayeva. (At a meet in Moscow, in August 1984, Tatyana Kazankina had sliced more than four seconds off Budd's outdoor mark of 5:33.15.)[6]

Mary's success did little to change the minds of those who felt she had acted badly in the aftermath of her fall at the Olympics, especially because of the way she had attacked Zola Budd.

As Craig Neff pointed out in an article for *Sports Illustrated* a week after her latest comeback, "All Mary Teresa Decker Tabb Slaney had to do was apologize. The public implored her: Please, Mary, just once say you're sorry. A simple statement of regret for having laid harsh words—and full blame—on Britain's Zola Budd after their famous collision in the Olympic 3,000 meters final last August could have saved Decker from a fusillade of criticism: reprimand from fellow runners, censuring letters to the editor, spoof awards for being Whiner of the Year (*USA Today*) and The Year's Sorest Loser (*Esquire*). But Decker," Neff said, "remained adamant."

Instead of apologizing she said, "I don't feel that I have any reason to apologize. I was wronged," adding snappishly, "I think it's time the press started telling the truth and not make up stories about me."

While her public image had suffered after the Olympics, her appearance fees had actually gone up by about $3,000, from $10,000 to $13,000. One promoter explained, "People just eat up this good-guy, bad-guy stuff."[7]

. . .

The Russians had not been in Los Angeles but after the games were concluded, they continued to run in Europe and seemed to set new records each time they ran. They held the top times at virtually every distance, and their dominance was complete, though how they did it was increasingly suspect.

In September 1984, after a 5,000-meter race in Paris, the Russian handlers of Kazankina told her to refuse to submit to a drug test. They insisted that she would submit to a test only if a Russian doctor administered it. None was present and she refused the test.

The International Association of Athletics Federations finally took action. Citing her refusal to submit to testing, the IAAF banned Kazankina from competition for life (later reduced) and she abruptly retired.[8]

. . .

Mary Slaney's 1985 indoor season ended prematurely but not without controversy when she was injured once again.

After LA she ran in San Diego, because Richard wanted to train down there. She won and returned to Eugene. Soon after, while running on a bike path in the woods in Eugene, she was attacked by a mugger," Dick Brown said. "Mary had been bruised in the attack but had run away from the guy. I insisted she report the attack to the police. But when they arrived to take her statement, Richard wouldn't allow the police to take photographs of her bruises. As a result the local cops didn't file an official report."

A few weeks later Mary Slaney dropped out of a race at the Meadowlands in New Jersey. "Mary told a reporter there that she had been attacked back home before the race," Brown recalled. "When the reporter checked with the local police back in Eugene, he found there was no record of any attack.

"The reporter filed his story in New York and said, in so many words, Mary had lied again. It didn't help her reputation at all."[9]

. . .

For some time Richard Slaney had been undermining the relationship between Mary and Dick Brown.

"We disagreed too much," Brown said.

It was becoming apparent to Brown that Richard wanted Mary to switch coaches. "He wanted Luiz de Oliveira to train her." The former Brazilian soccer coach had trained Joaquin Cruz, the Olympic 800-meter champion.

"One day I rode my bike over to their house and told Mary, 'Look, I want to be your friend,'" Brown said. "I could see the relationship was tugging at her, and I told her it would be better if we parted. Richard was her husband, and she loved him. She needed him more than me."[10]

The man who had trained and carefully cared for Mary Decker Slaney for four years, including the most spectacular year she, or anyone else, has ever had, was gone.

Under her new coach and his training methods, Slaney now prepared for the outdoor season. She planned to run on the new sixteen-meet Grand Prix circuit and hoped to qualify for the final in Rome in September; it offered $542,000 in prize money.

She would begin her outdoor season in the friendly confines of Eugene in the Pre Classic, a race that was part of the Grand Prix circuit and named after the late Steve Prefontaine.

Her goals, she said, were to run ten races in Europe at distances of 800 to 5,000 meters and to set personal bests at all those distances. And, she added, to stay healthy. "Under my new training program chances of staying healthy are greater," she said. "I'm doing more conditioning for all over my body. I don't think I did enough before, and that's why I got injured."

Doing more and running faster were familiar refrains to those who knew Decker.

"Dick Brown held me back," she now claimed. "His training philosophy was functional for a time. I felt like I sort of hit a wall. I felt like I wasn't training enough."

Functional?

Only Mary Decker could have the temerity to describe her achievements under Brown's careful tutelage as functional.

She was now in another's hands, and she was already feeling the pleasure of unbridled pursuit of her goals. She intimated that she now believed Brown's training methods had left her vulnerable to injury.

Luiz's philosophy, she said, was more in tune with her own.[11]

The Slaneys had what they wanted. How it would work out remained to be seen.

FIFTEEN. World Champ

Zola Budd was back on British soil and would begin her 1985 indoor season in Cosford at the British championships in a 1,500-meter race on January 25.

Zola won, but her return reflected her emotional condition as she posted a 4:11.20 mark over 1,500 meters, a distance she had covered in a world-record 4:04.39 less than a year earlier.

She then ran in the southern counties cross-country championships in Ipswich and clocked a time of 18:55 over 5.7 kilometers while running barefoot in very cold weather. Mel Batty of Brooks, whose shoes Zola had endorsed, was not pleased and neither was Pieter. "They both wanted me to wear spikes, but I wasn't that comfortable in them and decided to run barefoot," she said.[1]

Next she raced in a 3,000-meter event with an international field against the West Germans. It would be her first race representing Great Britain against international competition since the Olympics. "People should realize that Zola can beat the world," said Sue Crehan, her British teammate in the event.

Zola told a reporter that she had the British record set by Paula Fudge in her sights. "The people here (R A F Cosford in Wolverhampton) have been very good with their support. They have helped my running and I would like to do something special for them," she said.[2]

She did. She won in 8:56.1, setting a new Commonwealth record.

Zola Budd's first few races back in England had, as usual, produced a few antiapartheid protesters, but they were kept in check as they unfurled banners and signs aimed at Zola, who otherwise was warmly greeted by the crowds.

In fact she had become "the Pied Piper of English racing," as one paper put it, as her ability to draw crowds and television exposure surpassed that of Sebastian Coe in the past.[3]

In the *Daily News* of Durban, South Africa, Alan Robinson noted, "Indoors, outdoors, city streets . . . it is all the same to Zola Budd. The tiny waif just goes on collecting trophy after trophy, record after record in her quest to become the greatest woman runner the world has ever seen." Her recent performances were all that was needed, Robinson said, "to warm the hearts of the rapidly multiplying Zola Budd fan club."[4]

A club of a decidedly different kind awaited her at her next stop, Liverpool, on Saturday, February 16.

. . .

At about the same time, across the Atlantic in East Rutherford, New Jersey, Mary Slaney was crying and once more being carried off the track in tears by Richard, this time at the Meadowlands. Streaking ahead of the field, she had opened a twelve-meter lead when she clasped her right calf and limped to the infield and out of the race.

Dick Brown said it was too soon to tell how extensively she was injured. But Slaney's indoor season was over after just three starts.[5]

. . .

The weather in Liverpool was definitely nothing like South Africa's in February. It was cold and snow was falling when Budd arrived for the race. "I was wondering how I would run in that kind of weather," she said.[6]

The next day the snow had stopped, but temperatures were still cold, and a slight wind made it seem even colder. The crowd was large, and numerous police, some mounted on horses, were trying to keep the crowd in check.

Zola remembered the course as "unruly and boisterous" when she arrived. She also recalled feeling "a bit embarrassed" because her appearance had caused so much distraction for the other runners.

Angela Tooby, a leading cross-country runner from Wales, sped off at the gun and had the lead after the first circuit of the course. Budd was closing the small gap between them when a group of protesters, described as "a handful," surged out onto the course, blocking her path.

"I remember only that they reminded me of characters from a nightmare," she said. But this was no dream. "Suddenly they were all standing in front of me. I realized that if I tried to run on, or past them, I might get hurt."

It was real, and the demonstrators were screaming abuse and grabbing at her arms.[7] "They seemed so ugly and intent on causing harm that I swerved off the course to get away from them," Budd said. As she did so, she crashed through a patch of bramble bushes that tore at her bare legs. "I really thought my life was in danger, and I had to get away from them. I felt like I was suffocating." To evade the mob she crashed on through the brush, tears streaming down her face and blood streaming down her legs.

The bramble bushes did not cause the tears. "It was the injustice of it all," she said. "I had a right to finish the race."

Police and her adviser quickly whisked Budd, crying tears of frustration, away from the mob and the course.

After a tetanus shot and treatment for her scratches at a local hospital, she left.

She remembers feeling then that the British antiapartheid protesters were now demonstrating their willingness to use increasingly visible and dangerous moves to protest her presence in England. "They wanted to force me out of the country," she believed at the time.[8]

She was right.

"It is evident that the attitude of Zola Budd and the British Amateur Athletics Board towards her is still an issue," said an antiapartheid spokesperson, who vowed his organization would continue "to hound her for using her British nationality as a flag of convenience."[9]

. . .

The threats prompted the International Association of Athletics Federations to send a delegate to Lisbon to make certain security measures for its World Cross-Country Championships were adequate, with the British IAAF member adding, "We don't know if [the protesters] will go as far as Lisbon to make their protests."

Covering his political ass with the numerous African and Caribbean IAAF delegates who felt strongly that Zola should be banned, the British IAAF representative added, "It's not a very smart move, her going back to South Africa" to visit family and train.[10]

. . .

Despite not finishing the race in Liverpool, Budd was selected for the national team that would represent England, protesters' wishes notwithstanding, in Lisbon on March 24.

Ignoring what the British IAAF member had said, she quickly

booked a flight to return to South Africa to train there for the championships.

Before returning to Bloemfontein, she had a date on March 2 in Phoenix, Arizona, in the 10k Continental Homes road race that also featured Wendy Smith-Sly. Budd's advisers had negotiated an appearance fee of $20,000, and Budd finished a respectable second in 32:20, just six seconds behind Smith-Sly.

Then Budd returned to the welcoming sunshine of South Africa to prepare for Lisbon.

. . .

For runners, cross-country is the truest test of speed and stamina. It differs greatly from track racing. The courses are laid out in a roughly 5k loop of natural terrain. The undulations and length of the loop make it difficult to judge your position relative to that of the other runners.

On a track, you can see all the other runners, and you know exactly where you stand and how much distance you have to make up. On a cross-country course, the changing terrain often obscures the runners in front of you and you have no real idea just where you stand.

The world championships are held every year, and they are regarded as the defining event of running ability and rank, just below an Olympic event in terms of status for runners.

It is also a team event with scoring based on the places turned in by the top finishers in each race: the top six in the men's senior race and the top four in the women's junior and senior races and men's junior race.

The IAAF World Cross-Country Championships of 1985 featured a star-studded field of runners for the senior women's race: Aurora Cunha of the host country, along with Rosa Mota, the Portuguese who was the European marathon champion; Grete Waitz of Norway, a five-time winner; and Ingrid Kristiansen, a Norwegian who was the prerace favorite. A strong American team was headed by Cathy Branta; it did not include Mary Decker Slaney.

Great Britain, whose team included Ruth Smeeth but not Wendy Smith-Sly or Jane Furniss Shields, had never won the team championship since the inception of the team event in 1973, although it had produced several great distance runners.[11]

The crowded field of elite runners would make Zola Budd's task a difficult one. "To win would be an incredible performance by the 18-year-old South African–born wonder girl," opined a writer for the *Daily News* in Durban.[12]

. . .

Before the event, the British team manager, Vera Durden, said she felt that "all that business at the English National is behind her [Budd] now. I hope Zola can get up among the leaders in Lisbon and I expect a couple of other runners to be there with her. I am sure she can put it all out of her mind and concentrate on the race. I think she will have settled down by now and has the ability to do very well."[13]

Easy for her to say.

Cornelia Bürki, the Swiss champion many times over, had been training for Lisbon with Zola in Stellenbosch, South Africa. There they had trained with two men who were outstanding Swiss marathoners. Both men expressed their amazement at "how strong and fast Zola was" in training.

Bürki told reporters as she left South Africa that "Zola Budd will win a medal and must have a good chance of winning the gold" in Lisbon.[14]

The time in South Africa and the training with Cornelia and the Swiss marathoners had prepared Budd well. "Anything can happen in a cross-country race but Zola fortunately is in the most relaxed mental frame of mind in which I have seen her," Bürki said of her friend and competitor. "She is also so relaxed physically. If everything falls into place in Lisbon I shall be surprised if she does not win a medal."[15]

Budd's chances of fulfilling Bürki's prophecy increased when Maricica Puică and two Russian runners pulled out of the race at the last minute. But the competition would still be stiff and would provide Budd her sternest test since she lined up for the start at the Olympics.

Her frame of mind going into the race was enhanced by comments from an unlikely source. Pat Butcher, who had been a critic of the process that had brought Budd to England, while "admir[ing] her greatly as an athlete," told her that she would win the championship.

The *Times* of London writer had met her twice in England before her trip to Lisbon. Butcher was also a former club runner, and he had gone on a training run with Budd during which she told him that she didn't think she had a chance. After the training run, he told her emphatically, "You're going to win it out of sight."[16]

"Coming from one of my harshest critics, I was surprised but happy to hear that," she said.[17]

The course had been laid around the stadium of the Sporting Clube de Portugal, better known as Sporting Lisbon, and was relatively flat. Durden, the British team manager, figured that Zola would benefit from the layout.

She was right.

Flashing to the front, Zola Budd streaked across the course and blitzed the strong international field, winning easily by more than twenty-three seconds over her closest pursuer. "I started fast because I was on the inside of the field of 150 runners, and I wanted to get out of the pack quickly," she said.

Budd had the lead at the first bend and continued her fast pace, shaking Kristiansen off at the steep mounds as she negotiated them with ease. "I just told myself to 'relax and concentrate,'" she recalled.[18]

It worked.

Bürki and Butcher were right. And Zola Budd, just eighteen, was a world champion. The title, unlike a world-record time, would be hers forever. Cathy Branta of the United States finished second, and Ingrid Kristiansen was third.

On the medal podium, Zola took in the scene. "There was a large crowd all around, and I was too shy to raise my arm. Cathy grabbed my arm and lifted it for me."

Zola remembered feeling a strong sense of satisfaction after the win. "For the first time I felt that I had achieved something worthwhile," she said. "It was the greatest moment of my life."[19]

. . .

The only thing that marred the day was the conduct in the stands of Budd's South African advisers, who were whooping and hollering with gusto over Zola's win.

Their antics attracted the attention of Pablo Nebiolo, head of the IAAF, and Andy Norman, the British IAAF delegate. Both saw and heard the boisterous South African duo of Jannie Momberg and Graham Boonzaier celebrating a win by their "South African" runner.

They were not pleased—Norman gave them hell for being so indiscreet. And the IAAF would remember.

. . .

After the world championships, Zola returned to South Africa, where she would prepare for the outdoor season. She was still a reluctant runner and still "was under the influence" of Labuschagne, who had convinced her that she needed to run or she would descend into oblivion. She also was convinced she needed Pieter to win internationally.

When she left her mother's house in Bloemfontein to return to Stellenbosch to train with Pieter for the 1985 outdoor campaign, Zola was crying. She loved to compete, but felt "trapped in a web of unfavorable circumstances which made running overseas both appealing and repugnant. Graham, Jannie, and Pieter thought they could free me by slowly slotting me into different races in the hope that, once I started running well, I could make my home in England," she said. "To do that, though, they reasoned that they had to wean me away from my family, whom they regarded as a bad influence."[20]

She was unhappy in Stellenbosch—"I hated it and wanted only to go back home." She finally left and drove the ten hours back to her mother's home. It took Momberg and Boonzaier three weeks to coax her back. They had help from Pieter, who again reminded her of her fate if she didn't run internationally. And this time he added that he "didn't want to coach schoolchildren anymore."

Zola interpreted that remark to mean Labuschagne was interested in coaching her only if she were "an elite runner on the world stage" and bringing him prestige through his association with her.[21]

Pieter had been the recipient of a significant part of the money from the *Daily Mail*, and while overseas all his expenses were being paid by the Zola Budd Trust or her sponsors. Once again, Zola was reminded that Labuschagne was yet another person who was using her.

Still, she continued to train under the only coach she had ever known and by June was running as many as 160 kilometers (99 miles) a week in preparation for the season.

Her advisers had been busy compiling a schedule based on the lucrative appearance fees offered by the many race promoters eager to have Zola Budd in their races.

The race everyone in Europe and elsewhere in the world wanted to see, of course, was the rematch of Budd and Mary Decker Slaney.

They would get their wish.

SIXTEEN. Rematch

· ·

After taking time to heal from the injuries she suffered at the Meadowlands, Mary Slaney had begun preparing for the 1985 outdoor season under the guidance of her new coach, Luiz de Oliveira, who was now in Eugene with his outstanding runner, Joaquin Cruz.

Slaney's return to running with her new coach and the freedom he would allow her began in June.

"Luiz told me after the season was over that he wanted to thank me for having Mary in such fine condition when he took over," Dick Brown recalled.[1]

She proved she was in top form as she won her first outing in Eugene in the Pre Classic and then took another race in Vancouver, British Columbia, with ease, both during the summer.

Mary Decker Slaney was back.

The world took notice.

· · ·

In her second start after returning to England in June, Zola faced a strong international field that included French and Soviet runners and won the 3,000-meter race at Gateshead, on June 29, in 8:44.5.

But she faltered in her next start on July 4 and finished sixth in a 5,000-meter race in Helsinki, soundly defeated by Maricica Puică.

Budd's next test, arranged by the British promoter Andy Norman, was fast approaching. It would come on July 20, in the Peugeot Talbot Games at the Crystal Palace in London.

For the first time since the Olympics, Mary Decker Slaney and Zola Budd would be on the same track in the same race at the same time. The world would be watching. ABC had acquired the broadcast rights to the race and was estimating an audience of 100 million around the globe.

The hype that accompanied the rematch rivaled that whomped

up for their meeting at the Olympics eleven months earlier. Anticipation and appetite for the rematch had grown with every passing month. It was the race of the year, or so ABC and the BBC would have you believe.

The BBC devoted fifteen minutes of prime airtime to a preview of the race, with analysis of both runners accompanied by interviews with them. Jim Rosenthal of the BBC hosted the preview show and began by describing the event as a race between the "two leading ladies of the track world" in a race "that just had to happen" and one that "would end months of speculation and argument."

A replay of the incident at the Olympics was shown and Rosenthal claimed it had been replayed more than any other event.

During her interview by the BBC Slaney told viewers that she felt "something good had to come out of the incident in Los Angeles," and Zola Budd said that she was "looking forward to the competition." Slaney blamed the media for "creating expectations that she [Zola] wasn't ready to live up to" in Los Angeles.

Budd was calm and understated in her comments, avoiding any direct comments about the cause of the controversy. "I just want to have a good race," she said in her soft, barely audible, voice. "I don't really think about what the newspapers think or what people say" about what happened at the Olympics. "I've trained really well this week and I am confident I can run a good race."[2]

Before the race the *New York Times* quoted Zola as having told a *Runner's World* interviewer, "Frankly, I don't think I can beat her. If you look at the situation there is an eight-second difference between her best time and mine."[3]

Slaney told the BBC interviewer, "Beating Zola Budd is not what I'm after. What I'm after is to win the race. That's what I am always after."[4]

The telecast also pointed out the discrepancy in the best times recorded by each runner in 3,000-meter races. The edge was decidedly in Slaney's favor, almost nine seconds faster than Budd's best race time.

Despite the wide gap between the two on paper, sportswriters regarded the race as a head-to-head rematch that would settle the question left unanswered for eleven long months.

Who was better? Mary or Zola?

On a cloudy and overcast evening before a Crystal Palace crowd that was below capacity, because ABC had insisted the race be moved back a day to accommodate its scheduling, the answer would be forthcoming.

As the runners came onto the track and were greeted by applause, Slaney in her red, white, and blue warm-ups reached out to Budd, in a black-and-white warm-up suit, and extended her hand. The handshake was slight and quick but many would see it as a symbolic resolution of the conflict that had embroiled both for nearly a year.

Now it was race time.

The BBC had enlisted Wendy Smith-Sly to provide commentary. "Mary, I think, will go out and try to dominate the race," Wendy Smith-Sly predicted. "I think Zola will try to hang on and around the middle of the race see how she is feeling. Both runners have had a long time to prepare mentally and physically for this race. It will be interesting to see what happens."

Also entered in the race were Cornelia Bürki, Ingrid Kristiansen, and Christina Boxer, a two-time British Olympian; Maricica Puică was absent. According to Kenny Moore, writing in *Sports Illustrated*, the Romanian Federation had demanded that the promoters match the appearance fees paid to Slaney and Budd.[5] When the promoter refused, Puică stayed home and ran an 8:40.16 in a 3,000-meter race. "Take that," she seemed to be saying with the performance.[6]

As the runners warmed up, the overcast skies of late afternoon faded to a dim dusk. The BBC's Alan Barrett said, "Let's hope we see nothing of the demonstrations that have been going on." He said Slaney had summed up what transpired the last time the two had met by saying, "I will forgive, but I won't forget."

Just before the race, the BBC cameras panned the crowd, then focused on a man in a tan sports jacket—Frank Budd.

He and the millions watching on television would soon get to see a vintage Slaney performance.

. . .

In South Africa the evening news was under way. The government had declared a state of national emergency. Graphic footage of the latest in an increasingly violent number of racial riots and demonstrations beamed into homes across the land.

The cameras then showed a black woman, suspected of being a police informant, who was being "necklaced." The term describes a particularly horrific form of vigilante justice that involved killing a person by placing a burning tire around her neck.

When the footage ended, the announcer told viewers that next they would see the race in England between Mary Decker Slaney and Zola Budd.

And they would watch with rapt attention. For a few moments the graphic images of violence and death they saw each evening would take a backseat to the athletic prowess of a young woman who, they considered, would run for South African fans starved for athletics, her British citizenship a mere formality.[7]

. . .

Attired in bum-hugging shorts and her bright red, white, and blue Lycra top with the Athletics West logo, Slaney looked to have her game face on. Budd, looking relaxed, warmed up in her white singlet and her black shorts, which hung loosely although they had been designed for a skin-tight fit.

Just before the start, an antiapartheid demonstrator with an armful of leaflets jumped the fence onto the track about a hundred meters ahead of where the fifteen runners were lining up. Police quickly dragged him away.[8]

The starter's pistol fired.

Slaney quickly sprinted from her starting position near the far outside to grab the lead. As they reached the first turn, Budd had made her way up and was on Slaney's right but gave her a wide berth. Then Budd dropped into lane one behind the American by about two strides, with Kristiansen third and Bürki fourth.

Slaney turned in a speedy first lap of 66 seconds, with Budd trailing by about three strides and the field strung out behind them. For the second lap, Slaney slowed her pace to 69 seconds, and Budd, sensing the change, moved up to Slaney's right shoulder, just outside her swinging elbow.

At the 3:13 mark, Budd mounted her charge and moved directly alongside Slaney. The two ran in tandem, separated by inches, down the stretch with the crowd getting louder with their every step.

This is what everyone had wanted to see.

Slaney held off Budd's surge, and Zola dropped a half-stride behind with four laps to go. At 4:33 and heading into a turn, Budd mounted another challenge. Slaney had slowed the pace again, but now she picked up her pace and fought Budd off. Budd dropped back, about two strides behind.

As they entered the homestretch in front of the crowd, Budd fell farther back and was passed by Kristiansen with two laps to go. Slaney's lead had widened to about ten meters.

At 6:44, with a little more than a lap remaining, Bürki moved past Budd. Decker was running about fifteen meters ahead of Kristiansen and was moving away with every long, graceful, effortless stride. For Budd it was all but over.

At the bell for the final lap, Slaney held a commanding lead over Kristiansen and Bürki. The only thing in doubt was the margin of her victory and her time.

On the final turn, as she raced past the billboard touting Kodak, whose products she endorsed, Slaney kicked. Down the straightaway she ran, leaving Bürki nearly forty meters behind, and streaking across the line in 8:32.9, her second-fastest time ever for 3,000 meters. She had run the last lap in 64.2 and looked like she could have run even faster. Kristiansen was third in 8:40.34 and Budd fourth in 8:45.4.

Accompanied by about a dozen photographers and camera operators, Mary Slaney flashed a wide toothy smile and waved to the crowd as she ran a victory lap. Zola Budd, hands on her slim hips, wandered into the infield alone, pulled on her Brooks T-shirt and warm-up suit, and, with water bottle in hand, jogged off.

It was over.

"We can only hope," the BBC's Barrett intoned, "that this won't have too profound an effect on Zola Budd."[9]

. . .

Sports Illustrated used a photo of Slaney and Budd running side by side on the cover of its July 29, 1985, edition, which carried Kenny Moore's story about the race.

Slaney had beaten the time posted by Puică only a week earlier. Mary was back on top. "I'm just happy we could have a good race," she said. Without Puică in the field, Slaney said, "This doesn't prove anything. Puică is the Olympic champion and nothing can change that."[10]

The headline on the *LA Times* story the day after the race was "This Time Mary Runs Zola into the Ground," and the sportswriter, Mike Littwin, quoted Budd as saying, "I think all that has happened between us is in the past."[11]

Maybe so, but the race promoters were still eyeing the cash that having Budd and Slaney in the same race could generate.

. . .

Budd ran a mile race in Edinburgh on July 23 and won easily, but her advisers and her coach were still not satisfied. "They had warned me about my performance and said if I didn't perform better, I would not be able to pick the races I wanted," she said.[12] She had always run for personal fulfillment, but now she was running for money.

Her relationship with Pieter was deteriorating. "I felt that he was afraid my poor performances would hurt his reputation as a coach," she said. "He seemed to be more concerned about that than about me."[13]

Demonstrators had hoped to interrupt her race in Edinburgh and gain television coverage. When they refused to remove their banners, the ITV network chose not to televise the race. That didn't stop one protester, who managed to get onto the track during the second lap and was removed after the runners passed him in the outside lanes.

. . .

After Edinburgh, Zola spent some time in Switzerland with her friend Cornelia Bürki. They trained together, and Zola felt after the sessions that she was beginning to regain her form.

She was right.

During the next month, she would race as well as she ever had.

In her next start, at Gateshead, England, on August 9, she ran a personal best of 4:22.9, which confirmed her feeling that everything was coming together.

And just in time. She was entered in the Europa Cup, 3,000 meters to be run in Moscow on August 17. Because he held a South African passport, Labuschagne was not able to accompany Budd to the important event.[14]

It didn't matter. She took the lead at the gun and never looked back. In the process, she defeated the Russian Zamira Zaitseva, as well as the East German star Ulrike Bruns, and set a new British record of 8:35.3 for the distance.

It marked the second straight event in which she established a new personal best time, and the defeat of the Eastern bloc runners and their suspiciously powerful closing kicks was proof that she was indeed in top form as she held them off.

"It was my best race," she would recall.

. . .

Budd's second race against Mary Slaney was scheduled for the Weltklasse in Zurich on August 21, and this time Puică was in the star-studded field.

The mile race would pit the Romanian runner against Slaney for the first time since her fall had overshadowed Puică's gold medal-winning effort at the LA games. Slaney stayed true to the form she had used her entire career. After the designated rabbit in the race, Delisa Walton-Floyd, an 800-meter specialist, had set a modest pace for the first half, an impatient Slaney took over.

Puică was running along the inside in fourth with Budd stalking Slaney on the outside.

Later Slaney would concede, "I felt Puică's presence all the time," after the Romanian moved up right behind her with 400 meters to go.

The three were still closely bunched at 200 meters.

Only five days earlier, Slaney had broken her own U.S. record for 800 meters and was feeling good despite tape around her right calf to protect her tender Achilles.

Then, coming off the final turn, with the crowd roaring, Puică made her move. "I better get going," Slaney said to herself. Her head seemed to dip just a bit as she gathered herself for the sprint to the finish.

Budd stayed on the rail behind Slaney, hoping she would move out to head off Puică's challenge and give Budd an opening inside. Puică's straw-colored hair bounced wildly as she tried to summon the speed to overtake the American. But Slaney simply lengthened her smooth stride and finished four strides in front in a new world record of 4:16.7, bettering Puică's three-year-old mark of 4:17.4.

Budd finished strong, nearly catching Puică while establishing another personal best with a time of 4:17.5, an improvement of more than five seconds over her previous best for the mile.

Mary Decker Slaney, Maricica Puică, and Zola Budd were now the three fastest women in the world ever to run a mile.

Slaney said after the race that it was "so rare to have a race like today. You have to have the competition to push yourself."[15]

. . .

Budd's time set a new Commonwealth record, and her split for 800 meters was another personal best.

She hadn't won, but she had faced the two most dominant runners in the world at the same time and proved a worthy adversary. More important, she proved to all the naysayers that she belonged in their elite class despite her age and relative inexperience.

Four days later Slaney and Puică faced off again in Cologne, and the American continued her remarkable season by defeating the Romanian and a strong international field that did not include Zola Budd. Once again Slaney was able to hold off the powerful Puică's closing sprint and establish a new American record of 8:29.69 while doing so.

But the debacle at the Olympics was never far from Slaney's mind. After her second straight win over the woman she felt she had to defeat to prove herself, she said, "All this proves is that I'm a good enough athlete to be in contention at the Olympics."[16]

Whether she was referring to the last or the next is unclear. But she clearly was trying to reorder the images of LA, when Puică took the gold that virtually everyone had conceded was Slaney's.

. . .

Five days after her strong performance in Zurich, Zola Budd was back in London for another test at 5,000 meters, with one of the world's best at that distance, Ingrid Kristiansen. Budd and Kristiansen had agreed beforehand to take turns setting the pace.

The race on August 16 at the Crystal Palace came at a time when "everything just seemed to flow for me," Zola said. She had been bettering her own personal bests with every recent effort, and this race would continue her remarkable skein. Running as relaxed as she had in a long time, she bested Kristiansen and in the process established a new world record for 5,000 meters.[17]

It was the second time Budd had set a world record for that distance. The first had been unofficial, of course, coming as it did in South Africa, in January 1984, and it was the catalyst for everything that had come after.

This time her record would go into the books.

. . .

Mary Decker Slaney continued her triumphant return to a form unseen since her 1983 record-smashing season.

Her next meeting with Zola Budd would come at 1,500 meters in Brussels on August 30. The Van Damme meet was a highlight of the European season, and Budd's advisers had tried to get the promoter to pay her the same appearance fee that Slaney was to receive. They had even threatened to withdraw Budd from the race if the promoter failed to match Slaney's fee.

"It was unreasonable," Budd said years later. "Mary was having a peak season, and I resented the fact that Jannie [Momberg] and Graham [Boonzaier] would try to threaten the promoters to get more money."[18]

Although her advisers were doing well for her financially, she felt a bit disconcerted that money seemed to be the determining factor in all their decisions. "It just put more pressure on me, and it would hurt my performance, knowing that they had managed to pressure the promoters into paying more just to get me to race," she said.[19]

In Brussels Slaney again dominated the field, turning in another winning performance as she continued her march through Europe to the Grand Prix circuit final in Rome in September. Her time for the 1,500 meters was 3:57.2, with Budd finishing third in 3:59.56, her first time under the four-minute mark and another personal best.

While both women were enjoying remarkable seasons, Slaney had maintained her edge over her younger foe every time they met. The difference in their ages explains some of the difference as middle-distance runners seldom peak until their midtwenties or later. Puică, for example, was in her midthirties in 1985, and the Eastern bloc's leading runners were all older than Zola. While Budd had not beaten Slaney, the younger runner had shown an ability to stay with her that had the media believing that Budd was ready to compete with anyone at any time despite her years.

. . .

The end of the 1985 outdoor season in Rome in early September was another replay of the Olympics, at least the Olympics as Mary Decker Slaney would have us see them. She managed to end her extraordinary undefeated campaign with another convincing win in the Grand Prix final, finishing in 8:25.8.

Budd, who said she "was tired from all the racing" and travel she'd done, managed to stay right with Slaney for seven laps before fading to third again in 8:29.8, giving Budd another Commonwealth record as a consolation prize.

. . .

Mary Decker Slaney had not only come back from the ill-fated 1984 Olympics, she had overcome her early-season injury and turned in another sparkling season of dominating the world's best runners. She was once more at the very top of her sport.

After Rome, Slaney decided to take a season off. With few new world records and track firsts to conquer, she announced that she and Richard would be trying to have their first child. They were successful, and the pregnant Mary Decker Slaney was absent from the track scene for the entire 1986 season.

For her the highlight of the year was the birth of her daughter, Ashley Lynn, on May 30, 1986.

SEVENTEEN. World Champ Again

Zola Budd returned to South Africa after the 1985 Grand Prix finals in Rome and took a much-deserved rest. She completed some of her university work before she headed back to Europe to begin the 1986 season.

Her training regimen had been geared toward defending her IAAF World Cross-Country Championship at Neuchâtel, Switzerland, on March 23. At home she'd been running as many as 160 kilometers, or nearly a hundred miles, a week.

"I overdid it," she said. Her hamstring muscle problem flared up in July under the added mileage.

When she told Pieter about the injury his reply was, "It's all in your head."

Actually, it was in her leg.

Zola Budd had seldom encountered serious injuries and was not as familiar with the recovery process as one who has endured a string of injuries through the years. Because her coach ignored her complaints, she was left with no well-conceived plan for easing off and recovering.

On top of that, when she returned to England in early 1986, she did so without Pieter Labuschagne. Her coach had taken a new teaching position in Stellenbosch, and he would be staying behind. It would mark the first time that she would be essentially on her own. "He gave me a note when I left that told me to do my very best," Budd said.[1]

She placed the note in her Bible and would refer to it for encouragement throughout the coming months.

. . .

Waiting for Zola in England was another letter, from the secretary of the Women's Amateur Athletic Association (WAAA).

The lengthy letter outlined the conditions for competing in the Commonwealth Games that summer. It pointed out that to qualify for the games a "competitor must have resided in the country for a minimum of 6 months during the prior 12 months prior to the closing date for entries." The letter went on to assure Budd she could put the eligibility matter to rest if she let the WAAA know "whether your plans are such that you will have resided in England for at least six months during the 12 month period ending July 6th."

Also, the WAAA wanted to know "whether you would satisfy the alternative requirement that your domicile, 'permanent home,' or normal place of business is in England." Zola, sensing nothing amiss, responded promptly, writing, "I see no difficulty in meeting the residency requirements as outlined in your letter," adding that she was "looking forward to taking part in the Commonwealth Games in Edinburgh in July."[2]

Her pattern of commuting between Britain and South Africa had become a matter of interest to members of the athletics hierarchy in Great Britain. Her advisers' zeal in celebrating her victories as if they were South African victories had raised more than eyebrows. The warning flags were flying even if Zola couldn't yet see them.

. . .

Being back in another damp and dreary English winter while her coach was at home, basking in sunshine, did little to brighten Zola Budd's mood as the racing season began. She was, she said, "miserable and alone."

Mel Batty, of Brooks running shoes, had picked her up at the airport. When he arrived at her Guildford home the next day, he found her depressed, lonely, and, with no one to coach her, reluctant to race. He became concerned and called her advisers. After several phone conversations with Graham Boonzaier and Jannie Momberg, Zola once again deferred to them and decided to run.[3]

Her stay in gloomy Guildford became easier to endure when another South African, D. B. Prisloo, arrived to train with her. Had he not been barred from competing internationally, Prisloo would have been a world-class steeplechaser. He had been dispatched to England by Zola's advisers, to help her prepare properly for the season in Labuschagne's absence.

He and Zola ran in the freezing, often rainy, snowy streets together, and Prisloo helped her as they ran 1,200-meter repetitions together and did a 5K run that was part of her preparation for Switzerland.

Her first race in England on January 25 at Cosford, 1,500 meters over a steeply banked track, did nothing to help her hamstring pull, but she managed to win in 4:06.7, a new record for Great Britain.

On February 1, she again won in a cross-country event, at Peterborough. As she made her way to the awards ceremony, the promoter Andy Norman warned her about her absences from England. He made clear that international track officials would not tolerate for much longer her repeated visits to South Africa.

While Zola understood his concern, she was increasingly unhappy with the climate, the absence of her family, and having to work without a coach. While training with Prisloo one day, shortly after Norman's warning, she just "gave up. It's hopeless," she concluded. "I just can't concentrate."

Training without Pieter for just two weeks had left her feeling lost and abandoned. A phone call to her coach helped, but she was not a happy runner. It also helped that Pieter had obtained a short leave from his position and would be in England before the cross-country championships. Budd was still highly reliant on her coach. He was the one constant influence in her life at the time, and his presence gave her reassurance and confidence.[4]

Despite feeling "quite depressed," and slacking off in training, her next start on February 8, again at Cosford, in a meet between Britain and Hungary, she somehow pulled herself together and won in 8:39.7, a new indoor world record for 3,000 meters.[5]

After the record-breaking win, Zola thought that she had finally shown the British press that she was worthy of more than criticism because of where she had been born.

"With each step I seemed to make up for all the political wrangling, the constant criticism that I wasn't 'British' enough, all the hateful things that they were writing about me in the press. The fact that I ran well and established a personal best meant more to me than anything else."[6]

Although she was proud of herself, she had difficulty explaining herself when Yvonne Murray, another British team member, asked how she felt after the race. "[Running is] a very personal thing and private thing for me, and I am not comfortable talking about it with other people. I know inside how I feel and that is enough for me," she said.[7]

Her daily training with Prisloo, who was then engaged to Elizna van Zyl, Zola's old friend and former competitor, was instrumental in helping Budd reach a level of fitness that gave her confidence as she left for Switzerland in early March.[8]

Despite her unhappiness with the weather in England, Budd was determined to defend her title at Neuchâtel. She had been feeling depressed since her last race and was having trouble focusing on her training. "I felt like giving up," she remembered.

As it turned out, her training prepared her better than she could have known. She arrived in Neuchâtel on a rainy, drizzly, damp day.

The grass course was slippery from the rain and muddy in spots along the 5K course. Conditions were far from ideal for someone who preferred to race barefoot. Zola decided to do so anyway. It was her most natural and comfortable style, and she wanted to do her best at the world championship.

She did. Despite the treacherous footing, she successfully defended her title and for the second year in a row was crowned IAAF World Cross-Country Champion. The American Lynn Jennings finished second.

Budd did not feel the exhilaration her title in Lisbon had brought. Instead she felt a "great sense of relief" at having come out of the race with a win and no injuries.[9]

. . .

Zola again strained her hamstring muscle in May, and she knew that this time it was more serious. But she rested it for a while. Pieter, in whom she had placed all her trust, once again questioned whether she really was unable to run. That led to more arguments between the two.

At the same time, she was encountering renewed controversy and questions about her true place of residence. She remains convinced to this day that the issue flared anew as a result of political pressure exerted by the antiapartheid lobby, which had never abandoned its efforts to send her packing. Five African nations were now threatening to boycott the Commonwealth Games if Zola was a member of the British team.

"I was sick of it all," she recalled.[10] Zola Budd was tired of fighting. She sought to escape the press, which was camped at her doorstep, by taking day trips into London and to port cities. Anything, anywhere, just to change the scenery and get away from all the uproar.

When Pieter finally got to England, the two discussed the upcoming European Championships for which he was readying her.

Labuschagne asked what her expectations were, and Budd replied, "A medal." He replied that a medal "isn't good enough. You must want the gold."[11] She found her coach's retort more than a little disturbing. It told her he expected her to be at her very best when she knew that she was far from physically fit. Obviously he still doubted her.

Another problem for her to deal with.

Her injured hamstring notwithstanding, on June 7 Budd won a WAAA 1,500-meter race in Birmingham in 4:01.9. Two more wins followed in 800-meter races at St. Gallen and Meilen in Switzerland on June 15 and 22. She won yet again in Belfast in wet conditions in a 3,000-meter race at the Ulster Games on June 30. Her time there was 8:34, and she wore spikes to protect her ailing hamstring.[12]

Fortified by a handful of anti-inflammatory pills to offset the increasing pain, she next raced at the Crystal Palace in the Peugeot Talbot Games on July 11. But the tablets did little to ease her pain, and she finished a poor third to Maricica Puică and Yvonne Murray. "My leg was really hurting afterwards. I could barely walk," she recalled. Pieter nonetheless insisted her poor result owed to a lack of motivation.[13]

On July 13, before the Commonwealth Games began, the Commonwealth Games Federation issued a finding that she was ineligible because of a failure to meet residency requirements. Budd retained an attorney to contest the finding but later dropped her appeal.

Just two days later Pieter and Zola went to Barcelona, where on July 16 she would race in an 800-meter event, a distance that requires maximum exertion. Her time was a pedestrian 2:07 and she finished fourth.[14]

It seemed to her that her time, her slowest clocking in three years, should have confirmed to Labuschagne that she was far from herself. Instead he again questioned her motivation. In a conversation after the race, he told her, "You haven't raced well since I have been over here with you. There is no use, that I can see, to me staying here any longer."

She was shocked by his statement.

"What am I to do, without you?" she asked.

"Well, you can always go to Switzerland and stay with Bürki," he said offhandedly.[15]

The man she had trusted and whose guidance and advice had taken her to the pinnacle of the international track scene was in effect writing her off.

After they returned to England, Pieter told a still shocked and hurt Zola, "Don't worry—everything is going to be all right. We'll find a way to work things out." This 180-degree turn threw Budd for another loop. Her coach had gone from abandoning her to taking her back under his protective wing in the space of a single day.[16]

Although the change in his attitude eased Budd's mind in the short term, it would be a point of contention between them for several months. Their long-standing relationship was on very shaky turf.

On August 13, she returned to Zurich and the Weltklasse event against a strong field headed by Ingrid Kristiansen over 3,000 meters. Budd finished third, more than twelve seconds behind the winner, Kristiansen. Budd was simply unable to run any better on her still-ailing hamstring, yet she continued to run.[17]

In a 1,500-meter race on August 17, in Hendon, England, against the Polish national team, Zola turned in a winning performance with a time of 4:05.56. The win was especially gratifying because Pieter, who had returned to South Africa again, had told her he didn't think she could win.[18]

Next were the European Championships in Stuttgart at the end of August. Despite her injury, she was entered in both the 1,500- and 3,000-meter races. Doubling in middle-distance events is difficult for the vast majority of runners. Being hampered by injury makes it even more difficult. And the weather in Germany was wet and miserable.

Zola had been popping anti-inflammatory pills as if they were M&M's but they hadn't helped much. She was also seeing the British team physiotherapist for treatments to relieve the pain.

To gain any traction on the wet surface, Budd would have to wear spikes for the 3,000-meter race. Nonetheless, she decided she would run hard from the outset and try to have enough left to hold on for a medal of some kind.

Zola led from the start and her plan was working until the gun lap. Then the Russian Olga Bondarenko, who was mainly a long-distance runner, and Maricica Puică began to accelerate and pass Budd. Zola was still third and seemed certain to win a medal coming down the homestretch.

But moving ever closer was Yvonne Murray, her British teammate. Murray reached Budd's shoulder, and at that moment Budd's leg gave out. Murray streaked past as Zola eased up and coasted home in fourth.[19]

No medal.

Pieter was not happy. Zola, considering her injury and the manner in which it had affected her performance, was not displeased with her results. She did ask, though, to drop out of the 1,500, uncertain whether her leg would hold up under more stress, and then decided to try despite the soreness she felt.

Her coach, still casting a dubious eye at his runner's claims of injury, advised her to make her move with 800 meters remaining, a tactic designed to remove the threat of any powerful kickers' catching her.[20]

She tried to follow Pieter's plan. With two hundred meters to go, struggling on her bad leg, the other runners passed her. She hobbled home in ninth place. Her season was over, and in retrospect, she deemed Pieter's race strategy silly.

Labuschagne and Budd left to return to South Africa, and Pieter was quiet for most of the long flight. When he finally opened up and spoke, what he said wasn't what Zola wanted to hear. "How," he asked, "am I going to explain your poor results back home? I am going to have to take the blame for your poor showing."[21]

Zola thought it was as simple as saying that she was injured. But at this stage in their relationship, nothing was simple anymore. The bond between the two had gotten stronger after her father had ceased to be a part of her life, but by now it had been fraying for a long time.

Her advisers assured her they would get her expert medical treatment for her leg. In Bloemfontein doctors treated her with cortisone injections, anti-inflammatories, physiotherapy, and rest, but nothing helped.

After two weeks in Bloemfontein, Pieter called to ask her to return to Stellenbosch and resume training. By now it was early September. Zola asked for another week to recuperate. Pieter insisted she return.

Then Zola learned from Elizna Van Zyl that Pieter planned to leave his position in Stellenbosch and move to a new post in Saldanha Bay. The move would leave her without a coach because she had no intention of following him there to train.

He was the only coach she had ever known, and he had not even had the decency to inform her of his plans.

As bad as the situation was, it made one decision easier. It had been Pieter who had insisted she return to South Africa so frequently to train with him. And those visits were what had caused her so much trouble back in England.

Now she could return to England on a more permanent basis and go on with her life there. She decided now to go back to England and to "spend just holidays with her family in South Africa." It was, she felt, the best solution.[22]

. . .

Andy Norman, the race promoter, was in South Africa, and Budd met with him, with Pieter present, in the fall of 1986. She and Norman decided that Harry Wilson, the well-respected coach of Steve Ovett and the British national team, would supervise her training in England. Pieter got up and left the room without a word.[23]

She spent the next two months resting her hamstring. Then, at a track event in December, Budd ran into Labuschagne. He talked about his latest running sensation, Zola's friend Elizna van Zyl, and how well she was doing under his coaching.

But he was less friendly during a subsequent telephone call. "It was as if he had become bored or tired with me when I no longer could perform at a high level that would gain him attention," she said years later.[24]

. . .

When Zola returned to Guildford after Christmas, her friend Minke van der Walt accompanied her so that she would not be totally alone and adrift in England. Zola was looking forward to resuming her training under Harry Wilson and was exploring the possibility of enrolling in college in England.[25] Her future was looking brighter than it had in years.

EIGHTEEN. Mother Mary

Six days after giving birth, in May 1986, Mary Slaney went out and ran a mile.

Within a month of delivering Ashley Lynn, whose arrival had been preceded by nine hours of difficult labor, the new mother was back in training at her usual rigorous pace.

Soon she suffered for her impatience. During labor she had sustained a small crack in her pelvic bone, apparently suffered during her labor contractions and aggravated further by her training. It forced her to stop training.[1]

When she resumed yet again, a series of injuries would force her to stop periodically. She missed nearly the entire 1986 season. She entered the New York Mile in September, her first race since September 1985, but finished far behind Maricica Puică, who won and was awarded a new Mercedes that the Romanian government was persuaded to let her keep.[2]

During the New York trip, Puică was told she could make millions of dollars if she would defect to the United States. But she was closely watched by the Romanian secret police—they followed her everywhere—and Puică rejected the overture, fearful of the consequences her family would suffer if she did defect.[3]

Puică's fears were justified. Angelique Muha Mayer, a former member of the Romanian national team, said, "If we were to travel outside the country to compete, before leaving, two family members had to sign affidavits vouching for our return to Romania. If we did not return they would lose their housing, their jobs, and the extra benefits they were receiving for gasoline, sugar, et cetera.

"It was the method the communists used to make sure we were not tempted to defect," she said.[4]

. . .

Slaney, who had told reporters before the race that she was 75 percent fit, ran sixth, more than two seconds behind Puică.

"I'm satisfied with my performance," Slaney said after the race. "I never like to lose, but when you haven't raced for so long, it's not easy. It was fun. I was surprised that I was able to have fun and not really compete." Then she added, "But I don't want to learn how to do that."[5]

She would have to. She had been running with some bursitis and tendinitis in her left foot, the latest in a rash of injuries.

She ran in Brazil later in September and won a mile race in lackluster fashion. Shortly after that appearance her Achilles tendon injury flared up again, and she underwent yet another surgical procedure in November.[6]

By the end of 1986, she was reduced to making special appearances at meets rather than competing. Asked how she felt about all the injuries and setbacks she had endured, the now twenty-eight-year-old runner said, "I think about it, sure. I wouldn't be human if I didn't. Every time I'm injured or something else happens, I think, 'Why me? Why again? Is there never an end to it?'"

Then she added, "If you're patient things will work out. I'm in the middle of the patience thing right now."

That a patient Mary Decker Slaney was an oxymoron didn't seem to occur to her.

. . .

The 1987 season would be yet another lost year for Slaney as she battled more injuries. Racing appearances were announced, soon followed by cancellations.

In a February interview at her home, she told Randy Harvey of the *Los Angeles Times* that after giving birth she was "even more ambitious to get back. I'm really hungry at the moment, really anxious about the world championships and the Olympics."

Asked whether she felt other women runners were jealous of her success, she responded, "I'm sure it pleased a lot of them when I fell at the Olympics. I don't want to sound conceited, but I've increased the value of the sport in this country. Actually, what happened at the Olympics has helped the sport. One thing a lot of people are going to remember about the '84 Olympics is my fall."[7]

In February she traveled to Japan for a relay marathon won by the Portuguese team. The next month she raced in Phoenix and won a 10K, beating Kristy Wade of England and setting a course record.

"I went out fast, finished fast but the middle was slow," Slaney said, adding, "It's a case of not having raced in a while."[8]

In May she told reporters at a press conference that "training is going really well." Two weeks earlier she had said her ultimate goal was to be the first woman to run a four-minute mile.[9]

On May 16 she pulled out of the Pepsi Mile after experiencing pain in her Achilles tendon during warmups.[10]

A week later she pulled out of the Bruce Jenner Classic. Now she was pointing toward the June events.

In the first week of June, she had yet more surgery on her right Achilles tendon. Luiz de Oliveira said, "We thought it would be minor." Even so, his runner said she hoped to compete at the Athletics Congress meet in San Jose in late June. She was not able to.[11]

After the surgery she also pulled out of a June meet in Eugene and served as an analyst for ABC during the Pan-Am Games in August. On August 6, de Oliveira told *USA Today* that Slaney was "probably out for the rest of the year." And she was.

Mary, ever hopeful, said that she was working out in a pool and doing some light running and that she was "hopeful of running again in the fall."[12]

She would see her hopes dashed. Slaney had not run since February, and a rash of recurring injuries kept her sidelined, as her coach had predicted, for the remainder of the 1987 season.

In December she told reporters that "winning an Olympic medal is now the major goal of my career."[13]

Just around the corner was 1988, an Olympic year.

NINETEEN. Banned

· ·

Zola Budd was back in England in January 1987, but the balky hamstring that had been bothering her since August was still giving her trouble.

She was living in Guildford with Minke van der Walt and dutifully keeping her various medical appointments. But none of the treatments was working.

On the advice of a South African javelin thrower from Bloemfontein, she sought treatment in Freiburg, Germany. There a doctor who had earned a good reputation among athletes treated her injury with a series of injections. After four days of injections and ultrasound treatments, he told her she could resume training.

Back in England she attended a press conference organized by the race promoter Andy Norman to announce that Harry Wilson would be taking over as her coach.

Zola had not told Pieter about the formal change of coaches and was concerned about his feelings. "I wish I had told him about it personally, but he had to read about in the paper," she said.[1]

Then her relationship with Wilson got off to a rocky start. At her first training session with him Wilson asked her why she had chosen him. "I didn't know how to explain to him that the decision had been made by others for me," she said.

Zola had no answer for Wilson. "When he asked me about leaving Pieter, I burst into tears," she recalled.[2]

The highly regarded Wilson must have wondered what he was getting into. Then his new charge began limping and complaining about her injury on the second day of training.

Wilson recommended she see the physiotherapist who treated the British national team. "It didn't help at all, and I was not convinced he could help me recover," she said. So she returned to Freiburg for more treatments; the doctor there told her she had trained too hard, too fast.

More injections followed. But the hamstring was not responding to treatment, and she was unable to resume training. "I went back to Guildford feeling that my running career was over," Budd remembered.[3]

Without being able to train and race, Budd found she was soon being ignored by all those who had cheered when she was racing well.

Unable to run meant no promoters were calling.

Unable to train meant no interest from her new coach.

Unable to defend her title, she was reduced to watching the IAAF World Cross-Country Championships on television in March.

Unable to train and stuck in Guildford, Zola and two friends headed for two weeks of sunshine in the Canary Islands. While there she encountered her doctor from Freiburg. After explaining that her condition had not improved, he chided her again for resuming training too soon, and he administered more injections.[4]

Back in England her leg was no better. But at least the two weeks in the sun had relaxed and refreshed her.

Graham Boonzaier arrived from South Africa to see how everything was going. He quickly learned that her leg was preventing any meaningful training and that her relationship with Wilson was strained at best.

Boonzaier and Budd talked at length about her plan to attend college in England as well as her running future. "I was determined to get back into running even if I had to take a year off to recover," she said.

While Graham's visit was welcome and helpful, back in South Africa Jannie Momberg, her other adviser, was raising eyebrows as an active supporter of a former ambassador to England who was running for minister of constitutional development and planning. Momberg's high profile in the politics of South Africa was duly noted by antiapartheid lobbyists in England.

Zola, meanwhile, decided to return to South Africa for her twenty-first birthday on May 26. The surprise visit delighted her and her family, and Zola was able to continue swimming, the only exercise she could do to try to maintain her conditioning, in the university pool in Bloemfontein.

Leon Botha, a track coach and South African athletics federation member, suggested a potential solution to her hamstring problem. He told her about a doctor whom he knew had enjoyed significant success with injured runners in the past, even if his treatments were considered a bit unconventional. She decided to take Botha's advice. She made an appointment for the next day in Johannesburg. When Zola had second thoughts about keeping the appointment, her mother pointed out that she had nothing to lose and convinced her to go.[5]

Dr. Ronald Holder turned out to be a chiropractor who dabbled in kinesiology and had developed a treatment that had produced significant results with runners who had gotten nowhere with conventional therapy.

Fanie van Zijl—a world-class athlete who once defeated Jim Ryun and had benefited from the treatments—and his wife, Corrie, met Zola at the airport in Johannesburg.

On the way to Holder's office, van Zijl raved about the miraculous cure and explained that the treatment involved inserting wedges in her sneakers to correct muscular imbalances and doing exercises while using the orthotics, which were made from pages ripped from phone books. It wasn't exactly cutting-edge medicine, but, according to van Zijl, it was highly effective in helping injured athletes recover quickly.

On May 18, 1987, Holder examined Budd and inserted the wedges in her sneakers. "It is a date I will never forget," she said.[6]

With the thick wedges in her sneakers, she ran four kilometers that night and experienced little discomfort. It was, she said, the best birthday present she could have received.

In the weeks that followed, she continued to use the wedges and received vigorous massages of her hamstring.

The van Zijls invited Zola to stay at their home during her frequent visits to Johannesburg to see Holder. Fanie van Zijl became a source of encouragement and strength to her. Soon she was running under his watchful eye. Not long after, he and his family visited her in Bloemfontein, and he became her coach.

At first they kept the elevation of his status to themselves.

• • •

Brakpan and Randfontein. Chances are you have never heard of either of these South African communities.

Located in Gauteng Province, west of Johannesburg, Brakpan and Randfontein are in a region where coal and uranium deposits were found early in the twentieth century.

On June 6, 1987, Zola ran ten kilometers in the morning in forty-one minutes, according to her diary. Then, still in her running clothes, she accompanied the van Zijls and their son, Stephan, to a cross-country meet in Brakpan. "I was just going along to watch and support them as they competed," she recalled.[7]

After Stephan's race concluded, Fanie told her to run a few laps around the outside of the cross-country course. But she was mindful that any connection between her and competitive running in South Arica was dangerous and at first demurred. But Fanie assured her, "Don't worry. Nothing will happen. Just stay on the outside of the course." Budd recalled later that she had a "bad feeling" about the idea, but she complied.[8]

She took off on a twenty-minute training run. At one point, to avoid obstacles in her path outside the course boundary, she had to run for a short distance over a part of the course where some men were competing in a race.

"I never crossed the start-finish line," she said. "It was strictly a training run and I wasn't taking part in the race. Mixed races are not permitted in South Africa anyway."[9]

After she completed her training run, Budd watched Corrie's race and then they all left.

• • •

While working to regain her form, Zola had been busy on another front. She had decided to wind up the Zola Budd Trust and sent Momberg a letter in mid-July telling him she wanted to end her association with him and Boonzaier.

The letter also pointed out that Momberg's political activities had made "things very difficult for me in England and I don't want to become involved in politics." Finally, Zola asked Momberg to forward an accounting of the Zola Budd Trust, which had been the recipient of all her earnings, as well as of the bank account in Stellenbosch that was used to disburse the funds. Ending the letter with a grateful thank-you for past services made it clear that she still considered Momberg a friend but no longer her adviser or manager of her affairs.

Momberg's curt reply in late July stated that the trustees planned to continue their activities and responsibilities until November 1988, the original expiration date more than a year hence.

Zola replied a week later that she had been in contact with the other two trustees and that they did not agree with Momberg. She also declared that she did not believe the terms of the trust to be legally binding on her.

The accountants went through the books, and in the settlement, 15 percent of Zola's earnings from races, appearance fees, and endorsements went to Boonzaier to repay advances he had given her. His cut included 25,000 pounds (then more than US$40,000), a portion of the appearance fee for her rematch with Mary Decker Slaney.

When it was over, she was sad about the end of the relationships with two men she called uncles, as well as her relationship with her former coach.

. . .

Budd's comeback from her injury began with a low-profile, 5K race in Hyde Park in early September 1987. She won the race in 16:13 and was happy to find herself free of pain throughout.

The next outing was a two-mile cross-country event in Horsham on September 13. Zola wanted to keep her presence at the meet quiet to avoid any confrontations with demonstrators and entered under the alias T. Davies. But meet officials and reporters recognized her immediately.

She won the event, but her use of an alias was roundly criticized in newspapers the next day. "They had a field day exposing who T. Davies really was," she said.[10] It didn't help her image at all.

. . .

Her next parting of the ways was with Harry Wilson.

Fanie van Zijl had also arrived in England. Soon after, he insisted that she break off her association with Wilson.[11]

She felt beholden to van Zijl, crediting him and Holder with her recovery from injury. She also was aware that Holder and van Zijl were close friends. She feared that sticking with Wilson would cost her the support of both Van Zijl and Holder. Wilson, on the other hand, had not had much to do with her since her hamstring injury and trip to South Africa—she couldn't run, so she wasn't earning any money.

The choice seemed simple. Wilson would have to go if she were to keep her relationship with the doctor who held the key to her recovery. At a luncheon meeting with Wilson in August, she explained that she needed more independence and that, while she would continue to consult him, she was now going to seek another coach.

She later acknowledged that her reluctance to make a clean break with Wilson was a mistake. But she was mindful of his reputation and didn't want to appear to be an imperious twenty-one-year-old who thought she knew more than Britain's best-known coach.[12]

She was still unsure of herself and felt she needed van Zijl to succeed on the track. But she needed a front man to serve as her coach of record in Great Britain, and after consulting Andy Norman and Les Jones, both British racing officials, she decided to use John Bryant, the former *Daily Mail* features editor and an amateur runner, as her British coach. Bryant had since moved to another paper, the *Independent*.

Bryant was told the role he was to play to give the appearance of legitimacy to Zola's career as a runner for Great Britain. Bryant readily agreed, giving Budd a British coach of record. (Years later he said, "Her father bullied her and her coach bullied her," adding that she needed someone she could trust.)[13]

It was another case of problem solved. Or so it seemed.

. . .

Under the new coaching arrangement, Zola entered a 10,000-meter event, the Kodak Classic, on September 19 at Bangor, Northern Ireland. She was still uncertain how well her leg would hold up in stiff competition.

No protesters were present for a change, and adding to her enjoyment was that she ran well. "I experienced no pain at all, and was so happy that I could race again, I went out way too fast," she remembered.

Still, she had enough left to win in 32:17. The time was impressive after the long layoff, and she was pleased with the results: they convinced her that "I could still produce the goods."[14]

Another win followed in Chichester on September 26 before Budd headed to Italy for a big international competition on October 4, the first since her injury.

Biella, Italy, had attracted a strong field for the 3,000-meter race, including the Dutch runner Elly van Hulst, with whom Zola had literally tangled a year earlier in a race in Belgium. "She had bumped me from the inside lane all the way across to the third lane," Zola recalled.

That memory gave her incentive. She put van Hulst away with a strong finishing kick. Budd won her first major international test in her comeback season in 8:54.6.[15]

. . .

A celebratory trip to Amsterdam and then Germany followed.

After Fanie remarked that she didn't seem to be having much fun on the trip, Zola voiced a nagging concern. "I told him I was afraid he might drop me if things started to go badly," she said. "I still had the memories of my unpleasant experiences with my father, Pieter, Jannie, and even Harry Wilson on my mind."

Fanie was quick to assuage her fears, telling her, "Don't worry. I'll never drop you, Zola."

Even so, Zola said she "cried in the shower that night," fearing that the relationship with Fanie would end up like the water swirling into the drain.[16]

Then Zola made a short trip to Switzerland to see Cornelia Bürki before returning to South Africa.

Her frequent trips to the land of her birth had become a point of contention with British racing officials. Before her trip to Italy, she had met with the British Amateur Athletics Board, which agreed that the British Athletes Fund, which collected and disbursed funds for British runners, would pay for three trips to South Africa for her every year.

Acting as unofficial advisers, both Andy Norman and Les Jones approved of the plan but warned Budd that Fanie van Zijl needed to keep a low public profile and that John Bryant must be seen as her real coach. They also asked Budd to avoid the World Cross-Country Championships in New Zealand in April 1988 because they anticipated that, if she ran there, several African nations would organize a boycott of the event—and the last thing the International Association of Athletics Federation (IAAF) and its African members wanted was for Zola Budd to become three-time champion of one of the federation's signature events. Norman and Jones also tried to convince her that track meets were more important than cross-country and pointed out that she could earn more money and prestige there than in cross-country.

. . .

Back in Bloemfontein in October, Zola Budd was hearing a familiar argument.

"Fanie insisted that I needed to stay and train in South Africa, where I could train at altitude," she recalled. Also troubling her was Fanie van Zijl's obsession with her making money.

To her it was Pieter all over again.

"His [van Zijl's] attitude was that if I wanted to be successful, I needed to spend all my training time with him." He told her she needed to train at altitude to be successful in international meets. He wanted her to train in Randfontein (altitude: 5,344 feet, about the same as Denver), where he was located.[17]

Foremost in Budd's mind at the time was her desire to return to being among the top runners internationally. That desire led van Zijl to concoct a plan to try to conceal her whereabouts from the public and especially the press.

In November she made a quick trip back to England, where she attended an awards banquet. Afterward, while on a training run, her left leg just collapsed. "I had never had trouble with that leg. It was always the right one," she said.

That evening she called van Zijl and reported her concerns about her left leg. His only advice: take a few anti-inflammatory pills and don't "worry too much about the injury."[18] She continued with her training regimen in preparation for a race in Portsmouth on November 15 in which Fanie had entered her. In her autobiography she describes his prime concern as getting her into races with the biggest purses—"I began to notice . . . how he placed so much emphasis on making money."[19]

She ran that race with new wedges inserted in her sneakers and managed to win despite developing blisters and having her leg give out again during the race. She was limping badly at the awards ceremony. Budd knew something was seriously wrong and that a few pills were not the answer. She needed to see Holder and returned to South Africa the next day.

Much experimenting with wedges followed. She would run with new wedges, and then Holder would examine her. It was a painful and drawn-out process, but eventually they determined that the injury to her right leg had caused her to overcompensate with her left, and that had led to the recent injury.

. . .

Van Zijl was in Randfontein, the other small town you've never heard of, promoting a race meeting on New Year's Eve 1987.

Zola wanted to celebrate the New Year in Bloemfontein with her family and had planned to do just that when Corrie asked her for a favor. "'Fanie has done so much for you and he thinks you should go along and support his race,'" she told Budd. Zola remembers the plea made her feel guilty, so she agreed to accompany them to the race.[20]

She took her bike along in the back of a pickup truck, and once at the course she rode it around the course, following the runners in one of the races.

Later van Zijl called her name over the public address system and summoned her to the rostrum, where the awards were being presented to the runners. On the podium a young girl gave her a small bouquet of yellow roses, and the crowd chanted her name. Van Zijl thanked her for being there, and she left the podium.

A few reporters spoke to her afterward, but Zola, ever mindful of any publicity associated with her and a race in South Africa, declined to pose for any photographs. The reporters were not pleased.[21]

The next day, January 1, 1988, Zola made the long trip back to Bloemfontein. She continued her training under the guidance of van Zijl and Holder. The results continued to prove that orthotics were the answer to her hamstring problem.

. . .

By mid-January 1988, she was again training without pain and returned to England to prepare for the IAAF World Cross-Country Championships—despite the warnings from Norman and Jones that she should not race there.

Marea Hartman of the British Amateur Athletic Board soon asked Budd to meet with her and Mike Farrell, another board member, on January 21. The subject was the Brakpan appearance back in June. It was "starting to cause trouble," Hartman told Budd, and the board wanted her to explain.

. . .

At the meeting with Hartman and Farrell, Zola gave a truthful and full account of her activity.

Then they asked about her plans. Did she intend to stay permanently in England? Was she going to attend school there?

The tone and line of questioning had Zola's antennae for trouble twitching. It seemed obvious to her that the board was under considerable pressure about her from the IAAF and its member nations.[22]

It wasn't paranoia.

Budd did her best to assure the board members that she intended to spend as much time as possible in Great Britain but added that she needed to be able to visit her doctor in South Africa whenever she had to.[23]

The meeting led to more speculation in the media about her true allegiance, her real coach, and real intentions. Those articles fed the antiapartheid lobby's fires. The demonstrators were back in force at the trials for the national cross-country team on January 30.

Although she was still less than 100 percent fit and facing yet another jeering band of demonstrators that reminded her of their aggressive Liverpool antics, she managed to qualify for the British team.

She won a cross-country race on February 7 at Epsom and followed that with another win in Shere, on the twenty-third. Zola was pleased with her progress and that her injury was slowly resolving itself.

She was feeling good about her chances in New Zealand at the IAAF World Cross-Country Championships when she was summoned to yet another meeting of the BAAB.[24]

. . .

John Bryant accompanied her to the meeting, again with Hartman and Farrell, at the British Amateur Athletics Board offices on March 1.

"It was apparent from their questions that they were coming under a lot of pressure about me. They asked for detailed information on how much time I spent in South Africa and on my 'connections' there," she recalled.

So much for Fanie van Zijl's plan of deception.

This time the board was much more insistent that Zola provide details about the time she spent in South Africa. "They said they had received notice that if I competed in New Zealand, there would be a boycott of the event" by African nations that belonged to the IAAF.[25] Apparently, what had been rumored for sometime had now become official IAAF policy.

The BAAB asked Budd to sign an affidavit detailing the time she had spent in South Africa over the past year. She refused to do so out of fear the information would result in her being declared ineligible to participate in New Zealand as a British citizen.

She explained that she spent most of her time in South Africa with Holder, who was treating her injury. But that didn't matter. She felt that if she signed the affidavit, she would be providing her opponents, who seemed to be more numerous by the day, with the ammunition they needed to bar her from competing.

Budd left the meeting convinced that something was about to go very wrong.

She finished her preparation for the championships by winning again at Aldershot on March 5 at the Combined Services Meet. With armed soldiers at the gate, no demonstrators had appeared.

A week later she raced in Belgium in rainy weather and finished third behind Angela Tooby of Wales.[26]

Zola Budd was ready for the championships.

On March 14, the IAAF came out from behind the curtain where it had been hiding while passing on ominous threats to the BAAB.

In a letter to the British board, the IAAF asked that Zola Budd be removed from the British team while referring to the incident at Brakpan—a seemingly innocent appearance to cheer on members of her coach's family—as evidence she had competed or appeared at a competition in South Africa, which was forbidden by the IAAF.

Brakpan became the cudgel that the forces arrayed against her since 1984 would use to bludgeon her hopes.

To Zola Budd it seemed unfair. She felt she had not broken any rules. All she had done was take a few meaningless strides on a cross-country course at the insistence of her coach. What was wrong with that? If it had been anyone else, anywhere else, no one would have noticed.

But Zola Budd and her actions had been under the microscope and in the gun sights of the antiapartheid forces for years. Now it appeared they had her where they wanted her.

The IAAF had informed the BAAB that Budd was ineligible for international competition until the IAAF met on April 15, when it would consider her case further. The action angered British officials, who nonetheless feared the consequences to their national team at international meets if they continue to maintain she was in fact a British citizen.

Spearheading the case against her was the president of the IAAF, Primo Nebiolo, the Italian with a huge ego and ethics that were at best questionable. At around the time that his organization was preparing to destroy Budd's chances to compete, the Italian Olympic Committee issued a report saying Nebiolo's IAAF had conspired to fix an event to give an Italian a medal at the world championships in Rome the previous August.[27]

When caught and exposed by his own country as having participated in the conspiracy to commit fraud, Nebiolo, who harbored hopes of succeeding Juan Antonio Samaranch as head of the International Olympic Committee, merely shrugged his shoulders.[28]

Nebiolo would be acting as foreman of the jury hearing Zola Budd's case.

If kangaroos had been found in the hearing room, no one would have been surprised.

. . .

If things weren't looking bleak enough for Zola, on April 15 a small subcommittee within the sprawling bureaucracy of the United Nations added her name to its blacklist of athletes known to have participated in events in South Africa. She was in illustrious company: Chris Evert, Seve Ballesteros, Billie Jean King, and nearly 2,500 others. None of the others had attracted the same attention from the media, which had previously ignored the obscure subcommittee's announcements designed to periodically alert the world about who, it alleged, supported racism in South Africa.[29]

. . .

In his *Atlanta Constitution* column at the end of March, Ed Hinton protested the treatment Zola Budd was getting.

"The simplest, indeed the primal, athletic endeavor of mankind is to run free. Unrelenting love of such a simple act has brought upon Zola Budd an adolescence so cluttered and clandestine."

Zola, Hinton added, was a victim of a frame-up and was staying close to her Guildford cottage awaiting her fate. "Guilty until proven innocent she has always been, in the eyes of the world," Hinton observed.

Acknowledging that chastising South Africa's political leaders was the right thing to do, Hinton asked if it was also then right "to devastate a 90 pound barefoot girl, wherever she goes on this earth? It is prejudice, no matter how you stack it." Hinton ended with the observation many others would also make of the Budd controversy: "Political causes, no matter their righteousness or evil, are irrelevant to running free."[30]

. . .

By April the IAAF was issuing ultimatums to the BAAB: it would find *all* British track athletes ineligible to compete internationally if the British board failed to bar Zola Budd from competition.

Many saw the threat to be just what it was: "Moral blackmail," as the British runner Hugh Jones put it. The British board, said Jones, was spineless if it caved in to IAAF demands.[31] Margaret Thatcher took to the floor of Parliament to denounce the IAAF actions against Zola as repugnant.[32]

The meeting by the IAAF to decide Zola's future took place in a London hotel, and at the outset Tony Ward, a BAAB member, was still optimistic. "We are confident . . . that she will compete. Zola is very tired but she has had four years of this and is very patient," he said.

He probably hadn't heard the comments of the Kuwaiti committee member, Essa Al-Dashi, who had told reporters before the hearings, "It will go very badly for Zola Budd. We have many ideas about how she participated."

Ward indicated that Budd, who would not participate in the hearing, still might take her case to court.[33]

When the IAAF's decision was announced, it surprised no one who had knowledge of the case. The federation told Great Britain to suspend Zola Budd from international competition for a year or risk having the entire British team barred from the Olympic Games. The decision was based, the committee said, on a "breach of the spirit of the rules."

Committee members acknowledged that they could not point to a single rule that Budd had violated. Instead they used the sham argument of her having breached the spirit of IAAF rules, whatever that meant. The BAAB was given thirty days to comply.

In a classic case of British understatement, Tony Ward called the possibility of suspension "a veiled threat," one the BAAB would have to consider. It was all but over for Zola Budd.

The leading spokesperson for the antiapartheid lobby called the IAAF action a compromise, adding that it "fell short of what the Africans wanted, which was a total ban on Zola Budd."[34]

The jackals howled.

. . .

Recognizing that her fate had pretty much been decided, Zola said during a television interview in Great Britain, "I don't want to give up on my running. Running is the key to the rest of my life." She added she would fight any organization that tried to ban her.

"I want to live a happy life after running and if I don't go through this now, I think for the rest of my life, I will regret the decision," she said.[35]

. . .

In the week after the decision, sportswriters around the globe did something unusual: they acted like journalists and called out the IAAF. To their credit, they recognized the persecution of Zola Budd for what it was and told their readers about it. They added their voices to Ed Hinton's, identifying the vengeful pursuers, exposing the hypocrisy of their claims, and defending the right of Zola Budd to compete.

In his popular *Los Angeles Daily News* column, Ron Rappaport pointed out the flaws in the raging Budd debate. Comparing Zola to the active Kilauea volcano in Hawaii, he wrote, "Everywhere she goes, the sky is split with lightning and the air reeks of sulfur. . . . There is enough cynicism, enough hypocrisy and self-serving politics surrounding Budd's tortuous path through big-time track to fuel all the Presidential primaries and have enough left over for November."

Noting that the BAAB was being forced to choose between sacrificing its entire Olympic team or sacrificing Zola Budd, Rappaport wrote, "Whatever they [the BAAB and IAAF] do, she will be back at the beginning. A tiny athlete with a tiny voice and with battles she hardly understands raging all around her."[36]

Julie Cart of the *Los Angeles Times* traveled to Guildford to speak with Budd. When she arrived in England, a customs officer asked Cart why she was visiting. She said she was there to interview Zola Budd, and the officer responded, "Poor little thing. Everyone is always after her. I wish people would leave her alone."[37]

In the *Sacramento Bee* Bob Burns told readers that he thought "Zola Budd should be the torch bearer at the opening ceremonies of the 1992 Olympics. What a beautiful sight she'd be, circling the

Barcelona track in bare feet before tiptoeing up the steps, her thin arm upraised, flame burning brightly.

"Then, as she stands atop the majestic stadium, Zola should grab a fire extinguisher and douse the Olympic flame once and for all.

"It would be," Burns wrote, "a fitting gesture. The Olympics, in offering Budd as a human sacrifice, deserve to be sacrificed as well."[38]

Burns pointed out that Zola was being used by black-led African countries such as Kenya and Ethiopia. He acknowledged that South Africa's racial policies were indefensible, and then pointed out, "Here's Ethiopia threatening to skip the Olympics for the third time in 12 years when its own Marxist government beefed up its military while millions of its citizens starved."[39]

He didn't mention that East Germany and the other communist countries of the Eastern bloc had joined the black-led African nations in calling for Budd's ouster. He didn't point out that their leaders were dictators who practiced mass murder of those who exercised freedom of speech. Or the Middle Eastern countries that were crying out against Budd while denying women their rights. He didn't mention that many of those calling for Budd's ouster erected walls at their borders to keep their citizens from fleeing to freedom.

None of these sportswriters mentioned that these were among the most vocal IAAF member nations calling for the British to take action against Zola Budd, but maybe it was so obvious to all that it wasn't necessary.

. . .

The decision was met with outrage in Great Britain, South Africa, and elsewhere, but it was not one easily overturned.

The BAAB announced it would hold an independent inquiry to determine how to respond. By then—a week after its first pronouncement—the IAAF had backpedaled and dropped its threat to ban all British athletes from the Olympics but left in place its demand that Budd be suspended for a year.[40]

Zola and her representatives announced a lawsuit.

Norris McWhirter, a former runner and coauthor of the *Guinness Book of World Records*, tried to have members of the IAAF charged with blackmail for trying to get Budd suspended, but a judge rejected his gambit.[41]

In an article in *USA Today* on April 26, Dave Rossie gave a name to all that had transpired in recent weeks: "Hypocrisy is as much a part of the Olympics as are the torches."

Noting that the IAAF's decision was based on a loose interpretation of the "spirit of their rules," he asked what Budd's crime was beyond wearing a sweat suit to a track meet in her homeland. Then he suggested that if her crime had been as uplifting as "pulling guard duty at a forced labor camp in Siberia, or interrogating prisoners in one of Pinochet's dungeons in Chile, or pitching dissidents to the crocodiles in Zambia, she would, we assume, be acceptable to the simon-pure hypocrites of the IAAF. But show up as a spectator at a track meet, well, that's another story."

In Watertown, New York, near the St. Lawrence River and Canadian border, an editorial argued that "sports should not be held hostage to politics. An athlete should not have to pass a political test to compete. Nor should a competitor have to answer for any nation's wrongdoing. Miss Budd is the target of wrong-headed reverse discrimination. Zola Budd's a runner, not a policy maker. Banning her would not help apartheid's victims or budge Pretoria's cruel system close to extinction."[42]

Despite the public outcry from many quarters to let Zola run, the IAAF stuck to its position.

But Zola had won a huge contingent of new supporters who saw through the subterfuge and international furor and recognized a tiny barefoot woman who wanted nothing more than to run.

And now couldn't.

. . .

When I interviewed Zola for this book, she told me her opponents "had been shadowing and watching me for years, and finally they had something that they thought they could use to get me. And they did."[43]

Another media furor erupted in early May when the *Star*, a South African paper, ran a photo of Zola at the New Year's Eve race meeting she had attended in Randfontein. Then the *Mail* and other British papers published the photo, and it was all over but the shouting.[44]

Zola withdrew from competition voluntarily rather than risk other British athletes being barred along with her.

. . .

The IAAF ultimately suspended Zola Budd from competition for a year, which would keep her from earning a living and would bar her participation in the 1988 Olympic Games in Seoul.

It also left her in a rather awkward place in Great Britain, where her support by the BAAB had been less than stalwart.

She quickly made arrangements to leave the country, then consulted a doctor in London before she did so.

After examining her, Dr. Ken Kingsley decided she was "suffering from nervous exhaustion caused by stress." He recommended "rest and recuperation with the support of family and friends to regain her health." Kingsley would later tell an interviewer that the young woman he examined was "a pitiful sight, prone to bouts of crying and deep depressions . . . all the clinical signs of anxiety."

. . .

Budd's coach of record, John Bryant, told *Track and Field News* that he had "seen her crumble as a human being. She suffers from complete mental exhaustion. Doctors tell me she is no longer capable of rational thought."[45] Zola and Bryant, who once was employed by the newspaper that had so outrageously exploited her, had become close friends, and he spoke out on her behalf on numerous occasions. Indeed he was the only one of her coaches who seemed to have her best interests at heart.

But Zola Budd had been dragged through a personal hell for four long agonizing years. Her remarkable ability to dissociate from the events that would have destroyed any other person was at last exhausted. She had been vilified, attacked, labeled a racist, and stalked by a consortium of nations whose sole goal was to end her career.

She could take no more.

. . .

Zola issued a statement detailing the medical findings and announced her intention to return to South Africa as recommended. "I sincerely thank the many people in Great Britain who are supporting me in this time of crisis and I hope that in the future I will be able to represent them internationally once again."

Displaying a remarkably magnanimous attitude toward all, she left for Bloemfontein on May 9, 1988.

TWENTY. Heart and Seoul

· ·

While Zola Budd was battling the International Association of Athletics Federations in London, on the other side of the Atlantic, in drizzly Eugene, Oregon, Richard Slaney was watching his wife work out on a trail course in Amazon Park near South Eugene High School. It was an Olympic year, and Mary Slaney was eager to get back into peak form so she could chase the medal that had eluded her since she began running.

"Stay easy," Richard said as she passed him on a five-mile run.

"She's twice as fit as she's ever been before," Richard declared. "If she doesn't get hurt, nobody can touch her."

Luiz de Oliveira concurred: "I don't like to be too optimistic, but if Mary's healthy and can do all her training, with all due respect to the other runners, I can't see anyone beating her."[1] That was especially true now that Zola Budd was out of the running.

Decker Slaney was asked about Zola Budd so often that she had prepared a written statement that she handed to any reporter who dared pose the question. She would say she didn't want to be misquoted or misunderstood when speaking of Zola. The statement said in part, "I am most certain that Zola has many times felt betrayed and politically misunderstood. I know a lot of those feelings and for that I also have a great deal of sympathy for Zola."[2]

· · ·

Mary Slaney made her 1988 debut in a 1,500-meter race at a twilight meet in Eugene in May. As usual, she led from start to finish. Her time was a new meet record but twelve seconds slower than her own American record for the distance.

She said she "got over a big psychological hurdle" by winning the race. "I did exactly what I should have done tonight. People don't want to peak too early this year, because the Olympics are so late," she told reporters.[3]

During the months leading up to the U.S. Olympic Trials, Slaney, eager to avoid the usual spate of nagging injuries that caused her to miss valuable training and racing time, sought help from Dick Brown, her former coach.

"I told her I didn't want to do it," Brown said. "I did agree to monitor her training conditioning for her but that was all. I thought she was going way too fast too early."[4]

. . .

Decker Slaney's preparations for Seoul continued at the Bruce Jenner Classic at the end of May.

She won again in a Mobil Grand Prix event, covering 3,000 meters in 8:49.43, a U.S. record. The result was gratifying but far from her personal best of 8:25.83.

Afterward she seemed relaxed and pleased with her performance and even joked with reporters about her advancing age.[5]

On June 11 she entered a minimarathon of ten kilometers in New York. The race was sponsored by L'eggs, a pantyhose maker whose products Slaney endorsed. Her appearance fee was $30,000; Mary was now pulling in more than $500,000 a year from all sources, with the potential for even more if she did well.

All the top distance runners were entered in the race, which is run over the hard New York pavement. Her coach, de Oliveira, told her not to go. Dick Brown also advised against it, as did her orthopedic surgeon, Dr. Stan James, who knew just how fragile her legs were. Friends felt she was insane to go.[6]

She ran anyway.

She promised to hold something back and bank the competitive fire that burned within whenever she toed the starting line. Slaney finished fourth, forty-seven seconds behind the winner, Ingrid Kristiansen, which shocked everyone who knew Mary because she had managed to hold back from her usual front-running, catch-me-if-you-can form.

She was smiling as she crossed the line. She had run well and not extended herself to the limit.[7]

Two weeks later she was in San Diego for the Michelob Classic on June 25. Mary had asked meet organizers to scrap the mile race and add a 2,000-meter race. She told them she planned to attempt to set a new record for the distance. The promoter complied. Slaney ran the 2,000 in the unremarkable time of 5:36.65, which was eight seconds off the world record she had sought to better. Still, she had won again.[8]

Her preparations for Seoul were on schedule, and she had thus far avoided any injuries. She was running fifty to fifty-five miles a week, a light schedule for her, and using an exercise bike and a cross-country ski machine to save her fragile legs and Achilles tendon.[9]

So far it was working.

. . .

Slaney's final tune-up event before the Olympic trials was the Prefontaine Classic at Eugene's Hayward Field in the first week of July. The setting was familiar, and the race was named for a man who had been instrumental in bringing her to Oregon years earlier.

At Hayward Field a sign above the track just beyond the first turn reads, "There is no finish line."

Mary Decker Slaney saw it every time she rounded the turn.

For her the only finish line that counted, and had counted for more years than she cared to remember, was the one at the Olympics. She had yet to cross it a winner. This time, in Seoul, she would try once again.

And if she failed, she would try again. "My career wouldn't be complete without the gold," she would say.[10]

. . .

Slaney won the final mile event at the Prefontaine Classic in 4:21.25, which was four and a half seconds off her own world record set three seasons earlier.

The light schedule had left her as healthy as she had been in a long time, and she was ready for the trials in Indianapolis. She would have to make it safely through several elimination heats and keep advancing each time.

One bad race and it's over.

. . .

The trials were held from July 15 to 23 at the Indiana University stadium, and the wait for her race must have seemed interminable to Mary Decker Slaney. July in Indiana can be hot and humid, and it was in 1988. But finally she would get her chance to make the team and once more chase the medal that was never far from her thoughts.

On the eve of the trials, Mike Littwin, writing in the *Baltimore Sun*, took a long look back at Decker Slaney for his readers. He didn't particularly like what he saw. Acknowledging that she was as beloved as any American track star, Littwin wondered why. He attributed it to her longevity. But the picture Littwin saw was not that of a beloved sports figure. He saw the baton-throwing fit and her attack when Zola Budd attempted to apologize to her idol in Los Angeles.

Littwin wrote frankly about the Mary Decker Slaney all the writers knew: "She deserves our cheers. But I wonder how you'd like Slaney if you met her. She is a pouter. Her mouth is set that way, perhaps permanently. Some call what she does complaining. Others call it whining."

Littwin told readers what Slaney had said when asked about Budd's problems in Great Britain: "Do we have to talk about Zola Budd? This is the U.S. Olympic Trials."

Mary, Littwin added, had even complained about the weather and that television was dictating race times in the stifling heat of the afternoon. "She probably has a point. It was too hot. But it's the whine that gets me, the whine that is always so sour," he said.[11]

. . .

Mary Decker Slaney easily won her qualifying heat and then the final of the 1,500 at the Olympic trials. Her time in the final was 3:58.92. The only American to have ever posted a better time for the distance was little Mary Decker, when she had clocked 3:57.12 many years earlier, before she sustained so many injuries.

She was determined also to qualify for the 3,000 meters for Seoul. She managed to do just that, even though the 3,000 was held in the heat of the late afternoon, which left the second- and third-place runners staggering to the finish line and in need of intravenous hydration. "All I worried about," she said later, "was getting through the race without an IV."

Slaney came out of the Olympic trials with a spot on the team in both events. She reported that she was feeling good about her chances in the 3,000, which she said she wanted to win to "rectify the incomplete scenario" in LA.[12]

The coach of the U.S. women's team, Terry Crawford, said after the trials that Slaney was "at the same level she was when she doubled in Helsinki. I wouldn't want to think of less than that in Seoul."

Asked about the added pressure of running for her country in the games, Slaney said, "I run for me, not anybody else. I want to do well because I really want to do well. I feel good about running for my country in the Olympics but I am here because I want to be here, for me." She added her certainty that "I'll be able to run whatever kind of race I need to run comfortably and stay in control."[13]

Had she learned on the comeback trail to run from behind? Not if you look at her races—she ran all of them the way she had always run, from in front. She really didn't know any other way.

. . .

Because of the late start to the Seoul Olympics, and because she had so few races under her belt, Mary took advantage of the time between the end of the trials and the start of the games to head to Europe. Slaney was healthy and optimistic about her chances at the Olympics, so the plan was for her to earn some additional money and further prep for the games.

"I warned Luiz against it," Dick Brown said. "I thought she might get sick or hurt."[14]

The first stop was the Weltklasse in Malmo, Sweden, in early August; she won a mile event in 4:22.8, her best performance of the season. That was followed by a stop at Hengels in the Netherlands on August 13, when she won the 1,000-meter race in 2:34.65.[15]

In Zurich, Slaney found herself boxed in and lost to Elly van Hurst of Holland in a 3,000-meter race. The loss troubled her.[16] Getting boxed in and roughed up was not part of her plan.

Other than that setback, things were going well, but soon the plan, like so many others she had formulated through the years, went awry.

"She got sick in Europe," Dick Brown said.[17]

"Mary came down with a virus and had to go on antibiotics. She missed two weeks of training at the end of August and early September," de Oliveira said.[18]

It couldn't have come at a worse time, causing her to miss her final tune-up race at UCLA. The Seoul Olympics, where she would compete in both the 1,500 and 3,000 meters, were dead ahead.

To double in any international meet is difficult under the best of circumstances. To do so after fighting off a virus and facing the best runners in the world, all of whom would be in Seoul, was even harder. According to the schedule, Slaney would have to run five races in nine days in Seoul.

Nonetheless she pronounced herself ready to take on the world and to claim her gold at last. She made her case in an interview with Christine Brennan of the *Washington Post* on the eve of the games.

"For me the Olympics are the one thing I've never been able to be at, or be healthy for, or perform well at," Slaney said, summing up her frustrating experience with the games. "There's a lot at stake for me. If I screw up, I will have blown another Olympics. I have chosen to run the 3,000 as well as the 1,500 because of what happened in 1984. I left something unfinished and I'd like to finish it and do so successfully."

She also told Brennan: "In a lot of respects, a successful Olympics will get the monkey off my back. But bigger than the 1984 monkey is just staying healthy."[19]

Slaney made certain to tell Brennan that she already was planning to run past 1988 into 1992 and maybe beyond, if she could stay healthy.

That was always the big if for Mary.

. . .

In September, before she left for Seoul, Slaney granted a rare interview at her home in Eugene to a reporter who had covered her since she had arrived in Oregon. The result was a long, detailed profile by Cathy Henkel, now with the *Seattle Times*, that ran on September 11, 1988.

When Henkel arrived at the Slaneys' sprawling white home in the northernmost limits of Eugene, she noticed the vanity plates on Mary's Mercedes station wagon: DBLWC—double world champion.[20]

Henkel acknowledged that since the 1984 incident in Los Angeles, the runner's image had fallen even further than she had when she tumbled to the track.

In summarizing Slaney's miraculous comeback season of 1983, Henkel called it "her greatest conquest in a career that now spanned 19 years."

Asked about her current quest, Mary was predictable in her response: "I'm going to run from the front. I'm just going to go for it." That was no surprise but what followed was: "There's nothing wrong with getting beaten in that fast a race. Then you can leave the stadium with your head up."

The woman who "always needs to be first" actually said that.

In preparing her piece, Henkel spoke with Mary's former coach Dick Brown in an effort to determine why she was so much better than the other American runners. "She is genetically gifted, that's first. Next, she's been running half her life at a world-class level, and third, she has a definite need to excel," he told Henkel.

But, Brown added, "From the knees down she is made of glass."

Richard Slaney, who was present during the interview, revealed he had put his own career on hold to support his wife's. "If I went back to England to train and then if she lost by one tenth of a second, I'd feel it was my fault for not being there for her," he said.

By now a lot of people were there for Mary. She had Richard; her coach, de Oliviera, along with Dick Brown; her masseuse; a slew of doctors; her agents; and a small circle of friends, who were actually friends of Richard's, according to Molly Salazar, a member of the friend group; and always more doctors.

"She needs Richard," Molly said. "He's her anchor in the wind." When Mary curled up in the lap of her three-hundred-pound husband, Henkel observed, "It's almost as if she has found another father image in her husband."

Mary reported that for races she always wore a diamond heart around her neck, diamond earrings, and a diamond ring, all gifts from Richard.

Henkel was taken with the imagery. "It's almost as if the image of Mary Slaney is still turning on a kaleidoscope, sometimes sparkling like the diamonds, sometimes dark like the coal they came from. More than any of the images through the years—from Little Mary Decker, to Queen Mary, to Mary Quite Contrary to Mary the

Mom—she has been the Survivor. She has battled injuries and circumstance, always returning to top form. She has exorcized ghosts of ill-fated relationships and gone on to find happiness."[21]

Whether Mary Decker Slaney would experience the ultimate happiness in Seoul remained to be seen.

. . .

The Seoul Olympics would be remembered primarily for the rampant drug use. The Canadian sprinter Ben Johnson was among those who failed his drug test. The Russians and all the Eastern bloc countries were back, of course, with their pharmacologically enhanced teams. To the surprise of no one they dominated the games and didn't get caught.

Mary Decker Slaney was where she wanted to be, doing what she wanted to do, and hoping against hope that this time she would grab the elusive gold.

. . .

Her first opportunity would come in the 3,000, which she had said was her chance to rectify what had happened to her in 1984.

The final was vintage Decker from the start. She raced out to the lead and set a world record pace in the early going as the Russians and Romanians stalked from behind.

But this time her quick pace failed to shake them. After completing a third of the race, she began to slow. Like a clock winding down, she began to lose all momentum. At the halfway point, the field was tightly bunched right behind her faltering legs.

The woman who had dominated the world in 1983 and had mounted a sensational comeback in 1985 was not the woman on the track in 1988. At the 2,000-meter mark the field, led by the American Vicki Huber, sped by Slaney like she was standing still. The race was won by the Russian Tatiana Samolenko in a new Olympic record time, with Paula Ivan of Romania next and Yvonne Murray of Great Britain, Zola Budd's former teammate, third. Britain's Wendy Smith-Sly was seventh, and Lynn Kanuka Williams of Canada finished eighth.

All finished well ahead of a spent Mary Decker Slaney, who lost her balance briefly on the backstretch and wound up a weary-looking tenth. She'd rectified nothing except that she had been able to stay on her feet.

"It was a textbook example of what happens when you go out too fast," she said. "It wasn't a very good plan when you look at the outcome."[22] Later she would claim she had strained something when she had stumbled and nearly fallen. She admitted to "bitter disappointment" at the effort, but was looking forward to the 1,500 meters. But first she needed to qualify.

It almost didn't happen. In her qualifying heat Slaney, once again on the pole, was passed and then boxed in by a large pack of runners. Boxed in, she was forced to slow down, allowing others to pass her, before she could find an open lane on the outside. Then she had to expend significant energy to make up lost ground and barely managed to qualify. It was not the way she wanted it to go.

"I just don't run in packs enough to know how to get out of it," she said later. "In the final I'm going to have to come up with something different to keep from getting stuck on the pole. Otherwise, I'll have to do what I did today, wait until everybody goes by and then get out."

That strategy wasn't the way to win a race, she admitted. "I'm really worried about falling or tripping. What can I say? I tripped several times in the 3,000."

The runner who had spent her entire career running in front and away from trouble now was worried about running with a pack of elite runners. And for good reason.

The 1,500 was a replay of the 3,000. She managed to stay with the leaders, all Russians and Romanians, until they broke her. Kim Gallagher, also in the race but never a factor (she finished eleventh), said later that she had squeezed Mary's hand at the starting line and was among the many American runners who looked at Mary in awe for all she had accomplished.

"I kept saying to myself, 'Stay with them, Mary.' When I finally saw her break, it was so sad," said Gallagher, who had been the silver medalist in the 800 meters at the LA games.

The race was atypical for Slaney. She stayed in the second lane, just off the leaders' pace, but she faded badly and was shuffled back to fourth with 800 meters to go and continued to drop back, finishing in eighth place, far behind Romania's Paula Ivan and two Russians. Afterward Slaney said, "It occurred to me the other day that I've been in this sport 19 years. I found that hard to believe."

With sweat still beading on her brow, she admitted to the horde of sportswriters, "The dream all along was gold. But my life has been much better rounded the last three years [so] that the disappointment is less. I'm 30, and most middle distance runners keep improving until age 35. If my body allows it, I'll be back in 1992. The obsession is gone, but I'll still be trying to win," she said.[23]

No one present doubted that.

. . .

The writer John Jeansonne called Slaney the "Olympic Chicken Little," whose "doomed presence" in the 1,500 was a repeat of her drubbing six days earlier in the 3,000.

Referring to her abbreviated preparations, the runner herself said, "Obviously, it takes more than eight months to get ready for the Olympics. I think I prepared enough to be here, but I'm not prepared enough to run here. A lot of it is that I had two years off and I didn't race enough."[24]

Though she left without a medal, she insisted, "It doesn't mean I'm going to give up trying. After this, there is actual confirmation in my mind that I want to compete in Barcelona."[25]

Only Mary Decker Slaney could find a silver lining in two dismal performances.

. . .

In a post-Olympics interview with Dave Dorr of the *St. Louis Post-Dispatch*, Slaney acknowledged that after her 3,000-meter race she had been seriously "thinking of going home."

Asked if her obsession with the Olympics was still with her after Seoul, she told Dorr, "Up until now, I would have said yes. Getting through the last 12 days with the ups and downs, it's been a lot of pressure. I had such a let-down after the 3,000 because I wanted to do well so badly. That's why I went out so hard. Physically, I fell completely apart. But, you go on and try again the next time," she said.[26]

. . .

After she had been home for less than two weeks, Mary Decker Slaney entered the Mercedes Fifth Avenue Mile in New York. The event marked her first win in any event since August and atoned a bit for her dreadful performance in Seoul. "I wanted to end the season on a positive note," she said.

She had done so by running the mile in 4:20.3, just missing Puică's record time set in 1986.

Before heading home, Mary told *Newsday*, "I learned something this year. I learned how to lose. I had never learned that before. I was always programmed to win."[27]

She did not reveal how she would apply this newfound knowledge.

She left for Eugene and would take the rest of the season off.

. . .

While Mary Decker Slaney was racing in New York, a group of thirteen U.S. athletes, including her old nemesis, Ruth Wysocki, was racing in South Africa.

The Bandit Tour, as it was called, would place all the Americans in jeopardy. The IAAF's ban on competition in South Africa was still very much in force. "We did it for the money," Wysocki said recently. "My international career was winding down, and this was a chance to earn some money at the end of my racing days."

Three events were scheduled, in Pretoria, Cape Town, and Johannesburg. "The risks were all explained to us before we went," she said. "I decided it was a 'gray area' and decided to do it. Every concern I raised was answered clearly. There was no risk to our safety, and I decided to take my chances with the TAC [the Athletics Congress, the governing body for U.S. track] and went over.

"When we got there we found there were blacks and whites in the stands and on the track," she said. "The people were all very receptive to us and were happy we had come."

TAC acted swiftly.

"I was prepared to give a statement and explain my feelings but wasn't allowed," Wysocki recalled. "They said, in effect, 'We're a private organization and we can do what we want.' We were all banned for four years from competition. It was a done deal."

Later, at the Athletics Congress convention, she asked to appeal the decision.

"Another American athlete, Stephanie Hightower, had told the convention that we were all racists and should be suspended. I was appalled by the injustice of the TAC action. We weren't given a chance to explain our side."

Wysocki's appeal dragged on and on. Hearings were called, then canceled. On February 11, 1990, Nelson Mandela was released from prison. TAC finally heard Wysocki's appeal on Good Friday 1990 and promised a decision in ten days. August arrived, and still she had still heard nothing.

Then the IAAF announced that South Africa would be readmitted to the federation in 1992. Now a moot point, Wysocki's suspension was lifted.[28]

. . .

In December 1988, Dr. Daniel Hammer, a Manhattan specialist in physical medicine and rehabilitation, encountered Mary Decker Slaney and asked her if she took the food supplement DMG, also known as pangamic acid.

Hammer believed the substance, which was not among those banned, improved an athlete's VO2 maximum, the maximum volume of oxygen an athlete can use.

"She said no, she wasn't taking it," he told a reporter.

Hammer, who advocated use of the substance to build endurance and who had written a book extolling its benefits, added, "But she (Mary) said she had taken it at one time and then stopped. She said the results were equivocal."[29]

. . .

USA Today ran a story on December 21 in which Mary Decker Slaney reported she was pleased with the past year. "It's been a year since my last surgery," she noted. "Even with the disappointment of the Olympics I've been able to train a whole year."

She revealed she would be training in the future with another coach. Luiz de Oliveira was out, the latest in a long line of coaches who had failed to last with Mary Slaney. His replacement was Bill Dellinger, a disciple of the legendary Bill Bowerman.

"I think Luiz and I had personalities too similar to work together," she explained. "I need someone more conservative, more flexible."[30]

In fact de Oliveira had quit two weeks before the Seoul Olympics. "He told me he couldn't deal with Richard," Dick Brown said, reporting a more believable reason for the split. "He was too much in the way." Dick Brown said.[31]

Ron Tabb, Mary's ex-husband, offered yet another reason for de Oliveira's departure: "Luiz asked her to submit to weekly drug testing and she refused to do it."[32]

In late 1988 Mary Slaney was again talking about being the first woman to break four minutes in the mile. "If you don't think about it, you can't accomplish it," she said. Of course that would require her to stay healthy. Even she acknowledged that "everything would have to go right for an extended period of time—two or three years."

. . .

In her last interview of the year, Decker Slaney discussed her plans for the 1989 indoor season, saying she expected to enter the women's mile at the Millrose Games at Madison Square Garden in early February, and she talked about drugs.

She said runners throughout the world engaged in extensive drug use and that much of it went unpunished.

There was, Slaney claimed, "a big cover-up" of drug use. To clean up the sport, she called for "testing of all athletes by an 'independent' agency at any time during the year, not just at meets."[33]

TWENTY-ONE. Marriage and Murder

When Zola Budd returned to South Africa in May 1988, she was in a sorry state.

She needed to heal, not from physical injury but from a deeper psychological wound that had brought her to a state of near nervous collapse. She had been told to rest, and she followed the advice, spending time in bed and just staying away from everyone.

Well, almost everyone.

Two years earlier, she had met a young man, Mike Pieterse, when her sister Estelle had arranged a "sort of blind date" for the two.

Mike, then twenty-six, owned a liquor store with his brother in

Bloemfontein; they came from a prominent, well-to-do local family. Mike and Zola dated briefly before her globe-trotting life took her back to Europe. Since then the relationship had continued but had never gotten very far because of her frequent absences.

Now Zola was back but felt abandoned and alone.

Mike Pieterse was a big, handsome, warm, caring man. He and Zola renewed the relationship and began dating again. Not long after, Zola made up her mind.

She was going to pursue Mike until he caught her.

. . .

After only a few dates, Zola was in love and "knew my life was going to change."

But, she said, "I couldn't bear the thought of being hurt again." So the young woman who was so shy she whispered and blushed when praised, decided to speak up. After a little more than a month of steady dating, Zola—to everyone's surprise—popped the question.

"If you want this relationship to continue," she told Mike, "I need to have a commitment from you. Let's get married."

In her eyes Mike was just about perfect. He was solid, dependable, loving, and fun to be around. Mike was a sea of tranquility for a woman whose storm-tossed world had left her a stranded wreck high on the angry rocks of despair. In short, Mike Pieterse was everything she desperately needed in her life.

Mike wasn't as surprised as she thought he'd be. He readily agreed, and the two made plans to announce their betrothal in September. Zola wanted to keep the plans secret for a while.

For the first time since leaving South Africa in 1984, Zola Budd was happy. She was engaged to the man she loved, she was taking courses at the university, and she had even begun training again.

They set the wedding for April 15, 1989.[1]

. . .

In an article that appeared in the *London Star* on October 21, 1988, and was picked up by other papers and reprinted around the world, Zola Budd announced from her home in Bloemfontein that "I definitely want to run again at the international level. I've always loved running and you can't just give it up like that."

Apparently her rest and recuperation in South Africa was working. After the traumatic year of 1988, Zola Budd was mending.

. . .

In January 1989, Zola Budd did what those around her had urged her to do for nearly five years. She made a public statement on apartheid.

She had stubbornly insisted on her right to refuse to discuss the system that was the source of all her troubles. "I'm an athlete, not a politician," she would say.

Back in 1986, her advisers had given her a statement denouncing the policy as racist and wrong; it would have satisfied her most vocal critics. But she had refused, because no one was demanding that other athletes speak out on political matters.

What held her back was a combination of her unwillingness to offend anyone back home, a stubborn resistance to making her private thoughts public, and a lack of understanding of the history and complexities of apartheid. Her position had cost her dearly.

Now, with her running career at a standstill for at least a year, she spoke out on the subject that had been her albatross for years.

She decided to do so after the British filmmaker Kenneth Griffith released a film about her that she felt badly distorted her words on apartheid. The film included an interview she had done with Griffith for *ITV News* in Great Britain, in which she had fired back at Archbishop Desmond Tutu and the antiapartheid lobbyist Sam Ramsamy for targeting her personally. Viewers saw her remarks as favoring apartheid, and she was forced to set the record straight.

Zola Budd is a Christian. Her religion is an important part of her life. She doesn't proselytize or parade it in public, but her faith is strongly held and is essential to her as a person.

From her Christian upbringing, Zola knew that apartheid was wrong—very wrong—because it denied basic human rights to individuals based solely and entirely on their race.

Her statement, released on January 3, 1989, said in part:

> I object to being used as a political pawn and as a matter of principle do not think that my own political views, or those of any sportsman or woman, should be a matter of public concern. An athlete, however, does not have to be a politician to recognize that people everywhere

have basic human rights and I, as a Christian, hold that view. I do not support any political system that entrenches the superiority of one race over another.[2]

• • •

There. She said it. And, as she had predicted all along, the statement caused barely a ripple in the news.

In a follow-up interview with the *Sunday Star* of London, Zola said, "Because people misinterpreted my silence as tacit support for apartheid, the time had come to set the record straight."

Her statement did nothing to stop the escalating violence in South Africa, where a state of near civil war was threatening to topple the white government by one means or another.

• • •

In response to Zola's saying she wanted to run internationally again, British track officials announced in January 1989, right after she made her statement on apartheid, that they would reopen the probe into Zola's eligibility.

The International Association of Athletics Federations, meanwhile, was considering a new rule that would ban South African athletes from competing for two years after relocating to a new country. The IAAF planned to vote on the rule change at its September meeting in Spain. An IAAF spokesperson said that Budd "would be considered as a South African by the IAAF as she was making repeated trips to her homeland."[3]

In South Africa a spokesman for Zola said she was "not contemplating returning to competition at present—nor will she be making any plans—until the two bodies [IAAF and British Amateur Athletics Board] have made their standpoints clear."

He added, "Zola still has immense potential which is virtually untapped."[4]

And it appeared likely to remain so.

The British Amateur Athletics Board announced in March, undoubtedly in response to growing pressure from IAAF members, that Zola would "have to pledge to live the life of a normal British athlete" before being allowed to compete again internationally.

Tony Ward, speaking for the board, said, "We ask for clarification of Zola's position. We are requesting her to come to Great Britain and live as a British citizen, rather than this zooming back and forth. We also want to know how her marriage might affect this."[5]

Having already said all she could possibly say, Zola occupied herself with wedding plans.

. . .

She wanted a small wedding—just family and close friends and only a select few reporters by invitation only.

All brides-to-be find planning a wedding to be a nerve-racking experience. In Zola's case, it was even more so because of her father. Should she invite him to walk her down the aisle, as is customary?

For some reason Frank had always told his daughters that he was against church weddings where the "Wedding March" wasn't played.

Zola, aware of his opposition, had asked her brother, Quintus, to give her away. That's when the trouble began.

Frank threatened to disinherit Quintus if he walked Zola down the aisle. Quintus insisted he would do so, but then Frank sternly reminded his son who held title to the property on which Quintus's house was located.

To take Quintus off the hot seat, Zola asked Mike's father to walk her down the aisle. The irony was that after all Zola had gone through with her father, she had intended to invite him to the ceremony until he started threatening Quintus.

Now she decided not to invite him. "He probably would have used the wedding to sell a story to the papers," she said in retrospect.[6]

Zola got through the ceremony, although she was more nervous than at any time before a race. After it was over, she felt contentment and security in the knowledge that she would not be returning that night "all alone to an empty house."

"I wished I had been married to him earlier," she said.[7]

. . .

Frank Budd, who was now also living in Bloemfontein again, in a small farmhouse, inflicted yet another assault on the raw psyche of his youngest daughter.

As the wedding plans became public knowledge, a reporter asked Frank about the upcoming nuptials.

The day after the wedding, the *Sunday Times*, South Africa's largest newspaper, carried Frank's reaction in a front-page headline: "Zola, I Curse You!" The article quoted Frank as saying, "I don't have a daughter named Zola. To me she's dead and I curse her. May she never be happy."[8]

No one should have been shocked. This was, after all, the man who had sold his daughter's services to the *Daily Mail*, triggering a plan that had nearly destroyed his frail teenage daughter.

Zola read the remarks, as did others in her family, who were very hurt by them. But Zola decided to simply ignore Frank.

She never spoke to him again.[9]

. . .

On June 7, after she and Mike had settled in their home, Zola responded to the BAAB and the IAAF.

At a news conference in Johannesburg, she told reporters she was through as an international competitor. She also would not be returning to the United Kingdom to pursue her running career. She thanked the people of Great Britain for their support and said she bore no ill will toward those who fought against her participation in international athletics.

"I had a choice between my athletic career and me as a person, and I decided to make the best decision for me as a person," she said. At the time, she was content to be Zola Pieterse, and to her the decision wasn't as simple as running in South Africa or running overseas. "It was a choice between running and life. I chose life," she said, adding that she would henceforth limit her competition to events in South Africa.

In Eugene, Mary Decker Slaney was surprised by Zola's decision.

"I think she'll change her mind over time. I think she'll get back in shape and then get frustrated because there's no one to compete with in South Africa. I know how I am. Once I get fit, I can't wait to compete," said Slaney, who was recovering from yet another surgery.[10]

. . .

Zola was living with her husband in Bloemfontein and attending classes at the nearby university. She had resumed training and was enjoying it again.

In August she entered the 10k Phoenix Road Race in Johannesburg, her first race since leaving England. She won in 37:35, with spectators, black and white, cheering her all the way through the race.[11]

It was good to be home.

. . .

On the evening of September 22, 1989, at his small farmhouse a few miles from Bloemfontein, Frank Budd, fifty-nine, was murdered.

A neighbor found his body the next morning when he saw Frank's dog wandering outside the house. Frank's body was in the house. He had suffered two shotgun wounds to his left side, and Frank's gun and truck were missing.

The police began searching for a suspect who had done odd jobs on the farm and eventually apprehended him. He confessed to the crime but told police he had killed Frank in self-defense when Frank made homosexual advances toward him.

The man was subsequently tried and convicted. The court sentenced him to fifteen years in prison and cited mitigating circumstances in handing down the relatively light sentence. He served six and was released.

Frank Budd, described by a South African news service as a bitter man, still sought to control his family from the grave. His will forbade his daughters from attending his funeral and threatened to disinherit them if they did.[12]

Zola did not go, and it would be eight years before she could bring herself to visit his grave.

. . .

In November the autobiography that Zola had been writing with the South African journalist and author Hugh Eley was published.[13]

Most people promoting a book want all the attention they can get. Not Zola. At promotional events she would tell reporters that she had a simple request: "Leave me alone."

"I wanted to tell my side of the story, then for things to die down and disappear. I want to live a normal life," she said. "I see the book as the last of Zola Budd." Today she is known as Zola Pieterse.

TWENTY-TWO. Promoting L'eggs on Bad Legs

Mary Decker Slaney was back in Eugene with a new coach and a new endorsement deal as 1989 began.

She had been with Nike since 1974, when she was sixteen, and became the first woman athlete the shoe company had signed.

Her agent, Brad Hunt, of Advantage International in Washington DC, had tried to renegotiate her contract with Nike to permit her to sign a lucrative apparel deal with L'eggs, the North Carolina–based pantyhose manufacturer, for which she was already doing promotional work, while continuing on the Nike team as an endorser of shoes and clothes.

Nike nixed the deal, which was for a significant amount of money—more than Nike had been paying her, although she wouldn't say how much—and Mary left Nike.[1]

Attired in her new hot pink running outfit for the L'eggs Sheer Energy Racing Club, Mary made a successful debut. At an indoor meet sponsored by the *Dallas Morning News* in early January, she won her first indoor event since 1985 in an 800-meter race.

Early in the race she needed a stiff arm to protect herself from falling on the steeply banked wooden track. She survived the incident, sprinted to the front, and was never challenged.

"I felt like I was going to fall. I'm not used to starting on the outside, first of all, and then going right into the bank," she said.

It was her first 800-meter race in three years, and her time of 2:02.87 was, for her, proof that she could better four minutes in a mile race, which was her oft-stated goal. Eight hundred meters is about half a mile. "This race shows I have a good shot at the world record in the mile," she said afterward. "To me, it would be a more significant achievement than an Olympic medal."

Then Slaney announced that she planned to run four indoor races and her objective was to win all four.[2]

Her second appearance for her new team came a week later in her home state of Oregon in a 1,000-meter race in Portland. When it was over, Slaney, who led all the way, was two for two.

In her first try at the seldom-run distance, she set a new American record of 2:37.6, just beating the old mark set by Joetta Clark of Newark, New Jersey.

Speaking to reporters afterward Slaney revealed, "My legs felt a little tired after the first half from hard training."[3]

. . .

The next stop for Mary Slaney was the Panasonic Millrose Games in New York.

Ruth Wysocki and other American runners would not be testing her, as they had been banned from competition by the Athletics Congress as punishment for their Bandit Tour of South Africa.

But the mile event gave Slaney a rematch with the Romanians Maricica Puică and Paula Ivan, who had crushed the American in the 1984 and 1988 Olympics. Also entered was another Romanian, Doina Melinte, who had taken the gold medal at 800 meters at the 1984 games.

It was a top international field, stiff competition for Slaney. After taking the lead as usual, she gave it up with four laps to go as Ivan took over.

Then, with more than seventeen thousand cheering Slaney on, she fought back on the gun lap to reach Ivan's shoulder off the last turn. "I felt her," Ivan said later. "It spurred me on." Slaney finished a close second with the other two Romanians, Melinte and Puică, following.

"I let her get too far ahead of me and didn't give myself enough time to catch her. I learned," Slaney said. "I think next week will be different," a reference to the Vitalis Invitational at the Meadowlands in New Jersey, her final planned event for the indoor season.

"I feel like a new person," she declared. "I'm enjoying training, I'm having fun. I feel normal." She also noted that she had been escorted immediately to the drug-testing center. She found it ironic that she was chosen at random while none of the Romanians was.

"I feel like someone's giving orders," she said.[4]

. . .

A rematch with the swift Romanians was not to be. Slaney's indoor season ended after three meets. She was injured yet again.

"She's disappointed and frustrated, but it's a matter of a stitch in time saving nine," her agent, Brad Hunt, said. Mary had injured her left calf and Achilles tendon at the Millrose Games. She was out of the Meadowlands event.

She still planned to run in the 1,000 meters at the Los Angeles Times/Eagle Indoors meet a week later.[5]

Bill Dellinger, her new coach and the head track coach at the University of Oregon, told reporters on February 26 that Slaney had felt soreness in her Achilles tendon after the race in New York.

"It never responded to rest, so she came home and has been getting treatments and limiting her workouts to the water. We decided to forget about the rest of the indoor season, because outdoor is more important, and she has a long season ahead of her," Dellinger said. "I think she's okay now. She's running without pain, so she's resumed her workouts."

In the months that Dellinger, a disciple of the legendary Bill Bowerman (who had bowed out of coaching Mary after only six months), had been working with her, he had learned that Slaney "has a history of leg problems. But what I've found with her is, first, she's very, very talented, and second, she is very determined to do something with that talent. My goal is to keep her healthy, because if she's healthy and makes progression in her workouts, she can be very, very good."

Exactly what all her coaches had said about her.

Kerry Eggers, who knew her history, began his piece in the *Oregonian* with "Same ol, same ol: Mary Slaney's legs are bothering her again."[6]

The 1989 season wasn't two months old and Mary was sidelined.

. . .

In March, Slaney attended a 10K race in Carlsbad, California, making an appearance on behalf of L'eggs.

There she gave some advice to aspiring runners: "Once you start to rush—go too hard, too fast, too soon—you're courting disaster."

She was living proof of it.[7]

. . .

After taking a few weeks off, Mary had gone back to training for the outdoor season.

Her activity at meets had been limited to personal appearances on behalf of L'eggs to promote a running brochure published under her name that L'eggs was using to promote its products and the benefits of running for fitness.

That the oft-injured Mary Slaney was a most unlikely promoter of running for fitness was overlooked in the interest of getting something in return for the large investment in a runner who, well, wasn't running much.

She announced in April that she was planning to run again in mid-June at the Athletics Congress meet in Houston and then in New York in the L'eggs minimarathon at the end of June.[8]

. . .

Shortly after making her optimistic statement that she would run in Houston and New York, she underwent yet another surgical procedure on her ailing Achilles tendon to remove more lesions.

The latest setback didn't dim her enthusiasm for the 1989 outdoor season. She announced just two weeks after the procedure in late May that she was planning to resume training soon for the L'eggs-sponsored event on June 24 and another mile race in July before heading to Europe for the summer season there.[9]

It was a good plan.

. . .

Instead of lining up for the start, Slaney was reduced to making an appearance at her new sponsor's premier event as a not-too-serious jogger who was just there to have fun. She would run behind the leading competitors with the other recreational runners who had no chance of winning.

Her appearance made news nonetheless. Before the race she had attended a L'eggs press conference. During the questioning she claimed that when she was just nineteen, the track coach Chuck DeBus had approached her about taking performance-enhancing drugs. DeBus then was under investigation by the Athletics Congress, following claims by some of his runners that he had offered or provided them with banned substances. A year later TAC banned him for life.

"[DeBus] said I wouldn't be able to perform internationally if I didn't take drugs," Slaney said. "He was trying to recruit me for the Los Angeles Naturite Running Club he coached."

She said she had been horrified by his proposal. "I didn't believe in his methods, and I didn't want to participate in his system. I said I can't do that.

"At that time, and now," she continued, "I don't believe in drug usage. I haven't even touched my potential naturally, so why should I use them?"

Slaney went on to say she was aware that the Eastern bloc countries were using drugs back then and that she had thought they were the only ones until DeBus made his proposal.[10]

Slaney then told reporters that two years after the offer from DeBus, someone else, whom she refused to identify, had offered her an opportunity to use drugs. "I turned down the offer," she said. "I think people believe if you are going to get better, this is what you have to do."[11]

She conceded that her winning 1983 season had led to a lot of speculation about her preparation. "A number of people have accused me of taking drugs because I was so much better than everyone else," she said, addressing the rumors about her use of drugs during that season.

Then she voiced her approval of the random drug-testing system that the Athletic Congress was putting into effect on July 1. The best way to rid the sport of drugs, she offered, is to test continually.

"I think if more people get caught, it will help the situation," she said.[12]

. . .

Slaney jogged through the L'eggs event, which was won by Canada's Lynn Kanuka Williams, and finished 103rd. Aurora Cunha was the third-place finisher behind the Russian runner Yekaterina Khramnikova; Judi St. Hilaire was the top American, finishing fourth.

Slaney said she "had a good time. I tried to fade into the pack as much as I could. I tried to offer advice to some of the women who were working hard. I learned from it today—that competitive spirit isn't just among the leaders in the race."[13]

. . .

The easy jog had not spared Mary Decker Slaney's ailing Achilles tendon.

On July 17, a few days before her scheduled appearance at a mile race in New York, she was back in Eugene, where she underwent her fourth surgical procedure on her right Achilles tendon.

. . .

With Slaney out of action, new faces were emerging in women's track. Now PattiSue Plumer and Suzy Favor Hamilton were America's top middle-distance runners.

But neither had the name recognition that Mary had.

Plumer was still working as a server to earn money while attending law school and retain her NCAA eligibility. Hamilton didn't yet have the international résumé to command large appearance fees.

Slaney was living comfortably on her endorsement money while spending most of the year in recovery. She was earning her money by speaking at appearances arranged by L'eggs, which by now had, well, egg on its face for signing her to a lucrative contract and getting little in return.

By November 1989, when she was recovering from yet another surgery, this one in August, Slaney was reduced to speaking to a conference of osteopathic physicians in Los Angeles. Her topic was one she was eminently qualified to address: "An athlete's response to injury."

"I'm very good at giving advice. And I'm very good at knowing what I should do. I'm just not good at taking my own advice," she said.[14]

. . .

Slaney revealed that she planned to skip the indoor season in 1990 because she had gotten hurt indoors. Instead she would concentrate on outdoor races.

"I'm looking for a couple of short road races to do in February and March, just to do something competitively," she said.[15]

It didn't happen. She suffered yet another injury.

In Winston-Salem, North Carolina, the marketing guru who had inked Mary to a lucrative endorsement deal in the high six figures must have been worried. If things kept going the way they were, he'd probably be looking for a new job soon.

• • •

In February 1990, while she was still mending, meet promoters honored Mary Decker Slaney as "The Female Indoors Athlete of the 1980s."

They probably wished she could do some running and help them sell some tickets, but Mary wasn't ready to run yet.

That didn't stop her from running her mouth on several topics in the May/June issue of *Special Report—On Sports* published by *USA Today*.

"Among the top 20 men and women athletes in each event in the world . . . I would say 90 percent of them aren't clean," she declared. She repeated her old story of her observations in the women's restrooms at meets in Europe and thinking that she was in the wrong bathroom.

She also spoke about the different attitudes of women and men in track. Men are friendly with one another, she said, while women, "barely speak to one another. There's a lot of jealousy." Slaney's commentary on the social scene reflected the comments others had made about her through the years.

She also said that she believed there was nothing wrong with women athletes looking good on the track but that "some people carried it a bit too far."[16]

Hot pink bum huggers and skin-tight tops, perhaps?

• • •

A week later she was optimistically looking ahead to the outdoor season and announced she was back in training.

"The doctor said it's now 100 percent," she said of her Achilles. "He said it's coming along great." She said she would avoid the indoor meets and concentrate on the outdoor races, especially regaining her record at the mile from Paula Ivan of Romania and her 1,500 mark from the Russian Tatyana Providokhina.

"I feel like I have a lot left," Slaney said. "I haven't touched on my potential yet. I've been unlucky as far as injuries go. I envision running much faster in everything I've ever run."[17]

Whatever her shortcomings, they did not include a lack of confidence.

. . .

In May 1990 Slaney said she planned to run in the L'eggs minimarathon and later in the 1,500 at the Athletics Congress meet because she wanted to make the U.S. team for the 1990 Goodwill Games later in the year.

The Goodwill Games, she said, were "going to be in Seattle, an hour flight from where I live. It's perfect."[18]

. . .

However, she spent most of the 1990 season watching her numerous records fall to new runners.

Early in the season, Paula Ivan of Romania broke Slaney's indoor 1,500 mark, which had stood for ten years, and collected a bonus of $100,000.

The Romanian had trained for the race with bullets flying over her head as the Romanian revolution that toppled the dictator Nicolae Ceaușescu raged.

One of the many changes brought by the revolution was that now Ivan could keep her bonus money.[19]

. . .

Mary spent most of her training time in the pool or on a stationary bike, allowing her battered Achilles and calf injuries time to heal.

But as the Athletics Congress championship meet at Cerritos College in Orange County neared, she needed to race. She wanted to make the Goodwill Games team that would be selected after the TAC meet in July. Only the first two finishers in each event would automatically qualify.

On June 8 in Eugene, Dellinger hastily arranged a race for her at a Eugene all-comers meet. Slaney's first race outdoors since 1988 was a qualified success. She ran 1,500 meters in 4:17.9 in a race won by Shelly Steely, who was coached by Dick Brown and who outkicked Mary in the final hundred meters.[20]

The one downside to Slaney's comeback was that she found "I couldn't sprint," she said. "I kept saying, 'Go, go, go,' and I couldn't."[21]

. . .

At the Athletics Congress meet Slaney would be competing against some of the new young stars that had supplanted her as the top middle-distance runner in America during her absence.

She would face Suzy Favor Hamilton, the twenty-year-old University of Wisconsin star who had been running well while Mary was healing, and PattiSue Plumer, who was becoming the new face of women's track.[22]

Plumer, a Stanford Law grad, was now practicing law in Palo Alto. She would be named Female Track Athlete of the Year in 1990. She raced in sunglasses with a long auburn braid bouncing behind her. There was no way you could miss her in a race, and she was known as an aggressive runner.

Plumer was cool. In Europe she was as popular as a rock star; men proclaimed their love for her and she drew huge crowds.

Charismatic, and talented, she was, at twenty-eight, reaching her racing peak.[23]

. . .

Mary Decker Slaney's semifinal race at TAC was less than auspicious. She finished eighth and squeaked into the finals.

"I'm not fit to race," she said after the heat. "I haven't been on the track and I haven't done the interval training I need." Mary added she hoped to be ready in a month and was still predicting she'd run "a 1,500 in under 4 minutes by then."[24] Her comments were intended for TAC officials who would be making selections for the Goodwill Games later in the season; she wanted to be there.

To get an automatic berth she had to finish first or second in the 1,500 final. She didn't.

A tightness in her troublesome right calf forced her out of the race before it started. Now the only way she would get to the Goodwill Games was to buy a ticket—unless she was named to the squad by "special invitation."

Plumer finished a close second to Suzy Favor Hamilton in the final of the 1,500 and had already qualified in the 5,000 as well.

Plumer and Favor Hamilton were in.

The Athletics Congress extended special invitations to several athletes who, like Slaney, had failed to earn spots on the U.S. team. It wasn't a particularly popular move with other athletes.[25]

In July at the Goodwill Games, a Ted Turner production that had long since outlived its purpose and was less popular each year, Slaney pulled out of the event before it started.

Her Achilles tendon required yet more surgery.

. . .

As the year wore on, Mary fought to recover. There were the usual optimistic pronouncements of upcoming appearances followed by the inevitable no-show. She was becoming track and field's no-show equivalent of the country music star George Jones, who regularly disappointed fans by canceling appearances, although he was recovering from frequent bouts with the bottle, not surgery.

In September Julie Jenkins, a former Brigham Young University star, broke Slaney's 1,000-yard record.

Mary could only watch, frustrated, as her records continued to fall throughout the 1990 outdoor season.

TWENTY-THREE. Budd Blooms

While Mary Decker Slaney was spending 1990 approaching a record for most surgeries by a middle-distance runner, Zola Pieterse was enjoying her return to South Africa. She was happily married, among friends and family, and even starting to enjoy running again.

Her appearance had changed with her attitude. A late growth spurt had added two inches to her frame. She was also maturing physically, with her sparse body becoming more feminine and curvy.

No longer was her angelic face clouded by the dark frown that had marked it since her return from England. Her hair was longer, too.

In short she was being reborn and reinvented. Physically and emotionally, Zola Pieterse had blossomed, leaving behind Zola Budd, with all her traumas, troubles, and trials.

Zola Pieterse, happily married, was running freely again.

. . .

Though the winds of change were growing stronger with each passing month in turbulent South Africa, the nation was still isolated from the international track and field community.

Even after Nelson Mandela was released from prison, in February 1990, South African athletes continued to be limited to competition within their country's borders.

This suited Zola just fine.

In her absence from South Africa, other runners had been developing without fanfare or international attention. Zola's friend Elizna van Zyl, and Elana Meyer, were but two who had developed in relative anonymity during Zola's globe-trotting career. They would provide her with the competition she had lacked before she left for England.

At the end of 1989, she had run three races, winning two and finishing second in her final appearance that season.

She began her 1990 season in February.

. . .

Zola's return to South African track as "a lady, not a baby" was, by any measure, astounding.[1]

During the 1990 season, she competed thirty-two times, drawing large crowds that were obviously happy to have her back. Racing over distances from 400 meters to 18,000 meters on the track, the road, and cross-country courses, she would win all but seven events she entered. Her only foray outside the country was to nearby Tahaba Nchu, in Bophuthatswana.

Zola's running reflected her improved state of mind, and her body slowly assumed the condition that it had been in before her injury.

Much of the success of Zola Budd Pieterse can be attributed to her running at altitude since the very first time she ran through the veldt with her sister Jenny. Bloemfontein is at approximately the same altitude as Denver.

It is well established that running and training at altitude is ideal for conditioning middle- and long-distance runners. Training in thinner air develops the superior lung and heart capacity that provides an edge when the runner competes at sea-level venues. It is something like having a supercharger attached to a racecar engine. It wasn't by happenstance that the U.S. Olympic Committee selected Colorado Springs for its training center.

Zola's training at altitude, combined with her indomitable will and the pure joy that running brought her, was a winning combination. Especially in her early years, those who could not see beyond her slight frame and immature body never understood how she won. They were unaware of the strengthened heart and lungs that propelled her long legs into a high speed that she could sustain while others fell behind.

Zola Budd Pieterse was a well-designed racing machine mechanically. Her training program from the outset under Labuschagne had been designed using the popular Lydiard method, which some of Mary Slaney's coaches also used. Arthur Lydiard, a New Zealander, had toured South Africa in the late 1970s and introduced his program to coaches there.

Labuschagne was among those who listened and learned. The Lydiard program emphasized long training runs at moderate pace, coupled with shorter interval-training programs.[2]

Runners who followed the Lydiard program were known for their endurance and strength, able to run longer distances without incurring serious injuries. Zola would prove to be one of the top graduates of the Lydiard school.[3]

Now that she was also healthy emotionally, the machine that was now Zola Pieterse was humming and purring again.

. . .

Zola continued to rack up successes in 1991. As her conditioning improved and the orthotics kept her safe from injury, she again was among the top elite middle-distance runners in South Africa.

The competition with Meyer and others was a contributing factor—Zola thrived on it.

She still was firm about competing only in her native land, but with change coming rapidly to what was being called the "new South Africa," running internationally, as a South African, was a possibility.[4]

In her third start of 1991, a 3,000-meter race in Stellenbosch on March 11, she set a new South African record of 8:42.26, beating Meyer in the process. Her time would have made her the best in the world that year if the feats of South Africans had been recognized.

Zola Pieterse was getting noticed. And with President F. W. de

Klerk moving South Africa steadily out of the apartheid era, track fans were talking about whether Zola would resume her international career.

"At the moment I am not banking on anything beyond the South African Championships in April," she said. "But these are momentous times in South Africa and, with all that is happening, I hope it will be possible for me to run for my country internationally in the future."

To a reporter visiting her in the new home she shared with Mike, five dogs, and two cats, she "hardly seemed like the same person who trod, and tripped, through a political minefield" in Great Britain. "She is no longer a little girl lost, but a woman who has found contentment and confidence in marriage on a return to the land that, spiritually, she never left."

Pieterse acknowledged it would be another year before she was back in top form. If things worked out, she said, "Obviously I would like to try again for an Olympic medal."[5]

. . .

Zola Pieterse ran fifteen races on the track and road before tasting her first defeat in Pretoria on April 1. She finished second in an 800-meter race, not her strongest distance, to Zelda Pritorius, who established a new South African record of 1:58.5.[6]

She would lose again in late April to Meyer at 3,000 meters, again in Durban. Once again, it took another South African record performance to beat Pieterse.

The race in Durban drew a crowd of eleven thousand to Kings Park Stadium, which was built to accommodate eight thousand. It marked the largest crowd for a track meet since New Zealand's Peter Snell had raced there in 1964.[7] In South Africa, Zola's name was as good as her country's plentiful supply of gold. Inevitably spectators would begin the rhythmic chant of "Zo-la, Zo-la," as she motored forward, as if the crowd could, with its vocal support, carry her even farther and faster. She seldom disappointed.

By the end of the 1991 season, Zola Pieterse had competed in forty-five races, on the track, the road, and cross-country, losing only five times, and was displaying her old form under her new name. In her final start of the year, in December, she reached the Olympic qualifying time for 3,000 meters, running 8:54.02, more than two seconds faster than the minimum qualifying time.

Of course, there was no guarantee that any South African team would participate in the 1992 games in Barcelona.

. . .

In June 1991 the newly organized South African sports organization, which was open to athletes of all races and in all sports, had announced it would be seeking approval for its members to compete internationally.[8]

De Klerk had continued to dismantle apartheid, and by August, many people were betting that the International Association of Athletics Federations, the world governing body for track, would readmit South Africa at its August meeting during the world championships.

Only the month before, in July 1991, the International Olympic Committee had held a special meeting in Lausanne, and, urged on by black-led African nations, decided unconditionally to readmit South Africa to the Olympic family.[9]

That meant South Africa would be permitted to send a team to Barcelona and that the team would surely include a runner named Zola.

The various international sports bodies, including the IAAF, would soon all follow suit.

The IOC's lifting of the ban had a ripple effect far across the world. The Athletic Congress lifted the ban it had imposed on Ruth Wysocki and the others who had taken part in the Bandit Tour of South Africa. They too could run again.

. . .

Zola was pleased at the news of the IOC's decision, although at first she didn't believe it. Assured that it was true, she said, "I'm very positive at the moment. I'm excited about the prospects of running again, just being able to go to the Olympics."

Then she added her hope that the changes in South Africa would help heal old wounds and "promote unity." "South African sport is the biggest passion in the country. It doesn't matter what race or color or whatever you are, as long as you are from South Africa, everybody is behind you. And that unifies us. Athletics has done a lot for South Africa," she said.[10]

Tim Noakes, a South African professor of sports science and an author, was looking even further ahead, predicting, "Zola will peak at 28, even older if she goes for the marathon. Like many great athletes she has matured late."

Jannie Momberg, her one-time adviser, said, "Zola needs to be happy to run well. A happy Zola will break records."[11]

That could mean a lot of broken records ahead because, as Zola said, "I've never been happier in my life."[12]

. . .

In early August, a group of South African track athletes that included Zola wrote to IAAF president Primo Nebiolo asking to enter the world championships in Tokyo later that month. "We as athletes are aware of our rights and obligations and we believe that it is also our duty to take part in this important event," they asserted.[13]

Before Nebiolo was forced to decide, they withdrew the application, but international developments all pointed toward a South African team at the Olympics for the first time since 1960.

Zola was looking forward to the 1992 season, with the promise of a chance, at last, to compete once again against the best in the world at the Olympic Games in Barcelona.

She thought the most important thing about the games was that "it's not important how many medals we win. It's more important to go as a team, with the support of all South Africans."[14]

She told a reporter she had a new coach, Van Zyl Naude, who had her begin each day with an hour run before breakfast. In the afternoon she trained with the local university team that Van Zyl Naude coached. She thought South Africa would send a competitive team to Barcelona, adding, "Just to be there and to compete will be more than enough for me."[15]

She would be twenty-six when the games began. It had been a long eight years since Los Angeles.

TWENTY-FOUR. New Faces, Old Story

Mary Decker Slaney made a quiet 1991 debut at a low-key race in New York in May, finishing second, and then headed west for the Bruce Jenner Classic in San Jose two weeks later.

Like a flash from the past, she won the 1,500 meters in 4:04.92, the fastest time in the world that year. "This makes me feel like I'm back," she said.

Coming down the stretch, she had instigated a bumping incident with PattiSue Plumer.[1] Plumer was not pleased and would remember.

Slaney's optimistic declaration that she was back was a familiar refrain that had seldom proved to be accurate, but perhaps she was right this time. With Mary, you never knew.

"Most people thought I'd never run again," she said with a smug smile.

Some saw her latest comeback as "an extra chapter in an already eventful fairy tale of fame and pain." Slaney later acknowledged that she "probably [had] run harder than I should have" in San Jose.[2]

It would cost her.

• • •

The Prefontaine Classic in Eugene, on June 21, was next for Plumer and Suzy Favor Hamilton. But whether Slaney would enter was still doubtful. Earlier in June she had pulled out of a meet at Randall's Island in New York with leg cramps.

Plumer said she hoped Mary would be in Eugene: "I think Mary is really good for us. She just adds so much to the race. When she enters a race, she raises the level of acceptability."[3]

But Slaney's right calf wasn't responding to treatment, and she pulled out of the meet.

Favor Hamilton edged a lunging Plumer at the tape to win the 1,500.

Time was marching on. And Mary Decker Slaney was treading water, both literally and figuratively.

• • •

Mary's balky calf injury failed to respond, but she remained ever optimistic, telling *USA Today* in late June that she would be racing in Oslo and London in July. "By then, I think I'll be running as fast as anyone in the world. It's a shame. Maybe it's a trade-off for next year," she said.[4] For Mary Decker Slaney, as for the Chicago Cubs, there was always next year.

. . .

In July she appeared at the hot and humid New York Games at Columbia University's Wien Stadium. She was clearly not healthy and finished fifth, beaten by a high school student, Maria Mutola.[5]

Another layoff and more missed meets followed.

When Slaney finally recovered, she went to Europe and Australia at the end of the 1991 season and ran well there. She won the Diet Coke Mile in Sydney in October and was looking forward to the 1992 season and the Barcelona Olympic Games.

She planned to be there.

. . .

"I'm not putting a lot of pressure on myself," she told Ray Didinger of the *Philadelphia Daily News*, in April 1992. "I'm going to train as well as I can and whatever happens, happens.

"I don't want to make this (Olympic year) like it's the end of the world. I've made that mistake before. I'm not going to make it again," she said.[6]

Slaney was now running fifty miles a week in preparation for the Olympic trials in New Orleans later in the season.

Even as she spoke about her plans, she was recovering from yet another injury. A minor nerve tear near her foot had slowed her progress. Yet she remained upbeat. "Those people who thought they saw the last of me (in 1988) will have a rude awakening," she predicted. "I don't give up easily."

Richard, who as usual was sitting in on the interview, added, "That's an understatement."

Asked about retirement, Mary said, "I've put so much into my career. I can't bear the thought of leaving things unfinished. Winning an Olympic medal is part of it. It's something I've wanted for a long time. "Besides, I really love the sport. Despite all I've been through, I still love it."[7]

. . .

Things had changed dramatically for Mary Decker Slaney in the years since she was the highest-earning and most-sought-after female runner.

No large entourage of sponsors was urging her to make appearances; she had no personal trainer, not even a private coach. She was sharing Dellinger with the University of Oregon track team.

She had a new shoe company, Brooks, the company that had signed Zola Budd when she was running barefoot, and an agent who now checked with Slaney once a week or so.

Reflecting on her recent disappointments, Mary said, "You think about all the 'what-ifs' and 'what might have beens' and you wind up going crazy. I've taken the attitude, 'Okay, that wasn't my time. Maybe this will be my time.'"[8]

. . .

After a disappointing start to the 1992 season, when she finished ninth at the New York Games in May, she appeared at the Prefontaine Classic in June on her home turf.

No one except Mary expected much.

She finished second to Annette Peters, a former University of Oregon runner and another of the new faces emerging in the sport. As usual, Slaney led most of the way. Peters caught and passed her in the final few yards.

"I'm happy that I raced," Slaney said later. "I think this will do me a lot of good for the trials. I just wish I had two more weeks."[9]

. . .

Mary Slaney could control many things, but time wasn't one of them. The trials for the 1992 games loomed straight ahead.

Olympic trials are unforgiving events. Runners know there are no second chances. It's a lot like the men's NCAA basketball tournament: the mantra is survive and advance.

Lose and you go home.

But basketball teams get their next chance only a year later. If you don't make the team at the Olympic trials, you face a four-year wait for your next opportunity. Four years for a runner in her thirties is a long, long time.

. . .

Mary faced the do-or-die 1992 trials with typical optimism despite her nagging injuries.

"My goal is to win the gold," she announced. "But I'm not obsessed with it. If you put too much emphasis on it, and it doesn't happen, then the disappointment is that much greater. If I could have one more year without injuries, I think I would get closer."[10]

There's that *if* word again.

. . .

Bill Dellinger knew his runner all too well.

"Mary has already proven that she is the best in the world, but she's never been able to do it at the Olympics. That's still gnawing at her," he said on the eve of the trials.

In her preliminary heat for the 3,000 meters, Slaney faced Patti-Sue Plumer. Still not 100 percent after her latest surgery, to repair a torn tendon only fourteen weeks earlier, Slaney finished a strong second to Plumer. Mary had opened a large lead early in the heat, then eased off when she was assured of advancing, and Plumer pulled ahead to win.

"I didn't see any point to racing PattiSue tonight," Slaney said. "Monday night [the final] is what counts."[11]

. . .

New Orleans is hot and muggy in the summer. The air was thick and heavy as the field lined up for the final on Monday. The top three finishers would form the team for Barcelona.

Mary Slaney, true to form, took the early lead and led by as much as ten meters early in the race. She faltered after about a mile, and the others moved ahead of her. She finished a poor sixth, a hundred meters behind Plumer.

Plumer, Shelly Steely, and Annette Peters made the Olympic team. Mary Slaney did not. "I probably went out too fast," she said.

"I wanted an 8:30 pace, but obviously I was not ready to carry it through. If I went out at a slower pace, I might have run a better race, but that's not me."

Old habits die hard.

She had one last chance to achieve her dream. The heats for the 1,500 meters were scheduled for Wednesday. "The key is to run the qualifying races as easy as I can," she said.[12]

That would be something seen in a Mary Slaney race as often as confirmed sightings of Sasquatch.

. . .

On the eve of the qualifying heats for the 1,500, Mick Elliott, a *Tampa Tribune* reporter who described Mary as "one of sports' most confounding figures," asked her what she would do if she failed to make the team and finished her career without an Olympic medal.

She repeated the question, staring hard at the reporter before replying, "I've still got a lot of years to work on it. It's not like this is it."

There's always 1996 and Atlanta, she seemed to be saying.

"For all she had accomplished on the track," the reporter noted, "Slaney remains viewed as a now 33-year-old adolescent who's always crying over spilled Olympic gold."

After her latest failure in the 3,000, she said, "I'm thinking of running the 10,000 in Atlanta."[13]

. . .

As her last chance to advance loomed, Mary Slaney told John Lopez of the *Houston Chronicle*, "I really never had a chance because of everything that has happened, injuries and other various problems. But I'd like an Olympic medal. I really would like that a lot."

Still haunting Slaney, Lopez said, was "the stare, which froze the world with its iron-eyed look of disgust, despair and rage [during the 1984 Olympics]. It just won't go away."[14]

Dreams die hard.

. . .

She won her heat and advanced to the final.

"I feel better. Really, I feel a lot better today," she said.

PattiSue Plumer and Alisa Hill won the other two heats.

Slaney revealed, "I had an infection over the last week. I think I am getting over it. I think it is finally out of my system."[15]

With Mary, it seemed, there was always something.

• • •

As the final lap of the 1,500-meter final began, Mary was in second place, and it looked like she would see her dreams realized.

With about 250 meters to go, she was still second. All she needed to do was hang on and finish no worse than third.

Then Regina Jacobs passed her and so did Suzy Favor Hamilton as she came flying off the final turn.

Mary Decker Slaney, fourth, failed to qualify.

"I wanted to go to Barcelona. I really did," she said. Her body had once more failed to follow her will.

"It's coming, it's just not coming fast enough. I just couldn't make the move," she explained. "With 200 meters to go, my legs felt tired and sluggish."[16]

"I tried, I really tried," she said as tears spilled down her cheeks.[17]

Plumer, Jacobs, and Favor Hamilton would be in Barcelona.

Decker would be heading to Europe to run, but not to Barcelona. Or would she?

• • •

The door to Barcelona had seemingly slammed shut on Mary Decker Slaney. But there was one tiny crack through which she might squeeze.

It all depended on PattiSue Plumer. She had qualified for both the 3,000 and 1,500 meters at the Olympics, and trying to double is a difficult proposition. If Plumer decided not to compete in both events, perhaps Slaney would be named to replace her in Barcelona.

It was a long shot.

• • •

Asked by reporters if she might consider dropping out of one of the events, Plumer, who was suffering from a persistent cold, said, "I'll have to see how I feel after I get home and recover from my cold."[18]

Someone asked Slaney about the slim chance she still might go to Barcelona, depending on Plumer's decision. She shot back, "I wouldn't count on it."[19]

. . .

PattiSue Plumer made her announcement on July 3. She would be doubling.

"Most of the controversy generated over my decision was on the basis of a comment Mary made: that I would never give up my spot because I disliked her," Plumer said. She was referring to Slaney's response when asked if she thought the spot would open for her.

She had replied peevishly that she doubted it, because, as she told an unidentified friend near the end of the trials, "I think PattiSue hates me."[20]

Plumer then confronted Slaney about her remark.

"She didn't deny it. I said, 'I want you to know I would never base a decision on that kind of a personal notion. If I ever gave up the spot, it would be because I had only great respect for you as an athlete and thought you could do a better job than me.'

"I think she thinks no one likes her," Plumer said.[21]

Plumer said that at first she could not believe Slaney had said such a thing. "I can't think of anything I've ever said or done to her," Plumer said. "We're not really friends, but we've always been nice to each other."[22]

Mary at thirty-three was watching her hopes and dreams evaporate as new faces took over the spotlight, and she was having more than a little difficulty accepting that.

"I thought her response, that bit about me always hating her, was incredibly tragic," Plumer said. "She's always been sort of a loner. I'm the only person (among the athletes) that even talks to her. Some people run better when they're really miserable, and I think the depth of her drive came from being this neurotic outsider that nobody really understood. She's almost like a child, in some respects. I just thought it was a really sad commentary on what makes up the personality behind Mary."[23]

Plumer, a practicing attorney, had missed her calling as a psychoanalyst and didn't know it.

When the U.S. runners went to Europe to prepare for the Barcelona games and run in a few meets to sharpen up, Slaney joined them. Plumer ran without receiving appearance money, whereas Slaney still commanded handsome fees and drew crowds.

Her European season was successful and, despite lingering calf and Achilles problems, she would end it in October in a mile race on the streets of Sydney.

TWENTY-FIVE. Seems Like Old Times

Coming off a great 1991 season and eagerly looking ahead to Barcelona, Zola Pieterse picked up in 1992 where she had left off.

She began her season in January by setting a course record of 33:30 for 10,000 meters in Bloemfontein and by breaking her own record from the year before. She was stronger and faster despite adding about ten pounds to her frame.

Her winning way continued through February and March at distances from 800 meters to 3,000. She didn't taste defeat until April 10 when Elana Meyer edged her in both the 1,500 and 3,000 at the South African Championships in Bloemfontein and again in Dakar, Senegal, a week later at the African United Games, which marked the first international appearance of South African athletes in thirty-two years.[1]

Pieterse was now the second-best runner in South Africa but still the most popular by far.

Zola ran through the rest of April and May without a loss and finished May with an Olympic qualifying mark for the 3,000 of 8:53.15 in Durban on the twenty-fifth.

The Olympics were in July.

Zola then moved to Europe to earn some appearance fees and get ready for Barcelona.

Before she left, disaster struck.

· · ·

The African tick is a tiny, barely visible insect. Smaller than a pinhead in its larval stage, the adult tick packs a fierce bacterial wallop when it succeeds in injecting its saliva into the host's bloodstream.

It carries a disease called African tick bite fever.

And Zola, although she didn't know it, had become one of its victims. "I was sick. I thought it was a bad case of the flu," but it kept getting worse, she said.[2]

Pieterse ran in three events at the end of June and early July, finishing fourth, sixth, and eighth. That's no way to prepare for the Olympic Games.

. . .

Then she made an appearance in Great Britain on July 10 that would have made her sick, even if she hadn't been.

The race was her first back on English soil and it was a dreadfully familiar experience. She was racing when antiapartheid demonstrators rushed onto the track, impeding her progress. She was forced off the track and out of the race. "It was the same nightmare all over again," she said.[3]

Would it never end?

Stunned by the renewal of a bad dream, on July 15 she finished sixteenth in Nice, France, in the final event before the games.

Still sick and not getting better, she returned home before going to Spain. In South Africa she was finally diagnosed with tick bite fever—its symptoms include a rash, a high fever, and a severe feeling of fatigue—and given strong antibiotics.

Nonetheless, she arrived in Barcelona with the rest of the South African team and prepared to run.

"I was sick, and I couldn't do anything about it," she recalled. "I had to run."[4]

She finished ninth in her heat, more than seven seconds slower than the time she had posted before getting bitten.

Her Olympics were over.

. . .

Disappointed, Zola returned to Bloemfontein and some much-needed rest and recuperation.

In a very small percentage of cases, African tick bite fever remains in the host's system in a dormant state after the initial disease has run its course. Then the disease flares back up at times with no warning.

Zola would find that she was in that unlucky percentage. As she said recently, when that little tick clamped its incisors down on her, "[It] ended my running career."[5]

. . .

But she still had races to run.

After not competing since Barcelona, she responded to a lucrative offer from a promoter in Australia to compete in a mile race over the streets of Sydney. Among the other entrants was a familiar face and name—Mary Decker Slaney.

. . .

Jana Wendt (pronounced *Yanna Vent*) was the most popular television personality in Australia in the 1980s and 1990s as host of the highly popular newsmagazine show *Current Affair*.

Wendt, an attractive native of Hungary, managed to persuade Mary Decker Slaney and Zola Budd Pieterse to appear on her show before the Diet Pepsi Invitational Mile. Wendt sat in the middle at a long table, the two former adversaries at opposite ends, as far from one another as they could get, as Wendt posed her probing questions.

The differences between the runners were stark.

Slaney's hair was longer and darker than it had been eight years earlier, and her face seemed to be much sharper and more angular. She would respond to questions in a pointed and mildly heated manner, her voice rising to emphasize her point.

Same old Mary.

Pieterse also was sporting longer hair, as well as a few extra pounds, since 1984. As usual, she was noticeably uncomfortable in front of the cameras. She shrank into her seat, and her whispered responses were barely audible.

Same old Zola.

. . .

Not surprisingly, the highlights of the interview are the runners' responses to Wendt's questions about what happened in Los Angeles in 1984.

Slaney was emphatic in repeating her belief about what caused the incident that had become one of the most memorable moments of the Olympic Games.

Describing Mary as the golden girl of track and Zola as her arch-enemy, Wendt aired a clip of the fall. It included the soundtrack from the BBC telecast.

Then she aired a brief clip of the press conference from 1984 that showed Mary saying, "I don't think there's any question that she was in the wrong. And I do hold her responsible for what happened," then dissolving in tears.

Wendt began by telling the runners she would like to "take you down a time tunnel you're reluctant to go down" and asked Slaney how she regarded the incident eight years later.

"I look at it as history of the Olympics," she replied. "It was blown all out of proportion for two reasons. One: I was the favorite in the race, and two: it was in Los Angeles."

Wendt asked Zola about her memories of what happened. Pieterse said, "The most vivid memory I have of the Olympics in 1984 is when the crowd started booing." Then Zola laughed.

Did that frighten you? Wendt asked. "Yes," Zola replied.

Then Wendt asked, "When you were up against the crowd booing, how were you feeling?"

Zola laughed and said, "It's bad."

"It was hard to take," she added. "It's hard to distinguish between the incident and yourself."

Turning to Slaney, Wendt asked her the question everyone was waiting for: "Do you still hold her responsible?"

"If you look at the footage you'll see that she slowed down," Slaney replied. "If you look at the footage, you can tell someone is at fault. I don't hold her responsible that I didn't win a medal. I hold myself responsible in the fact that I ran the race the way I did. I put myself in that position."

Wendt wasn't giving up.

"You did say that you held her responsible, that she was in the wrong. When Olympic officials ruled that Zola was not, did you revise your—"

"No, no, no," Decker Slaney said, interrupting, sitting up straight, and leaning toward Wendt with her voice rising. "At first the Olympic official who was on the track right there put up the red flag. That decision was overturned with that official not present at the meeting. It was a political decision." She made the last comment while nodding her head and opening her eyes wide.

Wendt followed up: "Are you still convinced it was a political decision?"

Slaney: "Absolutely. The official that was on the track at that spot is not allowed to be heard?" As she replied she raised her eyebrows and arched her head questioningly

Wendt followed up by asking, "Then to this day you feel you were wrongly done by?"

"Yes, that race should have been run over. But, even if it had been, I couldn't [have] run because I had been injured. I hurt my hip when I fell," Slaney said.

Wendt then turned to Pieterse, asking, "Do you accept responsibility? Do you accept that you were in the wrong?"

Zola, her cheek resting on her left hand, her eyes downcast at the table, replied, "I don't like to talk about the actual details about what happened. There's been a lot written and said about it, Mary has blamed me and whatever. It's just something that happened."

Wendt then observed, "It's interesting from an observer's point of view that after eight years she still holds you responsible."

Zola smiled. "Yes," she said. "It is interesting." Her smile widened.

"What do you think of it?" asked Wendt.

"Oh, it's just something in the past," Zola said.

Asked how they felt about each other now, both women acknowledged that they didn't really know each other.[6]

. . .

The Diet Coke Invitational Mile was run on George Street, a main thoroughfare in downtown Sydney, on October 16. A crowd estimated to be in excess of 250,000 lined the route.

Mary easily bested a field of fourteen. Zola finished second, about 10 seconds behind.

. . .

Zola returned to Bloemfontein and ran three more times in 1992.

She won at 15K, 10K, and 4K, all on the road. In the last, she broke her own course record. She was feeling better.

· · ·

Mary returned home shortly after the Sydney win.

Atlanta and her next chance for an Olympic medal were four years in the future, a long time for a runner in her thirties. But Slaney's quest remained firmly fixed in her mind.

She would be thirty-seven when the games came to Atlanta in 1996.

She would be there. Of that she had no doubt.

TWENTY-SIX. Trials and Tribulations

Zola opened her 1993 season in January the way she had finished 1992: with a win in a cross-country meet.

She had a new sponsor in Saucony and had finished her education in computer programming at the Orange Free State Technicon Institute.

She followed her initial win with another, this time in a 2,000-meter race in Boksburg.

Nine days later she lost for the first time to the improving Elana Meyer in a 3,000-meter race in Stellenbosch. Two more wins followed, and Pieterse headed for Spain, where the IAAF World Cross-Country Championships would be contested. The two-time champion finished a strong fourth in her first appearance at the event since 1986.

Back home she raced and won in mid-April, but then on the twenty-third had to pull out of a race in Belleville with six hundred meters to go. She'd been ill and her stamina gave out. She recovered quickly and was back on the track ten days later, finishing second to Meyer in Port Elizabeth, in a 3,000-meter race there.[1]

The Mobil Grand Prix series event in Rome, the Golden Gala as it was called, was held on June 9 and attracted a strong field of international runners. Zola finished eleventh in the final, which was won by Yelena Romanova of Russia.

Three straight wins in South Africa followed. Then she returned, not without some trepidation, to Great Britain. There Pieterse competed in two longer road races without incident and finished third in both. Her season concluded with a trip to France, where she won her final race of the year, a cross-country event in Leffrinckoucke.

In all she raced seventeen times in 1993, despite bouts of fatigue caused by the lingering effects of the tick bite. "It prevented me from training too hard," she said. "When I do, my system is susceptible to the effects of the disease, and it flares up and I have to stop."[2]

It was a lighter schedule than she had undertaken the previous season, and it had included more longer-distance tests, but in all it was a successful season for her.

· · ·

The same can't be said for Mary Decker Slaney.

As usual, she began the year full of optimism, bravado, and lofty goals. And, as usual, the inevitable announcements of appearances were followed by the equally predictable announcements calling off those appearances.

In March 1993, she actually made it to the meet in Carlsbad, California, for the Carlsbad 5K.

While warming up she twisted her foot and pulled out.[3] The injury presaged another injury-riddled year punctuated by yet another surgery.

In May she had surgery on her left heel, causing her to cancel her appearance at the USA Outdoor Track and Field Championships in Eugene. The surgeon removed 75 percent of her heel bone to alleviate the irritation to her oft-injured Achilles tendon.

She recovered slowly from the procedure, which was but the latest in a list of operations so numerous she could not remember just how many she'd had.

This one was memorable because, as she said, "Unlike my other surgeries, which were muscle and soft tissue, this took a long time for recovery. I couldn't believe how painful it was."

In September 1993 she went back into training with Alberto Salazar, the distance runner who was now her primary coach.[4]

· · ·

That same month Slaney weighed in on the remarkable and highly questionable results being posted by runners from China.

When the Berlin Wall fell in 1989, so did the state-run doping program that East Germany had conducted for years.

China has had a wall for centuries, and behind it something strange was going on. Chinese runners were obliterating records nearly every time they stepped on a track. One had just set four new world records in less than a week.

"If they ratify these records, it will set women's middle-distance running back 25 years," Slaney said.

The runner Wang Junxia had just broken her own record by more than six seconds for 3,000 meters in a race in China. Her new mark was sixteen seconds faster than the old record, held by the Russian Tatyana Kazankina, who was running on something other than Gatorade when she set that mark.

Wang came back a few days later to break a seven-year-old record in the 10,000 meters, the oldest record in women's track, set thirteen years before.

In short, Wang had run under the world records four times in three events in the space of just six days.[5]

Whatever was going on behind that venerable wall didn't smell quite right.

PattiSue Plumer also caught a whiff of the spectacular performances. "I would love to jump up and down and say, 'Fabulous!' but to smash those records by that much, it needs investigation," said the current U.S. record holder in the 3,000 meters.

Another U.S. runner, Lynn Jennings, a three-time IAAF World Cross-Country Champion and Olympic bronze medalist, said she was "pretty bummed" about the news.

The IAAF announced it would review the records when China sent them in to be certified. Given the organization's reputation, that didn't give anyone a great deal of confidence.

Certification required the submission of urine samples provided by the athlete immediately after setting the record.

Yeah, right. That was gonna happen.

"I believe they are doing something chemically and that the results are not legal," Slaney said.[6]

The Chinese had hardly been a factor in international track before winning three titles at the world championships a month before.

A few people believed the astonishing results the Chinese were posting could be legitimate. Tom Sturak, an agent for runners, said, "I think the Chinese, like the Kenyans, are succeeding for cultural reasons." If he was right, that was some cultural revolution.

Chinese officials defended their runners. Ma Junren, the Chinese coach, said that his runners were not using anything magical. The only magic, he said, was an herbal medicine mixed with worms. He said the results were obtained from intense workouts and studies of the locomotion of ostriches and deer.[7]

Another Chinese official credited ingestion of a rare fungus found growing high in the Himalayas, where it is used as a food source for yaks.

Ever see a fast yak?

. . .

"If these suspicions aren't cleared up, it's a big problem for the IAAF and the IOC," said Ollan Cassell, the executive director of USA Track and Field (formerly known as the Athletics Congress, or TAC).

The ever-vigilant International Olympic Committee, concerned as always—not about drug usage but its own credibility—said through Arne Ljungqvist, a member of its Medical Commission, "There is no evidence whatsoever for these claims" of illegal substance use.

"It is mere defamation," he declared. "It's totally unfair to spread rumors of this type without any sort of evidence. It's a tragedy that any unexpected achievement is considered suspicious. It's a threat to sport when this comes up."[8]

What he really meant was that it was a threat to the IOC, but of course everyone knew that.

. . .

By November Mary Decker Slaney had returned to competition, winning a 10K race in Phoenix and setting a new course mark in the process.[9]

On Thanksgiving Day, she and Salazar ran in Manchester, New Hampshire. Before the race, Salazar predicted Slaney would "run very well. We did a 4-mile time trial at a 5:07 pace a few weeks ago. That pace will probably win the race."

"I don't feel a lot of pressure in road races," she said. "It's just like training—except with people."

Her training methods under Salazar had changed dramatically. He had forced her to run behind him in training sessions. "I can control her better that way," he said. Mary concurred, saying, "I've always been intense in my training. I'm taking more easy days, and my easy days are a lot easier."

She also was back in Nike running shoes again, and she felt they were helping prevent wear and tear to her Achilles.[10]

Salazar's prediction was accurate: Slaney easily won the race.

She next ran in Hartford, Connecticut, and won again.

Her last race of the season was the Runner's World Midnight Run in New York on New Year's Eve. Before the race Salazar predicted, "Mary will shock the world in 1994." She laughed when she heard what he had said. "Too many times everything has backfired," she said. "I'm taking things one week at a time."

She now was wearing orthotics in her Nikes to alleviate stress, and they seemed to be helping.

Salazar was convinced her natural speed plus strength-oriented training would keep her sound and produce new personal bests for his thirty-five-year-old runner. He had her doing only two tough weekly workouts—and he was controlling their intensity. "I'm getting used to running behind someone," Slaney said. "It's helping me in races."[11]

The day before the race Slaney told John Hanc of *Newsday* that she was feeling pretty confident. After what she called "five frustrating seasons," in which she had "undergone Achilles tendon surgery, plantar fascia surgery, bone surgery and you name it, I decided this year to start from ground zero," she said.

"I have thoughts about doing the 5K in Atlanta. And also making serious attempts at the 10K," she said, referring to the 1996 Olympics, which were always on her mind.[12]

Atlanta was now just two short years away.

. . .

If 1994 was any indication, Mary Slaney's hopes for Atlanta were going to be dashed.

She began the season with a surprise appearance in Salem, Oregon, in the Governor's Trophy Run on January 9. She ran the 10K race in 33:19, earning an easy victory. She told reporters she was in training for Atlanta in 1996.

Soon the all too familiar pattern of injury and recovery replaced races.

• • •

In February the Chinese runner Wang Junxia arrived in New York to accept the Jesse Owens Award, the highest honor given by USA Track and Field, which had once bestowed it on Slaney.

Wang's appearance didn't sit well with everyone. "There's definitely something crazy going on here," said Bob Sevene of the Boston Athletic Association. "It kind of points out there's a huge problem in this sport."

When told that the Chinese credited herbs and worms for their success, Sevene said, "I'll put it flat out: NO! It does not make sense to anything I know about running."

Sevene added, "Mary Decker Slaney is the greatest physical talent I've ever had the pleasure to watch, and [the Chinese are] on a whole new level." He had coached both Joan Benoit Samuelson and Judi St. Hilaire and knew what elite women runners were capable of doing. "They've (the Chinese) put up times that are unbelievable," he said.

Ma Junren and Wang met the press and faced reporters' questions. Wang said she trained twenty-nine miles a day at an altitude of 7,300 feet, seven days a week, ten to eleven months a year.

And she said that eating worms was okay with her, adding that she wanted "to run like a deer."

No mention was made of yaks.

A Chinese official added forcefully that the IAAF had found no evidence of drug usage in the tests it had performed on Chinese runners in 1992 and 1993.[13]

Big surprise there.

• • •

Mary Slaney underwent surgery in May and by September was back under the knife for yet another repair to her Achilles tendon, her 1994 season over.

She was still recuperating in October when she was informed she had been selected for induction into the Orange County Hall of Fame.

A reporter visiting her for a profile in *People* magazine said that an ultrasound photo of Mary's lower extremities would "discourage most people from even a casual jog."

Not Mary. She was predicting a return to racing in the late fall.

The reporter, Susan Reed, interviewed Salazar, who said he was limiting Slaney to just fifty miles a week, with some of that on a treadmill to reduce the stress on her legs.

"Mary's headstrong and stubborn," Alberto observed. "Athletes at her level tend to push themselves to the brink." When they fail, he told Reed, it's "because they trained too hard."[14]

. . .

Mary was not disappointed that she had lost most of another season. She said that she had enjoyed spending the summer with Ashley and that had "taken her mind off things."

But one thing was still very much on her mind. In 1996 the Olympic Games would be held in Atlanta, marking their first return to U.S. soil since 1984.

Slaney's friend Cathie Twomey Bellamy, an All-American runner at the University of Minnesota, said, "Mary's more focused on what she wants than ever."

What Mary wanted was an Olympic gold medal. "I dream about being healthy," she said. "That's all I need to be."[15]

. . .

In December she was still recovering but was back to jogging again when she was inducted into the Orange County Hall of Fame.

Slaney told Robyn Norwood, a reporter for the *Los Angeles Times*, that she had her sights set on the Atlanta Olympics.

Recalling the glory days of her spectacular 1983 campaign, Slaney declared, "Everything I've done has been done drug free."[16]

. . .

More injuries, surgery, a kidney infection, and rehabilitation marked 1995 as another lost year. But she wasn't through yet. The Olympics would return to the United States in 1996, and Mary Decker Slaney planned to be there.

With Alberto Salazar directing her training program, she began the Olympic year full of optimism and dedicated to making the U.S. team for the Atlanta games in July.

She and Alberto began the season in Florida, where she finished second to the Danish marathoner Gitte Karlshoj in the Citrus Classic, a 10K road race in Winter Park. Mary had led from the start; Karlshoj passed her with a mile to go. "I wanted to run comfortably," Slaney said. "I didn't want to go out really fast and feel like I'm dying. I think for where I am in my training, it was a decent race."[17]

A week later she was in Atlanta for the opening of a USA Track and Field exhibit, "Images of Excellence." "There are no more aches and pains. I feel solid. I feel healthy," Mary told reporters, adding, "The Olympics are here, and I want my chance."

After recounting her numerous ailments since 1992, Slaney said, "Now I'm sticking to a program, and I hope to be ready when it counts. I don't want to be impulsive."[18]

. . .

Slaney had come out of her first race still healthy, with the runner herself noting, "Nobody expects me to run this year, no less do well. I think people are surprised I'm still running."[19]

A month later, back in Eugene, she ran in the April 13 Twilight Invitational, the field for which included Vicki Huber, also on the comeback trail, and Suzy Favor Hamilton.

Slaney continued to exhibit the merits of Salazar's program. In the 5,000-meter race, on a breezy day, she blew past runners as much as twenty years her junior. With 3,500 mostly hometown fans cheering her on, she pulled away from the field and won easily. But her time of 15:38.61 was well within what she needed to get into the U.S. Olympic Trials in June.

"I like doing this hometown stuff," a relieved Slaney said.

She had surmounted the first hurdle in her comeback attempt.[20]

. . .

Now that she was eligible for the trials in the 5,000, she wanted to qualify in the 1,500 as well. A month later, in Eugene on May 11, Huber outkicked Slaney in the stretch, but both runners were well within the Olympic trials qualifying time for the 1,500.[21]

. . .

Slaney gave a lengthy interview to the *Orange County Register*, in which she said, "I have a point to prove. I want to prove that I'm not done at 37. That I can still be as good as I want to be."

Slaney acknowledged that at her lowest point, in 1994, she was crying, not sleeping, and slipping into deep depression. "I honestly thought I was not going to be able to walk normally again, let alone run," she recalled.[22]

Salazar's methods had transformed someone who was almost completely disabled into a woman who was now qualified for two events at the Olympic trials.

. . .

The Mobil Grand Prix series, a tune-up for the Olympic trials, attracted a strong field to Eugene's Hayward Field on May 26, a cold windy day.

Mary Decker Slaney finished fifth in the 3,000-meter race, behind a strong field led by Sonia O'Sullivan, who posted a world's best time of 8:39.33 for the year in front of fifteen thousand fans.

Slaney had run conservatively in less than ideal conditions and emerged from the race relatively healthy except for a kidney infection from which she was recovering.[23]

Much to Salazar's displeasure, she went out and ran a hard 3,000 the very next day.

Old habits die hard.

"She wanted to prove to herself that she could still do what she had done before," Alberto said of his runner's unsupervised workout.[24]

. . .

The Olympic trials began on Friday, June 14, in the stadium that would host the games in Atlanta.

Mary Decker Slaney won her heat for the 5,000 meters on opening night, advancing to the final with a chance to make her third Olympic team. "I was very, very comfortable and I'm starting to feel like I used to," she said.

Mary admitted to having experienced some butterflies at the starting line. "If you're not nervous for an event like this, you must be crazy," she said.[25]

. . .

On Monday Slaney finished second in the final of the 5,000 meters. She had made the Olympic team.

It almost didn't happen.

Coming into the last two laps, she was in fifth place. Only the top three finishers would make the team.

She began to move up with eight hundred meters to go. As she did so, her feet became momentarily tangled with those of another runner, Amy Rudolph. Slaney stumbled slightly toward the infield in a way that was eerily similar to what had happened in 1984. This time she recovered her balance and managed to catch the leaders. Lynn Jennings won, with Slaney right behind her.

The two women hugged after the race, definitely reflecting a new Mary. And the woman who almost always looks like she just had her parking spot stolen beamed as she blew kisses to the crowd.[26]

"I'm ecstatic," she said after the race. "It's one of those things you wanted to do and sort of expected to do, but I didn't know if it was possible, I had doubts. Now I feel as if I'm starting over again."[27]

The crowd of twelve thousand had cheered heartily for her in the stretch. Few knew her as anyone other than the runner who had fallen in 1984.

But she still held three U.S. records—in the 800 meters, mile, and 3,000 meters—that she had set in a twenty-two-day period during the glory days of 1985.

In fact, of the eight records she had set that year, only three had been broken by 1996.[28]

. . .

After the race, Slaney, like all the qualifiers, went directly to the drug-testing facility under the stadium to provide a urine sample. Her sample was coded, labeled, and processed along with the others.

. . .

The testing and then the press conference kept her up until 2:30 a.m. The heats for the 1,500 meters were that evening.

"I'm not counting myself out," Decker Slaney declared.

Having already gotten his charge into the games, Salazar was equally optimistic, saying, "Mary can win the 1,500 at the trials."

Reporters who had regarded Slaney as washed up after 1992 were now describing her latest incarnation as "a story for the ages."[29]

. . .

Slaney breezed through her heat for the 1,500, beating Ruth Wysocki, who was making her own comeback.

They had a day off before the semifinals for the 1,500.

Slaney finished eighth in her heat and was eliminated. But she managed to put a positive spin on it. "I think I have had a good effort here," she said. "My priority had been to run the 5,000 and make the team, and I did both."[30]

It was, some would say, nothing short of miraculous.

On the day that the IOC would extinguish the Olympic flame in Atlanta, Mary Decker Slaney would celebrate her thirty-eighth birthday—as an Olympian.

. . .

Mary arrived late at the games, avoiding the opening ceremonies on July 19.

Since the trials, she had been training every day with five or six younger male runners to prepare for the race.

At the press conference, she told reporters, "My goal is to qualify for the finals on Friday and then just go out and run a personal best after that."

Slaney also said her training with men in a pack had helped her prepare and to avoid any repeat of 1984. She added she had been using protein supplements recommended by Salazar and was at her physical peak.[31]

Since the beginning of the year, she had trained diligently with

Salazar, doing what few had thought possible: qualifying for the Olympics. Her oft-stated goal to win an Olympic medal was within reach.

On Friday, July 26, she wilted badly in the qualifying heats, finishing seventh in her heat and twenty-first of the forty-six runners entered, and was eliminated. She had dropped to tenth midway through her heat and never was a factor. "I thought I would feel better and could pick it up on that last mile but I just didn't have it. The lead pack got away from me," she told reporters. "Sure, I'm disappointed because I wanted to be in the finals. But I have to be happy I'm just running again."

She simply was not fast enough to grab the prize she had lusted after for as long as she could remember. But that didn't mean she was ready to hang up her cleats. "By no means does this mean I'm finished. I'm just starting to make the transition from a middle distance to a distance runner," she declared, adding, "I can see trying for another Olympics."[32]

Steve Bisheff, who had covered Mary for years at the *Orange County Register*, said of her still-unfulfilled quest, "Nobody, absolutely nobody, ever chased it harder or any longer" than Mary.

That, Bisheff wrote, would be her legacy.[33]

Maybe.

Maybe not.

. . .

After the Olympics, Mary Decker Slaney ran some road races and wrapped up the season in Honolulu in the Waikiki Mile, sponsored by Nike.

Sonia O'Sullivan, the Irish middle-distance runner whose star had eclipsed Mary's, won the race. Mary finished a tenacious second. Both women broke the existing course record.

"I'd still like to beat her," the thirty-eight-year-old said of her much younger rival. "Health permitting, I still think I can run as well as I used to in all my events but the 800."[34]

The fire still burned.

. . .

For Mary Decker Slaney, 1997 would mark the beginning of her own personal purgatory.

The urine sample she had provided at the U.S. Olympic Trials had been found to have an impermissibly high level of testosterone. Slaney would be labeled a drug cheat by the IAAF and later by USA Track and Field, which had succeeded the Athletics Congress in 1992 as the governing body for the sport. It was not the kind of legacy Steve Bisheff had envisioned for her.

In May 1997 the *New York Times* broke the news of Mary Decker Slaney's failed drug test at the 1996 U.S. Olympic Trials eleven months earlier.[35]

Papers around the country quickly picked up the story, and subsequent stories reported that she and her attorney had suspicions about the leak behind the *Times*'s story. Her lawyers alleged that the leaker was someone who held a grudge against his client. Slaney and her lawyers also were critical of the nearly yearlong investigation.[36]

The test she had failed measured the ratio of testosterone to epitestosterone, a natural isomer of testosterone. Both substances occur naturally in men and women, and their normal ratio is 1:1. The test allowed for fluctuations that might be seen in athletes in training, and the U.S. Olympic Committee had established 6:1 as the highest acceptable ratio. Anything higher would indicate that testosterone, in natural or synthetic form, had been introduced into an athlete's system. Drug tests at the time could not detect testosterone that had been introduced into the body; the tests could detect only a ratio too high to be the result of natural fluctuations.

The University of California at Los Angeles laboratory conducted the test and found Mary Decker Slaney's ratio to be 9.5:1 in one sample and 11.6:1 in the other. Her previous tests had shown her ratios to have been 3.1:1 or lower. The infamous East German women swimmers, whose government had supervised the drugging of athletes, were found to have testosterone ratios of 8:1, 10:1, and 12.5:1. Slaney's level was as high, or higher, than the levels of some of the East German women swimmers.[37]

The UCLA lab reported the results to the USOC and the IAAF; the IAAF then investigated whether Slaney should be found in violation of the rules and, in February 1997, determined that her "specimen [was] positive for the prohibited substance testosterone."[38] Both USA Track and Field and the IAAF suspended her from competition, and USA Track and Field ordered an investigation.

It did not look good.

Mary, her husband, and her attorneys, the husband-and-wife team of James and Doriane Coleman of North Carolina, were quick to answer the allegations. "There is an investigation to determine if there is a doping charge," said James Coleman, who noted that his client had taken and passed three subsequent urine tests. "We're very upset about it," said Coleman, a professor at Duke University Law School.

Richard Slaney was incensed. "Someone has smeared her name deliberately," he charged. "Nobody should be treated like this." He alleged that someone within the USATF had leaked the information and swore he and his wife would pursue legal action.[39]

In the opinion of Dr. Linn Goldberg, a physician at Oregon Health Sciences University, "Testosterone can do a lot to improve a woman's performance. An athlete intent on cheating could use testosterone as an anabolic steroid to increase her muscle mass, improve the speed of her muscle contractions and hasten recovery from hard workouts. With the right cycle, the athlete could use the substance without being caught."[40]

Doriane Coleman, a former Ivy League track star, thought the source of the leak was the five-member board of former athletes and coaches that oversaw drug cases for USATF and was known as the Custodial Board. Its members were Larry Ellis, the Princeton track coach who had been the U.S. men's coach for the 1984 Olympics; Alice Jackson, a top quarter-miler in the 1980s; Larry James, a runner who won gold and silver at the 1968 Olympics; Chad Bennion, a top-ten U.S. marathoner in 1992; and PattiSue Plumer.[41]

• • •

Under the rules of both the IAAF and USOC, USA Track and Field had to hold a hearing on whether Mary Decker Slaney had committed a doping offense. But the organization had not yet scheduled one.

Richard Slaney was not pleased.

"This is preposterous," he said. "We've provided them (IAAF and USATF) with proof that there was no drug taking. This is a lot of malicious crap that's just doing a lot of harm. It's ridiculous. This should have been dismissed nine months ago."

The IAAF was also unhappy with the delay. On May 31, 1997, just before the national track and field championships in Indianapolis, the IAAF suspended her pending the results of the hearing.

"If the Federation [apparently a reference to USATF] is reluctant to act immediately in accordance with IAAF rules, then the IAAF council will now suspend the athlete from competition until the national federation decides a ban or not," IAAF president Primo Nebiolo said.[42]

The IAAF decision was not based on guilt but on the delay by U.S. officials. The IAAF also invoked its "contamination rule, whereby anyone who competed with a suspended athlete (in this instance Slaney) would themselves be suspended." The Custodial Board waited ten days, then suspended her "pending a hearing before the USATF Doping Hearing Board."[43]

• • •

The public first statement from Mary Decker Slaney herself declared, "This is an attack on my integrity. It is an attack on everything that I believe to be good for the sport."[44]

Her comment to the *Eugene Register-Guard* was consistent with her stated opinions about drug use and dopers in track. She had repeatedly decried the practice while emphasizing that she had competed clean against those who were obviously not. She had not wavered in her feelings about drugs and drug use to enhance performance.

The facts of her positive drug test results would seem to say that something was amiss.

The possibilities were endless.

They would be explored and examined in detail in the months and years that it would take to decide her case. It would also put Slaney on the sidelines for a long time while the process wound its way through the IAAF bureaucracy and then the U.S. federal court system.

Not a place she wanted to be.

Now her main competitive appearances would be largely limited to hearing rooms and courtrooms, not tracks or roads.

• • •

Jim Coleman was quick to respond to the news that his client had been suspended by the USATF. "They have completely disregarded

Mary's rights and treated her in a way that is disgusting," her lawyer said.[45]

Mary asked the doping board to promptly schedule a hearing on her appeal of her suspension. She was facing a ban of as long as four years and the possibility of being stripped of all her placings since the 1996 tests.

Salazar, the coach who had supervised Slaney's training and the dietary supplements he'd added to her regimen, was also upset. "Mary has been pushed into a corner. She's fighting for her life. Now, unless she goes to court, she's going to have been seen as having used drugs," he observed. "Because of their stupid rules—their inflexible rules—they've put themselves in this position. And Mary is going to win in the end."[46]

Richard Slaney continued to be a vocal critic of the accuracy of the test itself and the actions taken by the IAAF and USATF. "That's the greatest runner this country has ever had, and this is how they [the USATF] reward her for 25-26 years of service," he said.

Many had criticized the test Mary Slaney had failed as not accounting for the normal hormonal changes that women experience. Mary Slaney would claim that her results were skewed because she had changed birth control pills and had begun menstruating during the testing.[47]

However, her ratio of testosterone to epitestosterone, as measured by regular testing through the years, never had exceeded 3.1:1 previously.

The IAAF was, in fact, cognizant of the problems with the test and was in the process of investigating other test options. But at the moment, the established ratio of 6:1 was in force.

Slaney had exceeded that ratio, and she would base her defense on the questions about the efficacy of the test.

Slaney's ban by the IAAF and suspension by USATF cast an ominous shadow over her career accomplishments. Over the next four years, the shadow would only darken.

• • •

Decker Slaney was scheduled to appear before the doping board of USA Track and Field in September to plead her case for reinstatement.

Like most national organizations that were under the umbrella of the IAAF, USA Track and Field did not hold the sport's international governing body in high regard. (Many also did not hold the USATF in high regard, convinced that it had spent years covering up for drug cheats among U.S. track athletes.)

USA Track and Field regarded the international organization as being much more concerned with its own financial welfare than it was about actually ferreting out those who were cheating.

The IAAF reflected the philosophy of the IOC's former head, Juan Antonio Samaranch, who believed the discovery of dopers would be bad for business and wasn't interested in learning that athletes had failed drug tests at the Olympic Games. The IAAF had adopted a similar attitude at its version of the Olympics, the track and field world championships. The number of competitors found to be using drugs was miniscule.

Perhaps Slaney's own criticism of the IAAF and its lackadaisical approach to ferreting out drug cheats helped land her in the predicament in which she now found herself. Finding her guilty of doping would be a win-win for the IAAF—it would shut up a high-profile critic and burnish the organization's bona fides as a drug cop.

• • •

On September 16, 1997, at a hearing in Chicago, USA Track and Field's doping board, well aware of the threatened litigation, and facing an array of experts assembled by Mary Decker Slaney and Nike, cleared her unanimously.

She had attended the hearing with two attorneys, a pharmacologist, a statistician, and an endocrinologist, all paid for by Nike. While Mary and Richard were celebrating having the ban overruled and crowing about Mary's exoneration, others in attendance were not so sanguine about the decision.

In the audience at the hearing was Dr. Don Catlin, America's foremost authority on drug testing.

The arguments put forth by Mary's team of supporters, insisting that the test results were invalid due to a change in birth control pills, and/or her menstrual cycle, did nothing to sway Catlin's faith in the test results.

Dr. Catlin had another reason for Mary's "victory."

"They lied," he said.[48]

The ruling should have made her happy.

Not so.

A week after she was cleared by the USATF panel, Mary Slaney made her first public comments, which amounted to an ultimatum to the organization: change its drug-testing procedures within the month and compensate her for her lost season or she would file suit. Richard Slaney said they would be seeking six figures.

After a month, Mary Slaney said, "If I have to, I'll go into litigation and I'll take no prisoners." She also wanted the telephone records of the custodial panel members so she could determine who had leaked the test information to the *New York Times*. She said the leaker "should be absolutely banned from the sport. That's what they tried to do to me." She added that she believed the leak "was done vindictively. Why would someone do it? The word that comes to mind is jealousy."[49]

Who could she be targeting?

Mary Slaney went on to tell reporters that "this is the most horrible experience I've ever been through. It's far more difficult than what happened in '84," she said, referring to her tangle with Zola Budd.[50]

• • •

Mary Slaney had not competed since the Penn Relays in April 1997. Her focus now was on challenging the test results, changing the testing methods, and being reinstated by the IAAF. It would consume her for the next four years.

Throughout, and in fact to this day, she refers to the decision by the doping board as her exoneration.

The jury, in the form of the IAAF, however, was still out. But by the end of September 1997, the federation, unhappy with the USATF's decision, had decided to seek arbitration. IAAF rules required that all disputes about testing procedures and eligibility that might arise between the IAAF and its members, in this case the USATF, be submitted to an arbitration panel.[51]

• • •

In January 1998, Mary Slaney pulled out of the Scott Mile in Santee, California, citing her ongoing battle with the IAAF.[52] She was still eligible to compete abroad pending her hearing but did not.

Then she pulled out of the Drake Relays in April with a hamstring pull.[53]

By May the runner, now just two months shy of her fortieth birthday, was having difficulty sleeping.

"If I think about all this, I have difficulty sleeping. A large part of it is because I'm an icon for the sport. A large part is because I'm an American. And a large part is because of my age. If I wasn't finished [as a competitor], they'd feel the need to do something immediately and replace the tests with something. It's like they'd rather die than admit they're wrong," she said. "Of course I'm concerned about my reputation. I have no idea how people will perceive me in history."

Mary Slaney would continue training but would forgo her lucrative stops in Europe that summer.

"Why go someplace where you're not wanted?" she asked.[54]

. . .

In May 1998, Slaney won a 5,000-meter race with what turned out to be the fastest time by any woman that year. She did so at the Prefontaine Classic in Eugene, and she was preparing to run in both the 1,500 and 3,000 meters at the USATF Championships in June in New Orleans.

She told reporters she was healthy, strong, and better prepared than a year earlier.

She had tried to put the IAAF out of her mind, saying, "It's laughable on one hand. But it's serious, because these people have tried to destroy everything I've done for 28 years."

"She has something to prove," Alberto Salazar said. "She wants to show these people that, not only did they not stop her, but they may have made her stronger. Made her hungrier."[55]

With the IAAF suspension hearing hanging over her head, Mary withdrew from the USATF Championships. She and her team of lawyers and experts were preparing for the IAAF hearing, to be held in Monte Carlo.

The hearing was scheduled, then postponed, and a new date was set for early January 1999—fifteen months since the IAAF announced it was taking her case to arbitration.

It is not the purpose of this book to detail the complicated and drawn-out legal process that ensued as Slaney sought relief from the U.S. federal court system in a suit she ultimately brought against the IAAF and the United States Olympic Committee.

The IAAF arbitration hearing that began at the end of January was adjourned, then reconvened several times. It was scheduled to resume on April 24, 1999.

By April 12, Slaney's legal team was out of patience and sued the IAAF and the USOC in federal court in Indianapolis.

Looking down their patrician noses from their swank headquarters in Monte Carlo, IAAF officials, through their spokesperson, sniffed imperiously, "The IAAF cannot be under the jurisdiction of a court in Indiana. IAAF rules are enforced in 209 countries and are the same for everyone. Sports rules must be enforced by the governing body of the particular sport." He promised a swift decision would be forthcoming.[56]

On April 26, 1999, the IAAF arbitration panel determined that Mary Decker Slaney had failed a drug test in 1996 at the U.S. Olympic Trials and stripped her of the silver medal she had won at the 1997 world championships.[57]

She was banned from competition for two years, retroactive to the time of the test.

One of the Colemans called the decision "legal fiction."[58]

But it was done.

The governing body of the sport Slaney had once ruled had found her to be a drug cheat.

The lasting legacy that only a few years earlier the writer Steve Bisheff had hoped would be hers now would be replaced by inclusion of her name on a long list of athletes whose accomplishments were regarded as suspect.

Not a list that Slaney wanted to be on.

Her legal team pursued her case through U.S. District Court to the U.S. Court of Appeals for the Seventh Circuit.

On March 27, 2001, nearly six years since she had submitted her urine for testing, the appellate court rejected each argument Slaney had made and upheld the district court's ruling that it had no jurisdiction in the matter.[59]

She appealed to the U.S. Supreme Court, which refused to hear the case.[60]

The results would stand.

Mary Decker Slaney, the best middle-distance runner the United States ever produced, would be forever seen by some with a scarlet *D* on her forehead.

The decision of the IAAF was controversial then and remains so today. Many agree with Slaney's argument that the test was flawed for certain women. Others believe, just as emphatically, that she had been caught doing what she had so often accused others of doing, confirming that she had been a fraud all along.

There are no easy answers in her case.

...

When, in recent years, honors have been bestowed on Mary Decker Slaney—as when she was admitted to the Millrose Games Hall of Fame and then to the University of Colorado Hall of Fame—the message boards of Internet sites were afire with indignant protests.

...

By the time her case had been fully adjudicated, by the sports federations and the U.S. courts, she was effectively through as a competitive runner, even though she was now eligible to run.

In 1999 she had surgery on both legs and her feet. The surgery was supposed to make her healthy, "help me enough to train . . . I was looking to train for marathons. Well, this surgery, it just destroyed what there was left.

"If I could get healthy, I would go out there and see how much an almost 51-year-old healthy body can do. But, I can't get healthy enough orthopedically," she told an interviewer in 2009.[61]

A reporter asked about her lost chances for Olympic gold, and in a reflective moment she replied, "I always felt like there would be another chance."[62]

But for Mary time had run out.

TWENTY-SEVEN. War and Peace

Zola Pieterse ran in South Africa and a few times abroad in 1994 on a much-reduced schedule once more.

In early 1995 she learned with joy that she was pregnant—"I had always wanted to have children," she said.[1]

Her daughter, Lisa, was born in October. Zola returned to training soon after, but now motherhood and the attendant demands on her time reduced her serious running appearances. Elana Meyer had replaced her as South Africa's best hope.

. . .

With little preparation and a flare-up of the tick bite fever, Zola Pieterse failed to make the South African squad for the 1996 Olympics. After she recovered, she ran some road races in the United States, managing a third-place finish in the Boilermaker, a 15K road race held in Utica, New York, and then a second to the Kenyan Catherine Ndereba, who set a course record in a 10K race in Danbury, Connecticut. In late July, Pieterse raced in the Bix 7, a road race in Cedar Rapids, Iowa.[2]

Before returning to South Africa and her eight-month-old daughter, she told reporters that she too would like another shot at the Olympics, perhaps in the marathon. She said she was hoping to run her first marathon in 1997, in New York or London.[3]

But life has a way of changing the best-laid plans. In 1997 she again became pregnant and gave birth to twins Michael and Avelle in April 1998. Now, with three children younger than two, Zola had her hands full, and her serious competitive days were "pretty much over after that," she said.

She still ran, because running is a part of her life and will always be. But it was no longer her main focus.

Still, when the next Olympic Games began in Sydney in 2000, she would be thirty-four, which is not considered old for a marathoner.[4]

. . .

While Mary Decker Slaney was spending the late 1990s in a protracted legal battle, Zola Budd Pieterse continued to run in South Africa and occasionally abroad.

Her schedule was limited by the time she felt she could afford to be away from her children and by the effects of the tick bite fever, which continued to reappear periodically, making serious training difficult, if not impossible, for weeks at a time.

As it turned out, she did not compete in her first marathon until 2003—in the London Marathon. She had old ghosts to lay to rest. "People here hated me and I never knew why," she told reporters upon arrival.[5]

In anticipation of her arrival, Ian Wooldridge, the *Daily Mail* sportswriter who had discovered her years earlier, had urged Londoners to "welcome her back. After all we put her through," she deserved it, Wooldridge wrote.[6]

The Londoners lining the route cheered her heartily, but fatigue forced her to drop out about nine miles from the finish.

· · ·

Zola's running appearances were largely confined to longer-distance road races and the occasional marathon whenever she was healthy enough to train properly for the strenuous event.

She appeared at several marathons in the United States, though her appearances grew less frequent through the years.

In 2005 she told reporters that she was content with her life even if it no longer included a lot of competitive running. "I have my children and my husband, whom I love dearly," she said.

Life for Zola Pieterse was good, but once more it was about to change.

· · ·

To men one of the great mysteries of life is women's intuition.

We do not understand how it works or how often it seems to be (annoyingly) accurate. Among the failings of male beings is our inability accurately to read a woman's moods and emotions. Women's intuition is nevertheless well known to us, and we fear and respect it, even if we don't understand it.

In 2006 Zola's intuition told her something was amiss in her marriage. Her hunch was not predicated on the usual clues of lipstick on the collar or carelessly discarded trousers with a pocket containing a matchbook with a strange name and phone number on it. But she knew something was going on. Her intuition told her so.

She hired a private detective, hoping all the while to be proved wrong. In short order the detective confirmed her worst fears. The realization was devastating.

When confronted with overwhelming evidence of infidelity, the automatic age-old defense for men is deny, deny, deny. We always see denial as our best defense. Philanderers do not regard as appealing the alternative to outright bald-faced prevarication: admitting guilt and begging for forgiveness. That places men in a distinctly inferior position for the rest of their life: the one who done her wrong. This is a decidedly uncomfortable position for men, not least because women's memories are notoriously long.

So, like any man with sense, Mike used the standard defense and denied, denied, denied. Of course, it didn't work. The evidence against him was overwhelming. He had maintained an apartment for the other woman and, given the hours he frequently chose to visit, they seemed to be engaging in something other than a friendly landlord-tenant chat. He'd also provided her with a car.

It was bad enough that just a year earlier Zola had declared herself to still be madly in love with her husband. But he had strayed with a woman who had the headline-friendly name of Pinkie, a twice-divorced former Mrs. South Africa who was blonde, younger, and very attractive.[7]

After Zola filed for divorce in April 2006, Pinkie's picture ran alongside lurid headlines in tabloids worldwide. That Zola had to endure such a public humiliation after all she had been through in her life was difficult for her to manage. "On a pain scale of 1–10, I'm at a nine," she said, describing her heartbreak.[8]

Then things got even uglier. Mike had ended the affair, and Zola believed that Pinkie was responsible for poisoning the family dog. Zola reported receiving threatening phone calls at two in the morning and hearing a woman say, "This is a fight to the death."

Zola, concerned for her children, sought a restraining order against the woman in July, which generated yet more headlines.

Zola described in court why she could not ignore Pinkie's "emotional instability"; Zola also said she feared for her life and the lives of her children.

Pinkie also threatened suicide, and police were called to negotiate with the disturbed woman. The gun she was threatening to use turned out to be one she had stolen, along with other items, from Mike's residence, when he had given her an eviction notice. Zola also expressed concern to the court about what other "rash actions" Pinkie might try.

The judge signed the restraining order and ordered Pinkie to undergo a psychiatric evaluation.[9]

Now Zola had to figure out what to do about Mike, who continued to plead his case for reconciliation, for the sake of the children, if nothing else.

Pinkie was long gone, engaged to another man within two or three months of the issuance of the restraining order.

. . .

By September Zola had relented, and she took Mike back.[10] Her decision had taken a lot of tears and a lot of prayers.

Among the constants in her life was that men let her down. She was still not used to it and never would be.

"I think God must be a woman," she said recently.[11] If she's right, that's something else that will mystify men.

. . .

Zola received an invitation to the IAAF's end-of-season gala in Monte Carlo in November 2006. She wasn't sure why she'd been invited but went anyway.

Lamine Diack, the IAAF president, invited her on stage at the Sporting d'Eté Club. She drew the loudest applause of the evening.

Diack, from Senegal, had refused to present her with her gold medal for her second World Cross-Country Championship in Switzerland in 1986. Now he personally welcomed her with open arms into the IAAF family.

"I had a lot of admiration for her as a runner because, even barefoot, she proved that Africans can win major competitions," he said. "I refused to present her with her medal because for a lot of years I was fighting apartheid and she was a symbol of it. Zola was a young girl and not responsible for what was happening, but we were not prepared to make any sort of compromise."

When called to the stage, Zola was visibly moved by the gesture and the warm applause from the black-tie crowd.

"I felt proud being called onto the stage, but there was more sorrow. In my career I missed out a lot in terms of medals but also emotionally because of what happened," she said, referring to her suspension and her hounding by the antiapartheid forces. "I am trying to train once a day every day. It's a bit like old times."[12]

• • •

In 2008 Mike and Zola built a home in an upscale development south of Myrtle Beach, South Carolina.

There the children would benefit from an education system that is better than South Africa's, and Mike, an avid golfer, would benefit from the plethora of courses in the area. The mild year-round climate also would be conducive to Zola's need to run on a daily basis.

"Running is cheaper than therapy" reads a bumper sticker on her car.

The Pieterses have permanent resident status in the United States and still return to South Africa a few times a year.

• • •

Zola still competes in masters' events and local road and cross-country events in the United States and in South Africa.

In 2011 she finished second in her age group in the 8K cross-country race at the World Masters Championships in Sacramento. "It was great. I probably started out a little too fast, but it was good, healthy competition and I really enjoyed it," she said.[13]

She has a new sponsor in Newton running shoes. The brand, headquartered in Boulder, Colorado, mimics barefoot running; she helps to promote it through personal appearances at several events a year.

In 2012, she competed in the Comrades Marathon, the most popular sporting event in South Africa. The Comrades is a fifty-four-mile ultramarathon, more than twice the distance of a marathon.[14]

She finished eleventh in her age group in a race that attracted fifteen thousand entries and a national television audience. In 2014, Zola finished sixth among women in the Comrades.

"I didn't have a very good race," she said of her effort in 2012.[15] That didn't matter to the thousands of spectators, black and white, who lined the route and cheered, "Run, Zola, run," urging her on. She finished in less than eight hours and received her medal for doing so.

Budd Pieterse won the Charleston, South Carolina, marathon in 2014 and continues, at fifty, to do amazingly well in half-marathons and marathons, both here and in South Africa.

On a windy, brutally cold day in Charleston, she was less than thirty minutes behind Ethan Coffey, the thirty-year-old who won the men's division, and she was sixteenth overall in a field of fifteen hundred runners.[16]

• • •

Zola Budd Pieterse remains the most respected and beloved woman athlete South Africa has ever produced. She is the object of attention and affection wherever she goes.

A street in Bloemfontein is named for her, and the small minivans that are used as taxis, and are a principal mode of transport in the predominantly black townships outside major cities, are called Zola Budds because they are small and fast.

Some call the larger conventional buses Mary Deckers, because they are bigger and have more accidents.

Thirty years and seven Olympics later, the two women are still linked.

They are likely to remain so.

Epilogue

In the quiet, cozy sunroom of her substantial home on fifty-five acres outside Eugene, Oregon, Mary Decker Slaney, now fifty-eight, pursues her favorite hobby, quilting. She is now blonde and a bit heavier than when she ran her last race. She grants few interviews and makes few public appearances.

She and Richard share their home with some dogs they raise and seem to be content with the solitude of their surroundings, paid for with her earnings from racing and endorsements. Their daughter, Ashley, has graduated from college and is pursuing a teaching career in Arizona.[1]

The woman whose career spanned more than twenty-five years and saw her transformation from little Mary Decker to Queen Mary, who ruled the world of women's middle-distance running, is long retired.

Except for an Olympic medal, she had accumulated all the honors, titles, and awards her sport could convey. But her career ended after she had earned the one title with which she will be forever tagged: drug cheat.

It isn't a title she relishes, and she vigorously rejects it as unfair and unwarranted, but it will remain attached to her forever. For some the stigma obscures her marvelous accomplishments. For others it gives rise to questions about how she managed the performances that have never been equaled. She remains the only athlete to have held every U.S. record for distances from 800 meters to 10,000 meters. Some still remain unbroken.

But then, with Slaney, there was always going to be controversy, criticism, and questions.

She also will always remain linked to Zola Budd Pieterse. No matter how Slaney may try to extricate herself, the joining of their names is permanently fixed in the collective memory of millions.

The battered legs that endured nearly thirty surgeries now enable Mary Slaney to do little more than jog. In her sunroom, she stitches quietly and alone, creating a patchwork of brightly colored patterns she attaches to a larger fabric. For a woman whose life was a tapestry of alternating patterns of triumph and tragedy, quilting seems somehow fitting.

Out of the public eye for nearly two decades, Slaney recently was the subject of an ESPN documentary that the network commissioned to celebrate the anniversary of the enactment of Title IX, the federal legislation that opened equal athletic opportunity to women.

The network series, *Nine for IX*, aired one episode a week for nine weeks in the spring and summer of 2013.

The producer was Shola Lynch, a former runner who now directs documentary films—ESPN had given her a choice of subjects, and she chose her one-time heroine, the greatest middle-distance runner on the planet, Mary Decker Slaney.

Lynch called her film simply *Runner*.

In 2016 a documentary film on Mary Decker Slaney and Zola Budd Pieterse was produced by Academy Award–winning Caitrin Rogers and directed by Dan Gordon. It brought the two women together in Los Angeles at the Coliseum where, thirty-two years before, they had created the most memorable moment in modern Olympic history.

The greatest fear of any athlete is that they will be remembered for their most embarrassing moment. In the case of Mary and Zola, their collision in 1984, much to their mutual chagrin, has forever linked them in our collective mind.

That it should do so to the exclusion of their respective spectacular careers is as tragic as the collision itself.

. . .

The woman who answers the door is immediately recognizable. Her appearance hasn't changed much through the years. Her light brown sun-streaked hair is still short, her form is still relatively slim, and she is, of course, barefoot.

Zola Budd Pieterse is now fifty years old and lives outside Myrtle Beach, South Carolina, with her husband, Michael, and their three children, Lisa and the twins, Michael and Avelle.

As you would expect, there are plenty of pets around her—three small dogs, two beautiful parakeets, and a gerbil.

She still runs every day in the warm and humid climate of the low country, sometimes twice a day. It keeps her fit, and she says she needs to run for her own well-being—running brings her peace. But, she adds, at this age something always hurts.

Zola Pieterse is an assistant track and cross-country coach at Coastal Carolina University in nearby Conway. They are pleased to have her, and she enjoys working with the athletes.

Her older daughter, Lisa, has proved that genetics are hard to ignore: in 2013 she won the South Carolina state AAAA title for 3,200 meters.[2]

In 2016 she was among the first of her mother's recruits for Coastal Carolina.

. . .

The South Africa Zola returns to now is still a land of wild beauty.

But it is a land where the insidious AIDS virus has reached pandemic proportions, affecting millions and leaving streets filled with orphans.[3] Those stricken with the virus are treated like lepers once were. They are shunned, abandoned by their families and shut away, out of sight.

. . .

Outside Bloemfontein, along a rural road, sits a nondescript, whitewashed building, one of many such buildings in South Africa erected to house those in the late stages of the AIDS virus. It is a hospice.

In a small, dimly lit room lies a woman who is waiting to die. Nothing can help her. No serum or miracle will save her.

She is sick and dying.

By her side sits a small woman visitor whose gentle hand caresses hers and whose barely audible voice whispers words of comfort, solace, and peace.

The small hand is white, and it belongs to a woman who was once famous around the world. She was the subject of debate in Parliament. She was once the target of worldwide animosity because of her national origin. She was cursed at, abused, and condemned as a symbol of racism by protesters, chided by a Nobel laureate, and branded a known racist by a subcommittee of the United Nations.

The people who hounded her for so many years are nowhere to be seen. Nor are still photographers, television camera operators, national leaders, or Nobel laureates anywhere in evidence, not here, not now, not ever.

The small woman would have it no other way. She seeks no publicity, no notice, no photo opportunities. She is there anonymously and seeks only to help. She is there to do what little she can for the dying woman in the bed.

Her soft words and compassionate stroking of the shriveled, black hand she grasps lightly and lovingly to her breast bring comfort to a woman otherwise abandoned to her fate. The dying woman is at peace. Someone cares for her. She doesn't know the small woman's name; it doesn't matter. But the small woman knows the value of a loving hand, of a kind word and genuine caring. She knows because she once was wrongly branded and reviled throughout the world, back when her name was . . . Zola Budd.

NOTES

1. Starting Line

1. In 1935 Flemington had had a brief brush with fame when it served as the setting for the trial of Bruno Richard Hauptmann for the kidnapping and murder of Charles Lindbergh's infant son. But for that fleeting moment in the spotlight, it remained a quiet community.

2. Kenny Moore, "Yesterday's Child," *Sports Illustrated*, May 1, 1978.

3. Moore, "Yesterday's Child," *Sports Illustrated*, May 1, 1978.

4. Moore, "Yesterday's Child," *Sports Illustrated*, May 1, 1978.

2. First Steps

1. Budd and Eley, *Zola*; Zola Budd Pieterse, interview by author, March 2013, Myrtle Beach SC.

2. Budd and Eley, *Zola,* 10. This, like Zola Budd's subsequent comments on her early years, was verified and/or slightly altered by her in interviews on October 1, 2012, and March 5 and 7, 2013, in Myrtle Beach; and telephone interviews on April 11, and May 14 and 21, 2013.

3. Budd and Eley, *Zola*, 14.

4. Budd and Eley, *Zola*, 13–14.

5. Budd and Eley, *Zola*, 15.

6. Budd and Eley, *Zola*, 15.

7. Budd and Eley, *Zola*, 17.

8. Pieter Labuschagne, email to author, October 30, 2012.

9. Labuschagne, email to author, October 31, 2012.

10. Budd and Eley, *Zola*, 18.

3. Off with the Gun

1. Bob Hickey, telephone interview by author, October 26, 2012.

2. Don DeNoon, telephone interview by author, October 20, 2012.

3. Hickey, interview by author, October 26, 2012; DeNoon, interview by author, October 20, 2012.

4. DeNoon, interview by author, October 20, 2012.

5. Murphy, *Silence of Great Distance*, 144.

6. DeNoon, interview by author, October 20, 2012.

7. DeNoon, interview by author, October 20, 2012.

8. Kenny Moore, "Yesterday's Child," *Sports Illustrated*, May 1, 1978.

9. DeNoon, interview by author, October 20, 2012.

10. Dave Distel, "Decker: Too Fast Too Soon?" *Los Angeles Times*, February 26, 1974.

11. Distel, "Decker: Too Fast Too Soon?" *Los Angeles Times*, February 26, 1974.

12. Distel, "Decker: Too Fast Too Soon?" *Los Angeles Times*, February 26, 1974.

13. Hickey, interview by author, October 26, 2012.

14. Hickey, interview by author, October 26, 2012.

15. DeNoon, interview by author, October 20, 2012.

16. Bob Seaman, telephone interview by author, October 18, 2012.

17. DeNoon, interview by author, October 20, 2012.

18. DeNoon, interview by author, October 20, 2012.

19. Hickey, interview by author, October 26, 2012.

20. DeNoon, interview by author, October 20, 2012.

21. Mal Florence, "Prefontaine Wins; Borzov Falls," *Los Angeles Times*, February 10, 1973.

22. Murphy, *Silence of Great Distance*, 146.

23. Another outstanding young runner of the era was Robin Campbell, who defeated Russia's best over 800 meters at the age of fourteen. Robin too was young, had a charming personality, and was supremely talented. She was also black, and her media appeal suffered for it.

24. DeNoon, interview by author October 20, 2012.

25. Anita Verschoth, "Mary, Mary, Not Contrary," *Sports Illustrated*, April 22, 1974.

26. Distel, "Decker: Too Fast Too Soon?" *Los Angeles Times*, February 26, 1974.

27. DeNoon, interview by author, October 20, 2012.

28. Seaman, interview by author, October 18, 2012.

29. DeNoon, interview by author, October 20, 2012. See also Anita Verschoth, "Mary, Mary, Not Contrary," *Sports Illustrated*, April 22, 1974.

30. Hickey, interview by author, October 26, 2012.

31. Hickey, interview by author, October 26, 2012.

32. Harley Tinkman, "Van Zijl Surprises in 4:04.4 Mile; Liquori Finishes 2nd," *Los Angeles Times*, January 20, 1974.

33. John Hall, "Spaghetti Kid," *Los Angeles Times*, February 5, 1974; AP, "Decker Sets Meet Record in Nationals," *Los Angeles Times*, February 23, 1974.

34. Distel, "Decker: Too Fast Too Soon?" *Los Angeles Times*, February 26, 1974.

35. Hall, "Spaghetti Kid," *Los Angeles Times*, February 5, 1974.

36. Hall, "Spaghetti Kid," *Los Angeles Times*, February 5, 1974.

37. Times Wire Services, "Mary Decker Wins 800 Meters, Goes 0 for 2 in Baton Throw," *Los Angeles Times*, March 3, 1974.

38. Times Wire Services, "Mary Decker Wins 800 Meters, Goes 0 for 2 in Baton Throw," *Los Angeles Times*, March 3, 1974

39. Harley Tinkham, "Mary Decker's Tomboy Image Is Changing," *Los Angeles Times*, April 23, 1974.

40. Murphy, *Silence of Great Distance*, 150–51.

41. Murphy, Silence of Great Distance, 150–51; Moore, "Yesterday's Child," *Sports Illustrated*, May 1, 1978.

42. Dick Bank, telephone interview by author, October 20, 2012.

43. Superior Court of California, County of Orange, re: *Decker v. Decker*, Case D-78622, December 28, 1973.

44. John A. Decker, Declaration re: Modification, *Decker v. Decker*, September 4, 1975; *Decker v. Decker*, transcript.

45. Rich Castro, telephone interview by author, October 25, 2012; Dick Brown, telephone interview by author, October 18, 2012.

46. Mel Watman, *Athletics Weekly*, November 1983.

47. Dave Distel, "Little Mary Hurt," *Los Angeles Times*, January 26, 1976.

48. Murphy, *Silence of Great Distance*, 152; Mel Watman, *Athletics Weekly*, November 1983; Gary Burns, "New Lady Buff Decker Aims for 1980," *Boulder Daily Camera*, January 27, 1977.

4. Healing the Body

1. Murphy, *Silence of Great Distance*, 154.

2. Rich Castro, telephone interview by author, October 25, 2012.

3. Castro, interview by author, October 25, 2012.

4. Castro, interview by author, October 25, 2012.

5. Murphy, *Silence of Great Distance*, 155.

6. Murphy, *Silence of Great Distance*, 157.

7. Castro, interview by author, October 25, 2012.

8. Castro, interview by author, October 25, 2012.

9. Castro, interview by author, October 25, 2012.

10. Castro, interview by author, October 25, 2012.

11. Castro, interview by author, October 25, 2012.

12. Nobby Hashizume, email to author, October 25, 2012.

13. Hashizume, email to author, October 25, 2012. Hashizume is the head of the Lydiard Foundation in Plymouth, Minnesota.

14. Hashizume, email to author, October 25, 2012.

15. *Track & Field News*, February 1978.

16. Mal Florence, "Eamonn Coghlan Wins Times Mile," *Los Angeles Times*, February 4, 1978.

17. *Women's Track & Field News*, March 1978.

18. *Track & Field News*, February 1978.

19. *Boulder Daily Camera*, February 9, 1978.

20. *Track & Field News*, February 1978.

21. John Jeansonne, *Newsday*, reprinted in *Boulder Daily Camera*, February 19, 1978.

22. Elizabeth Wheeler, "It's Big Mary Decker," *Los Angeles Times*, June 5, 1978.

23. Bob Wischnia, "Mary Decker," *Runner's World*, November 1979, 49.

24. Murphy, *Silence of Great Distance*, 154.

25. Castro, interview by author, October 25, 2012.

26. Moore, *Bowerman and the Men of Oregon*.

27. Dick Brown, telephone interview by author, October 18, 2012.

28. Brown, telephone interview by author, October 18, 2012.

29. Brown, telephone interview by author, October 18, 2012.

30. Alan Greenburg, "Mary Decker's Life on the Run," *Los Angeles Times*, June 9, 1980; Francie Larrieu Smith, telephone interview by author, November 15, 2012.

31. Elliot Almond, "Decker Is Tough Off Track Too," *Los Angeles Times*, April 6, 1980.

32. Almond, "Decker Is Tough Off Track Too," *Los Angeles Times*, April 6, 1980.

33. Mark Heisler, "Decker: Flying Feet Not a Problem," *Los Angeles Times*, February 21, 1980.

34. Wallechinsky, *Summer Olympics*, xxix.

35. Mel Watman, *Athletics Weekly*, November 19, 1983.

36. *Runner's World*, November 1979.

37. *Track & Field News*, August 1980.

38. *Track & Field News*, August 1980.

39. Mel Watman, *Athletics Weekly*, November 19, 1983.

40. Murphy, *Silence of Great Distance*, 169.

41. Brown, interview by author, October 18, 2012.

42. *Track & Field News*, December 1980. The American swimmer Shirley Babashoff had complained about the East German women swimmers after their near-medal sweep in the 1976 Olympics. Her remarks were considered highly controversial and set off a strong backlash against her. Since then no track competitor had openly questioned the physiques of the communist women athletes.

5. Dirty Little Secret

1. In one of the greatest injustices ever perpetrated against an athlete, Thorpe was later stripped of his Olympic medals for professionalism. Long after Thorpe's death, and after years of attempts to do so, the medals were restored to Thorpe's family. Avery Brundage, during his twenty-year tenure as IOC president, had resisted all entreaties to do so.

2. Brundage continued in power on the USOC and was elevated to the head of the IOC in 1952, a position he held for twenty years.

3. Dick Pound, telephone interview by author, August 17, 2012.

4. Pound, interview by author, August 17, 2012. See also Pound, *Inside the Olympics*, 58–59.

5. Pound, interview by author, August 17, 2012.

6. Ungerleider, *Faust's Gold*. For another excellent source of information on the subject, see Alison Rooper, dir., *Doping for Gold*, May 7, 2008, aired as part of the PBS series *Secrets of the Dead*.

7. Ungerleider, *Faust's Gold*, 19, 38–39, 44–45.

8. Pound, interview by author, August 17, 2012.

9. Ungerleider, *Faust's Gold*. For anyone interested in the extent to which the communist states went to assure their athletes' success while blatantly ignoring the physical damage they were visiting on the athletes, this is the book. The subsequent acknowledgment of guilt, nearly twenty years later, by physicians and

administrators in a landmark court case in the reunified Germany (522–40/99, July 30, 1999), is at once fascinating and terrifying.

10. Simson and Jennings, *Dishonored Games*, 81, 21.

11. Simson and Jennings, *Dishonored Games*, 62, 102.

12. Simson and Jennings, *Dishonored Games*, 262.

13. Pound, interview by author, August 17, 2012.

14. Pound, interview by author, August 17, 2012.

15. Pound, interview by author, August 17, 2012. See also Pound, *Inside the Olympics*.

16. Pound, interview by author, August 17, 2012.

17. Samaranch was an imperious personage who saw himself as a world leader. He insisted on meeting heads of state wherever he traveled (he traveled a lot), and he had the carriage and attitude of one who demanded respectful deference wherever he went. His hubris extended to seeking for the IOC a seat at the United Nations as an observer. That idea may have died aborning, but throughout his tenure, which lasted until the end of the 2000 games, Samaranch was the haughty public representative of the Olympics around the world. That the enormous financial success of the games was the work of Dick Pound was something Samaranch would never publicly acknowledge, and when Pound sought to succeed him as president of the IOC (after a few years of scandalous revelations had tainted Samaranch's reign with corruption), Samaranch worked behind the scenes, as usual, to help defeat him.

6. Running for Jenny

1. Pieter Labuschagne, email to author, November 1, 2012.

2. Budd and Eley, *Zola*, 18.

3. Budd and Eley, *Zola*, 20; Zola Budd Pieterse, interview by author, October 1, 2012, Myrtle Beach SC.

4. Budd and Eley, *Zola*, 20; Budd, interview by author, October 1, 2012.

5. Budd and Eley, *Zola*, 20.

6. Budd and Eley, *Zola*, 20–22.

7. Budd and Eley, *Zola*, 21.

8. Pieter Labuschagne, email to author, October 31, 2012.

9. Peter Hawthorne and Kenny Moore, "A Flight to a Stormy Haven," *Sports Illustrated*, April 9, 1984.

10. Budd and Eley, *Zola*, 22.

11. Budd and Eley, *Zola*, 22–23.

12. Labuschagne, email to author, November 1, 2012.

13. Budd and Eley, *Zola*, 23.

14. Budd and Eley, *Zola*, 23.

15. Budd and Eley, *Zola*, 24.

16. Budd and Eley, *Zola*, 25.

17. Budd and Eley, *Zola*, 26.

18. Budd and Eley, *Zola*, 27.

19. Budd and Eley, *Zola*, 27.

20. Budd and Eley, *Zola*, 20.

21. Budd and Eley, *Zola*, 26–27.

22. Budd and Eley, *Zola*, 27–28.

7. The Kid Comes Back with a Swoosh

1. Dick Brown, telephone interview by author, October 18, 2012.

2. Brown, interview by author, October 18, 2012.

3. Brown, interview by author, October 18, 2012.

4. Frank Martin, "World Champion Mary Decker Settled for Tie—with Marathoner Ron Tabb," *People*, May 3, 1982.

5. Ron Tabb, telephone interview by author, November 21, 2012.

6. Martin, "World Champion Mary Decker Settled for Tie," *People*, May 3, 1982.

7. Brown, interview by author, October 18, 2012.

8. Martin, "World Champion Mary Decker Settled for Tie," *People*, May 3, 1982.

9. Tabb, interview by author, November 21, 2012.

10. Tabb, interview by author, November 21, 2012.

11. Tabb, interview by author, November 21, 2012.

12. Bob Hickey, telephone interview by author, October 26, 2012.

13. *Track & Field News*, August 1982.

14. "Mary Decker Slaney," NNDB.com, http://www.nndb.com/people/601/000025526/.

15. Brown, interview by author, October 18, 2012.

16. Brown, interview by author, October 18, 2012.

17. Cathy Henkel, *Eugene Register-Guard*, June 20, 1983.

18. *Track & Field News*, August 1983.

19. Murphy, *Silence of Great Distance*, 179.

20. Cathy Henkel, *Eugene Register-Guard*, June 15, 1983.

21. *Track & Field News*, August 1983.

22. Francie Larrieu Smith, telephone interview by author, November 15, 2012.

23. *Eugene Register-Guard*, July 27, 1983.

24. *Eugene Register-Guard*, July 27, 1983.

25. Brown, interview by author, October 18, 2012.

26. Simson and Jennings, *Dishonored Games.*

27. Simson and Jennings, *Dishonored Games*, 189–90.

28. Simson and Jennings, *Dishonored Games*, 189–90.

29. Brown, interview by author, October 18, 2012.

30. Murphy, *Silence of Great Distance*, 182.

31. Larrieu Smith, interview by author, November 15, 2012.

32. Kenny Moore, "She Runs and We Are Lifted," *Sports Illustrated*, December 26, 1983. See also Murphy, *Silence of Great Distance*, 183–86.

33. Alexei Srebnitsky, *Canadian Runner Magazine*, September 1984.

34. Cathy Henkel, *Eugene Register-Guard*, August 11, 1984.

35. With her father's denial of her still festering and her strong insistence,

expressed to writers after her marriage to Tabb ("Don't call me Decker"), Decker may not have been pleased, but the moniker would stick.

36. *Eugene Register-Guard*, August 15, 1983.

37. Moore, "She Runs and We Are Lifted," *Sports Illustrated*, December 26, 1983.

38. Wallechinsky, *Summer Olympics*, 254.

39. Moore, "She Runs and We Are Lifted," *Sports Illustrated*, December 26, 1983.

40. Brown, interview by author, October 18, 2012.

8. Out of Africa

1. Berna Maree, "Zola Budd, South Africa's Barefooted Wonder Runner," undated clipping from unidentified newspaper in the Zola Budd Pieterse scrapbook. This article, as well as many others, is contained in a large scrapbook compiled by a fan and sent to Zola Budd. Many of the clippings fail to identify the name of the publication or date. When possible, I have listed the source and author. But in many cases the source, date, and page numbers are missing.

2. Peter Gamabaccini, "Olympian Sydney Maree Released from South African Prison," *RunnersWorld.com*, March 18, 2013. Maree was sentenced to prison in South Africa for embezzlement and was released after serving twenty-one months.

3. Zola Budd Pieterse, interview by author, March 7, 2013, Myrtle Beach SC.

4. Budd Pieterse, interview by author, March 5, 2013, Myrtle Beach SC.

5. John Bryant, telephone interview by author, May 22, 2013, and follow-up by email, February 21, 2014.

6. Sarah Wooldridge, telephone interview by author, August 9, 2012; John Simpson, telephone interview by author, August 15, 2012. To avoid a long waiting period when applying for British citizenship, Zola would have to file before she was eighteen. Even so, the wait for minor children was usually three years. The *Mail*, Simpson recalled, was certain it could expedite the process through its connections to the Thatcher government.

7. Budd Pieterse, interview by author, March 7, 2013.

8. Cornelia Bürki, telephone interview by author, July 19, 2012.

9. Budd ran four races in which she set South African records and would have set world junior records but for the boycott during the period that the talks with the *Mail* were taking place. She ran distances ranging from 800 meters to 5,000 meters with records coming in races at 1,500, 2,000 and 3,000 meters.

10. Bryant, email to author, February 21, 2014.

11. Simpson, interview by author, August 15, 2012.

12. Simpson, interview by author, August 15, 2012.

13. Budd Pieterse, interview by author, March 5, 2013. Labuschagne was to accompany his athlete, and his expenses while preparing his young charge for the Olympic Games were to be paid from the money the *Mail* supplied.

14. Budd and Eley, *Zola*, 39.

15. Amby Burfoot, telephone interview by author, September 11, 2012. Burfoot, former marathon runner turned writer for *Runner's World*, had been the first writer to visit Zola on the farm in the fall of 1983. He found her, he said, to

be "more like fourteen," and surrounded by pets and stuffed animals. *Runner's World* had begun tracking Zola six months before her record-shattering race in January. "We thought with that name and the fact that she ran barefooted, she must be a poor little black kid."

16. For the definitive story of the Ovett-Coe rivalry, which would be supplanted by the Zola Budd controversy in Great Britain, see Butcher, *Perfect Distance*.

17. Budd Pieterse, interview by author, March 5, 2013.

18. Budd Pieterse, interview by author, March 5, 2013.

19. Budd and Eley, *Zola*, 40.

20. "From Bethlehem to Bedlam—England's First Mental Institution," www.english-heritage.org.uk. The definition is from *Webster's New World Dictionary*, 4th ed. (New York: Pocket Books, 2003).

21. Ian Wooldridge, "The Race to Win a Waif Named Zola," *Daily Mail*, March 6, 1984.

22. Simpson, interview by author, August 15, 2012.

23. David Miller, "Record Breaker Is Racing to New Life," *Times* (of London), March 27, 1984.

24. Tim Taylor, "Zola Go Home!" *(London) Daily Express*, March 28, 1984.

25. Neil Wilson, "Zola—'I'll Run My Heart Out for Britain,'" *Daily Mail*, April 7, 1984.

26. Budd and Eley, *Zola*, 56.

27. Budd and Eley, *Zola*, 50.

28. Budd and Eley, *Zola*, 41.

29. Budd Pieterse, interview by author, March 5, 2013.

30. Budd Pieterse, interview by author, March 5, 2013.

31. Budd and Eley, *Zola*, 44.

32. Simpson, interview by author, August 15, 2012.

33. Simpson, interview by author, August 15, 2012.

34. Budd Pieterse, interview by author, March 5, 2013.

35. Budd and Eley, *Zola*, 45.

36. Budd and Eley, *Zola*, 45, 46.

9. Gathering Storms

1. Strasser and Becklund, *Swoosh*, 372.

2. Strasser and Becklund, *Swoosh*, 373.

3. Strasser and Becklund, *Swoosh*, 373-74. There is no evidence that the bills were connected to treatment for Mary Decker, and the authors made no such assertions.

4. In recent years the procedure has received an inordinate amount of publicity because of its popularity among bicycle racers, including Lance Armstrong and other members of the USA Cycling team.

5. When I interviewed him, Tabb denied using drugs and asserted that he never observed Mary using them (Tabb, telephone interview by author, November 21, 2012). In light of later events, her 1983 results remain suspect, but they remain in the record books. After Decker failed a drug test in 1997, the sports pages were full

of stories questioning whether her 1983 performance had somehow been enhanced by the use of banned substances or techniques such as blood doping.

6. Strasser and Becklund, *Swoosh*, 374.

7. Strasser and Becklund, *Swoosh*, 376.

8. Dick Brown, telephone interview by author, October 28, 2012.

9. When the divorce was granted, Tabb still was not happy. He recorded a message for his answering machine that greeted callers to the couple's old number with "Here's today's trivia question: What American athlete fell flat on her face during the women's 3,000 meters race during the Olympics? If you get the right answer, you're entitled to a free Mary Decker doll.... It does have a flaw, though. It has a tendency to fall down when it tries to run. We've also developed the Richard Slaney doll, though, to pick it up and put it on its feet again. If you want to order it, leave your name and number after the beep." Cathy Henkel, "Older, Wiser, Faster," *Seattle Times*, September 11, 1988.

10. Henkel, "Older, Wiser, Faster," *Seattle Times*, September 11, 1988. Richard Slaney would finish twelfth in the discus at the LA games as a member of the British team.

11. Brown, interview by the author, October 28, 2012.

12. According to Ron Tabb and others, her income was more than $600,000 from all sources. It is likely that she was the highest-paid woman track athlete in the world and that the figure was probably higher by the time the Olympic Games began. Tabb, interview by author, November 21, 2012.

13. Rick Reilly, telephone interview by author, September 12, 2012.

14. Brown, interview by author, October 28, 2012.

15. Brown, interview by author, October 28, 2012.

16. Brown, interview by author, October 28, 2012.

17. Gallagher was a small but gifted runner. She was coached in her early career by her father and at the age of eight ran the fastest mile ever for a girl that age. Later she would become muscular, and her changed physique would give rise to rumors that she was using steroids. Gallagher consistently denied doing so. Yet her later history raises serious doubts about her denial. She developed cancer and, after beating it, later developed another cancer that ultimately led to a stroke that ended her life at only thirty-eight. Her medical history and problems are, in many ways, similar to those of the East German athletes who were administered steroids by the East German government.

18. Budd had run the 2,000 meters in London on July 13 and had established a world record of 5:33.15 for the seldom-run event. That was the record Decker was referring to.

19. Brown, interview by author, October 28, 2012. While Mary would grow increasingly dismissive and angry about being compared to Budd ("I'm tired of seeing her name in the same paragraph as mine," she would tell reporters at a news conference before the Olympics), she obviously had Budd on her mind more than she was willing to admit.

20. Brown, interview by author, October 28, 2012.

10. Rings of Fire

1. Zola Budd Pieterse, interview by author, March 7, 2013, Myrtle Beach SC.

2. Neil Wilson, "Wonder Girl Zola Ready to Face Any Challenge," *Daily Mail*, April 11, 1984. Smith-Sly would avoid all races with Zola in England before the Olympic Games. Smith-Sly's times had already qualified her for the team, and the BAAB would select her for the team without requiring her to compete for a berth at the trials.

3. "Mrs. Sly Chases Fitness, Not South African Rival," *Times* (of London), March 29, 1984; "Zola Go Home," *Daily Express*, March 28, 1984.

4. H. R. G. Nickolls to the editor, *Daily Express*, April 4, 1984.

5. Budd and Eley, *Zola*, 47.

6. "Labour to Seek Inquiry into Daily Mail Link to Zola Budd Passport Application," *Home News*, April 9, 1984.

7. Argus Foreign Service, "A Power Game That Could End in Tears," *Argus* (of South Africa), April 16, 1984. Normal attendance at the meet was about one hundred, and the volunteer staff was hard pressed to handle the crowd.

8. Budd and Eley, *Zola*, 50.

9. John Bryant, telephone interview by author, May 22, 2013.

10. Budd Pieterse, interview by author, March 5, 2013, Myrtle Beach SC.

11. David Emery, "Zola: How the Cynical Manipulators Have Turned Her into a Circus Act," *Daily Express,* April 16, 1984.

12. Emery, "Zola," *Daily Express,* April 16, 1984.

13. Colin Hart, "Carry On, Zola," *Sun*, April 16, 1984, 28.

14. Richard Pound, telephone interview by author, October 17, 2012.

15. Alastair Campbell, "Zola's a True Brit," *Daily Mirror*, April 7, 1984.

16. Tony Snow, "Lefties Battle to Ban Zola from Race," *Sun*, April 18, 1984.

17. "A Mixed Reaction Greets Zola in Britain," undated clipping in the Zola Budd Pieterse scrapbook, 53.

18. Vic Robbie, "Jibes Have Zola in Tears," *Daily Mirror*, April 26, 1984, 31; Frank Keating, "Barefoot Zola Runs in Tears to Record," *Guardian*, April 26, 1984.

19. Christopher Hilton, "Zola Upset After Protest Mars Record," *Daily Express*, April 26, 1984, 40.

20. Christopher Hilton, "Now Time to Set Zola Free," *Daily Express*, April 27, 1984.

21. Budd Pieterse, interview by author, March 7, 2013.

22. William Oscar Johnson, "Endurance Test: Distance Running Star Zola Budd Has Survived Turmoil on and off the Track," *Sports Illustrated*, June 24, 1991.

23. Budd and Eley, *Zola*, 175; Pieterse, interview by author, March 7, 2013.

24. Budd and Eley, *Zola*, 175; Pieterse, interview by author, March 7, 2013.

25. Budd and Eley, *Zola*, 175; Pieterse, interview by author, March 7, 2013. See also Budd and Eley, *Zola*, 174–76, for detailed discussion of the issue of apartheid, portions of which form part of the basis of the narrative here.

26. Hilton, "Now Time to Set Zola Free," *Daily Express*, April 27, 1984.

27. Jenny Johnston, "'People Hated Me and I Never Knew Why,'" *Mirror*, April 9, 2003.

28. Budd Pieterse, interview by author, March 7, 2013.

29. From an undated clipping with no headline in the Zola Budd Pieterse scrapbook.

30. "Zola Proves Her World Class," *Natal (South Africa) Mercury*, July 5, 1984.

31. Brian Vine, "Passport to the Future: Zola Cuts Ties with South Africa," *Daily Mail*, May 16, 1984.

32. Budd and Eley, *Zola*, 55.

33. Christopher Hilton, "Zola Kisses Them Goodbye," *Daily Express*, May 28, 1984.

34. Neil Wilson, "A Kiss for a Champ," *Daily Mail*, May 29, 1984.

35. "Zola Budd Racing in Cwmbran on the 28th of May 1984," YouTube video of BBC broadcast, https://www.youtube.com/watch?v=lhCoUQN9rY8.

36. Wilson, "A Kiss for a Champ," *Daily Mail*, May 29, 1984.

37. Budd and Eley, *Zola*, 56–57.

38. John Simpson, telephone interview by author, August 15, 2012.

39. Ian Wooldridge, "Zola Deserves Warm Welcome After All We Put Her Through," *Daily Mail*, April 9, 2003.

40. "GLC Threat to Sports Centre over Zola Budd," *Times* (of London), June 7, 1984.

41. Chris Brasher, "Zola—Not in Decker's Class," *(London) Observer*, June 10, 1984.

42. Frank Keating, "A Mite Defying Winds of Change," *Guardian*, June 25, 1984.

43. Christopher Reed, "LA Double for Decker Is Cancelled," *Guardian*, June 26, 1984.

44. "Zola Budd 'World Record' 2000 Metres," YouTube video of BBC broadcast, July 13, 1984, https://www.youtube.com/watch?v=FGSjpUIGbZs.

45. Her time for the mile within the race also established a new British junior record.

46. The endorsement deal that John Simpson secured for Zola Budd from the Brooks athletic shoe company must rank as one of the greatest coups ever pulled off in athletic management. Budd, who raced without shoes, was paid by Brooks, a small American firm, to endorse its product. The company's ad agency came up with a novel and unforgettable way to exploit the discrepancy. An ad that ran in running magazines and newspapers showed a photo of Zola's bare feet juxtaposed with a pair of Brooks's shoes. The only text read: "Next to her feet, Zola Budd prefers Brooks." If it didn't win an award, it should have, and Simpson should be applauded as a genius.

47. Kevin Francis, "Zola Zips to World Record," *(Johannesburg) Daily Star*, July 14, 1984.

48. Dick Brown, telephone interview by author, October 18, 2012.

49. Dr. Bradley Donohue, interview by author, April 5, 2012, Las Vegas.

50. Budd Pieterse, interview by author, March 7, 2013.

51. D. B. Prisloo, telephone interview by author, May 11, 2013.

52. "Citizenship Lost," *Times* (of London), July 28, 1984. The article said the revocation had been announced in the *Government Gazette* in Johannesburg and was effective as of May 30.

53. Budd Pieterse, interview by author, March 7, 2013.

11. Dream Chasers

1. Maricica Puică, interview and English translation by Simion Alb for author, August 2012, Iasi, Romania.

2. Puică, interview and English translation by Simion Alb for author, August 2012.

3. Puică, interview and English translation by Simion Alb for author, August 2012.

4. Puică said she was given vitamin B and iron tablets. Puică, Alb told me, insisted she never took drugs.

5. Pat Butcher, telephone interview by author, March 19, 2013.

6. Puică would race until she was thirty-nine, when she finally retired with persistent injuries. Her career is among the best of any European middle-distance runner. She now divides her time between her home in Aisci, inherited from her husband's family, and a small cabin in the Carpathian Mountains, where she lives modestly. She takes in, and cares for, stray dogs and describes herself as too poor to do more than she is doing for them. The Securitae's fears that she would defect were well founded. She said that after winning a road race in New York, she was offered $2 million by Fred Lebow of the organizing committee to defect to the United States. She declined because of the fear, well founded, of the reprisals and punishment her family in Romania would suffer. Her earnings from racing were considerable, but the government kept 75 percent for taxes; after deductions for training expenses, she got to keep only 2 percent. Her Olympic gold medal, however, brought her a $1,500 per month annuity for the rest of her life, and she was permitted to keep the Mercedes she won in New York. She remains active as a member of the Romanian Athletics Federation and is a revered heroine in Romania. Puică, interview and English translation by Simion Alb for author, August 2012.

7. Wendy Smith-Sly, telephone interview by author, October 16, 2012.

8. Smith-Sly, interview by author, October 16, 2012.

9. Smith-Sly, interview by author, October 16, 2012.

10. Lynn Kanuka Williams, telephone interview by author, July 21, 2012. Kanuka Williams would go on to a successful career in middle-distance running at an elite level. In 1986 she won the 3,000 meters at the Commonwealth Games. Her performances in Canada were so far ahead of the competition, some of her records set there in the early 1980s still stand.

11. Lisa Gaumnitz, "Going the Distance," *Sports Illustrated*, October 30, 1995.

12. Gaumnitz, "Going the Distance," *Sports Illustrated*, October 30, 1995.

13. Gaumnitz, "Going the Distance," *Sports Illustrated*, October 30, 1995.

14. Cornelia Bürki, telephone interview by author, July 19, 2012.

15. Bürki, interview by author, July 19, 2012.

16. Bürki, interview by author, July 19, 2012.

17. Phil Hersh, "Running Out of the Shadows," *Chicago Tribune*, October 25, 1990.

18. Joan Hansen, telephone interview by author, July 21, 2012.

19. Hersh, "Running Out of the Shadows," *Chicago Tribune*, October 25, 1990. Cunha moved up to longer distances after 1984 and found much success. She won several major marathons and continued to compete into the 1990s. She appeared in three straight Olympics from 1984 to 1992.

20. Hansen, interview by author, July 21, 2012.

21. Hansen, interview by author, July 21, 2012.

22. Hansen, interview by author, July 21, 2012.

23. Hansen, interview by author, July 21, 2012.

24. Dianne Rodger, telephone interview by author, October 15, 2012.

25. Rodger, interview by author, October 15, 2012. Dianne Rodger and her husband, who made the Olympic team as a rower, became the first couple from New Zealand to represent that country in the same Olympics. Their oldest son, born in 1989, would become a member of the New Zealand rowing team.

26. Profile of Agnese Possamai at All-Athletics.com.

27. Brigitte Kraus, interview by Dick Hein for author, April 22, 2013, Germany.

28. Kraus, interview by Dick Hein for author, April 22, 2013.

29. Zola Budd Pieterse, interview by author, March 5, 2013, Myrtle Beach SC.

30. Cindy Bremser, telephone interview by author, July 27, 2012.

12. A Split Second That Will Live Forever

1. Randy Harvey, "With Budd, Puică in 3,000 Meters, Decker Is Anything but a 'Shoe In,'" *Los Angeles Times*, July 30, 1984.

2. Grahame L. Jones, "IOC Ban Fails to Curb Press in South Africa," *Los Angeles Times*, August 8, 1984.

3. Amby Burfoot, telephone interview by author, September 11, 2012.

4. The press conference is shown in the film *Runner*, directed by Shola Lynch for the ESPN series *Nine for IX*; *Runner* first aired on August 12, 2013.

5. Richard Walker and Elaine Durbach, *Cape (South Africa) Times*, headline and date missing, in the Zola Budd Pieterse scrapbook.

6. Mike Waldner, interview by author, September 13, 2012.

7. Betty Cuniberti, "OK, World, This Budd Is for You," *Los Angeles Times*, August 8, 1984.

8. Dick Brown, telephone interview by author, October 28, 2012.

9. Budd and Eley, *Zola*, 64–65.

10. Budd and Eley, *Zola*, 70.

11. Budd and Eley, *Zola*, 67.

12. Zola Budd Pieterse, interview by author, March 7, 2013, Myrtle Beach SC.

13. Budd and Eley, *Zola*, 74.

14. Budd and Eley, *Zola*, 71–72.

15. Budd and Eley, *Zola*, 69.

16. Jim Murray, "Win or Lose, Citizen Budd Already Has Her Medal," *Los Angeles Times*, August 9, 1984, 11.

17. Budd and Eley, *Zola*, 75; Budd Pieterse, interview by author, March 7, 2013.

18. Budd Pieterse, interview by author, March 7, 2013. See also Budd and Eley, *Zola*, 76–77.

19. Burfoot, interview by author, September 11, 2012.

20. Steve Bisheff, telephone interview by author, October 26, 2012.

21. Wendy Smith-Sly, telephone interview by author, October 16, 2012.

22. Rich Castro, telephone interview by author, October 25, 2012.

23. Budd Pieterse, interview by author, March 7, 2013.

24. Butcher, *Perfect Distance*, 71.

25. Smith-Sly, interview by author, October 16, 2012.

26. Lynn Kanuka Williams, telephone interview by author, July 24, 2012.

27. Cindy Bremser, telephone interview by author, July 27, 2012.

28. Joan Hansen, telephone interview by author, July 21, 2012.

29. Dianne Rodger, telephone interview by author, October 15, 2012.

30. Hansen, interview by author, July 21, 2012.

31. Maricica Puică, interview and English translation by Simion Alb for author, August 2012, Romania.

32. Budd and Eley, *Zola*, 76.

33. Lynn Kanuka Williams, telephone interview by author, July 21, 2012.

34. Puică, interview and English translation by Simion Alb for author, August 2012.

35. Burfoot, interview by author, September 11, 2012.

36. Puică, interview and English translation by Simion Alb for author, August 2012.

37. Smith-Sly, interview by author, October 16, 2012.

38. BBC commentary with feed of ABC telecast of the race, August 10, 1985, for British audiences, www.youtube.com/watch?v=10Qys5W-aKE.

39. Kanuka Williams, interview by author, July 21, 2012.

40. Brigitte Kraus, interview by Dick Hein for author, April 2013, Germany.

41. Budd Pieterse, interview by author, March 7, 2013.

42. Budd Pieterse, interview by author, March 7, 2013.

43. Kanuka Williams, interview by author, July 21, 2012.

44. Kanuka Williams, interview by author, July 21, 2012.

45. Cindy Bremser, interview by author, July 27, 2012.

46. ABC telecast. Zola Budd has never watched the film of the race and told me, "I never will."

47. Marty Liquori, telephone interview by author, July 31, 2012. Liquori had no opportunity to interview Decker. She did an interview with Kathleen Sullivan of ABC the next morning. When approached about appearing with Liquori, Decker snapped, "I've already done an ABC interview," and refused to do it. The day after the race Liquori amplified his opinion about what had happened, deciding "no one was at fault," but his statement was lost in the wake of Decker's early morning interview with the ingratiating Sullivan, who allowed Decker to blame Budd without being challenged.

48. Rich Perleman, telephone interview by author, July 17, 2012.

49. ABC telecast.

50. Cornelia Bürki, telephone interview by author, July 19, 2012.

51. Randy Hartman, "Experts Back Zola as Mary Raves On," photo in *Rand (South Africa) Daily Mail*, August 13, 1984.

52. Colin Gibson, "Zola's Dream of an Olympic Gold Ends in Nightmare," *Daily Telegraph*, August 12, 1984, Zola Budd Pieterse scrapbook.

53. Bürki, interview by author, July 19, 2012. There are a number of versions as to what was said in the tunnel. I have used Bürki's because it comes from someone who was near both parties. Budd Pieterse claims that she said no more than "I'm sorry," to which Decker screamed, "Go away," which Budd did, saying nothing further. Budd Pieterse doesn't remember crying after the exchange, but others present said she was in tears. The version I have used also appears in *Newsweek*, August 20, 1984.

54. Bürki, interview by author, July 19. 2012.

55. Perleman, interview by author, July 17, 2012.

56. Murphy, *Silence of Great Distance*, 201.

57. Patrick Collins, "Crash Go Those Dreams of Gold," *Mail on Sunday*, August 12, 1984.

58. Steve Bisheff, telephone interview by author, October 26, 2012.

59. Betty Cuniberti, "ZOLA: Post Race Rebuke by Decker, Her Idol, Bewilders Youngster," *Los Angeles Times*, August 11, 1984.

60. Steve Friedman, "After the Fall," in Willey, ed., *Going Long*, 130; Budd Pieterse, interview by author, March 7, 2013.

61. Greg Harney, telephone interview by author, September 12, 2012.

62. Hartman, "Experts Back Zola," *Rand (South Africa) Daily Mail*, August 13, 1984, 2. See also Steve Bisheff, "If Anyone Is at Fault It Is Our Mary," *Orange County Register*, August 13, 1984. Three decades later Dick Brown told me Decker suffered a strained groin muscle. But all other contemporary accounts cite the hip muscle, which is the area that Decker is seen clutching on video as she writhed on the ground. Brown, interview by author, October 28, 2012.

63. Harney, interview by author, September 12, 2012.

64. Bisheff, interview by author, October 26, 2012.

65. Christopher Brasher, "Inexperience and Iron Determination—Elements That Led to Disaster," *(London) Observer*, August 12, 1984.

66. Allan Greenberg, "Mary: The Queen of Track Becomes Frightened Child," *Los Angeles Times*, August 11, 1984.

67. Brasher, "Inexperience and Iron Determination," *(London) Observer*, August 12, 1984.

68. Greenberg, "Mary: The Queen of Track," *Los Angeles Times*, August 11, 1984.

69. Brown, interview by author, October 28, 2012.

70. Larry Stewart, "What the Games Meant to Television," *Los Angeles Times*, July 28, 1985.

71. Brown, interview by author, October 28, 2012.

72. Stewart, "What the Games Meant to Television," *Los Angeles Times*, July 28, 1985.

73. Mike Littwin, "Real Heroes? Decker Falls Flat and Lewis Is a Long Jump Away," *Los Angeles Times*, August 14, 1984.

74. Rodney Hartman, "Decker Must Take the Rap," *Rand Daily Mail*, August 13, 1984.

75. Frank Keating, "Mail Train Survives the Crash," *Guardian*, August 13, 1984.

76. *Athletics Weekly*, August 25, 1984. See also "Why Mary Decker Was Wrong," *Times* (of London), August 13, 1984.

77. Bisheff, interview by author, October 26, 2012; Bisheff, "If Anyone Was at Fault," *Orange County Register*.

78. Undated clipping from unidentifiable source, in Budd Pieterse scrapbook.

79. Undated clipping from unidentifiable source, in Budd Pieterse scrapbook.

80. Rich Roberts, "Decker's Coach Defends His Star, Talks of Europe and Next Olympics," *Los Angeles Times*, August 12, 1984.

81. Rich Roberts, "Ryun Felt the Pain When Decker Fell," *Los Angeles Times*, August 11, 1984.

82. This was the same Olympics that saw the severely dehydrated Swiss marathoner Gabriele Andersen-Schiess stagger around the Coliseum to finish the race though twisted grotesquely by the agony she was suffering in the attempt. She finally collapsed into the arms of officials after crossing the finish line in thirty-seventh place. But she finished. The differences between Decker and Schiess were not lost on writers and fans.

83. "Somebody Ought to Be Asking: Is Zola All Right?" *San Diego Evening Tribune*, August 11, 1984.

84. Budd Pieterse, interview by author, March 7, 2013.

85. Colin Gibson, "Los Angeles Breathed Life into the Olympics," *(London) Daily Telegraph*, August 14, 1984.

86. Pound, *Inside the Olympics*, 67-68.

87. Pound, interview by author, August 17, 2012; Perleman, interview by author, July 17, 2012.

88. Dr. Don Catlin, telephone interview by author, April 22, 2013.

89. Perleman, interview by author, July 17, 2012.

90. Colin Gibson, "Death Threat Guard for Zola Budd," *(London) Daily Telegraph*, August 14, 1984.

91. Budd Pieterse, interview by author, March 7, 2013.

13. Coming and Going

1. Zola Budd Pieterse, interview by author, March 7, 2013, Myrtle Beach SC.

2. "Press Left Standing as Budd Returns Home," *Times* (of London), August 17, 1984.

3. *Rand (South Africa) Daily Mail*, clipping with no headline, August 13, 1984, in the Zola Budd Pieterse scrapbook.

4. "Brill Jumps to Zola Budd's Aid," *Vancouver Sun*, August 16, 1984.

5. "Decker Rips Letter," *(Torrance CA) Daily Breeze*, August 17, 1984.

6. *Rand Daily Mail*, August 13, 1984.

7. Steve Friedman, "After the Fall," in Willey, ed., *Going Long*, 130. Other accounts give the date of the letter as February 1985 and say the marathoner Alberto Salazar delivered it to Budd in Phoenix, Arizona.

8. Peter Tory, "Zola the Movie," column, *Daily Mail*, August 17, 1984.

9. Leon Botha, telephone interview by author, October 7, 2012.

10. Budd Pieterse, interview by author, March 7, 2013.

11. Budd and Eley, *Zola*, 91.

12. Clipping from South African newspaper in Zola Budd Pieterse scrapbook, date and paper not identified.

13. Michael Hornsby, "Zola the Person Puts an End to International Run of Zola the Athlete," *Times* (of London), November 2, 1984.

14. "Short Sad Tale of Little Zola," *(UK) Daily Mirror*, 30.

15. John Simpson, telephone interview by author, August 15, 2012.

16. Budd and Eley, *Zola*, 91.

17. Budd and Eley, *Zola*, 91–92.

18. Budd and Eley, *Zola*, 94.

19. Zola Budd Pieterse, telephone interview by author, April 17, 2012.

20. Budd Pieterse, interview by author, April 17, 2012.

21. Budd and Eley, *Zola*, 94.

22. Budd Pieterse, telephone interview by author, April 17, 2012.

23. Budd and Eley, *Zola*, 94.

24. Budd and Eley, *Zola*, 95. The announcement appeared in both the British and South African press.

25. Budd and Eley, *Zola*, 96.

26. Simpson, interview by author, August 15, 2012.

14. The Phoenix Rises

1. Dick Brown, telephone interview by author, October 28, 2012.

2. Brown, interview by author, October 28, 2012.

3. Mal Florence, "Wysocki Does a Number on Decker," *Los Angeles Times*, January 9, 1985.

4. Julie Cart, "Scott Supports Wysocki, Calls Decker a Baby," *Los Angeles Times*, January 10, 1985; Steve Bisheff, "Mary Will Probably Bounce Back, but Can Zola Ever Break Free?" *Orange County Register*, August, 13, 1984.

5. Ruth Wysocki, telephone interview by author, August 11, 2012.

6. Wysocki, telephone interview by author, August 11, 2012; "Decker Sets 2,000 Record in Triumphant Return," *San Diego Union Tribune*, January 19, 1985; "Tatyana Kazankina Bio, Stats, and Results," n.d., Olympics at Sports-Reference.com; Mika Perkiömäki, "Track & Field Statistics: World Record Progression in Women's Running Events," January 26, 2014, http://www.saunalahti.fi/~sut/eng/wwr run.html#2000.

7. Craig Neff, "Mary, Mary, Still Contrary," *Sports Illustrated*, January 28, 1985.

8. Murphy, *Silence of Great Distance*, 206-7.

9. Brown, interview by author, October 28, 2012.

10. Brown, interview by author, October 28, 2012

11. "Decker Sets 2,000 Record in Triumphant Return," *San Diego Tribune*, January 19, 1985.

15. World Champ

1. Budd and Eley, *Zola*, 97.

2. Clipping from *Natal (South Africa) Witness*, February 9, 1985, in the Zola Budd Pieterse scrapbook.

3. Alan Robinson, "Zola Fan Club Growing," *(Durban, South Africa) Daily News*, February 11, 1985.

4. Robinson, "Zola Fan Club Growing," *(Durban, South Africa) Daily News*, February 11, 1985.

5. Andrew Walker, "Mary Crashes but Maree Bounces Back," *(Durban, South Africa) Daily News*, February 11, 1985.

6. Budd and Eley, *Zola*, 97.

7. Daily News Foreign Service, "UK Anti-Apartheid Demos Vow to Harass Zola Again," *(Durban, South Africa) Daily News*, February 18, 1985.

8. Zola Budd Pieterse, interview by author, March 7, 2013, Myrtle Beach SC.

9. Daily News Foreign Service, "UK Anti-Apartheid Demos," *(Durban, South Africa) Daily News*, February 18, 1985.

10. Daily News Foreign Service, "UK Anti-Apartheid Demos," *(Durban, South Africa) Daily News*, February 18, 1985.

11. "England Pins Hopes on Budd," *Natal (South Africa) Witness*, February 3, 1985.

12. "Tough Time for Zola," *(Durban, South Africa) Daily News*, March 21, 1985.

13. Partial undated article, headline obscured, from *(Durban, South Africa) Daily News*, Zola Budd Pieterse scrapbook.

14. Alex Eales, "Zola's in Line for a Gold, Says Cornelia," *Natal (South Africa) Mercury*, undated clipping in Zola Budd Pieterse scrapbook.

15. Eales, "Zola's in Line for a Gold," *Natal (South Africa) Mercury*, undated clipping in Zola Budd Pieterse scrapbook.

16. Pat Butcher, telephone interview by author, March 19, 2012.

17. Budd and Eley, *Zola*, 101.

18. Budd and Eley, *Zola*, 102.

19. Budd and Eley, *Zola*, 102-3.

20. Budd and Eley, *Zola*, 105.

21. Budd and Eley, *Zola*, 105-6.

16. Rematch

1. Dick Brown, telephone interview by author, April 20, 2013.

2. Quotes from BBC broadcast of the July 20, 1985, race as posted at YouTube, https://www.youtube.com/watch?v=LAzrLwpRUuQ.

3. R. W. Apple Jr., "The Decker-Budd Rematch: Who Will Rise After the Fall?" *New York Times*, July 18, 1985.

4. BBC broadcast of preview show, July 20, 1985, as posted at YouTube, https://www.youtube.com/watch?v=YMzlISfEMq4.

5. Kenny Moore, "Sweet, Sweet Revenge," *Sports Illustrated*, July 29, 1985. Budd Pieterse recalled the payment to her was 90,000 British pounds. The *New York Times* reported the amounts as $125,000 for Budd and $75,000 for Slaney and that the money came from ABC, which had obtained the TV rights. "$200,000 Re-Match," *New York Times*, October 30, 1985.

6. Moore, "Sweet, Sweet Revenge," *Sports Illustrated*, July 29, 1985.

7. Richard Mayer, email to author, April 24, 2013.

8. Moore, "Sweet, Sweet Revenge," *Sports Illustrated*, July 29, 1985.

9. BBC broadcast of the rematch race, July 20, 1985, as posted at YouTube, https://www.youtube.com/watch?v=LAzrLwpRUuQ.

10. Moore, "Sweet, Sweet Revenge," *Sports Illustrated*, July 29, 1985.

11. Mike Littwin, "This Time Slaney Runs Budd into the Ground," *Los Angeles Times*, July 21, 1985.

12. Budd and Eley, *Zola*, 108.

13. Budd and Eley, *Zola*, 109.

14. He was able to attend other international events with Budd because they were held in England.

15. This account is heavily based on the BBC broadcast of the women's mile at the Weltklasse, August 21, 1985, Zurich, as posted at YouTube, https://www.youtube.com/watch?v=_NPhihJ2kMg, and Kenny Moore, "Banner Week in the Record Business," *Sports Illustrated*, September 2, 1985.

16. Kenny Moore, "Banner Week in the Record Business," *Sports Illustrated*, September 2, 1985.

17. Budd and Eley, *Zola,* 110–11.

18. Zola Budd Pieterse, interview by author, March 7, 2013, Myrtle Beach SC.

19. Budd and Eley, *Zola*, 112.

17. World Champ Again

1. Budd and Eley, *Zola*, 113–15.

2. Budd and Eley, *Zola*, 115–17.

3. Budd and Eley, *Zola*, 117.

4. Budd and Eley, *Zola*, 119.

5. Budd and Eley, *Zola*, 119.

6. Budd and Eley, *Zola*, 120.

7. Zola Budd Pieterse, interview by author, March 7, 2013, Myrtle Beach SC. See also Budd and Eley, *Zola*, 120.

8. Van Zyl and Prisloo would later marry. Today Prisloo teaches at the University of the Free State in South Africa.

9. Budd and Eley, *Zola*, 123.

10. "Commonwealth Games Bar Budd," *(Torrance CA) Daily Breeze*, July 14, 1986; Budd and Eley, *Zola*, 124.

11. Budd and Eley, *Zola*, 124.

12. Budd and Eley, *Zola*, 124.

13. Budd and Eley, *Zola*, 125.

14. Budd and Eley, *Zola*, 125.

15. Budd and Eley, *Zola*, 125.

16. Budd and Eley, *Zola*, 126.

17. Budd and Eley, *Zola*, 126.

18. Budd and Eley, *Zola*, 127.

19. Budd and Eley, *Zola*, 128.

20. Budd and Eley, *Zola*, 128.

21. Budd and Eley, *Zola*, 129.

22. Budd and Eley, *Zola*, 130.

23. Budd and Eley, *Zola*, 130.

24. Budd Pieterse, interview by author, March 7, 2013.

25. Budd and Eley, *Zola*, 127.

18. Mother Mary

1. George Vecsey, New York Times News Service, "Slaney Right on Schedule with Her Life," *Los Angeles Daily News*, August 24, 1986.

2. AP, "This Run Is Just for Fun," *Newsday*, September 12, 1986.

3. Maricica Puică, interview and English translation by Simion Alb for author, August 2012, Romania.

4. Angelique Muha Mayer, telephone interview by author, April 29, 2013.

5. Sarajane Freligh, "Slaney 6th as Puică Wins Mile," *Philadelphia Inquirer*, September 14, 1986.

6. Mercury News Wire Services, "American Track Stars Register Dull Victories in Brazil," *San Jose Mercury News*, September 22, 1986; Wayne Lockwood, *San Diego Union Tribune*, December 13, 1986.

7. Randy Harvey, "Homelife Is Fine, but Slaney Longs to Compete Again," *Los Angeles Times*, February 8, 1987, as reprinted same day in *Chicago Sun Times*.

8. Harvey, "Homelife Is Fine, but Slaney Longs to Compete Again," *Los Angeles Times*, February 8, 1987.

9. Gary Jones, "Back on Track," *Los Angeles Daily News*, May 3, 1987; Katie Castador, *USA Today*, April 23, 1987.

10. Wayne Lockwood, "Mary's Decision Shows New Maturity," *San Diego Union Tribune*, May 17, 1987.

11. "Slaney Has Surgery on Tendon," *San Jose Mercury News*, June 3, 1987.

12. "Still Running," *USA Today*, August 6, 1987.

13. AP, "Injured Slaney Will Skip '88 Indoor Season," *Dallas Morning News*, December 25, 1987.

19. Banned

1. Budd and Ely, *Zola*, 133.

2. Budd and Ely, *Zola*, 134.

3. Budd and Ely, *Zola*, 133–34.

4. She never knew just what was in the injections. She did say that after undergoing the series of injections she "was glad I wasn't racing at the time," because drug testers might have discovered some banned substance in her system.

5. Leon Botha, telephone interview by author, November 12, 2012; Budd and Ely, *Zola*, 140.

6. Budd and Ely, *Zola*, 141.

7. Budd and Ely, *Zola*, 148.

8. Budd and Ely, *Zola*, 149.

9. Budd and Ely, *Zola*, 149.

10. Budd and Ely, *Zola*, 152.

11. Budd and Ely, *Zola*, 155.

12. Budd and Ely, *Zola*, 156.

13. Budd and Ely, *Zola*, 156.

14. Budd and Ely, *Zola*, 157.

15. Budd and Ely, *Zola*, 158.

16. Budd and Ely, *Zola*, 158.

17. Budd and Ely, *Zola*, 159–60.

18. Budd and Ely, *Zola*, 160.

19. Budd and Ely, *Zola*, 158.

20. Budd and Ely, *Zola*, 149.

21. Budd and Ely, *Zola*, 149–50.

22. Budd and Ely, *Zola*, 163.

23. Budd and Ely, *Zola*, 163.

24. Budd and Ely, *Zola*, 163–64; booklet prepared for the media by filmmaker Peter Schiller Jr. in 1993 for a documentary film about Zola Budd, who lent me her copy.

25. Budd and Ely, *Zola*, 164.

26. Budd and Ely, *Zola*, 163–65.

27. Simson and Jennings, *Dishonored Games*, 164–73.

28. Simson and Jennings, *Dishonored Games*, 273.

29. Marshall Reed, "Budd's Name Is Added to UN Group's Black List," *Newsday*, April 15, 1988.

30. Ed Hinton, "Zola Budd Won't Be Allowed to Run Free," *Atlanta Journal*, March 29, 1988.

31. "Budding Discrimination," *Richmond Times-Dispatch*, April 23, 1988.

32. "Budding Issue," *USA Today*, April 20, 1988.

33. Andrew Warshaw, "IAAF Will Decide Budd's Future Today," *Lexington Herald Leader*, April 16, 1988.

34. AP, "Zola Budd May Be Banned from Olympics," *Seattle Times*, April 17, 1988.

35. A P, "Budd Says She Refuses to Give Up Fight to Run," *Los Angeles Daily News*, April 24, 1988.

36. Ron Rappaport "Small and Shy, Zola Budd Inspires Powerful Debate," *Los Angeles Daily News*, April 22, 1988.

37. Julie Cart, "Problem-Plagued Budd Finally Speaks Out," *Los Angeles Times*, April 24, 1988.

38. Bob Burns, "Run, Zola, Run. Sacrifice the Olympics, Not Zola," *Sacramento Bee*, April 24, 1988.

39. Burns, "Run, Zola, Run. Sacrifice the Olympics, Not Zola," *Sacramento Bee*, April 24, 1988.

40. "Decision on Budd Deferred a Month," *Chicago Sun-Times*, April 25, 1988.

41. "Court Denies Appeal on Zola Budd Case," *(Torrance CA) Daily Breeze*, May 6, 1988; "Appeal to Court Fails in Budd Row," *Glasgow Herald*, May 6, 1988.

42. Editorial, *Watertown (NY) Daily Times*, April 27, 1988.

43. Zola Budd Pieterse, interview by author, March 7, 2013, Myrtle Beach SC.

44. A P, "Photograph of Budd in South Africa Sparks More Controversy," *Charlotte Observer*, May 5, 1988.

45. Cathy Henkel, "Mary Decker Slaney Plans to Keep Her Feet on the Ground and Win Gold," *Seattle Times*, September 11, 1988.

20. Heart and Seoul

1. Kerry Eggers, "If Eugene Isn't Rainy Look for Slaney," *Oregonian*, May 7, 1988.

2. Cathy Henkel, "Older, Wiser, Faster, Mary Slaney Plans to Keep Her Feet on the Ground and Win the Gold," *Seattle Times*, September 11, 1988.

3. Shannon Brownlee, "Moms in the Fast Lane," *Sports Illustrated*, May 30, 1988.

4. Dick Brown, telephone interview by author, April 20, 2013.

5. "Slaney Runs US Best," *Dallas Morning News*, May 29, 1988.

6. Henkel, "Older, Wiser, Faster," *Seattle Times*, September 11, 1988.

7. Henkel, "Older, Wiser, Faster," *Seattle Times*, September 11, 1988. Henkel produced a major profile of Slaney for the *Seattle Times*, where she was the assistant sports editor. She had previously worked at the *Eugene Register-Guard*, where she covered Decker Slaney for eight years. The feature ran in the *Times* on September 11, 1988. It is the most comprehensive profile of Mary Decker Slaney ever produced. It may be retrieved in its entirety through http://nl.newsbank.com.

8. "Slaney Takes It Slow and Easy," *Orange County Register*, June 26, 1988.

9. "Slaney Not Done Yet," *USA Today*, June 3, 1988.

10. Henkel, "Older, Wiser, Faster," *Seattle Times*, September 11, 1988.

11. Mike Littwin, "Queen Mary's Whining Getting Old," *Baltimore Sun*, July 22, 1988. The story ran in many A P newspapers along with photo of Mary at the trials.

12. Chris Jenkins, "Front Runner," *San Diego Union Tribune*, September 23, 1988.

13. Jenkins, "Front Runner," *San Diego Union Tribune*, September 23, 1988.

14. Brown, interview by author, April 20, 2013.

15. Brown, interview by author, April 20, 2013.

16. Dave Dorr, "Slaney Tries to Analyze Keys to Latest Comeback," *St. Louis Post-Dispatch*, October 2, 1988.

17. Brown, interview by author, April 20, 2013.

18. "Slaney's Illness Forced Two Week Hiatus after Trials," *San Jose Mercury News*, September 9, 1988.

19. Christine Brennan, "One Goal Left for Injury-Prone Slaney—A Golden Moment," *Washington Post*, September 16, 1988.

20. Henkel, "Older, Wiser, Faster," *Seattle Times*, September 11, 1988. Local residents of the area referred to the Slaney home as "South Fork," after the mansion that was home to the Ewing family on the popular television show *Dallas*. All it lacked, Henkel said, was a moat.

21. Henkel, "Older, Wiser, Faster," *Seattle Times*, September 11, 1988. Henkel retired from the *Seattle Times* ten years later. She was one of fewer than a dozen women who had occupied the top job in sports departments at American newspapers. Her departure was our loss. While working in Wichita, Kansas, earlier in her long career, she had broken the BTK serial killer story.

22. "Olympics," *USA Today*, September 25, 1988.

23. Tom Cushman, "Slaney Again Fails to Medal," *San Diego Evening Tribune*, October 1, 1988.

24. Dorr, "Slaney Tries to Analyze," *St. Louis Post-Dispatch*, October 2, 1988.

25. John Jeansonne, "Americans Lag in 1,500," *Newsday*, October 1, 1988.

26. Dorr, "Slaney Tries to Analyze," *St. Louis Post-Dispatch*, October 2, 1988.

27. John Jeansonne, "Decker Ready to Go Extra Mile," *Newsday*, October 15, 1988.

28. Ruth Wysocki, telephone interview by author, August 1, 2012.

29. Gordon Slovut, "DMG Could Use More Tests," *Minneapolis Star Tribune*, December 4, 1988.

30. Dick Patrick, "Revitalized Slaney Puts Misfortune Behind," *USA Today*, December 21, 1988.

31. Brown, interview by author, April 20, 2013.

32. Ron Tabb, telephone interview by author, November 21, 2012.

33. AP, "Slaney: Extensive Drug Use, Limited Punishment in Track," *St. Louis Post-Dispatch*, December 22, 1988.

21. Marriage and Murder

1. Budd and Eley, *Zola*, 181–83.

2. Budd and Eley, *Zola*, 177.

3. AP, "New Rule Could Halt Budd Plans," *San Francisco Chronicle*, January 12, 1989; "Budd Seeks Clarification," *Houston Chronicle*, January 17, 1989.

4. "Budd Seeks Clarification," *Houston Chronicle*, January 17, 1989.

5. AP, "Budd Could Be Eligible If She Stays in Britain," *Dallas Morning News*, March 30, 1989.

6. Zola Budd Pieterse, interview by author, March 7, 2013, Myrtle Beach SC.

7. Budd Pieterse, interview by author, March 7, 2013.

8. "Zola, I Curse You!" *Johannesburg Sunday Times*, April 16, 1989. The story was picked up and ran in papers in England, the United States, and elsewhere.

9. Budd and Eley, *Zola*, 183–84.

10. John Hanc, "Recovering Decker Will Run for Fun," *Newsday*, June 22, 1989.

11. AP, "South African Eases to Victory," *Houston Chronicle*, August 27, 1989.

12. Budd Pieterse, interview by author, March 7, 2013. See also UPI, "Zola Budd's Father Found Murdered; Suspect Sought," *Seattle Post-Intelligencer*, September 23, 1989.

13. Budd and Eley, *Zola*. The *Daily Mail* had issued an earlier autobiography, also titled *Zola*, but she'd had little to do with the book. Its production was part of the deal Frank had signed with the *Mail* in 1984. In working with Eley, Zola recorded her words and Eley then edited and shaped them into the manuscript. The book was published in South Africa, Australia, New Zealand, and England. Eley was a well-known writer for the *Weekly Mail*, a South African publication for which he wrote under the nom de plume Merv Hughes.

22. Promoting L'eggs on Bad Legs

1. Kerry Eggers, "Slaney Puts Her L'eggs in One Basket," *Oregonian*, January 12, 1989; Phil Hersh, "Race Bonus No Boon to Chicago," *Chicago Tribune*, January 17, 1989.

2. Mark McDonald, "Slaney's Rough Start Takes a Turn for the Better," *Dallas Morning News*, January 15, 1989.

3. Kerry Eggers, "Slaney Sets 1,000 Mark," *Oregonian*, January 22, 1989. Clark was one of the running daughters of the controversial Newark school Principal Joe Clark, whose methods were the subject of much debate and resulted in the biographical movie *Lean on Me,* released in 1989.

4. Dick Patrick, "Track and Field," *USA Today*, February 4, 1989.

5. Patrick, "Track and Field," *USA Today*, February 9, 1989.

6. Kerry Eggers, "Slaney Aims to Get Back on Track," *Oregonian*, February 27, 1989.

7. Gerald Secor Couzens, "An Expert's Advice: Run, Don't Rush," *Newsday*, March 25, 1989.

8. Wesley Chapel, "Decker-Slaney Looks Ahead to Bright Future," *St. Petersburg Times*, April 12, 1989.

9. Kerry Eggers, "Promoter Has Post Pre Classic Blues," *Oregonian*, June 12, 1989.

10. Dianne Williams, a gold medal–winning sprinter at the 1984 games, was one of the athletes who took DeBus's advice. She admitted she was one of more than twenty who had tested positive for steroids at the 1984 Olympic trials. Her graphic and poignant testimony about the horrific side effects of the drugs, which she said had turned her body into a man's, came during a hearing on the allegations in July 1990 before a three-member panel of TAC. DeBus denied the allegations of Williams and two others, but he was eventually found guilty and suspended from TAC for life. See Julie Cart, "DeBus Suspended for Life," *Los Angeles Times*, July 18, 1990.

11. Julie Cart, "DeBus Suspended For Life," *Los Angeles Times*, July 18, 1990.

12. AP, "Slaney Says She Rejected Coach's Pressure to Use Drugs," *Houston Chronicle*, June 23, 1989.

13. Jim Brady, "Canadian Only Eyed the Finish," *Newsday*, June 25, 1989.

14. Gary Jones, "Injured or Not, Track Star Slaney Sets Blazing Pace," *Los Angeles Daily News*, November 16, 1989.

15. Jones, "Injured or Not, Track Star Slaney Sets Blazing Pace," *Los Angeles Daily News*, November 16, 1989.

16. "Slaney on Media, Men, and Steroids," *USA Today*, April 20, 1990.

17. AP, "Slaney to Concentrate Outdoor Circuit," *Seattle Times*, February 25, 1990.

18. Gary Jones, "Injured or Not, Track Star Slaney Sets Blazing Pace," *Los Angeles Daily News*, November 16, 1989.

19. "Romanian Sets Two World Records," *Chicago Sun Times*, February 2, 1990.

20. Brown also coached Vicki Huber and Suzy Favor Hamilton during the most successful parts of their respective careers. He had great success in bringing them to peak form for meets, just as he had with Mary. He had also adopted some of the Lydiard methods, which Bill Bowerman had introduced him to in the 1990s. Later Brown put out a training pamphlet of his own based largely on the Lydiard principles. In 1996 both Huber and Favor Hamilton went to the Olympics.

21. *Washington Times*, May 13, 1990.

22. David Osterman, "Slaney Enters 1,500 Mobil Meet," *Orange County Register*, June 13, 1990.

23. Sam Whiting, "Plumer Still Has Heart Set on Gold," *San Francisco Chronicle*, December, 16, 1990.

24. Ken Wheeler, "Lewis Shines, Slaney Falls Short," *Oregonian*, June 16, 1990.

25. AP, "Slaney, Borsheim Invitees," *Seattle Times*, June 18, 1990.

23. Budd Blooms

1. Alan Hubbard, "Zola Budd Has New Name and Renewed Dedication in New South Africa," *London Observer*, February 22, 1991. The article appeared in most Scripps Howard papers in the United States.

2. Nobby Hashizume, email to author, October 25, 2012.

3. Pieter Labuschagne, email to author, November 20, 2012.

4. With her marriage to Michael Pieterse she was again a South African citizen.

5. Hubbard, "Zola Budd Has New Name," *London Observer*, February 22, 1991.

6. Booklet prepared for the media by filmmaker Peter Schiller Jr. in 1993 for a documentary film about Zola Budd, who lent me her copy.

7. William Oscar Johnson, "Endurance Test: Distance Running Star Zola Budd Has Survived Turmoil on and off the Track," *Sports Illustrated*, June 24, 1991.

8. Ironically, the head of sports organization was none other than Sam Ramsamy, who had been the most vitriolic and vocal opponent of Zola's when she arrived in England. See Johnson, "Endurance Test," *Sports Illustrated*, June 24, 1991.

9. John Jeansonne, "IOC Ends South Africa Athlete Discrimination," *Newsday*, July 10, 1991.

10. "IOC Decision Was Big News to Budd," *Los Angeles Times*, July 21, 1991.

11. Stephen Taylor, "Returning to the Olympic Fold Budd Could Dominate with Restored Eligibility," *Washington Times*, July 10, 1991.

12. Hubbard, "Zola Budd Has New Name," *London Observer*, February 22, 1991.

13. Joe Arace, "South Africans Ask to Compete in World Meet," *USA Today*, August 7, 1991.

14. Taylor, "Returning to the Olympic Fold," *Washington Times*, July 10, 1991.

15. "Running Back . . . Older, Wiser Zola Budd Gains a New Perspective," *New York Times*, November 17, 1991.

24. New Faces, Old Story

1. "Decker Slaney Runs Like a Champion," *Seattle Times*, May 26, 1991.

2. "Slaney Runs All the Way Back," *San Diego Union Tribune*, May 26, 1991; "At 32, Slaney Has Shot at World 1,500 Title," *Washington Times*, May 30, 1991; "Slaney Back on Track," *Kansas City Star*, June 1, 1991.

3. AP, "Big Names in Prefontaine Track but Slaney May Not Be Able to Run," *San Francisco Chronicle*, June 21, 1991.

4. Dick Patrick, "Slaney Looks Optimistically to July Races in Europe," *USA Today*, June 27, 1991.

5. AP, "Lewis, Farmer-Patrick Heat Up New York Track," *Seattle Times*, July 21, 1991. Mutola would break Slaney's 800 meters indoor record in March 1992 in New York.

6. Ray Didinger, "True Grit Slaney Refuses to Abandon Quest for Medal," *Philadelphia Daily News*, April 21, 1992.

7. Ray Didinger, "With Pressure on Others, Slaney Tries for Spot on Team, Medal in Barcelona," *Philadelphia Daily News*, May 17, 1992.

8. Didinger, "True Grit Slaney," *Philadelphia Daily News*, April 21, 1992.

9. Abby Haight, "Slaney Surprises Spectators with Strong Showing at Pre," *Oregonian*, June 10, 1992.

10. "Heart of Gold: Mary Slaney," *New Orleans Times-Picayune*, Olympic Special Section, June 17, 1992.

11. Jimmy Smith, "Plumer, Slaney Impressive in 3,000 Meters," *Times Picayune*, June 20, 1992.

12. Bob Kenney, "Olympics Track and Field," *USA Today*, June 22, 1992.

13. Mick Elliott, "Mary Never Got Her Due from the Fans," *Tampa Tribune*, June 23, 1992.

14. John Lopez, "Injuries, Mishaps Mar Slaney's Illustrious Career," *Houston Chronicle*, June 23, 1992.

15. Bob Kenney, "New Orleans," *USA Today*, June 24, 1992.

16. Bob Kenney, "Olympics," *USA Today*, June 28, 1992.

17. Larry McMillen, "Is Slaney Almost Out of Time?" *Times-Picayune*, June 29, 1992.

18. PattiSue told me she never considered giving up her spot. Plumer, telephone interview by author, July 12, 2013.

19. Steve Brandon, "Lewis, Slaney Hold Fourth," *Oregonian*, June 19, 1992.

20. Bruce Jenkins, "How Slaney's Bitterness Cost Her Olympic Berth," *San Francisco Chronicle*, July 3, 1992.

21. Karen Rosen, "Plumer Won't Step Aside for Slaney," *Atlanta Constitution*, July 4, 1992.

22. Jenkins, "How Slaney's Bitterness Cost Her," *San Francisco Chronicle*, July 3, 1992.

23. Jenkins, "How Slaney's Bitterness Cost Her," *San Francisco Chronicle*, July 3, 1992.

25. Seems Like Old Times

1. Booklet prepared for the media by filmmaker Peter Schiller Jr. in 1993 for a documentary film about Zola Budd, who lent me her copy.

2. Zola Budd Pieterse, interview by author, March 7, 2013, Myrtle Beach SC.

3. Budd Pieterse, interview by author, March 7, 2013.

4. Budd Pieterse, interview by author, March 7, 2013.

5. Budd Pieterse, interview by author, March 7, 2013.

6. Jana Wendt, moderator, *Current Affair*, NBN Television, week of October 16, 1992, used with permission. The video is posted on YouTube at http://www.you tube.com/watch?=XT00tatX6Wg&feature=player_detailpage.

26. Trials and Tribulations

1. Results are from the booklet prepared for the media by filmmaker Peter Schiller Jr. in 1993 for a documentary film about Zola Budd, who lent me her copy.

2. Booklet prepared for the media by filmmaker Peter Schiller Jr. in 1993 for a documentary film about Zola Budd; Zola Budd Pieterse interview by author, March 7, 2013, Myrtle Beach SC.

3. "No Racing This Season for Slaney," *San Diego Union Tribune*, June 2, 1993.

4. Dick Patrick, "Slaney Refocusing with Salazar's Help," *USA Today*, December 30, 1993.

5. Sandy Keenan, "Out of This World, But Is Wang Too Good?" *Newsday*, February 1, 1994.

6. Phil Hersh, "Chinese Records Have Track and Field World Full of Accusations," *Chicago Tribune*, September 14, 1993.

7. Hersh, "Chinese Records," *Chicago Tribune*, September 14, 1993.

8. Hersh, "Chinese Records," *Chicago Tribune*, September 14, 1993.

9. AP, "Slaney, Butler Set 10K Course Records," *Arizona Daily Star*, November 15, 1993.

10. Lori Riley, "Ahead for Slaney: Unfamiliar Road," *Hartford Courant*, November 24, 1993.

11. Patrick, "Slaney Refocusing with Salazar's Help," *USA Today*, December 30, 1993.

12. John Hanc, "Midnight Sees Return of Slaney," *Newsday*, December 30, 1993.

13. Keenan, "Out of This World," *Newsday*, February 1, 1994. When the IAAF

started taking surprise urine samples a few years later, the times of Chinese runners returned to normal, and Wang disappeared back behind the wall.

14. Susan Reed, "Going the Distance," *People*, October 17, 1994.

15. Reed, "Going the Distance," *People*, October 17, 1994.

16. Robyn Norwood, "Orange County Hall of Fame: An Illustrious Track Record," *Los Angeles Times*, December 17, 1994.

17. "Kenyans Rule Citrus Classic," *Lakeland (FL) Ledger*, March 3, 1996.

18. "At 37, Runner Mary Slaney Isn't Giving Up on the Games," *Philadelphia Inquirer*, March 10, 1996.

19. "At 37, Runner Mary Slaney Isn't Giving Up on the Games," *Philadelphia Inquirer*, March 10, 1996.

20. "Women Take First Steps on Fast Track to Atlanta," *Oregonian*, April 14, 1996.

21. "Women Runners Light Up the Twilight," *Oregonian*, May 12, 1996.

22. "A Tough Road to Glory," *Orange County Register*, May 6, 1996.

23. "Three World-Leading Marks Are Set in Pre Classic," *Oregonian*, May 27, 1996.

24. Phil Hersh, "Slaney Runs with Pain," *Chicago Times*, June 23, 1996.

25. "For Johnson Trials Is Real Test, Slaney Fighting Past Failures, Easily Triumphs in Heat," *(Newark NJ) Star Ledger*, June 15, 1996.

26. "Slaney Healthy as She Aims at Another Olympics," Scripps-McClatchy Western Service, June 17, 1996.

27. Hersh, "Slaney Runs with Pain," *Chicago Times*, June 23, 1996.

28. "At 37, Runner Mary Slaney Isn't Giving Up," *Philadelphia Inquirer*, March 10, 1996.

29. "Since '84, Slaney Has Grown Up," *Press-Telegram,* June 19, 1996.

30. "Slaney Fails in Bid to Qualify in 1,500, Settles for 5,000," *Washington Times*, June 22, 1996.

31. "A Weary Mary Decker Slaney Isn't Fooling Herself," *Chattanooga (TN) Free Press*, July 24, 1996.

32. *USA Today*, July 27, 1996.

33. Steve Bisheff, "Slaney Loses a Race against Time," *Orange County Register*, July 27, 1996.

34. Pat Bigold, "Sullivan, Slaney Both Break Waikiki Mile Record," *Honolulu Star*, December 6, 1996.

35. Jere Longman, "Drug Inquiry Drags for Angered Slaney," *New York Times*, May 15, 1997.

36. AP, "Slaney Investigated for Drug Use," *Tulsa World*, May 16, 1997. This appears to be the AP version of the *New York Times* story.

37. Ungerleider, *Faust's Gold*, 35–39, 95.

38. *Slaney v. International Amateur Athletic Federation and U.S. Olympic Committee*, 244 F.3d 580 (7th Cir., March 27, 2001). The case clearly was brought against the IAAF, which is in fact the International Association of Athletics Federations, but its full name was for some reason given incorrectly in the pleadings and therefore the decision.

39. AP, "Slaney Investigated for Drug Use," *Tulsa World*, May 16, 1997.

40. Abby Haight and Ken Coe, "Slaney's Husband Asserts She Is Being Victimized," *Oregonian*, May 16, 1997.

41. Haight and Coe, "Slaney's Husband Asserts She Is Being Victimized," *Oregonian*, May 16, 1997; Larry Siddons, AP, "Slaney Investigated for Drug Use at the Olympic Trials Last June," *(Eastern CT) Day*, May 16, 1997.

42. "Slaney Suspended on Drugs," *Trenton (NJ) Times*, June 1, 1997.

43. *Slaney v. IAAF*, http:caselaw.findlaw.com/us-7th-circuit/1146530.html. See also "IAAF Orders Slaney Out of Nationals," column, *Seattle Post-Intelligencer*, June 11, 1997. Because of Slaney's expressions of animosity toward PattiSue Plumer, she recused herself from the deliberations of the Custodial Board.

44. "Slaney Suspended on Drugs," *Trenton (NJ) Times*, June 1, 1997.

45. "Slaney Won't fight U.S. Suspension," *Contra Costa (CA) Times*, June 12, 1997.

46. Abby Haight, "Disputed Test Gets Slaney Suspended," *Oregonian*, June 12, 1997.

47. Haight, "Disputed Test Gets Slaney Suspended," *Oregonian*, June 12, 1997.

48. Don Catlin, telephone interview by author, June 10, 2013.

49. AP, "Slaney Warns USATF: 'I'll Take No Prisoners,'" *Tulsa World*, September 24, 1997.

50. AP, "Slaney Warns USATF: 'I'll Take No Prisoners,'" *Tulsa World*, September 24, 1997.

51. Wire Services, "IAAF Sends Slaney Matter to Arbitration," *Philadelphia Daily News*, September 28, 1997; note 5 in *Slaney v. IAAF*.

52. Don Norcross, "IAAF Flap Causes Slaney to Pull Out of Scott Mile," *San Diego Union Tribune*, January 29, 1998.

53. Chuck Hoffner, "Slaney Hamstrung for Drake Relays," *Atlanta Constitution*, April 24, 1998.

54. Tom Kensler, "Mean Feet," *Denver Post*, May 12, 1998.

55. Abby Haight, "In Long Run, Slaney Determined to Go Own Way," *Oregonian*, June 17, 1998.

56. Steve Herman, "Slaney Sues IAAF, USOC," Associated Press, April 13, 1999.

57. "Last Chance Arbitration Panel Rules Against Slaney," *Seattle Times*, April 26, 1999.

58. Daily News Wire Services, "IAAF Strips 1997 World Silver from Slaney," *Philadelphia Daily News*, April 27, 1999.

59. *Slaney v. IAAF*.

60. "Court Refuses to Hear Slaney Case," *Seattle Times*, October 2, 2001.

61. Gene Cherry, "Slaney Still Yearns to Run," *Reuters.com*, July 27, 2009.

62. Gene Cherry, "Mary Slaney Still Feels Regret over Budd Race," Reuters, July 22, 2009.

27. War and Peace

1. Zola Budd Pieterse, interview by author, March 7, 2013, Myrtle Beach SC.

2. Sue Mott, "Zola Returns to Lay Ghosts to Rest," *London Telegraph*, April 12, 2003.

3. "Marathon May Be Zola's Ticket," *Hartford Courant*, July 28, 1996.

4. "Marathon May Be Zola's Ticket," *Hartford Courant*, July 28, 1996.

5. "People Hated Me and I Never Knew Why," *Daily Mirror*, April 9, 2003.

6. Ian Wooldridge, "Zola Deserves Warm Welcome After All We Put Her Through," *Daily Mail*, April 9, 2003.

7. Michelle Cahill, "Zola Left in Tears Again," IOL News.com.za, April 15, 2006.

8. "On a Scale of One to Ten I Think I'm Pushing Nine," *Mail on Sunday*, April 23, 2006.

9. "Zola Budd Wins Court Order Against Gun Siege Woman," *Daily Mail*, July 29, 2006.

10. "Zola, Mike Back in Race," News First Archives, September 5, 2006, www .news24.com.

11. Budd Pieterse, interview by author, March 7, 2013.

12. Tom Knight, "Budd in Emotional Return to Spotlight," *London Telegraph*, November 14, 2006.

13. Simon Turnbull, "Olympic Diary: Budd Rolls Back the Years," *(London) Observer*, July 8, 2011.

14. Any marathon longer than 26.2 miles is deemed an ultramarathon. Doug Rennie, "The Ultimate Ultramarathon Training Plan," *Runner's World*, no date given on website (runnersworld.com) but probably March 2013, judging from posted comments.

15. Budd Pieterse, interview by author, March 7, 2013.

16. David Quick, "Zola Budd Pieterse Wins Charleston Marathon," *Courier and Post*, January 18, 2014.

Epilogue

1. Gene Cherry, "Mary Slaney Still Yearns to Run," Reuters, July 28, 2009.

2. Zola Budd Pieterse, interview by author, March 7, 2013, Myrtle Beach, SC.

3. According to a recent report from the United Nations, the infection rate fell by a third in South Africa between 2004 and 2012. See "New HIV Report Finds Big Drop in New HIV Infections in South Africa," UNAIDS, January 17, 2014, http://www.unaids.org/en/resources/presscentre/featurestories/2014 /january/20140117southafrica/.

BIBLIOGRAPHY

Bascomb, Neal. *The Perfect Mile: Three Athletes, One Goal, and Less Than Four Minutes to Achieve It*. New York: Mariner Books, 2005.

Brant, John. *Duel in the Sun: Alberto Salazar, Dick Beardsley, and America's Greatest Marathon*. Emmaus PA: Rodale, 2006.

Budd, Zola, with Hugh Eley. *Zola: The Autobiography of Zola Budd*. London: Partridge Press, 1989.

Butcher, Pat. *The Perfect Distance*. London: Phoenix, 2005.

Connolly, Pat. *Coaching Evelyn: Fast, Faster, Fastest Woman in the World*. New York: Harper Collins, 1991.

Dwyre, Bill, ed. *The Los Angeles Times Book of the 1984 Olympic Games*. New York: Harry N. Abrams, 1984.

Friedman, Steve. "After the Fall." In *Going Long*, edited by David Willey. New York: Rodale, 2010.

Jennings, Andrew. *Foul! The Secret World of FIFA*. London: HarperCollins, 2006.

Jennings, Andrew, and Clare Sambrook. *The Great Olympic Swindle: When the World Wanted Its Games Back*. London: Simon and Schuster, 2000.

Lord Killanin, and John Rodda, eds. *The Olympic Games*. London: Barrie and Jenkins, 1976.

Mayer, Richard. *Three Men Named Matthews: Memories of the Golden Age of South African Distance Running and Its Aftermath*. Johannesburg SA: Red Lion Books, 2009.

McCloskey, John, and Julian Bailes. *When Winning Costs Too Much: Steroids, Supplements, and Scandal in Today's Sports*. Lanham MD: Taylor Trade, 2005.

Michaels, Al, with Jon Wertheim. *You Can't Make This Up: Miracles, Memories and the Perfect Marriage of Sports and Television*. New York: William Morrow, 2014.

Moore, Kenny. *Best Efforts*. New York: Doubleday, 1982.

———. *Bowerman and the Men of Oregon: The Story of Oregon's Legendary Coach and Nike's Cofounder*. Emmaus PA: Rodale, 2006.

Murphy, Frank. *The Silence of Great Distance: Women Running Long*. Kansas City MO: Wind Sprint Press, 2000.

Newman, Matthew. *Mary Decker Slaney*. Mankato MN: Crestwood House, 1986.

Noakes, Timothy. *Lore of Running*, 4th ed. Southern Africa: Oxford University Press, 2001.

Pound, Dick. *Inside the Olympics: A Behind-the-Scenes Look at the Politics, the Scandals, and the Glory of the Games*. Toronto: John Wiley, 2004.

Salazar, Alberto, and John Bryant. *14 Minutes: A Running Legend's Life and Death and Life*. New York: Rodale, 2012.

Scott, Steve, with Marc Bloom. *The Miler: America's Legendary Runner Talks about His Triumphs and Trials*. New York: Macmillan, 1997.

Simson, Vyv, and Andrew Jennings. *Dishonored Games: Corruption, Money, and Greed at the Olympics*. Toronto: SPI Books, 1992.

Smit, Barbara. *Sneaker Wars: The Enemy Brothers Who Founded Adidas and Puma and the Family Feud that Forever Changed the Business of Sport*. New York: ECCO, 2008.

Strasser, J. B., and Laurie Becklund. *Swoosh: The Unauthorized Story of Nike and the Men Who Played There*. New York: HarperBusiness, 1993.

Switzer, Kathrine. *Marathon Woman: Running the Race to Revolutionize Women's Sports*. Philadelphia: DaCapo, 2007.

Ungerleider, Steven. *Faust's Gold: Inside the East German Doping Machine*. New York: Thomas Dunne Books, 2001.

Wallechinsky, David. *The Complete Book of the Summer Olympics*. Woodstock NY: Overlook Press, 2000.

Wendt, Jenna. *Nice Work*. Carlton, Victoria AU: Melbourne University Press, 2010.

Willey, David, ed. *Going Long: Legends, Oddballs, Comebacks, and Adventures*. New York: Rodale, 2010.

Wilson, Harry. *Running Dialogue: A Coach's Story*. London: Stanley Paul, 1982.

Wooldridge, Ian. *Sport in the 80's*. London: Centurion, 1989.

INDEX

Italicized figure numbers refer to illustrations following page 142.